A Diplomat's Wife in Japan

MARY CRAWFORD FRASER

Mary Crawford Fraser

A Diplomat's Wife in Japan

Sketches at the Turn of the Century

edited by Hugh Cortazzi

New York • WEATHERHILL • Tokyo

This book is an abridgement of a two-volume work originally published in 1899 by Hutchinson and Co., London, under the title *A Diplomatist's Wife in Japan: Letters from Home to Home.*

The woodblock prints reproduced in the book and on the jacket are from the collection of the Maspro Denkoh Corporation, Nagoya, and are used with their kind permission.

First edition, 1982

Published by John Weatherhill, Inc., of New York and Tokyo, with editorial offices at 7-6-13 Roppongi, Minato-ku, 106, Japan. Copyright © 1982 by Hugh Cortazzi; all rights reserved. Printed and first published in Japan.

Library of Congress Cataloging in Publication Data: Fraser, Hugh, Mrs., d. 1922. / A diplomat's wife in Japan. / Abridgement of: A diplomatist's wife in Japan. 2v. London: Hutchinson, 1899. / Includes index. / 1. Japan—Description and travel—1801–1900. 2. Fraser, Hugh, Mrs., d. 1922. 3. Diplomats' wives—Great Britain—Biography. I. Cortazzi, Hugh. II. Title. / DS809.F84 1982 952.03 82–2589 AACR2 / ISBN 0–8348–0172–8

2211313

Contents

Illustrations appear following page 112

Map of Meiji Japan, page xxxii

v

Preface

When I came to Japan as British Ambassador in 1980 I was naturally interested in the history of the Embassy. In the course of my research my attention was drawn to Mrs. Hugh Fraser's book, *A Diplomatist's Wife in Japan: Letters from Home to Home,* published in two volumes in 1899. This work had an account of the first children's Christmas party at the Embassy (or Legation, as it then was) and a picture of the old residence, which became unsafe following the Yokohama earthquake in 1923 and was replaced by the present buildings, which were completed in 1931. I realised immediately that these were not, as I had expected, just another diplomatic memoir with rather dull accounts of diplomatic events. Instead, despite a certain Victorian tendency to overwrite, the author paints a picture in brilliant colours of a few years of life in Tokyo towards the end of the last century. More than most historical accounts, Mrs. Fraser's helped me to understand better what life in the capital had been like at that time. In addition, I was impressed by Mrs. Fraser's sympathetic approach to what must have been to her a very alien culture, by her ability to describe in a lively and personable style, and by her feel for atmosphere.

It is nearly ninety years since Mrs. Fraser's book was published. In that historically short span of time, war, earthquake, fire, and progress have transformed Tokyo into one of the largest cities of the world. That the great sprawling capital of Japan was once the attractive collection of gardens that Mrs. Fraser described is still difficult for me to imagine.

The present volume is an edited version of the second edition of Mrs. Fraser's book, which was originally produced by the London publishing firm of Hutchinson and Company and is now out of print. The first volume was 466 pages in length, divided into twenty chapters; the second, 439 pages divided into twenty-two chapters. Among the stories and events that Mrs. Fraser chose to include are many that have been more accurately presented elsewhere. Therefore I have taken the liberty of abridging the work, shortening it to approximately four-fifths its original length. Furthermore, I have deleted the numerous chapter headings and re-grouped the chapters, each originally simply numbered, under the five years of Mrs. Fraser's residence in Japan.

Not desiring to alter the flavour of the text I have retained the romanization of Japanese names and terms that Mrs. Fraser utilized. In many cases it agrees with that of the Hepburn system; in others it does not. For example, when we today would spell the Japanese name for pre-Meiji-era Tokyo as Edo, Mrs. Fraser has used the older spelling of Yedo. In the introduction and notes I have adopted the Western style of recording names, that is, with the given name first followed by the family name, for those people who figured in the events of the Meiji era (1868–1912); the names of those who lived prior to the Meiji era I have given in Japanese style, which is the reverse. All the explanatory notes, unless otherwise stated, are my additions; quotations from Murray's *Handbook for Travellers in Japan* have been edited for the general reader.

The portrait of Mrs. Fraser is taken from a later volume of reminiscences. The prints of Japan of the Meiji era are from the Maspro Denkoh Corporation collection. I am much indebted to Mr. Takashi Hashiyama for his kindness in giving permission for their reproduction. I should like to thank the editorial staff of John Weatherhill, my secretaries Vicki Turkington and Pam Simpson, as well as Jerry Matsumura and my son William for help in preparing the manuscript for publication.

HUGH CORTAZZI

Editor's Introduction

Japan has a long history of contact with the outside world. Some of the greatest strides in Japanese civilisation have followed hard upon the cultural influences brought about by such contact. But as is the case with almost any society, insular or not, each infusion of foreign ideas was accompanied by a certain amount of social and political unrest. When contact was established with China in the sixth century, Buddhism, Confucianism, and the Chinese language began to play an important role in Japanese culture. At the same time, the semblance of a central government was formed.

Even though new heights of sophistication were reached in the elegant court life of the capital during the eleventh century, the imperial government still exercised only limited control in the provinces where feudal lords were the effective rulers, and civil disturbances were a common occurence. From the thirteenth century onwards civil wars increased in frequency, and by the arrival of the Portuguese in the mid-sixteenth century much of Japan had been devastated by civil strife. Although this first period of contact with the West was extensive, it was to last less than one hundred years. For once Tokugawa Ieyasu established control over most of the country and founded a new government at Edo, modern-day Tokyo, contact with the outside world was severely limited. All that was allowed was intercourse with a small group of Dutch merchants on the island of Dejima in Nagasaki.

Contact with the West was only re-established in the middle of the nineteenth century with the arrival of the "black ships" of Commodore Perry. The Tokugawa shogunate was then in a period of decline and unable to resist the pressure from the outside world to open their ports to foreign trade. As a result Japan was forced to conclude the so-called "unequal treaties" of the 1850s. These agreements allowed foreign traders to operate in a limited number of ports in Japan and granted foreign governments extraterritorial rights over their subjects in Japan. The Tokugawa shogunate encountered, partly as a result of these treaties, increasing opposition from many influential daimyos, especially those of Satsuma in Kyushu and Chōshū in western Honshu. In 1868 the shogunate was overthrown, and the emperor was restored to power. The imperial court moved from Kyoto to Edo, which was renamed Tokyo. Japan had entered the Meiji era.

Most of the leading figures in the new government were originally middle-ranking samurai from Satsuma and Chōshū. They saw clearly that if Japan was to retain its independence the Japanese had to make radical changes not only in the structure of their society but also in their attitudes towards the outside world. Their long-range objective was nothing less than to catch up with the West, but to secure agreement to the revision of the unequal treaties was foremost in their minds. To these ends drastic steps were taken to abolish the feudal system and establish institutions in Japan that were modelled on Western prototypes. At the same time strenuous efforts were made to develop communication networks, build railways and ports, and start new basic industries. Education was also a very high priority. Western institutions and Western clothes and customs were officially encouraged, and contacts between government representatives and the small Tokyo diplomatic corps were frequent and friendly.

Japan's first attempt to secure agreement to amend the treaties ended in failure. A diplomatic mission led by Tomomi Iwakura, and supported by Toshimichi Ōkubo, Takayoshi Kido, and Hirobumi Itō, among others, was sent first to the United States and then to Europe. In Washington it was made clear to them that there was no possibility of treaty revision at that time. The same thing happened to them in London in 1872 and in Berlin in 1873. The mission returned with the realisation that a variety of reforms including a complete revision of Japan's legal system had to be made before a new agreement could be concluded; they also recognised the West's economic and military strengths and were convinced that they must step up the pace of modernisation.

In the years following the return of the mission, Japanese leaders made much progress in advancing necessary reforms. The army was reorganised along German lines, and the navy on British. A criminal code based partly on Japanese feudal law and partly on the *Code Napoléon* came into force at the beginning of 1882. It was not until 1890, however, that a civil code was promulgated. It aroused loud protests and was not finally approved until the turn of the century.

In 1885 a cabinet on European lines was established. This was followed by the creation of the Privy Council in 1888. One of the latter's first tasks was to approve a constitution which was promulgated on February 11, 1889. The constitution was drawn up largely by Hirobumi Itō, who had gone to Europe in 1882 to study European constitutions. He felt that the German and Austrian models were more suited to Japan and accordingly had started his investigations in Berlin and Vienna, only later visiting London and Paris. Under the new constitution many powers were reserved to the Emperor. He retained extensive rights to issue ordinances, and he could freely adjourn or prorogue the Diet. Some items of regular expenditure were altogether excluded from the consideration of the Diet. Significantly, if the Diet failed to pass the budget, the government was entitled to carry out the budget of the previous year. The Diet was bicameral, with an appointed House of Peers that had equal authority with the Lower House. Suffrage for the Lower House was strictly limited by a property qualification (there were only some 500,000 electors at the first election). Moreover, constitutional revision could only be initiated by the Emperor.

This oligarchic constitution was drawn up against a background of considerable political instability in Japan. Many of the former samurai were discontented with the way in which they had been treated by the new government, and the young Japanese who had been exposed to Western ideas and had had little or no political experience were vocal in their demands for increased rights. The Meiji leaders feared, therefore, that if they moved too quickly to establish a democratic system anarchy would result.

In these circumstances it was not surprising that when the Diet first opened, the government of 1889, led by Aritomo Yamagata, had a difficult time. When the session opened in November the Diet demanded heavy cuts in the budget and only reluctantly accepted a compromise. Masayoshi Matsukata, who succeeded Yamagata as Prime Minister, was forced to dissolve the Lower House in December 1891, having failed to get his budget accepted. The elections of February 1892 were marked by violence and intimidation.

It was during this turbulent period that renewed efforts were made to get the powers to agree to revise the treaties. The Japanese particularly wanted the abolition of the system of extraterritoriality and the right to adjust Japan's tariff on foreign goods. In 1888 Foreign Minister Shigenobu Ōkuma reopened talks and won general acceptance for the abolition of extraterritoriality subject to the creation of mixed courts for cases of appeal. When this fact was made known prematurely it aroused great opposition in Japan, and in October 1889 Ōkuma was wounded by a bomb thrown at his carriage by a nationalist fanatic.

Inevitably, with the opening of the Diet, treaty revision became more and more a matter of domestic politics. When talks were resumed in 1893 the then Foreign Minister pointed out that the Japanese would not be satisfied with less than the complete abolition of extraterritoriality. In July 1894 agreement was eventually reached with Britain providing that extraterritoriality should end after Japan's new civil code came into force and that foreign merchants, in exchange, should be allowed to operate outside the treaty ports: Hakodate, Hyōgo (Kobe), Nagasaki, Niigata, and Yokohama. Foreigners had also been permitted to reside in Tokyo and Osaka.

The promulgation of the constitution, the opening of the Diet, and treaty revision were accordingly key themes in Japan at the time when Mrs. Fraser was writing her letters.

Although Japan had made considerable progress in developing communications and industry by the time of Mrs. Fraser's arrival, it was, nevertheless, still a very poor and small agricultural country with a population of forty-one million (today there are over 115 million people living in Japan).

Mary Crawford Fraser was born the third child of Thomas and Louisa Crawford on April 8, 1851. Thomas Crawford, who was of Scotch-Irish stock, was an American sculptor who had come to Rome in the 1830s to study classical sculpture. His first important piece was a figure of Orpheus; his last was the Washington Monument, cast in bronze.

Louisa Crawford was a member of the Ward family. The Wards had fought under Cromwell, and an ancestor had fled to America at the restoration of King Charles II. The family lived in New York. More than one of her ancestors had been governor of Rhode Island. The family prospered, and Mary Fraser records that in the time of her grandfather Samuel Ward they had owned a large part of one side of Fifth Avenue in New York City. Samuel Ward married a Southern girl with much French blood in her veins; this French ancestry was reflected in Louisa Ward, of whom Mary writes: "Her loves and friendships filled her life; she never neglected, never forgot." Louisa met Thomas Crawford in Rome and over the objections of her family, to whom "the word 'artist' suggested everything impecunious, unstable, suspicious," insisted on marrying him. The wedding took place in New York on November 2, 1843. The couple settled in Rome, where Louisa with her love of languages mastered both spoken and written Italian.

The Crawfords lived in the Villa Negroni in Rome where Mary Fraser was born. The villa was built of materials taken from the baths of Diocletian, "whose huge sulky looking arches covered several acres of ground near us." Thomas Crawford, "who loved old grandeur and needed much space, fell in love with the Villa Negroni and took it on a lifelong lease from the owner, Prince Massimo, who reserved for himself a vast warren of rooms on the first floor and gave up all the rest to us." These apartments were "full of long galleries and dimly gorgeous rooms." The villa had been the home of Pope Sixtus V (1521–90) and provided the Crawford children with the opportunity to absorb the wonders of Rome. Mary describes how from her father's studio she "could slip out through a dark ilex grove, always full of singing birds, and climb a little hill on which sat a colossal statue of Roma Imperiatrix, looking down with stony eyes on her vassal city, while above her head waved the spires of some giant cypresses planted by Michelangelo." Alas, "It is all gone now. The railway runs where the ilex grove broke in gold and green nestlings over my head; the railway stands on the site of our studios; gone are the orange walk and the cypress avenue, and the lovely fountain court, guarded by stone lions and encircled by cypresses wreathed to their crests with climbing roses. The fountain had been playing for three hundred years."

In the spring of 1856 Mary Fraser made her first trip to the United States to visit her grandmother. Mary spent her fifth birthday in Paris, where she stayed in a house near the Champs Élysées. The family crossed the Atlantic from Le Havre on the Fulton, which she describes as "a labouring old tub with paddle-wheels, three or four stories deep, only the uppermost one having light or air." She was very seasick, and the fourteen-day journey was something of a nightmare. In New York they stayed at first with two bachelor uncles; the only bright spot was the kitchen where the Irish cook took pity on the children. From New York they went on to Newport and Bordentown and stayed on through 1856 and 1857. In the late summer of 1856 their father paid a fleeting visit to North America, and Mary, who adored him, saw him for the last time, for he died early in 1857. In Bordentown, Mary had a very frightening experience. She, her younger brother Marion, and her nurse were crossing a narrow railway bridge when they heard "the shriek of a whistle behind us, and turned—to see the volumes of smoke issuing from the funnel of an approaching engine." Fortunately the nurse did not lose her head and managed to grab the children and escape. But the nurse was also a sadist. When Mary was supposed to have gone to sleep the nurse would come to her bedside and peer into her face to see if she was asleep. "If I stirred or opened my eyes I was instantly severely whipped by way of calming my nerves. Whippings were inflicted on me day in, day out, but whatever happened I was dumb. . . . As I believed she was the most powerful person in the house and would flay me if I complained of her, nobody ever suspected anything was wrong." Back in Italy in 1858 the nurse nearly let Mary die from a hæmorrhage caused by nose bleeding.

Mary's brother, who was born in 1854, was given the odd name of Marion after their ancestor of the revolution, Francis Marion. He grew up to be a popular novelist and was admired and spoilt by his sisters.

Back in Rome from 1858 much of the fun in life seemed to Mary to have disappeared with her father's death the previous year. But she recalls in her reminiscences encounters in the cosmopolitan atmosphere of nineteenth century Italy with great men such as Hans Christian Andersen, who came back to Rome in his old age. "He played and romped with us, and when everybody was tired he proposed that he should tell us one of the fairy stories which we all knew and loved so well. The votes went for the 'Ugly Duckling' but he said that he could only tell stories with children on his knee! So he called two of us, golden haired Lucy Conrad (now the Marchesa Theodoli) and my fortunate little self, to him, and with one on either knee began to tell the tale."

She also met the Brownings in Siena in 1860. Mary was then nine and had largely recovered her health. She had learnt by heart a number of Mrs. Browning's poems and looked forward to meeting the poetess. But the meeting, if awesome, was something of a disappointment. She was taken to call by her mother. "From the blaze of the Tuscan summer noon we passed into a great dark room, so dark that it was some time before I made out a lady lying on a couch and holding out her hand to me. I felt my way to a stool on the floor and looked at her for quite an hour without daring to open my lips, while she and my mother spoke in rapturous whispers of the glorious epoch opening up for Italy. Everything was intense— the heat, the enthusiasm, the darkness and I tried hard to get keyed up to the proper pitch. But it was of no use. The poetess was everything I did not like. She had great cavernous eyes, glowering out under two big bushes of black ringlets, a fashion I had not beheld before. She never laughed, or even smiled, once, during the whole conversation, and through all the gloom of the shuttered room I could see that her face was hollow and ghastly pale." Fortunately she found Robert Browning more attractive: "His eyes, dark golden brown like his coat, were full of the sun; his face was a very noble one, clear and pale, with an aquiline nose and a beautiful mouth smiling under the gold brown beard!"

In 1861 Mary and her brother were inspired by reading Thomas Macaulay's *Lays of Ancient Rome*. They were also greatly encouraged by their English governess who enthused them about ancient Rome. Although brought up as a Protestant, Mary soon felt the Catholic atmosphere of Italy and in due course became a sincere and enthusiastic convert. It was at this time that her mother married again, to another American artist from New England, a Mr. Luther Terry, and the family in due course moved to the Palazzo Odescalchi, which remained her mother's home for the rest of her life.

It was shortly after her mother's remarriage that Mary first went to England. In 1862 she and her elder sister Jennie were consigned to the care of three women, each named Sewell, who ran a very select girls' boarding school at Bonchurch on the Isle of Wight. In her *Reminiscences* Mary gives a sympathetic and amusing account of this establishment. She and her sister found themselves installed in a great airy bedroom furnished with bright chintz. "A large bow window gave us the sun all day and a wide view of the sea. There was an open fireplace where for little Italians who might feel the cold a grand fire was always lighted for us in the evenings." The atmosphere was utterly foreign to anything she had so far experienced. "I had no complaints to make about indefiniteness now; in that little world there was never any doubt about belief or duty. The religion was Anglican and thorough; the manners those of my own dear mother; the language pointed and pure, and the morals so high and honourable that during all my stay under that kindly roof I cannot remember one case of deception or fibbing on the part of the girls. . . . There were no punishments of any kind. We found full reward or retribution in Miss Ellen's smile or frown on Saturday evenings when, one by one, she received us alone to inspect our registers." There were only seven girls in the school and for their care there were seven or eight maids. Ashcliff was not to be called a school—"It was a family home. . . . Since to the first pupils the Misses Sewell had been Aunt Ellen, Aunt Elizabeth and Aunt Emma, so they remained for every girl who came. . . . The minutiæ of our education would seem laughable to growing girls now. We were taught how to write notes to our equals, invitations, acceptances, enquiries for invalids" and so on. "Everything was thought of; we had to learn how to enter a crowded room with quiet self-possession. Aunt Ellen would be the hostess sometimes, and one was sent back again and again into the passage till one could enter smoothly and gracefully. . . . We did not have to be in the school-room till 7.30; there, plates of bread and butter, and in winter a warm fire, awaited us. An hour of study, prayers, breakfast (a great meat meal that made me open my eyes in amazement when I first beheld it), hours and hours of lessons out of which one hour was always taken for playing in the garden sometime in the morning to 'freshen' us up; the leisurely dinner (at which if we did not want second helpings to roast joints, puddings, pies, and beer, the Aunts looked anxious and sent for the doctor to prescribe a tonic), a two hours' walk—by ourselves, if you please, with any chosen companion, so that we might really enjoy it; afternoon tea, two more hours of study; a careful evening toilet, the highest of high teas, where everybody chattered all the time and the girls cut the vast cakes to suit themselves; then the great treat of the day, the evening spent in the big pretty drawing room, extravagantly lighted, while one of the elders read aloud and we occupied our fingers with our own pretty work; bed at nine thirty.

"The readings gave us in turn Walter Scott, Fenimore Cooper, Bulwer Lytton, Mrs. Gaskell, and other writers suited to all our ages; Dickens was considered 'vulgar and squalid,' and Thackeray too complicated for our minds." During a reading of *Cranford* by Mrs. Gaskell "we were all electrified when Aunt Elizabeth came to a full stop in the beginning of the part where the nephew plays a practical joke—something connected with a baby—on the old ladies. 'I will leave this out' said Miss Sewell, looking quite stern. Then she turned the page and took up the story further on."

In 1863 Mary and her sister Jennie went on holiday to Switzer-land, but then for two years they did not see their family, as the family's finances had been much reduced as a result of the American Civil War. Mary was able, however, to see something of English country life while staying near Sherwood Forest and in Warwick-shire. She also stayed at New College, Oxford, of which the aunts' brother was at that time warden. She was deeply impressed by Oxford, not least by the turf in the quadrangle. "That's fine," remarked an American multimillionaire to an English gardener.

"How do you manage to get it?" "Oh, it's quite simple, sir" was the reply. "You've only got to roll it for three hundred years."

At the end of June 1865 Mary and Jennie returned to Rome to the Palazzo Odescalchi in the piazza of that name. This was a more modern house than the Villa Negroni where she was born, but it too had an interesting history. It was built by Pope Innocent XI (1611–89). Opposite her window rose the bell tower of Santi Apostoli where Michelangelo used to go to Mass. "One of the doors in the ballroom was a sham one, put into the wall for the sake of symmetry. Behind it, from top to bottom of the house rose a great blind shaft, called in Rome the 'pozzo nero' (the black well)." This was used to brace the building and as a garbage dump.

Jennie died tragically of typhoid in 1866. Eighteen sixty-eight found Mary and her eldest sister Annie in Dresden where Annie, later to marry the Prussian landowner Erich von Rabe, went nearly crazy over her first experience of Wagnerian opera.

During these years, among the people Mary met were Generals Ulysses S. Grant and William T. Sherman. She made friends with the American poets Lowell and Longfellow. The latter she describes as "far and away the most interesting and lovable of our visitors."

In 1870 in the Alpes Maritimes she met Edward Lear. She became aware at table the day after her arrival that a gentleman on the opposite side was regarding her with benevolent if amused pity as she tried to understand the gabble of voices speaking the Lombard dialect. "He had a long white beard and very bright eyes." They soon became friends, and she realised who he was when he made a funny drawing for her young sister Daisy. "Never was there a man who could so live into the feelings of a child." Daisy took all her little disasters to "Uncle Lear" to have them "turned into joys by his rhymes and pictures. A frightful bump on her forehead was the origin of the 'Uncareful Cow' who got a similar one and was horrified to find it growing into a third horn which had to be rubbed away with camphor. The strange meats and unmanageable cutlery of the table d'hôte inspired the marvellous specimen 'Manyforkia Spoonfoolia' as well as most of the recipes for 'Nonsense Cookery.' But Uncle Lear did not always wait to be asked for his rhymes. Day after day Daisy would find on her plate some enchanting, highly coloured sketch with an appropriate poem. We all felt enriched when 'The Owl and The Pussycat went to sea in a beautiful pea green boat' and the mystery of the disappearance of 'The Jumblies' who 'Never came back to me' had an alluring gloom even for us grown ups." Lear later sent Mary a copy of his book on Corsica that was one of her "most treasured possessions." He often came to see the family in Rome in succeeding years.

The year of 1870 was a dramatic one for Europe with the Franco-Prussian War and the fall of the Second Empire in France. In Italy this was the year of the completion of Italian unity with the surrender of Rome. Mary was forced to remain in Florence, a city that she always associated with tragedy; her sympathy lay with Pope Pius IX (1792–1878).

At the age of twenty, in 1871, Mary and her elder sister, Annie, insisted on being emancipated from the irksome company of a chaperon on their walks. With their newly gained liberty they made many charming discoveries in and around Rome.

In 1873 at Lucca her sister Annie met Erich von Rabe, and Mary seems to have been caught up in the romantic attachment that Annie formed with the "very tall, very lame, very music loving German officer." Annie detested everything German and always spoke with Erich in French, but, according to Mary, they understood each other perfectly. They were married shortly after Christmas that year.

Mary herself was married the following year on June 15, 1874, to Hugh Fraser. Mary does not tell us where or when they met, but she says that "spring was a dream of beauty and every day took us out to some lovely villa. . . . When the end of April filled the house, the city, the villas with lilacs and lilies and roses, Hugh Fraser and I understood each other at last. He had been Second Secretary of the British Legation (as it was then) for two years, and had just been appointed to Peking, so no long delay was possible." Their engagement lasted only six weeks, and they spent a little leave in Venice. "I knew every stone in the place, but Hugh had never been there before, and he fell deeply in love with the silent beautiful Queen of the Adriatic, and ever afterwards, when life grew too strenuous for his rather indolent taste, he used to threaten to give up the Service and apply for the post of Consul there."

On August 21, 1874, Mary's diplomatic career began when they set sail for China. Her parting with her family was a tearful one, and the Adriatic was rough (Mary was always a bad sailor). They had to change ships three times before reaching Shanghai and ran into a typhoon outside Hong Kong. The typhoon had raked Hong Kong. "The Bund was swept away, not a tree in the Botanical Gardens was left standing, and half the buildings were roofless ruins. All haste was being made to bury the dead, for a pestilence was feared." (The plague remained a threat to life in Hong Kong into the twentieth century.) Mary found China "disappointing in the extreme, and the approach to Shanghai most depressing with those wastes of yellow, turgid waters." However, once housed in Jardine Matheson's "Palace" her spirits revived. They did not know anyone in the firm, but they were treated like "long expected relations." They had to stay briefly in Shanghai, if only "to buy furniture, nothing being procurable further north." (Mary had brought all her draperies and hangings from Rome.) The journey on to Tientsin by coastal steamer was uncomfortable, and Mary was dismayed by the preparations for the journey to Peking. "The Frasers," she wrote, "are all Spartans." A fleet of five boats was engaged, but there was not much room in which to sleep. "Our own apartment consisted of a tiny caboose sunk aft, just large enough for a mattress to be laid on the floor at night and replaced by a table in the daytime. . . . At night the caboose was closed in all round with wooden shutters, and in the morning poor Hugh used to hurry into his clothes and go on shore for a walk while I attempted to make my toilet, in all but darkness, with the help of one tin basin, muddy river water and a hand glass." The rains were heavy. Once they got stuck on a sandbank for twenty-four hours, and on another occasion they were without food for twelve. But her Hugh "was a splendid traveller" and entertained Mary with queer accounts of his former five years in China. They eventually reached Tungchow, where they were greeted by a "smart, friendly, British Constable," and Mary thankfully clambered into the waiting palanquin. "As we approached the town, the everlasting fields of millet stubble gave way before vast spaces of yellow dust, beyond which the enormous walls of the Manchu City stretched as far as I could see, four miles in an exact square, with huge out-standing buttresses all along their length and triple-roofed watch towers at every corner. It looked like a great sulky monster waiting to spring."

They stayed at first with Mr. and Mrs. Wade. Mr. Wade, later Sir Thomas, was the Minister at the Legation and a renowned Chinese scholar. By the time winter set in the Frasers had their own house, and Mary had begun trying to learn some Chinese. The cold was intense, but Mary suffered more from the heat of the huge fires, the soft coal for which was brought into the Legation com-pound "on camels, some twenty tied together, the nose string of one to the tail of the next." During the first two or three months Mary made few excursions, partly because what she had seen of the streets "was the reverse of attractive, partly because there was so much to interest one within our walls. . . . The place was a little world in itself; there was the 'big house,' the Envoy's residence, which consisted of a number of splendidly decorated Chinese buildings . . . houses for the mounted constables who constituted the escort . . . students quarters and the buildings used as a Chan-cery." There was also an arsenal, stables, and other offices. A "con-stant amusement" was the daily visit of one or more dealers in curios, furs, and embroideries. Mary found visits by Manchu ladies something of an ordeal. They might arrive at eleven or twelve o'clock and stay till sunset. They would "flit about from room to room fingering everything, trying on one's clothes, turning out wardrobes and asking the name of every article, and, strange to say, carrying off all the toilet soap in sight." Mary noted that during the cold months peoples' appetites were "portentous." They "fared royally on the frozen game brought down by the Mongols and sold in their own particular market near the Legation. . . . Except for one or two Heads of Missions who were usually engaged in extracting indemnities and apologies for the last crop of outrages, there was very little for anybody to do between December and April. . . . Everybody dined everybody else solemnly till the stores began to run short, for every atom of grocery and all the neces-sities of a civilised table had to come from Shanghai or—and most people preferred this method—from Europe. The arrival of dozens of huge cases twice a year from the Civil Service or the Army and Navy Stores was one of our great excitements; there was much secrecy about working out the lists from the fat catalogues beforehand and quite fierce rivalry between housekeepers to outdo each other in a fine display of European dainties. . . . The funny thing about all this entertaining was that each family in our compound, including the bachelor Second Secretaries, felt obliged to invite all the rest just so many times in the season. Our bungalows were scattered about the place; none were more than a stone's throw distant from another; but with the true English instinct for privacy, each was its owners' castle, and we sent each other cards of invitation as gravely as if we had been living in Mayfair." Mrs. Wade, who was much younger than her husband, soon went home, and Mary found herself "doing the honours. . . . I was not English at heart as yet, and found myself much more in sympathy with the French and Russians than with my neighbours in the Compound."

Mary Fraser, with her cosmopolitan background, inevitably found herself caught up in the affairs of the diplomatic corps. She became a particular friend of Madame de Prat, wife of the Secretary of the Spanish Legation. Secretary de Prat entered into a bitter personal quarrel with his chief, who was new to diplomatic life. This ended in a duel which took place in the compound of the Belgian Legation. Fortunately the duel, while highly dramatic and Latin, did not end in tragedy. A fusillade of shots caused a trickle of blood and a grand reconciliation.

In 1875 a young British official called Margary was killed in Yünnan. Wade, "who belonged to the Sir Harry Parkes School of Diplomatists, was bent on making the strength of the British position in China clear" and, determined to exact punishment, wanted to appoint Hugh Fraser as his commissioner to investigate the murder, but Mary pleaded strongly against this. She had given birth to a son and feared for the safety of her husband. The Minister agreed and appointed someone else.

Mary, whose health was always poor, found the Chinese summer very oppressive, but she obtained some relief in the western hills. The Legation rented five or six Buddhist temples there. Her first home was in the "topmost temple of all, . . . a grey and ancient retreat whence silent Buddhist monks had once looked out over the misty plain to the world they had renounced. It was an eerie place, reached by some hundreds of steps and surrounded by a high wall like that of a fortress." But the summer heat was terribly intense, and torrents of rain fell. The next summer the Frasers established themselves at another temple halfway down the slope and "a very much pleasanter residence than the other." She found the country people friendly, whereas "we were detested in the city and never passed outside the Compound without being made to feel it."

One of the Frasers' friends in Peking was Sir Robert Hart, the founder and autocrat of Chinese Imperial Customs. The customs service included Russians, Danes, Frenchmen, Italians, Germans, Britons and Americans. Sir Robert Hart ruled them very strictly and collected a princely revenue for the Chinese Government, which came, to quote Mary, to regard him "as a kind of demi-God."

Mary explains that most of the places of interest in Peking were then open for visits by foreigners. An exception was the Temple of Heaven, which the Emperor entered alone once a year. They also had permission to walk on the wall of the Manchu city, which gave them a splendid lonely promenade sixteen miles long. "The top of the wall was some fifty feet broad, smoothly flagged and protected by a breast high parapet. At each mile of its length, flights of steps led up from the Manchu side of the gate where the guardian who had orders to admit us received us gladly for the sake of his little 'cumshaw.'"

Mary found time to visit most of the interesting places between Peking and the Great Wall. Among these was the ruined Summer Palace built for the last Ming Emperor by the Jesuits. She much admired the ruins of the Italianate balconies and doorways, but she approved of its "sack and nominal destruction" by her compatriots in 1860 on the orders of Lord Elgin as "just and all too merciful punishment for the crime perpetrated" against Sir Harry Parkes and his companions who were "tortured and insulted." It took the Frasers some three days to reach the Ming tombs, but like so many other travellers before and since she was even more impressed by the Great Wall.

Mary Fraser found some aspects of Peking life very limited. She writes: "The severe seclusion of women among the educated

Chinese debarred me from personal acquaintance with their prominent men. . . . When Cabinet Ministers or other great personages came to the Legation, orders went forth that all Englishwomen were to stay indoors, and it was only through lowered blinds that I could watch the procession file in, the throng of mounted guards first, then the great man in his gorgeously decked palanquin and after him the equipages of his Staff, glorified mule carts with silken robed drivers, the animals sleek and well fed, and their harnesses shining with polished metal."

Mary's health had suffered much in China. Epidemics were common; sanitary arrangements, primitive; and contemporary medicine, inadequate. She also found the extremes of heat and cold difficult to take. So in the spring of her fourth year in China it was decided that she should return to Europe in advance of Hugh Fraser. She went straight to Rome to her mother's home in the Palazzo Odescalchi.

Hugh had been offered the post of Minister in Bogota, but having had an earlier experience in Guatemala he had turned this down. In her *Further Reminiscences* Mary explains that Hugh Fraser, after a delightful initial post in Copenhagen, was transferred to Guatemala. His chief there instantly went on leave, and Hugh remained as Chargé d'Affaires with responsibilities in five republics. "His headquarters were in the new town of Guatemala; his staff, a native clerk; and his only means of travel, a mule. He used to tell me how he would journey from capital to capital through the forest, in uniform, cocked hat and all, this latter for the benefit of any stray bandits that might have been drawn there for shelter. They would not touch a foreign representative in a cocked hat and gold lace, though they might have cut his throat in mufti. England was a word to conjure with in those times." After a year and a half "a dreadful doubt began to enter Hugh's mind. His mail grew scantier and scantier. His chief had not returned. Appeals for direction were unanswered and the F.O. [Foreign Office] turned a deaf ear to his suggestions of an exchange. They were beginning to forget all about him!" He decided he could stand it no longer. So one day he packed up, locked the Legation, and sailed away for England. When he reported shamefacedly, "authority was infinitely amused: 'Good Lord, my dear boy!' it said.

'We expected you home ages ago—we had no idea that you would last it out as long as that!' " (I have to say that things have changed!)

Hugh was sent as Secretary of the Embassy in Vienna, where he succeeded a former military officer who had got into trouble by forming a liaison with "a lady better known for beauty than virtue." After the officer had sat down with her at a table close to the one where his wife was sitting with his chief, Sir Henry Elliott, and Lady Elliott, he had to leave. In Peking Mary had not had much to do in society. In Vienna she was introduced to the grandeur and pomp of diplomatic life in imperial Austria, and before going to Vienna she had to be presented to Queen Victoria. She found this ceremony at Buckingham Palace a bore. She noted in the Viennese aristocrats an arrogance that she had never seen equalled. "Foreigners in general were looked upon as barbarians and their presence resented." Her first function was a dance at the German Embassy given by the Ambassador's wife, Princess Reuss. Here Lady Elliott presented her to Viennese society. "My beautiful grey-haired Chiefess laid her hand firmly on my arm and sailed away with me, through room after room, each fuller than the last, as it looked to me, of gorgeously bedecked dowagers with historical names, who gazed at me sadly over breastplates of diamonds, murmured a few polite words as I made my curtsey, and then faded out of my consciousness as I was hurried off to the next group. When it was over—it took almost all the evening—my monitress gave a big sigh, as well she might, and informed me that I must leave cards with every one of those women within twenty-four hours, and be sure to remember their names and faces when I met them again."

In the spring of 1882 Hugh Fraser was appointed at his own request Secretary to the Embassy in Rome. Mary felt that soon they would be sent far away from Europe, and she wanted to be near her own family for a year or two. Mary's account of these years contains much about illness. She suffered from malaria and her elder son was frequently sick. But she adored the Italian countryside and managed to travel if only for summer holidays outside the heat of Rome. One of Mary's holidays included a visit to Capri and Axel Munthe's wonderful villa at Anacapri. When she first saw the magnificent view from the balustrade she gasped and clung against the flank of a great white marble sphinx Dr. Munthe had brought from Egypt. "She is homesick, but she likes the view," the doctor explained.

In the spring of 1886 Hugh Fraser was appointed Minister to Chile. They sailed from Liverpool in June on the old cargo ship Cotopaxi that was carrying back a load of copper which for some reason had not been accepted in England. They had left their boys at school in Worcestershire and had had a happy holiday in Devonshire. Mary enjoyed her calls at Rio de Janeiro and Montevideo but found the Strait of Magellan cold and frightening. She was not impressed by the approach to Valparaiso and could not imagine how it got its name (Vale of Paradise). From the train to Santiago she got her first impression of the country, "its loneliness and dryness, and the poverty of the lower classes living in sparsely scattered mud-houses between fields of dried mud and stretches of drier sand." They arrived in the depth of the winter and found the house of their predecessor with its French windows and patios unbearable. She also found the heavy rain, which "washes holes for itself in the light roofs and flimsy walls and pours as steadily into the buckets in one's drawing room as into the gutters in the street outside. At the hotel I often had to sleep under an open umbrella, which did not prevent my waking up in a swamp of wet blankets in the morning." Not surprisingly, she suffered badly from rheumatism. She had her first experience of an earthquake while in the hotel. But although this was a "sickening" one, she gradually grew less apprehensive of the Chilean "tremblore," and it was not until she went to Japan that the true horrors of earthquakes were revealed to her.

Mary did not find life in Santiago easy. She had the inevitable servant problem. She had brought with her from England a butler, a cook, and a maid. This was an expensive mistake, but Hugh had insisted: "He would have one respectable manservant on the place, he said, and he refused to let himself be poisoned by the native messes, as he called them." The cook and the maid both soon struck up local liaisons. When Mary, who was then in a wheelchair, got very angry with her maid, the girl retorted "that they were English girls and not slaves, and that a little harmless amusement was not a sin." Harriet, the cook, indeed soon married the local English grocer, much to Hugh Fraser's anger. When the grocer offered to pay all the expenses incurred to bring Harriet to Chile Hugh's fury was extreme, and Mary had to be called in to smooth things down. She explained to the grocer that Hugh "did not really call him an impudent rogue. . . . It was a long business, for Hugh had entangled himself in the depths of that Highland temper of his, where I could not follow him." The cook was succeeded by a Chilean man and an assistant. One day the assistant, who had gone to market with one hundred pesos, did not return. So Mary told Hugh that the police must be called in. "Very well," said Hugh, blotting the letter he was writing, "we will go and rouse them. The walk will do you good, my dear." Mary had not expected this, and she was not pleased when she found out that it meant walking across half of Santiago. Hugh would not hear of a cab. "Hugh had come out for a walk, and he was going to have one. Square after square we crossed, street after street, and I was nearly ready to sit down on the pavement when, at last, we came upon the station." The police were surprised and amused by this visitation, and the boy was found. Mary wanted to dismiss him, but Hugh said that "they were all equally dishonest and unreliable," so the boy stayed.

In her accounts of life in Santiago she reveals another aspect of her husband's character. Hugh "knew Spanish, but quite refused to condescend to its employment."

Life in Santiago had few compensations, despite some performances by Sarah Bernhardt. As for "society, in our sense of the word, there was none, except that of the Corps Diplomatique. The natives never invited us to any of their functions, and we, consequently, could not invite them. True, the very rich and distinguished occasionally gave a dinner-party but these fearful affairs were, thank Heaven! few and far between. . . . I have known many nations that ate heartily, not to say greedily, but the Chilenos are alone in the consumption of solid food. They went through every course from soup to sweets, and often an extra dish of their own besides, sparing nothing. At lunch, when that was done, a savoury was brought on—a digestif—of red beef steak in the ration of a pound to a person; and what is more, they ate it up! . . . That same beef steak is the invariable accompaniment of every meal from breakfast onward."

Hugh Fraser's prime function in Chile was to complete the settling of the claims resulting from the war between Chile and Peru and Bolivia—the so-called Nitrate War. His main problem was compensation for the nitrate bond holders. "Suggestions poured in with every mail—suggestions not untinged with abuse. Hugh was very patient, and his Highland ancestry had given him a sense of humour . . . against whose edge the storm burst in vain. . . . Hugh was rather a queer person in some ways. When he might be expected, and reasonably, to lose his temper, he would be quite likely to laugh, or to display a gentleness so utterly impersonal and yet so understanding, so sympathetic and so selfless, that one looked up to him with a certain awe, as not being entirely of this world. At others, a trifle, unnoticed by anyone else, would stir that Scotch nature to its depths and for days he would brood over it, never speaking. One was left to conjecture what it might have been, but one never, never found out—except by accident."

Mary says little about Hugh in her letters from Japan, but these vignettes give us some idea of what he was like. Educated at Eton, the son of Sir John Fraser, a General who had served long years in India, he was obviously intelligent, with a strong moral sense. But despite the sense of humour which Mary mentions, we are left with the impression of a strong, silent man, hardworking and determined, but not very imaginative. That he was somewhat jealous of his romantic, sensitive, cosmopolitan, and delicate wife is clear from the remark of Mary's that she "had found it prudent to give up acting, myself, after three or four years of marriage. Violent love-scenes on the stage with good-looking men are not conducive to harmony at home!" Elsewhere she writes of him that "he was of philosophic temperament and he never wasted time and effort in complaint, when complaint was useless. Later in life he appeared not to notice ordinary discomforts and inconveniences at all. If he did, he never allowed anyone to know of it. I remember once in Japan, when I had been away from the Legation for a couple of days, I asked the English butler what he had given him for dinner the evening before. 'We gave His Excellency a very good dinner, madam,' he replied assuringly, 'a real old-fashioned English dinner—boiled bacon and cabbage, madam!' And Hugh had never said a word!"

Hugh and Mary Fraser had very different temperaments; his was very British, and hers rather Latin: "I always leave my real self in cold storage when I go to England, and my dear Hugh had very little use at any time for the Mediterranean born side of my personality." But despite these differences there is no indication in Mary's writings that the marriage was anything but a happy one.

After two years of dealing with Chilean claims Hugh announced that the majority of the court (himself and the judge) had decided to compromise the rest of the claims for one hundred thousand dollars. There were voluble protests, but Hugh Fraser insisted. And in the spring of 1888 he received his orders to proceed as Minister to Japan. It was a very welcome promotion for him. Mary recalled how in Vienna she had asked Lord Tenterden, the Permanent Under-Secretary of the Foreign Office, who had been one of Hugh's fags at Eton, to send her husband one day as Minister to Peking. "No," he said, "I shall not send Hugh to Peking; I think you would like Japan better." Indeed she did as you shall see from her book.

Pat Barr, in *The Deer Cry Pavilion* (London, 1968; p. 203), says of Hugh Fraser that he "remains a shadowy figure [in his wife's letters] wrestling with dispatches in his Tokyo office during hot summer afternoons, waltzing reluctantly with countesses, battling over the same terms of the trade treaties with each new Foreign Minister. 'His abnormally retiring disposition narrowed the circle of his appreciators and impaired the public's estimate of his capacity,' judged *The Japan Mail* in its obituary. 'But by all who served with him or under him he was loved and respected.'"

The Baroness D'Anethan, the English wife of the Belgian Minister, records in her memoirs titled *Fourteen Years of Diplomatic Life in Japan* (London, 1912; p. 75) that Hugh Fraser became ill on May 9, 1894, and "died peacefully at 8:45 pm, after great suffering" on June 4, 1894. He was buried on June 6. The Baroness records: "Preceded by a military escort, and followed by over sixty carriages and an immense concourse of people, Mr. Fraser was laid to rest at the Aoyama cemetery. A. [her husband] and I attended the funeral. It was very touching and so sad. I felt greatly for Mrs. Fraser."

Mary does not record much about her life after her husband's death in 1894. She seems to have spent most of her time in her beloved Italy, but she also must have lived quite a bit in England. (The prefaces in all her books give an English location.) Apart from her three years at Bonchurch she does not seem to have spent much time in earlier years in England. She does not write with any enthusiasm of London, where she used to stay at Brown's Hotel, that model of Victorian respectability. She did not enjoy Bath, the home of her parents-in-law, although she found Lady Fraser "one of the most charming types . . . of a bygone generation." But she eventually realised that Bath's "solemn calm was just what would appeal to men ready to retire from the wild hurly-burly of military service."

One person she came to know towards the end of the last century was Henry James, whom she met at her brother's house in Italy. She writes of him: "It was a treat to have Mr. James in the house. His keen interest in everything, his utter absence of 'side'; the exquisite urbanity which tempered every expression of his unnerving judgement of men and women; above all, his amazing humility about his own achievements, made a most endearing personality. He greatly admired [my brother] Marion, and would lead me on to talk of him on every opportunity." At one point she mentions in the context of Henry James some theatrical "pictures" played at Marion's house at Sorrento, adding "several of which I used in Japan in 1906, in a show given for the famine sufferers." So she must have revisited Japan at least once after her husband's death.

Only very occasionally does Mary refer to Japan in her lengthy *Diplomatists's Wife in Many Lands* (New York, 1911) and *Further Reminiscences of a Diplomatists's Wife* (London, 1912). But the following passage from the latter underlines her feeling for Japan: "In my two real homes, Japan and South Italy, beauty *lives*. It is not merely an exquisite scene that you behold, it is sight and revelation at the same time. Nature speaks some word at certain moments; it is for you alone—you cannot translate it any more than you can put a chord into speech; but it is clear, imperative, divine. Once, in Japan, after a period of great stress and preoccupation, I had been sitting up all night alone to finish a certain task. I was worn out; the coming day was programmed into a perfect chess board of engagements, public and private; and for a minute I felt as if sudden death would be a happy release from the unendurable responsibilities of life. The dawn made its way into the room—I opened a window and looked out. Already the world was white with morning and moist with dew. Just under my window, reaching up to show me its face, one great white lily had opened in the night; the sun had never seen it yet; its whiteness was the blue whiteness of snow in the shade; but from the immaculate heart of it the golden arrow heads had burst their bonds and trembled with their load of pregnant balm, whose perfume flooded up and kissed my eyes to just the few happy tears needed to wash away fatigue and despondency, leave sight clear, courage high, to meet the coming hours.

"That was Japan, the impersonal; one flower, one moment, and you are 'freed from the wheel' of self."

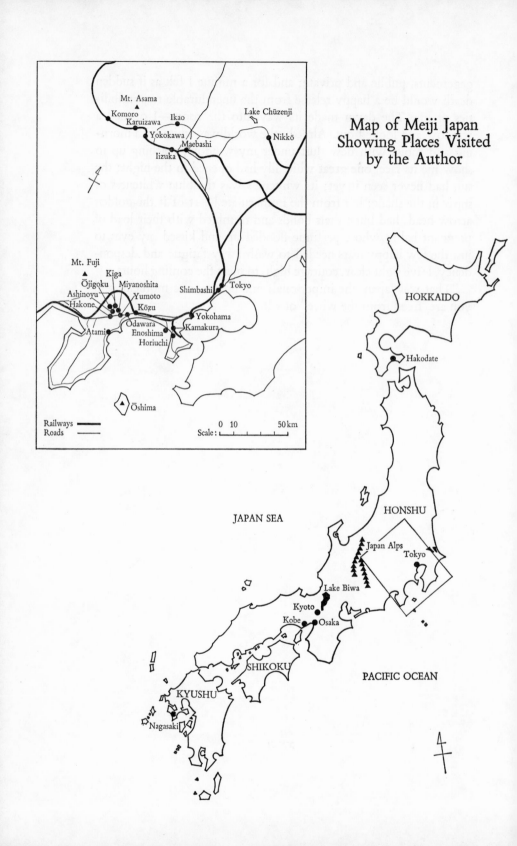

Map of Meiji Japan
Showing Places Visited
by the Author

A Diplomat's Wife in Japan

Author's Introduction

In the following letters, written during a three years' residence in Tokyo, no method was followed beyond the interests and the fancy of the moment; no detailed description was attempted of Japan, her history and her customs and her philosophies. In the times when every foreigner saw the same sights in the Island Empire, obtained the same stereotyped glimpses of the people's life, and was contented with the half-comprehended information given by his guide, it was easy, and alas! fashionable, to describe the "toy country" and its "fairylike" inhabitants with glib security in large print. Those times are gone for ever. Japan has set the doors of her secret shrines ajar, so that we can at any rate take the first step in wisdom, and realise how little we know. Those who, like myself, have had the privilege of spending long years in the country, with liberty to "visit any spot and remain in it for any length of time," become gradually aware of the many-sided and complex character of the people,—simple to frankness, yet full of unexpected reserves, of hidden strengths, and dignities of power never flaunted before the eyes of the world; surprising and majestic as some of those indescribable mountain views in the central hills, where from a flowery rise in a meadow the amazed traveller finds himself on the verge of a dizzy precipice, looking out on a world where the primeval forces appear to have that moment ceased their play, where some great city of giant towers and ramparts, temples and palaces, seems to lie at his feet, overthrown and tossed upon itself as the bricks that the child builds high, and then dashes down for the joy of their fall. The Japanese scenery is often like a book of pictures. The mists rise, and show you one beauty at a time, then close in behind you. The leaf is turned, and you wonder if it was true that you saw the sun shining on a bay and little islands covered with lilies floating on its bosom. You look back, and there is only blank mist. But the scene was the truth, the mist is the illusion.

And the people have the same way of wrapping themselves in colourless conventionalities. That which you expect from them is that which they would wish to show you, and very likely all that you will ever see. But if any shared emotion suddenly draws you closer together, then the veil is rent away, you behold the springs of action, and, lo! they are those which have swayed you in the best moments of your life; and if you are honest and humble-minded, you will say in your heart, "Brother, I misjudged thee. Perhaps thou art as near to wisdom and to love as I."

The years of my stay in Japan were those which will count in history as the first of its majority. With the proclamation of the Constitution on February 11th, 1889, Japan came of age, and assumed her full rights as a nation among the nations. The war with China in 1894 and 1895 showed that she knew how to maintain them. During the unnumbered centuries of her silent past, the two highest virtues of national life, love of country and sense of duty, had been growing, deep and strong, in the heart of the race. When the call to arms was heard, that root shot up its towering growth, and broke forth before the astonished world in the aloe flower of burning patriotism, the aloe fruit of hero deeds and hero faithfulness. The aloe dies with its rare blossom; but not until the swordlike shoot of a new growth has given promise of its resurrection to a future glory. The thunders and acclaims of war have died away; but the sense of shared strength and shared sacrifice, and even the memory of shared mistakes, remain. There is a new bond between ruler and ruled, between rich and poor, between the princes and the people. And should the years bring the moment back on their circling current, the Japanese people would stand again, shoulder to shoulder, to meet the shock.

4

I should like to call this book a record—and an appreciation. It deals mainly with events and persons connected with the different aspects of life in the capital, in which, naturally, most of our time was passed, and which is pre-eminently the centre of Japan's vitality to-day. I have described only such places as I visited, and more especially the remote hills where we took refuge from the summer heats, and whose every turn became as familiar and beloved as the garden of my childhood. Ill.health and many ties of duty generally put very long journeys out of the question; but the faithful and patient acquaintance made with those places where my lines lay, and what I may describe as the gradual absorption of the life atmosphere surrounding me, will, I hope, make up for the fact that this work is in no way a handbook or a history, but merely a humble and faithful effort to transcribe what I have seen and learnt, and thus to bring to-day's Japan a little nearer to the understanding and sympathy of to-day's England.

The letters came to a sudden end in the early summer of 1894, when I returned to Europe—alone. In the shadow of a great grief* one bright spot will stand out as long as memory lives—memory to recall the inexpressible kindness and sympathy of all my friends, European or Japanese: a sympathy so divine that it robbed sorrow of half its bitterness, a kindness so helpful and persistent that it still reaches out across two oceans to strengthen the link that binds me to the home which is home no longer. Dear people, dear kind friends, be thanked from my heart once more!

I must acknowledge my deep indebtedness to Captain Brinkley, the editor of the *Japan Mail,* for the rare and valuable information which makes it an education on Japanese subjects to read the collected volumes of his excellent newspaper. Two Japanese friends, Miss O'Yei Ozaki and Mr. Yasuoka, have given me many a quaint legend or detail of etiquette and family life, and have rendered signal help by going over these letters with me while I was preparing them for publication. As for books, the just and invaluable work of Rein has always been my companion; the *Murray's Japan* published in 1891 was compiled by Professor Chamberlain and W. B. Mason,

*Her husband, Hugh Fraser, the British Minister, died on June 4, 1894, having been ill since May 9, 1894.

5

both profound scholars of the language and history of Japan, and is as it were a good starting-point from which to read and study in different directions; the enchanting books of Mr. Lafcadio Hearn appeared after I left Japan, and take me back there whenever I open their pages; and most helpful is Mr. von Wenckstern's *Bibliography of Japan*, giving four hundred pages to recording and classifying the mere titles of the books which have been written about the Island Empire.

M. C. FRASER

THE WARREN, TORRINGTON
December 1898

1889

At Sea, April, 1889

I am no longer homesick, so I know that the journey is nearly done, and the new country is drawing me as the sun draws the sunflowers in the old gardens at home. I am looking forward to seeing this new old friend, Japan, with the certainty of happiness which absolutely fresh surroundings always bring me; for, dearly as I love the old, I love the new still better, and can hardly imagine a care or trouble which I could not lay aside amid beautiful scenery first beheld. But I am a little afraid of Japan! I would rather not have a host of first impressions of the ordinary kind, which, as it seems to me, satisfy meagre minds, and prevent their ever really understanding new places and races. I have talked to people who had brought nothing away from Japan but the recollection of a waiting-maid and a tea-house, or one brain photograph of a short dark man dressed in unbecoming clothes. Others have seen a procession, or a dinner with chopsticks, or a missionary school, and keep all their lives one silly memory of the strangest country in the world. And—I have thought that perhaps "Little Japan" had been laughing at them! I hope she will not laugh at me. I should like to understand a little, to love or hate, to praise discerningly or condemn dispassionately— to make a friend, in fine.

7

I think the friendship has begun. The landing at Nagasaki* and the sight of the Inland Sea have upset all my wise resolutions about first impressions. The only thing that came to me as I stepped on shore at Nagasaki was a fit of really light-hearted laughter—laughter of the joyous and unreasonable kind whose tax is mostly paid in tears. Life suddenly presented itself as a thing of fun and joy: the people, the shops, the galloping jinriksha coolies, the toy houses treated as serious dwellings by fathers of families, all combined to give me a day of the purest amusement that has ever been granted to me yet. For sixpence I would have changed places with a seller of cakes whom I met in the road. His clothes were of the impressionist kind, some rather slight good intentions carried out in cool blue cotton, the rest being brown man and straw sandals. He carried a fairy temple built of snowy wood and delicate paper, with a willow branch for a dusting-brush, and little drawers, full of sweets, which pulled out in every direction, as white and close-fitting as the petals of a moon-dahlia. All his dainty wares were white or pink, and at a distance one might have mistaken him and his shrine of sweets for a bundle of lotus blooms on two brown stems. It seemed unwise to change places with him, and might have caused confusion in the family; but I was sorry that H—— would not let me buy him, pack and all, and stand him up in the hall of the new home in Tokyo as my first curio.

And now we are in the Inland Sea; and it seems to me that I have been taken to the heart of the country, have seen the very essence of its beauty and remoteness, have been set in the presence of that by which it would choose to be judged. Our first hours were misty, and the sea was rough; but the mists rolled back from one dream

---

*Nagasaki was a small village until the arrival of the Christian missionaries in the sixteenth century. It became the centre of the Portuguese trade, and on their expulsion in the early seventeenth century the Dutch were allowed to establish a trading port on the small island of Dejima. It was among the first Japanese ports to be opened in the nineteenth century to foreign commerce, and a British Consulate was established there in 1859. It was usually the first Japanese port of call for ships coming from Hong Kong or China.

picture after another, and each was so lovely that one forgot to regret the last. Of all the things that I have seen none are so individually and weirdly beautiful as these pine-fringed hills of Japan, with their delicate, daring profiles rising in curves and points that no Western mountain ever knew, crowned with pines following each other in leisurely succession, and holding out dark-green branches for the mists to tear on, or coppery golden arms for the sun to strike. The mists are not thick rolling fogs like ours; they wave and hang, part and cling together, curl away from a breeze or sink back on a calm like a thousand veils of fine gauze, each moving with a will of its own.

It was a great deal to learn all that at once, to realise that the mist pictures of the Japanese are not fairy dreams, but faithful presentments of nature. Yet another and still stranger sight was in store for me. A fresh wind came tearing down some watercourse in the hills; it swept under the brooding mists, and rolled them up like a scroll; and then—we were on a sparkling sea, flooded with sunshine, enclosed by green mountains, and dotted with innumerable islands. On one, just before us, a lovely temple with a red *torii* (gate) stood right out on the flood, which bathed the feet of its sentinel pines. The deep was suddenly covered with that seemed like a flotilla of white nautilus shells, with sails all set, closing in round us with a flutter of wings, and the cool music of a hundred prows rushing through the water in the sun. Every fishing-boat from every village had put out on that liberating breeze, and the moving crowd of silver sails on the morning sea made a sight too bewildering to paint in words. The peculiar warm sheen of the junk sails, square above and round below, made in long strips, seamed and held together in a thousand lovely patterns by the interlacing ropes strained against the breeze, gave the impression of a web of silver against the blue; and the calm majesty of the silky rush on the water's surface made me feel that our great coal-fed, screw-driven liner was a blot on the universe, and had no title to travel with that fair company.

They, indeed, took little notice of the *Verona*, and treated us with gay disdain. They pressed in on every side, till we were completely surrounded by them, thick on the tide as the white lotus blooms that

smother the marble bridge in the pond of the Summer Palace.*
Then the wind changed, and they all floated away in a wide half
circle, which became a fringe of stars on the water after the night
came down.

I feel that the date at the head of this letter should mark an epoch in
my experience; but I am still too new to these strange airs to give
any clear account of what I have seen, am seeing all the time. I
cannot imagine a better cure for weariness of spirit than a first visit
to Japan. The country is absolutely fresh. All that one has read or
heard fails to give any true impression of this vivid youngness of
an atmosphere where things seem to sort themselves out in their
real, and, to me, new values.

We reached Yokohama on the 1st, and came up here at once.
As scenery Yokohama does not exist, so we will not talk about it;
but Tokyo is enchanting—so far! It strikes me as a city of gardens,
where streets and houses have grown up by accident—and are of
no importance as compared with the flowers still.

As I write, here on my upstairs verandah, so wide and cool that
every breeze sweeps through it from end to end, and yet so sheltered
that I can wander about and work or read in absolute privacy, I
am, as it were, at the heart of things; for there to my left, across the
green banks of the moat, and hid in the impenetrable foliage of the
gardens, is the Emperor's new Palace, which I am to see in a few
days when we have our audience. It stands, as in honour bound,
higher than any of the streets and buildings which lie round the
first moat; but no single gable can be seen above the dark roofs of
the pines, round whose red knees the smaller trees cling jealously
lest any glimpse of the life Imperial reach the outer world. All round
the crest of the hill run high walls, with here and there a beautiful

*In Peking.

gate. There is one, almost opposite our own, of ancient wood, soft and dull in colour, bound and hinged by sheets of beaten copper, which have taken on that wonderful blue patina that our old bronzes have in Rome. Above the gate the prophetic pines stretch their branches down to where the bank slopes away in a hundred yards of sheer green turf to the water of the moat. Here and there a pine or a cherry tree has been set, and some hang far over and dip in the water. Beneath their shade live a pair of white herons (I am sure they are royal lovers of the ancient time, bewitched by evil spells); and on the water swim great flocks of wild duck, tame, because no shot may be fired within sound of the Palace, but just now very much preoccupied as to summer quarters, and talking noisily all day as to the respective merits of the Kurile Islands, Mongolia, and Kamschatka. They cannot stay much longer, for the heat is all but upon us.

As I said just now, we are at the heart of things. For nearly three hundred years the tide of national life has set towards what was a humble fishing village (the name means the door of the bay), till Hideyoshi, the great usurper, pointed it out to his marshal Iyeyasu as a stronger and more central spot than the Castle of Odawara, which had fallen into their hands at the end of some murderous civil war. It seems to me that Tokyo, as I see it from my balconies, with its triple ring of shallow moats spanned by scores of solid bridges, with its vast area, and many miles of meandering streets and gardens, would be easier to take than to defend. Here and there, indeed, is some piece of gigantic wall, built with uncemented blocks like those in the *ager* of Servius Tullius in our old villa at home; but it generally frames in a wide gate, through which the armies of the world could ride with comfort. I should think it would take all the soldiers whom Napoleon slew to keep a fairly persistent invader out of Tokyo to-day. But I have not often seen a fairer city. Hill and valley, wood and water, wild-rose hedge and bamboo grove, stately pleasure-house and small brown cottage, palms and pines and waving willows —there the hills, leading up to the mountain of mountains, and there the sea, a silver line that speaks of home,—it all goes to make a picture so splendid in its breadth, and so alluring in its details, that I feel it is already growing into my mind as a necessary background to certain trains of thought. I am glad that we have come to stay for years, instead of having to rush away in a few weeks, as so many travellers do.

Our audience is fixed for the 17th; and as our social existence only really begins after H—— has presented his credentials, I am taking advantage of the intervening time to see all the flower shows and sights of the month. Beyond the 17th, life seems one long perspective of dinner and garden parties, of which I will tell you when they come—meanwhile I am enjoying myself! Our own gardens are quite lovely just now, with arbours of wistaria, and azaleas bursting out in masses of white and pink and orange blooms, while the great bed of lilies-of-the-valley outside the dining-room windows makes the whole air sweet round that side of the house. The lilies were a surprise to me. They do not grow in this part of Japan, but were brought down from Hakodate, where they are very plentiful, and have flourished and multiplied in the shady corner near the house. That is the corner presided over by poor Sir Harry Parkes' enormous watch-tower,* which he built as a fitting place from which to fly the British Flag. (Out here we always write it with a capital F.) The emblem of empire would, it seems, have been flying some inches higher than the Imperial roofs, so that project had to be abandoned, and the Flagstaff was planted on a mound at the other end of the grounds, where it looks very dignified and businesslike, and is known by the name of Haman's Gallows. But the tower remains, and serves as a reservoir for water, and as a constant reminder of the precariousness of life in these earthquake regions. It has been cracked rather seriously in the many shocks, and is bound and clamped with iron in every direction. They say it is safe enough; but in some slight shocks which we have already felt, it seems to set all that side of the house dancing and trembling ominously.

I am not new to earthquakes, and we have had no very alarming ones here as yet; but the Japanese papers are unkindly promising us a severe visitation shortly. It seems that the shocks are felt very strongly in Tokyo, as they are in all places where there is a large area of soft alluvial soil; and (consoling rider!) our house stands, so I am told, exactly where they all pass, no matter whence the

*The tower collapsed as a result of an earthquake on June 20, 1894.

12

current comes or whither it tends. It may be a distinction to live over a kind of Seismic Junction; but it is bad for the nerves—and the china!

I have not yet made the acquaintance of any of the Japanese ladies. The Ministers' wives all called at about nine o'clock on the morning of the 2nd; but I was not prepared for such an *aubaine,** and they were probably rather shocked to hear that I was not yet dressed. I hope to see something of them, if we can only manage to understand one another. It is terrible to me to be dumb in a new country. I have not experienced such a sensation since we landed at Tientsin many years ago. Our local authorities on the language look at me with indulgent pity when I announce that I mean to learn it. The Japanese Secretary† (that is to say, the Englishman who superintends the Japanese side of the Chancery) shakes his head, and tells me that, though he has been working at it for seventeen years, though he has translated three dictionaries and is now publishing one of his own, though he is examiner-in-chief for the Consular Service, he feels that he is but at the beginning still, and that many lifetimes would not put him absolutely in possession of the whole language as it is used by the learned Japanese to-day.

Tokyo, May 12th, 1889

I already feel quite like an old resident here; but that does not prevent me from having a hundred surprises a day. We have been driving about a good deal, and I begin to know a few landmarks in the town. Our first drive, indeed, was quite a sensational affair. We had arranged to try some very pretty and only half-broken ponies, and for a little while it seemed doubtful whether we or they should really be broken first; then I found constant excitement in

*French for godsend or piece of luck.

†J. H. Gubbins, C. M. G. (Companion of the Order of St. Michael and St. George).

13

watching our groom racing along in front of the horses, lifting fat babies out of the middle of the road where they sat confidingly, leading deaf old women politely to one side, and apparently saving a life once in every ten yards. What legs and lungs the man must have, to come in, as he did, fresh and undistressed after miles of this sort of thing!

I am trying to learn my servants' names, but have as yet only managed a part of two. Rinzo is a kind of head boy, who says, "Okusama, yes!" to every question, command, or reproach; and O'Matsu, his wife, is trying to teach my new English maid to wait on me. The Japanese woman already knows all my ways, and finds enough to do to fill up the tasks neglected by the other girl, who has but one real taste in life—her own amusement.

I have had a list made of the other servants' names, and keep it at hand for reference; but I think it is wasted trouble. I have only to cry "Boy!" or "Amah!" after the old barbarian fashion, and immediately I am surrounded by obedient genii, much nicer than those who waited on Aladdin, for mine smile and bow gratefully every time they are spoken to. The speech may be quite unintelligible, but they would rather die than confess it; at once they fly off, and do something or other just to show their goodwill. The *amah* brings tea or a shawl whenever the bell is rung; so I conclude that her last mistress was an invalid. One of the "boys," who has lived with a bachelor, always answers the summons with a brandy-and-soda *au grand galop*—let us not ask the name of that bachelor!

We are late for the cherry blossoms, and must wait till next year to see them in their glory; but, when the wind blows, the petals are stirred from where they have been lying in rosy heaps at the trees' feet, and go whirling down the paths like belated snowflakes. It is really wistaria-time, and I have been out to the Kameido Temple* to look at the famous arbours there. It is a lovely and amazing sight. The Temple grounds consist chiefly of flagged paths running round great tanks of water, shaded from end to

*Kameido Shrine, dedicated to Sugawara Michizane (845–903), political leader, scholar, and literary figure. Founded in 1662, it was especially revered by the Tokugawa shoguns and noted for its fine wistaria.

end by a thick roof of drooping flowers. The pale-purple clusters grow so thick that no glimpse of sky is visible between them, and their odorous fringes hang four and five feet deep in many places. Little breezes lift them here and there, and sway the blooms about, so as to show the soft shadings from pale lilac to dark purple; and the flowers as they move shed drift after drift of loose petals down on the water, where the fat red goldfish come up, expecting to be fed with lard cakes and rice balls. Low seats and tables covered with scarlet cloths are set by the edges of the tanks, and here people can refresh themselves with tea and *saké* (rice beer) as they sit to admire the flowers.

We found at one corner an arbour entirely overgrown with the white wistaria, which delighted me by its ethereal purity. Why is it that flowers which are usually deep in colour, such as wistaria or violets or pomegranates, are so astonishingly white, when the fancy takes them to leave their proper colour behind? White violets, white wistaria seem whiter than anything has a right to be in a sinful world, and new fallen snow would look almost dark beside a young white pomegranate!

This Kameido Temple seems poor and dusty, and is dedicated to more than one misty divinity; but the memory of a great scholar shares the chief honours with a marble tortoise and two stone ponies. There is a very high bridge over the central waterway, a bridge which describes exactly half a circle, with only slight bars cut in the stone by which to mount and descend. When we approached it, every head was turned towards us. My companion was Mrs. N——, a tall and handsome woman, who affects in her dress a good deal of brilliant colour such as is not worn by grown-up persons here; so there was perhaps some excuse for the staring. She and I wished to reach the other side of the grounds, and, like brave women, made for the most direct path towards it, followed by the interpreter and our *betto* (groom), both looking surprised and pleased. We scrambled up with some little difficulty, remarking to each other that one must be prepared for everything in these strange places; but when we reached the top, and looked down on the other side, our hearts misgave us. It was very dusty and very steep, we were both wearing nice little high-heeled shoes and fluffy silk skirts, and—a delighted crowd had assembled to watch us descend. The situation was a little strained. We did get down without a tumble, for which we were properly grateful; but I am afraid it was not a dignified proceeding, and after it was accomplished we learnt that there was another way round, and that the crossing of this dreadful little bridge was never undertaken except as an act of special devotion to the misty divinities of the Temple. Our attendants' surprise and pleasure were explained; but Mrs. N—— and I came home rather soberly.

I must tell you of a strange and touching ceremony which took place in Yokohama the other day. This was a requiem service in a Buddhist temple, for the repose of the souls of a number of officers and men who were drowned when the U. S. warship *Oneida** was sunk, by a collision with a P. & O. steamer, just in the mouth of the bay nineteen years ago. Lately the wreck was bought by some Japanese gentlemen, who discovered the bones of many poor fellows who had gone down in her. These they brought to shore, and buried beside the bodies of their comrades which had been recovered after the misfortune. Having laid the bones to rest, they thought that it would be kind to do something for the sailors' souls, and organised at their own expense a magnificent requiem service called *Segaki*, or the Feast for Hungry Spirits. They invited all the foreigners and the American admiral with his officers and men. Admiral Belknap was anxious to take some share of the heavy expense, but the five merchants would not hear of that at all. It seemed to me a kind and holy thought, this unasked benevolence shown to a handful of long-forgotten strangers. A local English newspaper describes the promoters of this charitable function as a "Japanese Firm of Wreckers"!

I was just going to begin talking about Treaty Revision, which is for us the question of the day; but the mail is going out, so that infliction must stand over till next week! Mail day seems to be the only inexorable fact in this land of leisure. A poor Englishman

*For an account of this tragedy see "The Loss of the U.S.S. 'Oneida' " in Harold S. William's *Shades of the Past: or Indiscreet Tales of Japan* (Rutland, Vermont, and Tokyo: Charles E. Tuttle Co., 1958, reprinted 1972), pp. 129-39.

who was drowned in Yokohama Bay a few days ago had to be buried in haste, and without any peroration over his grave, the clergyman explaining that it was impossible to break into mail day with what Jeames (was it not?) called "Igstranious subjicks!"

Tokyo, May 18th, 1889

The Emperor was away when we first arrived, so we could not have our audiences until yesterday. I was rather envious when H—— was carried off by a chamberlain in a Court carriage to present his credentials to the Emperor, whom I shall not see just now. But our visit to the Empress was most interesting. The weather was lovely, and the Imperial gardens were all bloom and sunshine as we drove up to the Palace, a long low building standing on high ground, and rearing a beautiful outline against the sky. It is quite new, and the sovereigns only took possession of it last winter, just before the proclamation of the Constitution, the old house which stood on this spot having been completely destroyed by fire. The new Palace is a wonderful achievement, of which its architects may be proud. The old Japanese lines have been everywhere adhered to in its construction, but so modified as to meet the requirements of the Court life of to-day. The whole building is of wood, a light fawn-coloured wood, giving out the most delicate aroma, a perfume which seems to be the essence of yet unembodied marvels of carving and lacquer. This rises into floreated gables, and sinks in richly painted eaves, where the blues and greens are strong and pure as those on a peacock's breast. One or two of these lovely creatures were watching us curiously from their perch on the wall of an inner garden, as we mounted the steps leading to the entrance hall of the Palace, a square room with two carved black-wood tables, on which lie the books, ornamented with gold chrysanthemums, where visitors may write their names for the Emperor and Empress. Here we were met by Marquis Nabeshima, the Grand Master of Ceremonies, and Mr.

17

Sannomiya, his second in command, a man so kind, so dignified, and liberal-minded, that it is impossible not to be drawn to him and the class he represents at once. I have only known him two weeks, and feel as if he were an old friend already.

These gentlemen took us for what seemed a long walk through broad corridors, lined, dado fashion, with shining orange and cedar woods, golden coloured, and scented; above them, an embossed leather paper, in flowing patterns of ivory, gold, and fawn, covers the walls to the lofty ceiling, with its carved beams and rich decorations. At distances of a few feet all along the wall the flowers seem to have taken separate life, and to have burst out in graceful bells and golden leaves inhabited by vital sparks of the electric light. As one goes farther into the Palace, these beautiful galleries lead off in every direction, through doors which are marvels of lacquer and painting. A favourite design is a rabbit in gold lacquer, on a ground of such indescribable polish that the eye seems to sink through its depths as through still waters, seeking in vain for a solid bottom. The gold bunnies, being creatures of earth, are on the lower panels of the doors, sitting up and gazing with ears erect, or playing with blown leaves and grasses; while the upper panels contain more airy designs of birds and flowers. In the heart of the Palace the rooms have glass slides instead of the usual Japanese paper ones, and get all their light and air from the wide surrounding corridors, which in their turn open on enclosed courts full of fruit blossoms and palm trees and the play of fountains in the sun.

At last we were ushered into a very large drawing-room with hangings and furniture of Kyoto silk in soft shades of grey and rose. In the middle of the room rises a kind of flower temple, in rich deep-coloured wood, almost like a circular chancel screen, whose every niche is made to hold a wonderful arrangement of flowers, the orchids and roses and lilies of the West mingling happily with the fruit blossoms and bamboos of the East. Divans and easy-chairs surround the flower temple; and against the walls are cabinets of old gold lacquer, subdued yet splendid as a sunset cloud. The ceiling of this great hall is divided by cross-beams into a hundred squares, each one painted with a different flower; and the doors are lacquered in colours also, blues and greens and crimsons that make one catch one's breath with surprise and pleasure. All this sounds, perhaps, too brilliant and varied for true beauty; but the great space and height of the hall, with the wide outlook all down one side to the flowery court, give so much atmosphere and perspective, that the vibrations of colour float slowly before the eyes, and never clash or jar on the sunny air.

Here we found five or six of the Empress's ladies, all in European dresses, pale blue and mauve and grey satins, made with the very long trains which are not worn in Europe now. I believe this is a part of Palace etiquette, recalling the immensely long robes of royal and noble women of Japan in times past. The little ladies were most kind and cheery, the two who spoke English translating for the others where I sat with them near the flowers, while the men in their brilliant uniforms stood together waiting for the summons to the Empress's apartments. At last the doors were thrown open, and we all started on another long walk through more glass corridors, till a hush fell on our companions, and we paused suddenly on a step, which ran all across the foot of a small square room, full of flowers, and draped with blue damask. After the three regulation curtseys, I found myself standing before a pale, calm, little lady, who held out to me the very smallest hand I have ever touched, while her dark eyes, full of life and intelligence, rested questioningly on my face. Her hair was dressed close to her head, and her gown of rosy mauve brocade had only one ornament—a superb single sapphire worn as a brooch.

In a voice so low that even in that hushed atmosphere I could hardly catch its tones, she said many kind things, which were translated to me in the same key by the lady-in-waiting, who acted as interpreter. First the Empress asked after the Queen's health; and then, when she had welcomed me to Japan, said she had been told that I had two sons whom I had been obliged to leave in England, and added that she thought that must have been a great grief to me. Her eyes lighted up, and then took on rather a wistful expression as she spoke of my children. The heir to the throne is not her son, for she has never had children of her own, and has, I believe, felt the deprivation keenly; but perhaps the nation has gained by her loss, since all of her life which is not given up to public duties is devoted to the sick and suffering, for whom her love and pity seem to be boundless.

When at last the little hand was held out in farewell, I went away with one of my pet theories crystallised into a conviction; namely, that it is a religion in itself to be a good woman, and that a sovereign who, surrounded by every temptation to selfishness and luxury, never turns a deaf ear to the cry of the poor, and constantly denies herself, as the Empress does, to help them, comes near being a saint.

When we found ourselves in the corridors again, Mr. Sannomiya asked if we would care to see the rest of the Palace, and we were led from one beautiful room to another till I was rather bewildered. The glass walls give an appearance of unreality to these splendid apartments, but they add greatly to the light and brilliant appearance of the whole. In all the Palace there is nothing which is not purely Japanese in workmanship, although the general design of the draperies and furniture are after European models. The silks are most artistic, many soft fabrics from the looms of Kyoto, in colours either of dazzling strength and purity, or of such tender cloud shades as one hardly expects to find imprisoned in the warp and woof of earthly tissues. Of ornaments, apart from the studied decoration of walls and floor and ceiling, there are few—a piece of lacquer, a bronze vase, or a fine carving here and there, just serve to break the long vistas; but everywhere there are flowers and flowers and flowers, so profuse, so artistically arranged, that it almost seems as if the Palace had been built for them.

Tokyo, May 25th, 1889

Our visit to the Empress was followed by several dinners at the houses of the Ministers. One does not learn much of Japanese life at these feasts, which are, as far as their appointments go, for all the world like official dinner parties in Rome or Paris or Vienna; but it is startling to find oneself between the host and some other big official neither of whom will admit that he can speak a word of any

European language. I believe they understand a great deal more than they like to confess for fear of being called upon to speak. There is generally an interpreter within hail, and three or four times in the course of the dinner my neighbour solemnly leans forward and instructs him to address a polite remark about the weather or the flowers to me, and I answer in the same three-cornered fashion, and then subside into silence once more. But the silence does not bore me. The new faces, the old historical names, the remembered biography of some hero who perhaps sits opposite to me in gold-laced uniform calmly enjoying the *foies-gras* and champagne as if there were never a blood-stained page in his country's history—all this appeals strongly to one's dramatic appreciations.

The women are really attractive with their pretty shy ways and their broken confidences about the terror of getting into European clothes. Some of them look wonderfully pretty even in these un-congenial garments. There is Countess Kuroda, for instance, the wife of the Prime Minister,* who has lovely diamonds, and always appears in white satin with snowy plumes set in her dark hair. She can talk a little English, and is intensely polite about everything European, as all the little ladies are; but I fancy in their hearts they put us down as big clumsy creatures with loud voices and no man-ners. The very smart people here affect the most impassive counten-ance and a low voice in speaking; and all the change of tone and play of expression which we consider so attractive is condemned in Japan as only fit for the lower classes, who, by the way, are the most picturesque and amusing lower classes that Heaven has yet created. My daily drives in Tokyo are as full of fun and interest as was my first jinriksha ride in Nagasaki. The distances are enormous, and it often happens that I make a journey of three or four miles between one visit and another; but every step of the way brings me to some new picture or new question, reveals some unimagined poetry or bit of fresh fun in daily life. There are parties of little acrobats, children in charge of an older boy, who come tumbling after the carriage in contortions which would be terrible to see did one not feel convinced that Japanese limbs are made of india-rubber. Then

*Count Kiyotaka Kuroda (1840–1900), samurai from Satsuma Province, now Kagoshima Prefecture, in southern Kyushu.

there are the pedlars; the old clothes-sellers; the pipe-menders, who solemnly clean a pipe for one rin as they sit on the doorstep; the umbrella-makers, who fill a whole street with enormous yellow parasols drying in the sun. Here a juggler is swallowing a sword, to the delight and amazement of a group of children; there the seller of *tofu,* of bean-curd, cuts great slabs of the cheesy substance, and wraps it in green leaves for his customers to carry away. I love watching the life of the streets, its fulness and variety, its inconvenient candour and its inexplicable reticences. I am always sorry to come in, even to our lovely home with its green lawns and gardens in flower. It is like leaving a theatre before the piece is over, and one wonders if one will ever see it again.

I went to a garden party the other day, given by Count Ito* on the occasion of his daughter's marriage with a rising politician, Mr. Kenchio Suyematsu. The wedding had, however, taken place some days before. The Count's villa at Takanawa is close to the sea, or as much of the sea as comes into the almost land-locked Tokyo Bay. The house stands on high ground, which overlooks Shinagawa and the Hama Rikyu Palace, the Empress's summer house, built half in the sea like poor Maximilian's villa at Miramar near Trieste. Count Ito's garden slopes down to the sea-level, clothed in a dark-green mantle of lordly pines with red-gold branches, lighted here and there by a cloud of rosy fruit blossom, ethereal as mist shone through by the sun. The views over sea and land are lovely, and we had plenty of time to wander from one point to another, taking it all in. There were crowds of people in brightly tinted dresses; but I saw hardly any Japanese costumes, even Countess Ito's youngest daughter being in European dress. No one seems to talk much at these gatherings; there is a tremendous feast, where we are all placed strictly according to precedence, and are expected to eat and drink as if it were eight o'clock in the evening instead of four in the afternoon! Count Ito has the cleverest face I have ever seen; it is not noble or elevated in any way, which is not strange, perhaps, since he did not originally belong to the higher class of Japanese,

*Hirobumi Itō (1841–1909), samurai from Chōshū, now Yamaguchi Prefecture, in western Japan. Itō served four times as Prime Minister and was later made a marquis and finally a prince. He was assassinated by a Korean at Harbin.

but for sheer intelligence and power I have seen few to beat it. Countess Ito is a very attractive woman, with a fine delicate face, and of course charming manners.

I am slowly learning to know one person from another in this big new circle. I heard a Japanese say that all foreigners looked alike to him, and I confess that for the first two weeks of my stay here I felt like a colley with a new flock of sheep. Now that the personalities are revealing themselves to me, I find my way about among them fairly well.

The great artist Kyōsai* is dead. His life forms a perfect example of God-given genius, served and cherished with complete and simple conscientiousness. Everything true was beautiful in his eyes, whether it appealed to the crowd or not. As a child of three he made friends with a frog on a long *kago* (or litter) journey, and drew its portrait as soon as his mother set him down at the journey's end. At seven he drew every aspect of the human figure as he could see it in the brawls and wrestling-bouts of the lowest quarters of the city, which he haunted patiently, sketch-book in hand, for weeks and months. At nine he captured the severed head of a drowned man from a swollen river, and brought it home to study in secret as any other child would treasure a toy or a sweetmeat. The horror was discovered by his family, and he was ordered to take the grisly thing back to the stream and throw it in. Reluctantly the little boy trudged back to the riverbank, the poor head in his arms; but before he threw it away, he spent long hours, sitting on the ground, copying every line of the awful countenance. The ordinary hopes and fears of humanity seem to have been spared him, and nothing daunted him where his imagination was roused by food for a picture. A wonderful story is told of how a fire broke out one winter night of 1846—a fire which threatened to destroy an immense number of rare birds kept for sale at a shop in the Hongo district. They had been carried out into a square where property was already deposited in quantities; but sparks fell on the cages, and they began to burn, so the owner opened them all, and let the birds loose to save themselves if they could. The whole flock rose up into the sky with wild

*Kyōsai (1831–89), an artist famous for his vigorous and humorous drawings and prints.

23

screams and whirring of wings, and instead of seeking safety flew straight towards the flames which were filling the night with tongues of fire and clouds of red light. Kyōsai was then fifteen, and seems to have been carried completely away by the sight of the gorgeous many-coloured wings turning and wheeling in the glare of the flames. Regardless of everything else, he sat down in the street and sketched with passionate eagerness, till he was bitterly reproached by his family for not lending his help to save their goods from the conflagration. Very humbly he begged to be forgiven his negligence, saying as an excuse that he believed no one had ever had a chance of drawing such a splendid spectacle before.

He got into terrible trouble once, as a young man, for following some ladies in a Daimyo's house, where he was employed in decorating a room. The girls fled from him, and he ran after them, down long galleries and across gardens, till they were terrified, thinking he had gone mad. Then he suddenly stopped, and returned quietly to his work. When reproved for his temerity, he produced his sketch-book, and showed a careful outline of a rare and antique pattern in the sash, or *obi,* worn by one of the girls, which he had caught sight of as she passed, and had sketched as he chased her.

A countryman and intimate friend of Kyōsai tells me that he possesses several of the great painter's drawings, obtained by an amusing stratagem. Kyōsai always refused, if asked outright for a sketch; so his friend began the negotiation by offering the artist an excellent dinner. When Kyōsai had drunk deeply (he pleaded to a love of wine as an aid to inspiration) and seemed in a mellow humour, his host would call for drawing materials, saying that he felt an artistic fancy taking possession of him. No one was surprised, as Japanese gentlemen often amuse themselves in this way after a feast. The servant then brought an enormous sheet of white paper, and spread it on the floor, with the brushes and Indian ink beside it. The crafty host, without looking at his guest, sank on his knees and began to draw, apparently absorbed in his occupation, but intentionally producing a few weak and incorrect lines. Kyōsai watched the feeble effort in silence and growing irritation, and at last jumped up, dashed the tyro aside, and tore the brush out of his hand, exclaiming, "Out of the way, you wretched bungler! *I* will teach you how to draw!" And the result was a priceless sketch, which remained in the possession of his wily entertainer. Again and again did the great artist fall into this snare, his generous soul unable to stand by and see his art wronged.

Once this same friend was travelling with Kyōsai in a region where the painter had not been before. After dinner Kyōsai had an attack of artistic frenzy, and in a short time had covered all the walls of the inn room with wonderful outlines, and filled in the low ceiling with a picture of an enormous black cat, fierce and lifelike to an alarming degree. More fierce and lifelike, however, was the wrath of the landlady, when she found her spotless paper walls and ceiling covered with strange shapes. The room was ruined, she cried; she would have justice; the miscreant must pay for new paper! Then the artist's friend whispered the name of Kyōsai in her ear. Her countenance changed, her curses turned into cries of delighted gratitude, and her reproaches became entreaties that the great painter would forgive her, and would have more dinners in more rooms of her favoured house.

He was a tender-hearted man, and made the fortune of one destitute old cripple by painting a picture for him, which the beggar showed for money, earning enough to buy a house, where he lived in comfort ever after. The subject was a strange one: on one side the poverty of the demons in hell, who were represented as starving to death, and sawing off their own horns to sell for bone-carving; on the other, the angels in heaven welcoming poor and humble penitents to eternal feasts.

He died, as he had lived, a great man with one thought. Three days before his death, when he was already so wasted that he could hardly stand., he sketched the shadow of his own figure, pitifully bent and emaciated, on the white paper wall beside his bed, but only as far down as the knees: below were a few ruthless lines in the shape of a coffin. After he had bade farewell to his wife and family in broken, gasping words, he gave a great cry, and called on the name of his picture-mounter, to whom he gave clear directions about one of his last drawings, and then died. Happy Kyōsai, happy mortal, who from life's dawn to its midnight, with single intention and undoubting faith, filled your place and justified your vocation!

Japan should make many artists. I went to a night fair two or three evenings ago, a humble show where little more than cakes and sweetmeats and straw sandals were sold; but there was one stall full of winged lights, tiny stars of green fire clustering all over it. I bought about a hundred Princess Splendours in a black horsehair cage, and brought them home with me. Do you know the story of Princess Splendour? She was, it seems, a tiny moon-child, so like a firefly that the old woodman (of fairy tales all the world over) picked her off a bamboo branch in the moonlight, and brought her home to his wife. She grew lovelier and brighter for twenty sweet years, till all the brown cottage shone with her beauty at night, and basked in it by day. Every one loved her, but most of all the Emperor, whom she loved too. But she could not marry him, because all her life was only to be twenty years, and the time was nearly up. And he hoped to keep her; but at last the day came when she had to go, and Princess Splendour travelled home on a moonbeam, crying silver tears all the way, till Mother Moon took her in her arms and folded her to her warm white heart, quite away from the Emperor's eyes for ever. And all her tears took wings, and go flying about the woods on warm nights looking for the Emperor still, though he died an old, old man hundreds of years ago. But the keeper of the strange stall at the fair (and I could hardly see it for the darkness) had captured scores of the winged lights, and sold them by ones and twos in a dainty cage two inches long, with a green leaf for provisions, for two rin, a sum so small that we have no equivalent for it. I stood for a minute before the firefly stall, and then told the interpreter to say that I must have *all* the fireflies in *all* the cages. People gathered round in crowds, and one curious face after another pushed itself forward into the dim circle of light, staring at the reckless foreign woman who spent money in this mad way! But the foreign woman knew exactly what she wanted. Princess Splendour's lovely successors were not to be sold away one by one in cages on this warm spring night. I carried them all home in the horsehair box; and when everybody had gone to bed, I crept out into the balmy darkness of my garden, opened the box, and set all the lovely creatures free. This way and that they flew, their radiant lamps glowing and paling like jewels seen through water, some clinging to my hair and my hands as if afraid to plunge into the garden's unknown ways. I felt like a white witch who had called the stars down to play with her. Some of our people thought the same, I fancy; for I suddenly became aware of a string of dark figures hurrying across the shadowed lawns in a terrified rush for the servants' quarters, and I noticed the next day that I was approached with awe amounting to panic.

In connection with fairs, of which there are so many at this time of year, I must tell you a strange thing that happened at a fair in Hakodate two or three weeks ago. The whole population was out of doors, celebrating the "Hill Holiday" by camping and feasting and wandering on the hills which surround the town. The weather was gorgeous, and the sun hot and dazzling. An old man had set out his wares in a little stall on a hillside, toys and sweets, and, alas! crackers—all laid out in bright and tempting rows. He was tired with the heat and the climb, and sat down to rest while waiting for customers. One cannot doze comfortably in spectacles, so he took his off (great round horn-rimmed things), and laid them down on a box of crackers, and fell asleep. Terrible was his awakening by an explosion of great noise and violence. The spectacles had acted as burning-glasses in the hot sun, and had exploded the crackers, which in turn set fire to the whole stall. When the flames died down, nothing was left except a quite ruined old pedlar and some terrified children who had been thinking of inspecting his cakes when the catastrophe occurred.

A new treaty has been signed, really signed. Not ours, of course; an event of such import would not have been treated of in a post-script at the end of my letter. The new treaty between Japan and Mexico is a most splendid and advantageous one for everybody concerned, and promises that, in return for Mexico's politeness in treating Japan as a grown-up nation capable of attending to its own affairs and administering its own laws, Mexicans may go where they like, trade where they like, and own any land they can pay for in Japan. The magnificence of these arrangements appears a little dwarfed on both sides, when we learn that the number of Mexican residents in this country is—one. Diplomacy seems an expensive luxury in such circumstances; but, there, the principle is everything, is it not?

One of the Japanese papers has been proposing that diplomacy should be utilised in a new direction. Why, says the *Yomiuri Shimbun*, not draft off to distant embassies those statesmen who are too popular to be disregarded, and yet who give some trouble at home? What more honourable employment for a chief of the wrong party than "plenipotenching on a dollar a day and his board," as the American politician neatly expressed it? The local paper even goes into details, and suggests that Count Okuma,* the present Minister for Foreign Affairs, shall be sent to England, in virtue of his splendid fighting powers; that Count Inouye,† a good talker, shall take Washington under his care; and that the mission of Peking (on account, I suppose, of the high standard of morals invariably maintained by the ten mendacious gentlemen who form one Minister for Foreign Affairs in the Tsungli Yamên) had better be confided to a man of purity and courage like Count Itagaki.‡ Purity and courage must be very alarming qualities, for Count Itagaki's return to a place in the Government after his long retirement seems to fill his countrymen with one desire—that he should depart from their coasts. The distinguished Liberal must at any rate be a generous man, for he has just procured the release from prison of a wretched fanatic who seriously attempted his life on political grounds some years ago. The pardoned fanatic insisted upon thanking his liberator, and a great deal of pernicious nonsense is being talked in the newspapers about purity of motive and true greatness, etc., etc. The national press does not yet stand high in Japan. I do not wish to be sweeping in condemnation, for one or two journals rank higher than the rest and show sound opinions on many subjects; but reckless misstatement, misdirected gush, and extreme gullibility make some of the daily papers anything but useful or elevating. All this enthusiasm about a forgiving victim and a high-minded assassin is rather nauseating when one remembers the terrible death of poor Arinori Mori§ (a friend of ours in Peking days), murdered for the same thin pretext of the 11th

---

*Shigenobu Ōkuma (1838–1922) played a prominent part in negotiating the revision of the "unequal treaties."

†Kaoru Inoue (1835–1915), Meiji statesman closely involved with the revision of the "unequal treaties."

‡Taisuke Itagaki (1837–1919), Meiji statesman and party politician.

§Arinori Mori (1848–88), a samurai from Satsuma Province who studied in England and the United States. A devout Christian and educator, Mori served as Minister to China and Britain and later as Minister of Education. He was murdered by a religious fanatic.

of February last when the whole country was rejoicing at the promulgation of the Constitution. Popular representation will point out many more victims to such high-minded assassins as Aibara or Buntaro; and it seems to me that the first work of the Legislative Assembly when it meets next year will necessarily be the protection of its members from the rancours of hidden fanaticism.

A fanatic of another kind attempted to blow up a newly erected temple in Kobe the other day. A great inaugural ceremony was to be held, and an unknown person sent five hundred candles as a gift in honour of the event. When the first one was lighted, a violent explosion took place and the temple narrowly escaped being burnt down. The remaining candles were examined, and it was found that they were all stuffed with dynamite.

Tokyo, June, 1889

It is a rainy day; everything is dripping in the grounds and steaming in the house. The maids creep from room to room with little square boxes of red embers, which they slip inside cupboards and wardrobes to keep the mildew from clinging where the damp has passed. It has rained so long that we have forgotten to count the days any more. There were twenty-seven wet days in April before we arrived, and I should think there must have been forty already in June! It is a mistake to pretend that a month can never go beyond thirty or thirty-one. Each day should count double when it pours like this. The streets, as I see them from these upper balconies, look like intersecting streams, paddled in by a few drenched creatures carrying huge oil-paper umbrellas, flat and large, like monstrous toadstools. Under the umbrella is more yellow-paper waterproofing, down to a few inches below the waist perhaps; and then come recklessly tucked-up skirts and bare legs. All the houses have their screens tightly closed, and nowhere is there a glimpse into the queer little homes, which are laid invitingly open to view on a fine morning.

29

I feel profoundly discouraged, for I have been reading in the *Japan Mail* an indignant protest against the crass ignorance displayed in English accounts of Japan and its history. A venerable firm, which we have been taught to regard as a kind of national educator, has just published a class-book of geography, in which Japan seems to have fared so badly as to rouse the just indignation of the English editor of the *Mail*,* an exceptionally intelligent man, who has lived for many years in Japan. The English newspapers seem to be as bad as the venerable educating firm; for they are handing round an idiotic story of how the Emperor (they call him the Mikado, a term which is never used here) keeps a beautiful jewelled sword, which he sends to turbulent Ministers when he wishes to have them commit *hara-kiri,* and take themselves out of his way. The story goes on to say that the last gentleman to whom this compliment was paid did not carry out the Emperor's wishes, but "ran off to Paris with the sword, and sold it for six thousand pounds."

It is of course very sad and bad that otherwise rational beings should believe all this nonsense; but—but Japanese history is nearly as complicated as Japanese customs, and both so foreign to European ways of thought that we must be forgiven a few mistakes. Being somewhat new to things as yet, I shall probably fall into some of these errors in trying to give you an idea of what Treaty Revision means. And yet no one in Europe will teach you anything, so perhaps you will be glad to learn what I have learnt, the bare outlines of our political ground of being in this half-way house of the world.

Do you remember, many years ago, when I was a child, that charming old Mr. Townsend Harris,† whom we young ones hailed so noisily on account of his enchanting stories of a world beyond our ken? I still feel the thrill which used to go through me when he described his hard-won audience with the "Tycoon." I have lived to see many idols shattered, and the unapproachable Tycoon has gone with the rest. As a matter of fact there never was such a person; but that does not in the least reflect upon dear Mr. Harris's veracity, because he firmly believed there was, having taken the

*Captain Frank Brinkley.
†Townsend Harris (1804–78), the first American Consul in Japan, arrived in 1856 to force Japan open to trade.

Japanese expression *Daigun,** the Great Regent, for a title in itself. The personage who received him with such tremendous ceremony that his square of standing place on the matting had to be marked out beforehand was the Shogun, not, as he imagined, the secular ruler in opposition to a Mikado who bore sacred sovereignty in Kyoto, but the hereditary Regent, the chief administrator, in whose hands all the real power most certainly lay, but who was quite as much a subject of the Emperor as the obsequious nobles who formed his Court.

Before the change of capital† was accomplished, the Emperor had consented to grant audiences to the Foreign Representatives; and the country learnt, in deep dismay, that the sacred countenance of the Emperor, hidden as a rule from his own subjects, was to be gazed upon by the alien barbarian. Poor Sir Harry Parkes very nearly lost his life on his way to enjoy that honour. He was attacked by two wild fanatics, who cut down nine men of his escort before they were captured; and it was said that, but for the valour and loyalty of Count Goto,‡ who had been appointed to accompany him, the great Britisher's work would have been cut short for ever that day. The Queen sent Count Goto a most beautiful sword in recognition of his services; and when I dined with him a few days ago, he showed me the sword with sober pride. He is a very handsome man, with keen dark eyes and snow-white hair; and his wife is one of the two Japanese women who have something like a political salon and count as an influence in public matters.

But I must finish my story, so that you may know why Treaty Revision is always coming to the front in our affairs. Sir Harry Parkes and the other foreigners who made the existing treaties with Japan could, to a great extent, count on the goodwill of the Government, but had daily reasons for distrusting the fanatical populace and the disappointed Daimyos of the north, who had lost power when the Shogunate fell. It was only natural that the foreigners who lived and traded in the newly opened treaty ports

*Literally, great prince.
†From Kyoto to Tokyo in 1869. Edo was given the name Tokyo, which means eastern capital, in 1868.
‡Shōjirō Gotō (1838–97), Meiji statesman and political party leader.

should require constant protection, so they were put under the authority of their own Consuls, who were constituted judges, and who tried all cases where foreigners or their interests were concerned. This arrangement, a learned friend (Mr. Montague Kirkwood) tells me, is of respectable antiquity, having been granted by an Egyptian king to a Greek colony long before the Christian era; and it was constantly in use during the Middle Ages for Christians resident in non-Christian countries. The Arabs, he says, insisted upon the privilege for their traders in China, who in the ninth century obtained permission from the Emperor of China to be solely under the jurisdiction of a Mussulman magistrate in Canton. On this principle foreigners were, and are, practically independent of Japanese jurisdiction, and can only be arrested or tried by their own countrymen; and this constitutes extra-territoriality. The concession or settlement in the treaty port is a piece of land handed over to the foreigners, where they do their own lawgiving, maintain their own police, and pay no taxes. Of course the English residents outnumber all those of the other nationalities put together, and each settlement is practically a bit of England planted where English people happen to want it.

All this seems very ideal, and perhaps was so twenty years ago, when a few enterprising merchants made large fortunes here and in China. But the accompanying restrictions which forbid foreigners to travel in the country outside the settlement, except with passports which can only be issued for a limited time (three months is the longest granted, except to officials)—restrictions which forbid them to own land or to trade outside settlement limits,—these are putting foreign trade under such disabilities, that our commerce absolutely requires their abolition at the first possible moment. The Japanese on their side say that they have reached a point on the road of civilisation when they can no longer allow foreigners to administer the laws on Japanese ground; and they demand that the old settlements, conceded while Japan was still emerging from her political swaddling clothes, shall be ceded to the Government; that foreigners, as in other countries, shall be tried by the laws of the land, now being framed on the most enlightened Western models (chiefly the Code Napoléon); and that extra-territoriality shall become a thing of the past. If we concede this, they in their turn promise to open up the country, and give every facility for the expansion of foreign trade.

The arguments on both sides appear quite reasonable, but unfortunately Japan is nothing like ready to be taken at her word; and as for us—well, a whole settlement of British merchants in every port, and a Chamber of Commerce just across the water, all absolutely contented with things as they are, and furiously opposed to any change which might enrich their country but impoverish individuals,—this constitutes a quantity which is not to be neglected at such close quarters; and the other great contracting party has still better reasons for not hurrying itself over the practical part of revision, although political decency requires that all sorts of polite things should be said about it. The truth is that very large and important classes of the population are as violently opposed to the inroads of the foreigner as they ever were, and a cautious Government finds it not easy to keep the retrograde party within bounds. It has its adherents in every class, and carries with it that tremendous factor in Japanese thought, veneration for the past and the horror of any sacrilegious rupture with national memories. Joined to this comes, among the more practical men, intense apprehension lest the all-devouring foreigner, once let loose in the country, should absorb all trade into his own hands; lest foreign money and foreign extravagance should destroy the valuable simplicity of Japanese customs; and behind these legitimate objectors is a vast body of newly made radicals, the outcome of the great army of *samurai* who were disbanded when the Daimyos gave up their power and the feudal system was abolished.

These men trained through the traditions of a hundred generations to consider fighting the only possible occupation for a gentleman, scorned all humbler employments, and for many years flocked round their old chiefs clamouring for leave to use their weapons. Some lost their chief; many were younger sons of *samurai*, and as such were not provided for in the retinue of the local Daimyos; and all these went wandering about under the title of *rônins,* or chiefless men, always ready for a little bloodshed, and nursing imaginary wrongs to keep up the fierce spirit of their class. Such were the men who attacked our Legation at Takanawa* in 1861 and 1862, and fought so ferociously that, as an eye-witness told me, the house ran with blood and looked as if two armies had been engaged there. Little by little the *samurai* have been drawn into the administration, into the police, into anything which does not lower their dignity in their own eyes; but the younger generation is a thorn in the side of the Government, and promises some serious obstruction to the progress of the country. They have received a modern education, believe in very little, and hate the foreigner with the inherited hatred of centuries. These boys (for they are little more) talk the wildest nonsense about "Japan for the Japanese." While affecting to discard any higher beliefs than those they have educed from Darwin, that unwilling heresiarch, or the rather sawdusty ethics of Herbert Spencer, they still claim profound veneration for the sacred institutions of old Japan, and declare that there will be no peace or prosperity for the country until foreigners are expelled and the old regulations put in force again. They are mostly very poor, and, as they only aspire to what they consider occupations of honour, present sometimes a pitifully forlorn appearance. They are so much in earnest that one cannot help being intensely sorry for them; but they are, as far as Japan is concerned, a potent cause of drawback and delay in the revision of the treaties, and, inasmuch as they do not confine themselves to words for the enforcement of their arguments, constitute a daily danger to the public peace. Swordsticks are their favourite weapons, probably because they seem to bear some relation to the two swords of which they have been permanently deprived.

The *soshi*† is a constant trouble and embarrassment in life. The other day, one, a boy of eighteen at the outside, got himself admitted into the Legation grounds on some pretext, walked into the Chancery, and demanded, rather imperiously, an interview with the Minister. The Japanese Secretary told him he could not see the Minister, and asked what he wanted, thinking from his poor clothes and

*The legation was housed in Tōzen-ji, a temple of the Zen sect. The temple has largely escaped damage from earthquake and war, and the rooms occupied by the Legation and the attractive garden remain much as they were.

†*Sōshi*, ex-samurai political bullies.

wasted appearance that he might be seeking work. The boy got quite excited, and said that he must see the Minister, who, he considered, was doing a great wrong in pressing Treaty Revision on the Government. He wished to explain his views to the British Representative, and to tell him that he was only one of many who would save Japan from foreign usurpation at all costs. Mr. G——,* I am sorry to say, got extremely angry with him, told him he was a mere child, and had better finish growing up before he asked to talk with men, and sent him away, poor boy, desperately unhappy. But many others come to the gate asking to speak to H——; and seeing their utter recklessness and their fondness for swordsticks, I am rather glad they do not get in.

The *soshi* are banded in clubs all over the country, and the Government seems to us a little weak in not dealing more summarily with them and their seditious speeches. They profess great veneration for the sacred person of the Emperor, but declare that he is surrounded by traitors, so their devotion does not make for peace and harmony.

I fancy we shall see some curious scenes when the first Parliament is opened next spring. As I have said, there are opponents of the new order here and there in all classes of society; but the visionary *soshi* are the only people who believe in the possibility of putting the world's clock back by thirty or forty years. The more educated reactionists have accepted foreign intercourse as an inevitable necessity, and are none the less polite to us individually because collectively they would like to see us sail away from their shores never to return. The law students, for instance, are protesting furiously against the codification of the laws, for which they declare the country is still unripe; but it is much suspected that their dislike to the new code is grounded on the fact that it is a task which can only be carried out by foreigners.

One of the Tokyo newspapers, the *Nichi Nichi Shimbun* (the day-by-day journal), has been giving a very just appreciation of the relative positions of Japan and China. It interests me from our having been so long in China before coming here. Though only five days distant, China has never been able to get a clear idea of modern Japan, and cannot lay aside a certain amount of swagger in her manner

*J. H. Gubbins.

to the younger nation, which was once her eager pupil, but never her tributary, as has so often been asserted. The journalist dwells on the great need of caution in dealing with China, who, half jealous, half contemptuous of Japan, is always ready to pick a quarrel, which would be profoundly disadvantageous to both countries. On the other hand, Japan has the proud consciousness of never having been worsted by China in fair fight, joined to the uncomfortable conviction of her neighbour's unmerited contempt. Quarrels seem imminent;* but the writer wisely reminds his countrymen that they would bring no good to either party, and would only give European powers a chance to seize territory and extend their influence under the pretext of restoring harmony. The Chinese seem to have very little in common with modern Japanese; and when we meet the Celestial diplomatists at official dinners, they give me the impression of people who are living among enemies under a flag of truce, and do not quite like the situation.

No one has been much surprised to hear that Count Itagaki's would-be assassin has found a follower in a gentleman who proposed to murder Count Goto for entering a Ministry which he condemned in public speeches last year. After all, that seems to be more Count Goto's affair than that of an obscure policeman; but the policemen evidently do a good deal of political thinking in this part of the world. A letter was seized in which the policeman confided his views to a brother, and he was arrested on his way to commit the crime. It must take some personal courage to be a Cabinet Minister in Japan.

But courage is certainly a national virtue. The other day two thieves armed with knives broke into a house where a woman was quite alone, and threatened her with death if she did not give up her property. She pretended to consent, apparently shivering with terror; and they took no more notice of her, and stuck their knives in the mats while they collected her few valuables. She waited until they were quite absorbed in their work, and then seized both knives, and attacked the robbers so valiantly that they fled, leaving their spoils on the ground.

*The Sino-Japanese War (1894-95) was basically a struggle over control of Korea.

The thieves here choose the most unmanageable kind of loot, it seems to me. Five ground pines, valued at over three thousand dollars, were carried off from a nursery garden last week! As soon as the rain will let me, I am going to some of the tree fairs, where you see everything growing the wrong way round, as it were.

I was very much amused, just after we came, to see the gardeners taking the pine trees out of their winter caging, built up to protect the delicate, shapely twigs from all danger of being broken by a heavy snow. This is done by planting a mast as a supplementary trunk beside the living one, and training a network like tent-cords down from its top to catch the larger branches and sustain their weight. From these, smaller cords drop and interlace, till every twig hangs on a string, and could carry a heavy weight of snow without injury. These supports were only removed in May, when all danger of a serious snowfall was past; and at the same time the bananas and sago palms were divested of their straw wrappings, and shook out pale-green shoots, which had been pushing up in the darkness; they soon lost their paleness in the hot sun and drenching rain which have visited us alternately for the last few weeks.

I was speaking in my last letter of the Empress's great interest in charitable work. Rather a touching little statement has been published of the way in which she has provided extra help for an institution of her own founding, the Tokyo Charity Hospital. The Hospital had outgrown its accommodation, and new buildings had become an absolute necessity; so the Empress started the subscription by cutting down everything that could be cut down in her private expenses (always heavily burdened with benevolent work), and as a result has sent to the Hospital the respectable sum of 8,446 dollars* and 8 rin. Ten rin go to one sen, of which a hundred go to a dollar, worth about two shillings; so you see with what loving conscientiousness the economy has been carried out. One of the Empress's ladies told me that for the last year her Majesty had hardly bought "a glove or a pocket-handkerchief," and that the thought of sick people being denied the help they needed was a source of profound pain to her. She constantly visits the hospitals, and on those occasions stops beside

*Dollar means yen.

every bed in every ward to say a kind word to the patients. The process begins at about nine o'clock in the morning, continues till one, when a light lunch is served, is immediately renewed, and goes on till about five, when even the Empress admits that she is tired, and her ladies say they "do not know where their feet are."

She has done as much for women's education as she has for the hospitals; and the "Peeress's School," taught in great part by English and American ladies, was founded by her. The Japanese girls fall quickly in love with the higher education, and work enthusiastically to obtain their diplomas. One curious outcome of this advance is a "Society for the Correction of Morals," composed of Japanese women, many of them Christians. They hold meetings, and get distinguished men to give lectures for them, and just now are preparing to petition the Government for a change of the laws relating to marriage, asking that unfaithfulness in a husband shall be punished as severely as the same crime in a wife, for which the penalties here are very heavy. It is not stated how they propose to deal with the legalised concubinage which, although diminishing, is still customary here, and which the pagan wife hardly resents, since it is not allowed to interfere in any way with her rights or dignity. To the Christian woman there is, of course, another side to the case. But I would like to say one thing on these subjects to my Japanese sisters—namely, that they are not the only women who have asked that men's morals should be put in petticoats and regulated by law; and that there is but one answer possible to the demand, whether it come from women of the East or women of the West, and it is this: the only law which can enforce a pure life must be a divine one; but the best policeman for your husband's heart is yourself. If you have not the sweetness and the wit to make him love you and you alone, you will appeal in vain to the magistrates to help you.

I am afraid this has been a very sombre day's writing! Please put it down to the rain, which makes one feel old and serious. If only the sun will dry things a little, you shall have something brighter next time.

A Japanese friend has been telling me stories about the Island Temple of Miyajima, which I saw at a distance when we were passing through the Inland Sea. It has more than one name, but this one means "Temple Island"; and the divinities, seeing how beautiful it was, evidently disagreed about it, for it seems to belong to two or three in part and to none entirely.

There is no country in the whole world which has been so drenched in bloodshed as Japan—it seems as if the very sap of the trees must be red; and yet nowhere does the spirit of peace brood visibly and everlastingly over sea and land, town and temple, as it does here.

One hears of terrific volcanic explosions, of earthquakes, and of disastrous floods, such as those which are now laying waste the villages of the south, where the rivers are gone mad, intoxicated by too much rain. But these things do not seem to break through the primeval calms of Japan. The ruined peasant does not indulge in lamentations, but smilingly rebuilds his hut the moment the soil can carry it. After whole streets of shops have been destroyed by the frightful fires which so constantly break out in Tokyo, one drives down to look at the ruin, and one sees business going on again cheerily in booths and sheds run up anyhow on the yet hot ashes of yesterday's disaster. The inevitable need not be the irretrievable; and this knowledge must make for peace, since only the irretrievable need cause despair. But there are deeper reasons for this manifest peace, and I fancy they must lie in some yet undiscovered harmonies and submissions of the national character, which has through so many centuries of isolation had time to fill out every corner and interstice of Nature's inexorable mould. It would seem that, for the perfection of a type, internecine wars and disturbances tend to develope rather than to modify its distinguishing characteristics. The vicissitudes result in the survival of the fittest, those in whom the national character finds its strongest examples. Among Western peoples we notice that the more highly educated and developed a class becomes, the more it resembles the corresponding class of any other country; aristocrats are first cousins everywhere in Europe, and original racial differences are often only shown in the peasant and the plebeian. But in Japan the case is reversed. The peasant might find his first cousin in the Chinese, the Cossack, the Corean, or even, as some have suggested, in the Tooltec Indian of Central America; but the Japanese aristocrat is as unmistakable as the thorough-bred. It would be more possible to confuse racers with dray-horses than to take him for anything but what he is, a fine gentleman, the outcome of a dozen centuries of pride, courage, and self-control. And this goes to support another of my theories (you know my weakness for generalisation), that the success of education, whether for school-children or nationalities, depends far more on continuity than on quality.

Such continuity has had full play here: that which is now thought good, or great, or beautiful has been thought so since the dawn of history; crimes and virtues have the same names that they bore in the days of Jimmu Tenno, the first Emperor; there has been no real change in the values of the important affairs of life; and those things which have been brought in, such as Buddhism and Chinese litera-ture, have become incorporated among Japan's properties without introducing any marked resemblance to the nation from whom she borrowed them. I think it must be this eclectic quality in the Japanese which causes them to be so severely criticised by Europeans, who see them take up new ideas with enthusiasm, and drop them again as easily. But the truth is that the "taking up," this "let us see what it is made of" system, is the only practical method of selection; and close observers will note that, although, for instance, German waltz-ing and French frocks are less popular than they were five years ago, the army is on a very much more German footing, an Imperial Prince, Kotohito Kanin, has just taken his certificate of proficiency in a French naval school, and the Empress sent the matrons of her Charity Hospital to get their training in London. All this is signi-ficant enough as to the true attitude of the more enlightened Japa-nese; but the education of Prince Haru, the heir to the throne,* is

*Haru no miya Yoshihito (1879–1925) became emperor on the death of Emperor Meiji in 1912. His reign from 1912 to 1925 is called the Taishō era. He was the father of the present emperor.

the most notable tribute to European ideas yet paid by this country.

The little Prince is ten years old, and is, I fancy, rather delicate. I saw him driving with his governor and two boy friends the other day. He has a fine pale face, and piercing dark eyes. Perhaps the paleness has misled me as to his health (I cannot but remember the rosy cheeks of our schoolboys at home) for his own people say that he is strong and healthy, fond of outdoor exercise, and already well-trained in fencing and single-stick. He is the first heir to the throne of Japan who has mingled with his future subjects at school and play. He goes every day to the Nobles' School,* a splendid building not far from us; and there he learns his lessons and plays his games just as the other children do. The innate reverence for the Imperial family doubtless prevents the games from becoming too rough, but I believe the lessons are very impartially dealt with. The Prince takes cold baths, eats meat, and will have no women to wait on him, an extremely legitimate prejudice, which recalls to my mind a family tradition of a certain Master John, one or two generations ago, who at the age of five refused to walk down the same side of the street as his nurse, saying that "men didn't care to have a lot of women hanging after them." The little Prince does not walk in the street, but is fond of a good romp on the seashore, and already delights in beautiful scenery. They say that he is kind and thoughtful to those around him and to his school friends. The whole description of the little character reminds one of the Prince of Naples at the same age. Prince Haru is fond of horses, and is sometimes taken to the mild races which are occasionally run here. The Emperor has just shown his interest in the subject by sending a thousand dollars for the new grand stand which is being built on the racecourse at Negishi, near Yokohama.

The papers tell us that the Shogun, Yoshinobu or Keiki, who so unwillingly abdicated in 1868, has arrived in Tokyo, and is staying with his relation, Prince Tokugawa Iesato. It must be rather sad for him to return as a private gentleman to this seat of the past glories of his line.

If I had my way, I would make a little supplementary world for

*The Gakushūin.

such splendid ghosts as Tokugawa Shoguns, and Danieli Doges, and old moons. It would make an admirable reformatory for new-broom radicals, and one might spend a few solemn days there oneself when one felt the novelty fever too strong upon one. By the way, a Japanese acquaintance told me that the title of Prince is never used by them except for a member of the Imperial family. The highest title ever given to a subject is that of Koshaku, which means Duke or Marquis, according to the character in which it is written. I protested, having seen this word Prince on more than one visiting card, and in the Court official lists.

"Why do you translate it Prince, if it is not Prince?" I asked rather indignantly.

"Well, you see" (my friend rubbed his chin, and looked at me with a twinkle in his eye), "we were translating—to the Germans!"

A most amusing book has just been published here, purporting to give the Japanese student a correct expression of his commercial aspirations and necessities in English. Why does our unfortunate language lend itself so easily to these absurdities? "English as she is spoke" was hardly a greater joy than this bold manual, and I cannot resist enclosing to you some extracts from the witty review in the *Japan Mail*. As I am beginning to collect curios, I shall at once send out to buy "sea-mouse," "dqe," "chanqhor," and "scrippers"! The writer states that the book is "for the gentlemen who regard on commercial and an official."

"Two dunning letters are given, and in both instances they are plainly intended to betray the natural irritation consequent upon long-deferred settlement of a debt:
"Page 16:

> 'I beg to draw your
> attention to the enclosed acc-
> ount, and to state that ip it
> is not settled for next week
> I shall be compelled to ploce it
> for atternegs hond.'

The one on the following page evinces still greater irritation at the very outset:

'Having applied to you Repeatedlg but ineffectuallg for a settlement, I have now to intimate . . . . . that I shall ploce it in my solicitois hands for Recovery.'

Note also the following:

> 'Gentlemen,
> we have this day forwarde
> to your care, per Orientoel slea-
> mer & co., 25 packages qer "yamasiromoru"
> consigned to Mr. Yamaugchi
> & co., of that port. Bill of
> landing, and statement of shi-
> pping charges, please transmit.
> At foot particulars of the shipp-
> ment We are,
> Jentlemen,
> your edient,
> particulars of shipment,
> M 15 cases 1500' pice chintr.'

"Somewhat less lucid still is the following announcement of a change in the style of a firm:

> 'we beg leave to infonu you
> that we this day admitted mr
> fujimura as partnor in our busi-
> ness here. In futu-
> re the otyll of our frim will
> be Yoshimwra & Co.'

The 'juniority' of the new partner in this case is admirably expressed by the want of capital letters in his name. Yoshimwra is evidently Welsh for Yoshimura, though why the author should prefer this language is not apparent. 'Otyll' we take to mean 'style'; but this, of course, must remain a mere hypothesis.

"Insinuating is the style of another letter (page 47), in which the writer requests a friend to 'glad me' with a loan, if it does not

43

intrench on the friend's 'oawn conwenien ce'; he mournfully states that he is being 'put to exceedingey persecution,' and is in 'painfule difficulty.'

"Still another writer is incoherently indignant about the state of certain goods forwarded him. He says:

> 'of the pared of sewed mu-
> lins I have had to reject fif
> ty picls as being un saleable;
> twenty pieces are tosn in siveral places
> and the others are without headivgs.'

"This must have been a fearful blow to the shippers, for their reply is indicative of great mental pressure, if not of incipient mania:

> 'Dear Sir,
> The contents of your favo-
> ur of yesterday's date sur prised
> considerably, us our wareho-
> usemen have explicit
> instru ctioni to supply our cus
> tomers with perfect goods only,
> and return the unsound to the
> manu foctuar. It is ebidient, ho-
> weves, thot they packed your
> goods without examininy them.
> We regvt excee dinglyect. . . .
> Trusting that you have not been
> seriously inconve nien-
> ced through the monifest remiss-
> ess of ovr ewpoyes.'

"At the end of the book is a list of commercial terms and names of exports, which repays perusal. 'Promissionary notes' has rather a religious than a commercial sound. 'Bankroptny' and 'bankruqty' are evidently so spelled with an eye to lessen the attendant disgrace. 'Gross waigh' is an unknown quantity. Among exports, 'soop,' 'scrippers,' 'sea-mouse,' 'quoin,' 'mouseline of lines,' 'dqe,' 'gold-

woteh,' 'chamqhor,' 'ass,' 'jam,' and 'frorid water,' are of interest
to the student."

These strange products of the far East are almost equalled by
some for which I was called upon to pay the other day. Ogita speaks
English much better than he writes it. Imagine my surprise on
receiving the following bill:

"Blue Showl   ...   .   2.   35.
7 7/10 yards Whitish brown? Race   ...   2.   31.
4   ”   ”   ”   ”   ...   1.   32.
10 4/10 yards mud colour Race...   ...   1.   66 4/10."

The arithmetic got very mixed in the addition, which, with some
other items, amounted to 7. 644 somethings—currency unstated.
The English of the signboards in the streets is equally graphic:
"Highly perfumed waters" turn out to be tins of kerosene; "Deal
beer," "Wine and other," require reflection.*

Any walk that one tries to take just now might well be described
as a mud-coloured race, for the rain still comes pattering down at
intervals, though not so persistently as it did in June. Meanwhile
the country is very green and beautiful to look at, and the view from
my upstairs verandah most alluring. I can see, I think, every house
in "Kojimachi," as this quarter of the town is called; but between
the houses are so many trees that one can hardly believe one is in
the heart of a great city. My windows look to the west, and Fuji,
the queen of mountains, bounds my world. In the dawn (and in
these long warm days I am glad to come out for a cool breath in the
early hours) Fuji looks cold and dimly white till the sun creeps up
over the bay, and then she takes the most lovely rosy flush against
the morning sky. The mountain comes to dominate outer life in a
curious way, and I do not wonder that folk-lore has crowned it as
a sacred and powerful personality. On the days when clouds hang
between us and it, I am dissatisfied, and homesick as for the face of
a friend.

But the near landscape gives me enough to watch through many

*The foreign visitor to Japan today will still encounter quaint English phra-
seology and spelling.

45

an amused hour. The houses nestle close among the trees, with strange gables and latticed upper windows, from which, perhaps, looks out some dainty little lady, with a pale face and dark eyes and marvellously dressed head. She pulls a flower or two from her tiny hanging garden, and goes in again to bring out a gorgeous silk quilt, which she hangs over the balcony to air. Sounds of strange music come floating up to my window from a house in the valley below our garden. My maid tells me that a teacher of music lives there, and the place is never silent. The twang of the *koto* is strong and pathetic, and very melodious in skilled hands; then there is the humming note of the *samisen,* which accompanies every festival or holiday-making in the humbler houses. Drums rattle farther off; the *masseur,* the blind *amma,* pipes thin sweet airs on his bunch of reeds; the medicine-seller or the newspaper-man, as he goes on his rounds, rings a little bell continuously, a tinkle as light and musical as a falling brook; far away a gang of coolies pushing some heavy load are marking time with a long cry and a short one; a beautiful phrase, worthy to be the theme of a fugue, comes up to me in a clear childish voice, moving quickly along the sunken street. I sent out to ask who it was, as it is repeated every evening at this hour; and O'Matsu, my *amah,* has just come in to say that it is a young girl selling millet cakes. And above all the rest, from the distant temple on the hill, rolls out the deep note of a great bronze bell, strong and low, and vibrating steadily on the warm air, while the lesser noises run to and fro and spend themselves below it.

As the evening shadows fall, and the rain ceases, all our servants' children come out to play in the more remote parts of the grounds, and I hear little shrieks of happiness, and see a kite tossing madly above the trees. Then one, two, three little heads will cautiously peep through the shrubs to see if any gardener is near. No, the lawn is empty, and Kokichi and his assistants have withdrawn to their quarters for the night—even the Dachs family are all engaged in digging for the toad who lives under the flagstaff; so three little people decide to commit a terrible breach of discipline, and come close to the house, first to try and have another look at the English "Okusama," who is always a most interesting object, and then to see if she is inclined to bestow any more wonderful pink cakes such as they got last Sunday! To Okusama, who is watching them as they hesitate, it looks as if the trees had suddenly bloomed into flowers; for the little maidens' garments are of the brightest colours, and in their small dark heads are set pins of silver roses and coral beads. Hand tightly held in hand, they patter across the soft grass, too fast for the smallest one, who soon drops a sandal, and has to be comforted and shod again by the motherly mite in charge of her. By the time they have reached the rose garden under my window, I am ready to meet them, with three pink cakes in three bits of paper, and one more for a baby brother at home. The quick Eastern night is already shedding its hush over the quiet gardens, so I tell the mites to run along to their mother, who lives in the gatehouse; and they nod wisely, and look round a little frightened at the distance to be traversed. When asked what they are afraid of, the eldest replies that there are tigers in the gardens, it is well known, and—nobody likes tigers! When reasoned with, she declares that she has often heard them roaring at night, and there is nothing for it but to send them back under the escort of O'Matsu, who is supposed to be quite capable of overcoming the casual tiger. O'Matsu convoys them away smiling (nobody can be cross with Japanese children), and when she returns tells me that the pink cakes were considered too fine to eat, and have been put in state on the table in the niche of honour, beside those which I gave them last week!

I have fallen deeply in love with a gentleman of uncertain age (two at the outside, I should think), whom the nuns at the Tsukiji Orphanage* have induced me to accept as a godson. He is so fat and round that he never remembers where to find his feet, and is always rolling over the mats in search of them. His mother, a widow, cooks the rice for three hundred people every day, and is very anxious about her son's manners. She says he is three years old; but Japanese counting is not to be trusted in that way, since a baby born on the last day of December is called two years old on January 1st, because he has existed during a part of two succeeding years. This small child is told to prostrate himself, *o'jigi*,† when I appear, and then the little bullet head goes down on his fat hands on the mat with

---

*Tsukiji was the area of Tokyo first used by foreigners. Today the huge Tokyo Central Wholesale Market is located there.

†*Ojigi* is a deep bow.

great readiness; but it is a terrible business to get it up again. If one gives him something, and he is told to say "thank you," he at once makes the sign of the cross; it is the only prayer he knows as yet, and the expression of his highest feelings. I was very much overcome, when he was baptised, by seeing the good missionary father pour the holy water over his head out of a nice little china teapot, kept by the nuns for the purpose.

The work these dear women do is most interesting, and I sometimes go and spend hours in the Convent, looking at the girls' sewing, or sitting in the quiet chapel. They are called here the Black Nuns, to distinguish them from the Sisters of Charity with their white *cornettes,* who have a school at the other end of the town. The establishment is divided into two sections: one a resident school for pupils, who pay from three to four dollars a month for board and teaching; while the other—which is, of course, kept quite separate—is the Orphanage proper, where just now there are about one hundred and eighty children of all ages, maintained and educated by the Sisters, who are occasionally in very low water, and much put to it to find money for the daily food of such a family. The Convent stands near the Catholic church in Tsukiji, which is the foreign settlement of Tokyo, and full of Europeans and Americans. It is close to the sea, and is cooller in these hot days than our own house farther inland. When I drive down there, it always delights me to watch the junks, with their huge sails, white or saffron, moving along the wide canal on the incoming tide, to watch the woodmen piling timber in the yards along the banks, to see the crowded ferryboats carrying the people from shore to shore. In the courtyards of the Convent it is a sea breeze that comes to play with the willow and wistaria trails, and that sometimes finds its way to the chapel, which is always full of sweet flowers.

When one turns in from the road, the big gate gives admittance to a square garden. Opposite is the two-storied wooden building which contains the chapel and the Sisters' apartments. To the right are the boarders' quarters—large classrooms downstairs, and airy dormitories opening on a long balcony above. To the left a single-storied wing holds the work and study-rooms of the orphans, whose sleeping apartments open into another courtyard behind.

A few European girls attend as day scholars among the boarders, and one or two who are the daughters of mixed marriages, extremely pretty, graceful girls. The Sisters always beg me to talk with them and show some interest in their work; so I listen to recitations and admire embroideries and drawings with a good conscience, for some of the pupils are really clever. Two or three of the girls are, alas! children who have been abandoned by European fathers when they found it convenient to leave Japan; and although no one pays for them, the Sisters give them the same education as the boarders receive, and keep them nicely dressed in European costume—a considerable expense here.

But it is the other side of the house which draws me most. There the big orphans help the little ones, and the sweet-faced Japanese lay Sisters teach the babies their prayers, and carry about the tiniest ones; and the whole place is desperately poor, but so sweet and clean that one forgets the poverty of it.

"Don't go there!" my conductress cries, as I step heedlessly on the boarded gallery which runs round the inner court; "it is so rotten that it will only carry *les toutes petites*." And I come down again, having put my foot through a board, which gave like pie-crust. A great crowd of the children follows me about, for I want to go everywhere; and the lay Sister suddenly marshals them in the sunshine, and says in Japanese, "Sing for the lady—one, two, three!"

"Les voilà parties!" exclaims the good nun at my side, as all the little voices break out together, with a clapping of hands and nodding of dark heads, in a hymn whose strains must be heard by the junks in the canal yonder.

The children are left below while I inspect the poor dormitories, sadly in want of new mats and wadded quilts, but still, so *much* better than nothing, as the cheery Sister remarks; and when we come down again, we go to the long barnlike room, where the children are having their evening meal. Ten and five are their hours for solid feeding, with Japanese tea and bread for early breakfast. I found them seated in endless rows of benches at little narrow tables in a kind of "weight for age" arrangement. Each child had at its place a cup of water and a little wooden saucer with a scrap of fish and some pickles and sauce. This was intended as a relish to the huge bowl of rice, which made the staple of the meal. The rice is brought in large wooden tubs, and served out by the elder girls, two of whom carry a tub between them up and down the long rows of benches, filling the bowls as the children hold them out. The rule is that as long as a bowl is held out it must be filled; and when the tub stops its walk, all the little mouths are absolutely satisfied. A whole *koku* (just under five bushels) of rice is cooked daily, and rice just now costs ten yen the *koku*. When no more bowls are held out, the order is given to stand up and say grace, which is done very heartily; and then the Sister in charge says, looking at me, "Allons, un bon Pater pour les Bienfaiteurs!" And an "Our Father" goes up to heaven with such intense goodwill, that one feels it was cheaply purchased by a small contribution to the rice-tub!

The religious question seldom creates any difficulty among the children, though occasionally a paying pupil will take offence at some word said, and stop coming for a few days. The Sisters are very uncompromising about certain things. When the girls first come, they and their parents are told that they will be required to attend the religious services in the chapel and to be present at the catechism lessons. Otherwise the subject of religion is not mentioned to them by the Sisters until they come, as they often do, to ask to be baptised. But some of the girls themselves are eager little apostles, and do all they can to persuade their pagan companions of the beauty and truth of Christianity. Sometimes the parents will not consent, for the old prejudices are still strong; and then there is long waiting and much prayer before O'Hana or O'Yone can receive the Christian equivalent of her name and wear a white veil in church, a privilege reserved only for Christians.

As for the orphans, most of them are taken in as babies, and are baptised at once. Where the child is older, she must receive instruction and really desire baptism before it can be administered; but there is no opposition of parents to retard conversion, and there is much less prejudice against Christianity among the extreme poor than among the richer classes. Besides, the child's young heart is softened and warmed with gratitude for material benefits, which the nuns rightly teach her to consider as much less precious than spiritual ones; so there are many more white veils on the side of the church where the orphans sit than on the other, which is occupied by their richer sisters.

It is a very pretty sight on these summer mornings to see the long processions of children coming down the road from the Convent gates to the church. All the heads, gentle and simple, have been carefully dressed for the Sunday Mass, the girls performing the kind office one for another; and from the rich *pensionnaire* of seventeen, with her beautiful gold or tortoiseshell ornaments crowning her elaborate rolls, down to the tiniest orphan toddler, whose hair is combed in a deep fringe over her forehead and tied in a knob at the back, every head shines like burnished ebony in the sun. The best robes and sashes are always kept for Sundays, and happy is the child who can display a scarlet sash or inner collar to her dress, red being here the colour of youth and joy. In church the reverent devotional bearing is most impressive, and the many white-veiled heads bowed in prayer make a lovely sight.

But not only youth comes here, marshalled by the black-robed Sisters, but bowed old people, men and women, forlorn paupers, whom their charity will not turn from their doors, and who have invaded the two or three matted rooms which were meant as workshops and porter's lodge just inside the gate. The old women are the cheeriest creatures, the deaf helping the blind, and both supporting the cripples. I entered one of these rooms by mistake one day, and found seven or eight of the dear old souls, quite past work, sitting on the floor making their tea. They were very glad to see me, and said all manner of pleasant things, finishing up with what rather distressed me, the ceremonious salutation, knocking their venerable heads on the mats at my feet. In the men's room were one or two sick men, patient and very ill, with only one dread, that they might be sent away. The Sisters have many scruples about keeping any sick people so near the children, and as soon as possible propose to take a little house outside, to be used as an infirmary. Meanwhile the poor folk must stay here; for, in spite of all that has been done in that way, there are not yet nearly enough hospitals in Tokyo for the sick among its one million of inhabitants, and the very poor suffer greatly from the overcrowding of their tiny rooms.

The sight of one of these all-embracing Convent Homes, God's Casual Wards, always puts me out of conceit with the leisure and the luxury of modern life. The great cool rooms and the wide lawns and deep shrubberies of the Legation filled me with something uncomfortably like shame after my visit to the Convent School at Tsukiji.

❖   ❖   ❖

The constant rain of the early summer gave me so much rheumatism that at last Doctor Baelz ordered me down here to boil it away in a course of hot baths. The heat in Tokyo has been rather wearing; and although we had decided not to make any solemn *villeggiatura* this year, I was delighted to get away and to see something of the country. As it was my first journey inland, everything was pleasantly fresh and interesting. As far as Yokohama† there was nothing new in the railway journey, except the wonderful beauty of the lotuses, which are in full flower for miles in the ditches on either side of the line. They do not reach the enormous size of the leaves and blooms

*Atami is described in Murray's *Handbook for Travellers in Japan* (1894) as a favorite winter resort of the Japanese higher official class. "The soft air, the orange groves and the deep blue sea of Odawara Bay combine to make of this district the Riviera of Japan. Atami is most easily reached from Yokohama by the Tōkaidō Railway as far as Kōzu, 1 1/2 hours, and then by jinrikisha for the rest of the way, nearly 5 hours, along the coast. The road is delightfully picturesque and representatively Japanese."

In those days the Tōkaidō railway went over the mountains via Gotemba. Now, on the Shinkansen, the so-called Bullet Train, Atami can be reached by the Kodama express trains from Tokyo Station in some fifty minutes. Atami has become a prosperous, brash, hot-spring resort, full of concrete hotels and bars. The new Kyūseikyō religious sect has, however, built a very fine modern museum, where their treasures of Japanese art as well as special exhibitions can be seen.

†The Tokyo-Yokohama railway was opened in 1872 and was the first railway to operate in Japan. Murray's *Handbook for Travellers in Japan* (1894) describes the journey as follows: "The journey from Yokohama to Tokyo occupies 50 min. The line skirts the shores of Tokyo Bay with the *old Tōkaidō highway* recognizable at intervals on the right by its avenue of pines."

in our old haunts in China; but it may be because these are wild, and those had been cultivated for centuries in the temple tanks and the ponds of the Summer Palace. Here they are called the flowers of death, and are only used for funerals. Another death-flower is blowing too, in every bank and hillock through the country-side, a vivid scarlet lily, growing in a full round cluster on one strong wine-coloured stem. It is quite a splendid sight, when the wind tosses these thousands of blood-red tassels all one way, in the sun.

The train put us down at Kodzu, a little town close to the seashore; and while our belongings were being piled into a tramcar which runs a few miles farther on the road, we had tea in a pretty inn room, whose windows command a beautiful wide view of the bay. Indeed the room was all window, as these Japanese rooms generally are in summer. The sight of a long white beach with splendid rollers breaking on its edge was too alluring to be withstood, for there never were such friends as I and the sea; so I found my way down through a tiny garden and a bit of road, till I stood under one of the great pine trees on the shore. There was a world of sea and sky, a picture all painted in three colours—deep sapphire blue in the rolling main and the arching heavens, white to blind you in the sunlit foam and dazzling shore, and black green in the huge old pines that stood like blind prophets on the dune, listening to the booming surge that said they could go no farther.

I went back to the inn in a dream, and did not wake up till the rattling tram set us down in Odawara,* a strange sad place that always seems to be mourning its departed grandeur. Odawara shows little of its old greatness, except in the splendid avenue of pines which leads to it from Kodzu. They say that it was fairly flourishing as an industrial town until a fearful visitation of cholera depopulated it. It lies low, and—smells horribly.

When the train left us in the market-place of Odawara, our good Ogita (friend, servant, interpreter, and *samurai*) had to charter a little army of jinrikshas to carry the party over the eighteen miles which still lay between us and Atami. An inspector of police in

*Murray's *Handbook for Travellers in Japan* (1894) comments that "the tram cars going to Yumoto change horses opposite the ruined walls of the castle."

spotless white uniform came to pay his respects and give his assistance. He also intimated that, although he was entirely at our disposal, and took the honourable interpreter's word for it that this was the British Koshi Sama* and his family, it would give him great satisfaction to see our passports. H—— began to feel in his pockets for a document over which we had laughed a good deal in the shelter of the Legation, for it did seem so absurd that he should have to grant himself solemn permission to travel about; but, alas! the despised paper had been forgotten, and the inspector really had to take our word for it that it existed somewhere. The good Ogita, who is of imposing presence and warlike deportment, talked the official quite dumb, and then sent violent telegrams off to Tokyo about the missing document. Meanwhile the servants had got the luggage started, and I was comfortably packed into my Hong Kong chair and trotted off by a team of four coolies, who ran splendidly, but would not keep step, I find jinrikshas frightfully tiring, so I carry the chair and its poles about with me, and delight in being elevated on the men's shoulders, since I thus get such splendid views over the country.

The road from Odawara to Atami runs for a great part of the way by the sea, and reminds me in many places of the Cornice. There are endless orange groves, still carrying late blossoms here and there, and pines in their wonderful variety of shape, the most interesting trees in the world. These are of the kind which the Japanese call *hama-matsu,* coast fir, and they seem to have no dread of salt water or sea breezes, for they grow as close to the water as they can, and in some places actually dip into it.

The day was nearly done when we at last reached the strange little village by the sea. It lies in a bay of its own, which sweeps inwards to the land in a lovely curve. The beach is narrow, for the houses climb down in terraces almost to the water's edge, and every street seems to lead but that one way. A plain of green rice-fields runs back from the town, rising gradually towards a horseshoe of hills, which close in the horizon on every side save one, and run high spurs into the sea on either hand, so that one is fairly cut off from the rest of creation. But from the beach outwards a great stretch of water rests

*Kōshi is Japanese for Minister.

the eye; there is a splendid roar of breakers on the shore; and far away, on the sun-touched edge of the world, a misty island* floats in the haze, and sends up a constant jet of thin smoke from its volcanic mouth.

We were housed in a *dépendance* of the hotel, a Japanese house, standing by itself in the garden away from the larger building, which looked uninvitingly European. Our rooms had soft mats and international furniture, of which the Japanese part pleased me best. I was especially delighted with an enormous clothes-screen in black lacquer, with wrought gilt clamps at all corners, built in the beautiful *torii* shape, and intended for hanging *kimonos* on, well spread out, so that they should get no creases. The walls were decorated with specimens of curious fern-stem work, very dainty and graceful, and having the deep colour of a ripe pine-cone. It is a speciality of this queer little place. My front windows looked right out to sea; but the side ones commanded a sweeping view of all the Japanese part of the inn, and in the course of the next few days I had watched many an amusing sight in the wide-open rooms, where life was conducted with no more regard to privacy than that which troubled the sparrows who came to roost in noisy thousands in an enormous oak which grew near our house. Our fellow-lodgers seemed to regret that our life was not as open-airy as theirs, and cast many curious glances at me when I sate at my window, which, as the house was solid on that side, *was* a window, and not a paper screen pushing back from a balcony.

I was so tired with the long journey that I was glad to go to bed early on that first evening, and fell asleep to the long roll of the breakers booming solemnly on the shore. Never was I in a place where the sea sang its old songs so loud. All through the night my dreams were set to its solemn measures, and they filled the first moments of my waking consciousness in the morning, when O'Matsu crept into my room and set the windows open to the blessed freshness of the seaside dawn. She amused me by recounting how the wife of our predecessor came down here with children and servants, intending to stay three weeks, but fled back to Tokyo the morning after her arrival, saying that she should go mad if she had

*The island described is Ōshima.

to listen to that booming sea for another day. To me the sea is such an old friend that I do not care what it says or how loud it says it, so long as it will talk at all.

The sparrows left their quarters in the evergreen oak with the first flush of dawn, and my neighbours across the garden were not much behind them in beginning the business of the day. I could hardly attend to my own affairs at all for the intense interest with which I watched them. I could see into eight or nine rooms, each of which seemed to show a typical side of Japanese existence. The weather was so warm that all the paper slides had been removed, and people were carrying on life quite as much in the narrow verandah balconies as in the rooms themselves. In one of these, however, a student was trying to escape distractions, and kept his eyes resolutely fixed on his work. He was a young man, with close-cropped head and a broad heavy face, redeemed by keen dark eyes and a very earnest expression. He sat on a thin cushion before a small table, which stood, perhaps, a foot from the floor—surely the most uncomfortable form of writing-desk ever invented. A bamboo cup held his writing-brushes, and a tiny bronze teapot and stone slab seemed to account for the Indian ink. Piles of pink newspapers were on the ground at his side, and two or three open books fluttered in the breeze, and turned over their mystic characters too fast for him apparently, for he frowned, and turned them back with evident irritation. He was dressed in a single blue robe, the cotton *yucata,* which certainly cannot count as heavy clothing; but the heat was intense and the student had turned his sleeves up to the shoulder and bared his chest in the desire for coolness. To him, towards midday, entered one of the hotel servants, a dear little maid in striped *kimono* and red sash, bringing some light food, which she pushed towards him on a tray as she knelt a few feet from him on the mats. She was pretty and smiling, poor little thing, and only meant to be kind; but he frowned at her and motioned her away, as if he could not bear to be interrupted in his work. After she had withdrawn, silent and chagrined, the student suddenly discovered that he had an appetite, and did full justice to the *musumë's** provisions. The cold rice and

*Literally, daughter, but used here to mean girl-servant.

pickles did not look very tempting to me, though the bowls and cups were charming, red lacquer and white china shining in the sun.

The apartment above that of the ambitious student was occupied by a father and two daughters, people of the merchant class I should think, come here to bathe in the hot spring or inhale the fumes of the great geyser of which I must tell you more anon. The father looks consumptive, and his daughters wait upon him devoutly. They are blooming lasses, and take tremendous interest in their head-dresses. The whole of my first morning in Atami they spent under the hands of the hair-dresser, an elderly woman, who, unlike her kind, did her work in silence. It took just four hours for the two. First one girl sat on the cushion in the verandah, and last week's coiffure was taken down (O'Matsu says that once in four or five days is considered often enough to repeat the ceremony), and the long black hair was washed with something very like egg, and spread out in the sun to dry. Tea and conversation beguiled this in-terval, and then the great business of the dressing began. Oh, the twisting and tying, the moulding and oiling of those black rolls! Shaped wires were inserted to hold out the hair in two long wings over the back of the neck, a twist of scarlet crape was knotted in at the summit, and one or two brilliant flower-pins, or *kanzashis,* planted precisely in the right spot; and the handglass was presented to the young lady so that she might gravely examine the effect. As the girl looked down into the mirror, moving it this way and that, in the sunshine, I saw that its reflection was cast up on the white ceil-ing in an oval of light, with a Chinese character which means hap-piness standing out clearly in the centre.

When the turn of the second sister came, the whole ceremony was minutely repeated; and then what looked like a very small sum in coppers changed hands, the Kami San bowed herself out, and the two girls ran off to gossip with O'Detsu, the daughter of Mr. Higuchi, our landlord.

Meanwhile a middle-aged man on the upper floor was suffering terribly from the heat, and his little wife seemed greatly distressed about him. All the screens had been opened; but it was a breathless day, and no breeze came to ring the little glass bells on the hanging fern-wreath in the verandah. The man had laid aside almost all his garments, and sat with his head in his hands groaning; while madame, kneeling on the mats behind him, fanned his back, and from time to time rubbed him down with a blue towel, an expression of the deepest respect and sympathy on her face. When he seemed a little better, she busied herself with preparing tea, which he drank eagerly, and of course made himself frightfully hot again, when she went back patiently to her fanning and rubbing.

By this time the ambitious student in the first room had given himself a fearful headache by poring over those maddening Chinese characters in the heat of the August day, and so an *amma* or *masseur* was called in to rub it away. The *masseur,* man or woman, is always blind, the old law having forbidden any person not thus afflicted to practise the trade so eminently suited for people whose eyes must be in their fingers. The man who came to the distressed student was young, with a serene countenance deeply marked with small-pox, the most usual cause of blindness here. He was led in with extreme politeness by the little maid of the red sash; the patient bowed to him quite as ceremoniously as if he had been a duke—with two eyes; and then the student sat down on his heels, the *amma* stood over him, and literally punched his head with violence and precision for something like a quarter of an hour. How the student bore it I do not know. It looked as if the process must hurt him more than the worst headache ever evolved from over-work. But when it was over, he jumped up with a beaming face, evidently convinced that he felt perfectly well; the *amma* received his fee wrapped up in a corner of paper, and tucked it inside his girdle; the little maid, who had been watching the process, gravely came and led him away; and the indomitable student went back to his books.

A little later in the day, when it could be supposed that we had recovered from the fatigue of the journey, Mr. and Mrs. Higuchi came to welcome us solemnly to Atami. They were accompanied by O'Detsu, their daughter, who told me that she had been educated in an American school in Yokohama, and could speak some English, which came in very usefully in translating for her parents. All the party were beautifully dressed and expressed their delighted readiness to place themselves, their hotel, and all their belongings at our disposal, and apologised profusely for a thousand short-comings which did not exist. O'Detsu seemed very happy when I told her that I like American cookery, and afterwards strained her invention to the utmost to feed us properly during the three weeks of our stay. The *menus,* it is true, were sometimes puzzlingly worded, and such items as the following are hardly reassuring:

> "Currots Soup.
> Fish fineherbs. (Seaweed?)
> Beef Tea Pudding.
> Dournat. (Doughnut?)
> Boiled Sponge.
> Praised oeufs devil Sauce.
> Eclairs ala Oujam.
> Fish Squeak
> Dam Pudding!"

You see I have written this last small on account of the bad language.

But you will not thank me for detailing all these minor experiences, and I must tell you something of the great wonder of Atami, the admirable geyser, which has made the prosperity of the place. Do not laugh at the adjective, which is really the right one. This spring bursts up in the middle of the village, only a few hundred yards from the shore, with an outbreak of boiling water, and such a thunderous roar of steam that it can be heard far away, while its thick, white smoke-cloud hangs over the place long after the spring has sunk back to the heart of the earth. I have been standing close to it, and felt the earth quiver under my feet even before the voice of its coming had reached the surface. Its mouth is arched over for a little way, in order to direct the outburst toward the canals which lead off to the different bathing establishments, and to the tank where it is collected to form an inhaling-room for those who are suffering from chest and throat troubles. Before this roof was laid over it, I believe it rose two or three yards in the air, and of course much was wasted. As it is, the scalding flood which rushes out from the low tunnel is a terrific phenomenon, filling the world for the moment with fearful noises and choking sulphurous steam. It comes with perfect regularity every four hours, continues for a few minutes (not for an hour and a half, as Rein erroneously supposed), and in that time pours out a volume of water sufficient for all the needs of the bathers, and so hot that it was never possible for me to plunge into it at any time without letting it cool in the bath, although it might have been standing for hours in the bathhouse reservoir since the last outbreak.

The people of Atami count upon their geyser with the easy certainty of familiarity; but it has its caprices, though they are few and far between. Terrible is the consternation when the geyser strikes work, and stays away for ten or twelve days together. There are no hot baths, visitors leave in disgust, and the inhabitants are left to await its stormy homecoming in deep anxiety. When at last the spring returns, it bursts out with a frightful roar and clouds of sulphurous smoke, which hang over the place for a whole day, while the geyser does its many hours of neglected work in one long spell, keeps all its forgotten appointments in a visit which lasts several hours without intermission, and threatens to drown the place in O yu, the honourable hot water.

During my first days in Atami, the geyser attracted my attention with a start every time it broke out; then it came only to mark the time; then I ceased to notice it altogether, as I had ceased to notice the booming of the surf, unless some excursion took us far inland out of reach of its voice, and then there seemed to come deadness on the air, an emptiness which the bird-songs or the wind-songs could not fill.

Atami is a seaside nest lying in the arms of two green hills, that slope down on either side of it (fragrant with lilies just now) to the gentle sea, that breaks in one long roll day and night on the smooth sands. Just where the hills meet the sea on either side is an attempt at a rock and a precipice; but even these are all gay with ferns, and lilies orange and white, so there is no effect of ruggedness. The lilies are a revelation, hothouse flowers showered down on the land by an indulgent Providence as a reward for its humble, faithful love of nature. The great white lily, with leaves like carved marble gemmed with crimson blood-drops—a thing as royal and remote as a maiden empress—here it raises its lovely head on every hillock, reaches gracious greetings out to me from all the hedges, and sends waves of perfume out to bless the workaday air. Down nearer to the sea it is a scarlet lily which spreads its bell to the sun and the salt wind. The other day we took a fishing-boat, and made the

lean brown men row us in and out of the rocks and caves and little
bays within the bay. It was a perfect summer afternoon, with the
fulness of the August sunshine lying on the water; and as we floated
in and out among the rocks, which rise, abrupt and inaccessible,
from the sea, it was beautiful to find every one glorified by these
scarlet lilies, each on a single stem, waving happy and undaunted
in the breeze. Close to the rocks the water lapped and tossed in
sudden foam; one heavy wave went racing through a long arched
waterway of the caves; and out flew two lovely sea-falcons, with
brown wings strained wide, startled by the sea's caprice. The men
sang at their oars weird cold songs, like reminders of death in the
golden glow of life, and one laughed, while the others shook their
heads at the sight of the birds as if at some evil omen.

This is a long letter already, I fear, so you must have the rest
about Atami next time.

Atami, August 5th, 1889

The rooms are so full of flowers that I can hardly move. I come in
from our expeditions with both hands full, and one of our servants
(rather an idle boy) spends three or four hours every day out on
the hillsides, and brings me little forests of hydrangea, white and
blue and lilac, with beautiful bright foliage, and lilies in hundreds,
bursting from their stem like white fireworks, the blossoms nearly
a foot in diameter, and growing high above my head. The blue
hydrangea throws long branches of bloom down the clefts of the
rocks, where they look like waterfalls reflecting the sky. The white
one reaches farther, but separates the clusters more; and they lie
like forgotten snowballs dropped in the little angels' play, for to-day
is the Feast of our Lady of the Snows, Sancta Maria ad Nives, and
I am reminded of the old picture in Siena where all the court of
heaven are standing round her throne with snowballs in their
hands. How glad we should be to see a little cool whiteness here!

The heat is overpowering, and I have been seeking refreshment in the green wood of the old temple* behind the town. It stands between the hills and the plain, with the most lovely grove of trees around it that I have ever seen. They have long-pointed shining leaves of the most brilliant green, and I think are entered on the civic lists of the forest as *Quercus acuta;* but who cares about the name? You may be sure it is not the one they call themselves by in those long whispered conversations that they carry on among the green arches far overhead. Their venerable feet are sunk in a carpet of moss, and ferns, and translucent creepers with leaves like green stars and tendrils soft as a baby's fingers. That brooding peace that I spoke of the other day is in all the wood, and seems to have promised that the ruined temple shall not fall, but crumble dreamily in the sunshine, unconscious of its own decay. Quite near it stands a colossal camphor tree (*Cinnamomum camphora*), so old that it has fallen apart with its own weight, and is like two trees in one, the two divisions measuring altogether over sixty feet round. In the odorous brown shadow inside is set a little shrine; but above, all is life and vigour. Every branch is smothered in fresh green foliage, the small pointed leaves shining like newly cut jade, and giving out a fine aroma on the warm air. It is supposed to be the largest in Japan; and I think Sydney Lanier away in Baltimore must have seen its waving palace of verdure in his dreams when he wrote—

> "Ye lispers, whisperers, singers in storms,
> Ye consciences murmuring faiths under forms,
> Ye ministers meet for each passion that grieves,
> Friendly, sisterly, sweetheart leaves,
> Oh, rain me down from your darks that contain me
> Wisdoms ye winnow from winds that pain me,—
> Sift down tremors of sweet-within-sweet
> That advise me of more than they bring,—repeat
> Me the woods-smell that swiftly but now brought breath
> From the heaven-side bank of the river of death,—
> Teach me the terms of silence,—preach me

*Most probably Kinomiya shrine. Murray's *Handbook for Travellers in Japan* (1894) refers to a grove of the finest camphor trees there.

The passion of patience,—sift me,—impeach me,—
And there, oh! there,
As ye hang with your myriad palms in the air,
Pray me a myriad prayer."

As I sat under the trees in the grove, Ogita told me the story of Atami and the temple and the boiling spring. I cannot write down for you the song of the wind in the leaves, or the long low roll of the sea on the distant beaches; I cannot paint the sunshine flecking now one spot and now another in the green carpet at my feet, or the grey and gold decay of the old shrine. Truly the eye is not satisfied with seeing nor the ear with hearing, when the story has to be written and sent away with all its magic left behind.

Have you had too much of Atami? I must tell you of one more scene which made a great impression on my mind. I noticed yesterday that the village seemed more animated than usual, and the people were hanging red and white lanterns on long strings from high poles down to the ground, and the houses in the chief street were all outlined with them, blowing about violently in a tearing breeze from the day. Strange-looking groups formed at the street corners, and immense excitement prevailed in and around a kind of barn, whose doors, thrown wide, showed a high car being decorated with wreaths and lanterns. An enormous drum stood in one corner, and was being doctored by a specialist, who kept banging the end with a bit of bamboo to see if it sounded loud enough. Little boys were jumping about, screaming and playing, and getting in their elders' way with the complete security of children who are never scolded.

Booths had been set up in the street, and all the shops were displaying their most tempting wares. At lunch, Ogita brought a message from our landlord to say that he was afraid his "rough and ignorant countrymen" would make a great deal of noise in the evening; but he had informed the police that they must on no account let it go on too late, for fear of spoiling our honourable rest. This civility quite overcame me; but to tell the truth, Atami was almost too quiet for me, and I thought, what I was ashamed to say, that a little excitement would make a pleasant change.

As we must soon go back to Tokyo, I spent the afternoon in

collecting some of the curiosities of the place—lovely camphor-wood boxes and fernwork; and of course was followed to the counter of every shop by a crowd of the natives, very anxious to find out what my clothes were made of, for those nearest to me kept feeling my dress, and asked Ogita so many questions that he got quite angry. But it was only good-natured curiosity, and I did not mind it at all. The one drawback to so much cheerful society is that, as all the shopping is done from the outside, with the wares spread on a low board or counter sloping out from the seller in the house to the buyer in the street, the assistants get between the purchaser and his object, and have to be removed by force before he can see what he will have.

As I have said, the little town was crowded with holiday-makers in bright dresses. Among others I noticed an Englishman, a tall smart-looking man, sitting in the native cotton dress on the step of the tea-house, laughing and chattering in fluent Japanese with a swarm of Atami girls, who all seemed very glad to see him. He looked at us, as we passed, with an amused smile, and his face seemed a familiar one, though I could not put a name to him. His dress was poor and common in the extreme. He was probably one of the harmless maniacs who travel everywhere without passports, and try to see the country from the Japanese side of life. He must have seen a good deal of it, to judge by the ease with which he was speaking the language; and he looked like such a pleasing maniac that I longed to talk to him. Of course I did not—does one really ever do the pleasant thing? But, whoever you are, my brother, your clear brown eyes and strong happy face will always make a part of my recollections of Atami.

When night fell, and a splendid moon was riding in the sky, we went out to have a look at the *Matsuri,* or festival procession. The street leading down to the sea was closely packed with people, and the air was full of the sound of drums and the songs of girls, who, sitting high in the great cars, played on brass cymbals and triangles as the men pulled them up the street. All the lanterns were lighted and swung in the breeze; their rays fell on the dark faces and brown limbs of the men, who, naked, and wild with *saké,* strained fiercely at the ropes, while the huge erection, its three tiers decked with flowers and packed with laughing girls in brilliant robes, went tottering and swaying up the sandy street. The moon and the lanterns showed that the wheels were wet; and the men shook the sea water from their limbs as they pulled, for they had taken the sacred cars out into the sea, to bless the fishes, as Ogita explained to me, and were now returning towards the geyser, perhaps meaning to bless that too.

As they moved very slowly in the deep ruts half choked with sand, we went on to wait for them at the other end of the street. We found no difficulty in getting through the crowd, which everywhere gave way kindly and cheerily to the two smart policemen who had us in charge; and soon we found ourselves standing on the step of a shop, whose owner had begged us to come in and watch a pretty sight which was going forward on the opposite side of the street.

On a scaffolding some ten feet high and heavily draped in black and white, a little dancing-girl was holding the enraptured attention of the crowd. She was so small and slight, and so brilliantly dressed, that as she turned and wheeled and set her great flowered sleeves flying on the wind, she put me in mind of some dainty humming-bird with fairy crest and gemlike plumage. Her little head was sparkling with ornaments, which threw out gold and silver fringes as the turned; and her dark eyes shone strangely in her small impassive face, which looked dead white, unrelieved by the usual dash of rouge on cheeks and lips. The child danced beautifully, her feet marking the time sharply through their soft white covering, her movements making precise yet constantly changing volutes of her skirts and sleeves, bewildering, manifold, and parti-coloured as the petals of a tiger-lily shaken by a storm. The cars were coming nearer up the street; the red glare of the lanterns seemed to have passed into her robes, the white shining of the moonlight into her face, when some electric thrill ran through the dense crowd, hoarse shouts broke forth which drowned the clang of the drums and cymbals, and a score of young men, wildly intoxicated and yelling like demons, broke from the car, leapt over the cord which had been drawn round the scaffolding, and began to swarm up it by its hanging ropes and draperies. The thing swayed to this side and that; a number of policemen threw themselves on the rioters, who fought frantically; the little dancer turned a shade whiter, but went on dancing her weird measure, though her *samisen*-players had fled; our own policemen pulled us farther into the shop, hurriedly told the owner to look after us, and dashed across the way to the aid of their comrades, who were far outnumbered by the naked assailants of the stage. But their interference and the delay it caused saved the little dancer, if any harm was meant to her; for now her master, a middle-aged man with a terrified countenance, appeared behind her, snatched her up, and dropped by some hidden steps from the back of the scaffolding and vanished, just as the mob, getting the better of the police, tore the whole thing to pieces. It fell crashing to the ground, its draperies huddled among broken boards and bits of theatrical properties which were stowed beneath it. Then (for I had again come out on the step, to the despair of the responsible shopkeeper) I turned my head, attracted by a flash of light in what had looked like a dark house on our side of the street. I saw a woman holding open a side door, through which the little dancer was borne on the back of her master, who flew with her up a long flight of wooden stairs. Her arms were clasped round his neck, her sleeves spread from his shoulders like scarlet wings, and as she turned her head at the top I saw that she was smiling. Then the door slid into place, and I never saw the little dancer again, nor, in spite of my intense curiosity, could I find out what it was all about. Ogita had abandoned us when the policemen went, and now returned rather shamefacedly to my side. He would only say when questioned that "Atami people very rough much, very common much; very sorry Okusama see tipsy people not proper!" The inspector of police apologised in much the same manner; and since there was nothing more to see (for the rioters had become instantaneously sober after they had wrecked the staging), I went back to the hotel, amused and puzzled, and very sorry not to have the key to the queer story.

I am glad to be writing to you from here once more, though the heat is stifling and persistent. Atami was not all poetry; there was too much hot water about for that! It is difficult to keep up pure intellectual enthusiasm, when twice a day one has to lie for an hour or two, a melting mass of limpness, buried under piles of flannel to continue the effect of twenty minutes' immersion in a bath at 120° Fahrenheit. No curl is left even in the most obedient hair, one looks too frightful to be described, and one's thoughts are mostly concerned with the next thing that can be got to drink. The cure draws all the moisture out of the body; a burning thirst is the result, and one is tempted to think that Niagara would not make such a very long drink after all. At last I had had enough of it, and began to pine for my own airy rooms, and, I am ashamed to say, for my own cook. H—— had been patience itself; so had Mr. G——, whom he had brought to help him bear the exile from civilisation; but I was greeted with applause, when I said one evening, "This family will return to Tokyo the day after to-morrow."

There was any amount of packing to do; for the more I travel the more luggage I carry, and the bare hotel rooms are always beautified by what the old American Consul used to call "layers and peanuts," the photos and books and odds and ends, which are the little familiar gods of daily life, filling up quite a place of their own in our naturally idolatrous hearts. My maid, who had completely collapsed in the heat, pulled herself together enough to do the same by my properties. Ogita the invaluable engaged eleven jinrikshas to pull the family and four coolies to carry me the eighteen miles to Kodzu, and early one morning the whole population turned out to see us depart. Old Mr. Higuchi the landlord, his daughter O'Detsu (iron), and Také (bamboo) the maid, and many others came to the farther bounds of the town to wish us good-bye and beg us soon to return. The grave policeman in gold-laced cap and spotless white clothes came some distance farther, and on the confines of another district made an amiable little speech, and solemnly relinquished all further responsibility on our account. You cannot imagine how admirable the police are in Japan, how quiet and authoritative—and ubiquitous—always there to be appealed to in any difficulty, and amiable as, I think, only

Japanese and Italians (out of office!) can be amiable. It is so amusing to find that many of them can speak English. Fancy a Sorrento *carabiniere* or a member of the Devon constabulary who could talk Japanese!

After we had said good-bye to our little guardian, our troubles began in earnest. Never that I remember have we had to travel over roads in such a hopeless condition. The mud nearly swallowed up the coolies, and spattered the occupants of the jinrikshas till they were almost unrecognisable. I had the best of it in my chair but I expected at every moment to be dropped into some black pool of mud, as my coolies swayed and slipped and recovered their footing and struggled on again. I am not very heavy; but I felt like a criminal for making them carry me at all. The men all behaved splendidly, and not one jinriksha was upset. Near Odawara we suddenly found ourselves mixed up with a huge *Matsuri* procession, which was making its slow way along on the seashore. Our own line of march was immediately broken; I do not know what happened to my companions, but I found myself advancing solemnly on my bearers' shoulders, between two huge cars drawn by flower-decked bullocks and full of screaming musicians, surmounted by a tottering image that swayed and shook as the car advanced. On one was the figure of a woman, life size, with a dead-white face and elaborate coiffure and long stiff robes of purple and gold. She seemed to be holding out her hands to me as she swung this way and that, far above my head. The other car had a huge phoenix, the Empress's bird, with blue and purple wings and a gold crown. It was a dark lowering day, and the sea was rolling in with a heavy roar on my right hand; while on the land side stood crowds of spectators, who cried out with delight when they saw me apparently taking part in the procession. I remembered the sacred bridge at Kameido, and hoped there was no journalist in the applauding crowd, who would at once publish an account of my conversion to Buddhism! As I could not say a word to the coolies, I was quite helpless, until Ogita found out what was happening, and rescued me from the absurd situation.

We had left Atami at half-past seven, and reached Kodzu at two—in time for the train which brought us home at 5.30 in the very worst downpour of the whole season. It seemed cruel to bring the pretty cream-coloured ponies out in it; but I was very glad to get back to my own rooms and the warm bath and the home dinner. We used to have that feeling at the Odescalchi, you remember, when we got back in the autumn after roughing it in the hills all summer.

The next morning the rain had ceased, and in the garden the locusts and all their noisy relations* were screaming aloud to each other that the heat would not last much longer, and that people who wanted to sing had better tune up and begin. No locust or wee-wee, or scissor-grinder prima donna has a note left when the thermometer falls below 85° ; so in these days they are all shrieking *à tue-tête,* and very distracting it is. These last heats are rather exhausting. My dachshund Tippoo Tib, popularly known as the Brown Ambassador, lies on his back between door and window, with ears all over the place, and fat brown satin paws (just like legs of mutton in gloves) turned up in the hope of catching a stray breeze and showing it the way to his nose. His nose is rather his weak point, for it has been damaged by coming in contact with more than one *gheta,* I am sorry to say. The *ghetas* are the wooden clogs which the Japanese wear in the street, and shed at the doorstep as they come in. All the servants have them for crossing the courtyards, and there is often a little army of the curious footgear ranged on a particular doorstep leading towards the servants' quarters. Tip is a dog full of original sin, and his great delight is to steal all the *ghetas* one by one, and bury them in some solitary place in the garden. After long search they are recovered; and then, since mankind is also full of original sin, I fear they are occasionally shied at Tip's offending nose. Before me he is treated with the most tender respect, and solemnly addressed as Tip San.

I think the Japanese servants make the theory of the transmigration of souls account for our extreme care of and kindness to our pets. The Russian Minister has a decrepit old pug (she was eighteen last birthday), who rules the family with a rod of iron. He told me that the other day he saw Gip tottering down the corridor, where she met one of the coolies carrying wood for the stove. The man at once stopped, ranged himself against the wall, and, making a deep bow as the pug passed, murmured respectfully, "Gip San!"

*Mrs. Fraser is here referring to the noise of cicadas (in Japanese, *semi*) and crickets.

The Japanese puzzle me in their treatment of animals. Sometimes they seem devoted to them, as kind and careful as English people are to their dogs and horses. At others they show quite a cynical callousness to their sufferings. As far as I can see, they are kind to their own creatures and indifferent to those of other people. One can take a kind of family pride in seeing one's own pampered *chin* dog wearing a frilled collar *à la* Toby, and swaggering about in the sun; but there is no satisfaction to be got out of the dog of one's neighbour's grandmother, as Ollendorff would say.

To tell the truth, the dogs of Tokyo are not attractive as dogs. There are only four kinds: the coarse wolfish house-dog, only a shade less repulsive than the pariah of Peking; a middle-sized brown mongrel, smooth-haired, thick-set, and cowardly, who is much *répandu* in the dog world; and two kinds of lap-dogs, a degenerate King Charles (the *chin* above mentioned), and a smooth, rather bald beast with spots—both kinds have prominent eyes, and their sight is weak from having been brought up in the half light of Japanese houses. They generally wear Toby collars of scarlet or purple to mark their rank, and are much petted by their own masters. Even the pet cat wears a collar; and there is a woman I often pass on the Koudan hill near our gate who takes her pussy out for an airing wrapped in the folds of her own *kimono*. This is of course a tailless cat, the ugliest thing in Japan! Like all other foreigners, I have been much puzzled by this destitution of Japanese cats. Ogita declares that they are born without tails in Dai Nippon, and adds that it is a good thing too, since it is well known that a cat with a long tail is a most dangerous creature, and always turns into a witch when it grows old.

Perhaps it does! We have two weird cats here, imported with great trouble by Lady Plunkett* some years ago. They come from Siam, and are a pale biscuit colour, with black ears, paws, and tails. Such tails! Longer than their whole bodies, and lashing the ground furiously when they are waiting for a spring; then their pale-green eyes shine diabolically between the black ears above and the black

---

*Wife of Sir Francis Plunkett (1835–1907), British Minister at Tokyo from 1883 to 1888.

nose below; and their long lean bodies fly through the air in leaps that would not disgrace a panther. The servants are horribly afraid of them; and so am I, and so is Tip. They wait for him on the branch of an over-hanging tree, and drop on his smooth brown back as he saunters along in his lordly way. Then there is a fearful battle, from which Tip returns a lacerated conqueror, with tags of biscuit-coloured fur between his teeth.

The Emperor is fond of dogs, and has one especial pet, a tiny long-haired terrier, which was a present from Madame Sannomiya. The little creature is quite a personage in the Palace, and during this hot weather has a servant who sits beside it all day to fan the flies away and put bits of ice into its mouth. No one is allowed to wake it from sleep; and I believe there was terrible trouble one day when some unlucky person trod on its tail.

I wish some kind fairy would fan me all day and put bits of ice into my mouth! The heat is still over-powering, and I rather rebel against it, because as a rule I find warm weather inspiring and in-vigorating. This last week has been apoplectic. By half-past six or seven in the morning the sun is blazing; and if a cloud does drift across his face in the course of the day, the air only seems the hotter for it. I wander from room to room, in the thinnest of white gar-ments, seeking for something to breathe. Just now I have been sitting on the stairs, in the hope of catching a stray breeze; and Tip, limp and panting, came and sat down beside me. All the doors and win-dows are wide open, and have fine blinds of split bamboo hanging loose in them, giving out a strong grassy smell as the sun smites them from the other side. The wide staircase is half in twilight, and so is the hall below, where the palms are hanging, without a quiver on the breathless air; and the "Heavenly Bamboo" trained on great screens has not shaken its bright-red berries once to-day. Outside in the garden everything is simmering in the heat; not a servant is to be seen, except the slave of the hall door, who has fallen asleep on his bench; but a hum from the farther courtyard tells me that the rest of my household is gathered there, every one at the door of his room under the shady verandah, probably in the sketchiest of cos-tumes, smoking the afternoon pipe and consuming the afternoon tea. My English housekeeper tells me that very funny scenes are

71

enacted in that courtyard, where she, being a great favourite, comes and goes at will. On the doorstep my *amah,* who is a bit of a character, will sit and scold her husband, the head boy, by the hour, bewailing the day when she married such a fool as Rinzo. Rinzo takes it all quite patiently; and when she has done, hands her his pipe to clean, and suggests tea. Opposite, the pantry-boy, who has aesthetic tastes, is arranging flowers in a vase to put on the stand under a much-prized picture in his room, and remarks that he is not sorry he left *his* wife in the hills. Next to him "Cook San" is helping his little girl to dig up her toys from a corner where Tip buried them carefully this morning; while Mrs. Cook, who has been washing, is ironing her clothes by spreading them very tightly on a board, where the sun will bake them dry and stiff. Cook San's aides-de-camp, two idle youths in white cotton clothes, are pretending to wash vegetables for to-night's salad, but find it tempting to splash each other with the clear water from the tap. Okusama is not supposed to enter this courtyard except at stated hours; but cannot resist the pleasure of occasionally watching, through the closed blinds of an upper window, the many-sided, brightly coloured life of its inhabitants, of listening to the hum of chatter which rises from the human hive.

Really, servants in Japan ought to be very happy! Each man may bring his wife and children and mother to live with him, when he enters our service. I have drawn the line at grandmothers, on account of overcrowding, and also because it is impossible to impress these very elderly people with the necessity and propriety of wearing clothes in warm weather. They scoff at modern ideas, and doubtless talk of the good old times when they were young and all these absurd decency fads had not cropped up. Who wants clothes except for warmth, or to look smart in on proper occasions? Why be bothered with them in the house, in August? And so it happened that, when Cook San's grandmother was met in the kitchen one warm afternoon without a shred of raiment on her old brown body, then I found that there really was not room for more than three generations in our very inadequate servants' quarters, and a lodging was found for the old lady elsewhere.

Of course we do not keep house for this army of people. If we did, my good Mrs. D—— would have her hands full and her larder empty all the time. The servants' wages cover their food expenses (the wages are low on the whole*), and we provide a cooking-house and fuel; each man is given one, or, at the most, two little rooms, and then he does as he pleases about filling them. Some kind of supervision has to be exercised, and this is done by D——, our good head man, who has made himself much respected by the Japanese servants; and I occasionally make a tour of inspection, accompanied by him and his wife, when I express great approbation of the tidy pretty rooms, and look unutterable things at less well-kept ones. Now there is quite an ambition about it, and the going round brings me a little more into contact with the wives and children, who amuse me greatly. Little presents to the babies also go a long way towards establishing confidence between us, and some of the tiny ones get themselves brought upstairs occasionally to see me or bring me flowers.

On one point I have trouble, and that is their dislike to foreign doctoring, and their obstinate clinging to their own queer medicine-men, who are constantly smuggled in through the stable-yard to attend them, while the illness is carefully hidden from me in its first stages. When the local quack, half herbalist, half fortune-teller, has failed to help them, then I am told that So-and-so has just been taken ill, and may they send for "Baelz Doctor San"? Doctor Baelz arrives, looks into the case, and comes, full of righteous rage, to report to me that the patient has been ill for a week, and has been poisoning himself with the prescription of the Japanese medicine-man. Scolding is of no use. All one can do is to give good nursing and proper remedies a chance of overcoming the mischief that has been done—and that will be done again at the first opportunity.

Of course I am not now referring to the Japanese doctors properly speaking. They are a body of serious and learned men, educated either in Europe or here under Doctor Baelz, who is the medical professor at the University, and whose name is familiar to scientific men all over the world. In surgery the Japanese do wonderful work, their calm nerves and delicate hands fitting them to undertake the most difficult operations. They are as far removed from the strangely

*This is no longer the case!

clad practitioner of my back yard as our great physicians and surgeons are from the quack who sells medicines from a cart at a country fair.

Doctor Baelz tells me that, like medical students at home, the young men are occasionally turbulent and unmanageable. His predecessor had had much trouble with a class, and the first time that Doctor Baelz took it they threatened mutiny of a violent sort. So, as soon as he could make himself heard, he told them in a few pithy words that they had come to him with the worst reputation in the University, that he was not in the least afraid of them, but wished it clearly understood that if they were unruly there would be no lectures to attend, and since they had all to gain from him and he nothing to gain from them, perhaps they had better reflect on it till the next day, when he would be glad to hear what conclusion they had come to. They broke up in silence, came the next morning to his first lecture, and never gave him the slightest trouble afterwards.

I could listen to his lectures with rapt attention. He has made a study, as only a German can do, of the Japanese, their bodies and souls, their country and their customs. Our people take their learning more spasmodically, and do not give it out so well. Doctor Baelz has won a great position for himself here, and is so constantly appealed to by Japanese and Europeans that he hardly has the time to follow up the questions of research which interest him most. I am glad he is the Legation doctor. One could not fall into wiser or kinder hands.

On August 26th the three hundredth anniversary of Tokyo's existence as a capital was celebrated, very noisily and dustily, but with much enthusiasm. A kind of popular festival was inaugurated at Uyeno Park, where there is a racecourse, and a temple dedicated to Iyeyasu, the hero of the day.

Uyeno, the park where the tercentenary festival took place, was one of these *yashikis*,* the residence of the Daimyo of Todo, who gave it up to the Shogun Iyemitsu (the grandson of Iyeyasu) for the erection of some magnificent Buddhist temples, which were intended to remove the prevalent superstition that the north-eastern quarter of a town must always be the most unlucky one. But there

*Daimyos' houses.

74

was another motive for the erection of these great buildings. The second Shogun, to protect himself against any possible intrigues on the part of the Emperor in Kyoto, invested an Imperial Prince (the son of his own daughter, who was the reigning Empress) with the dignity of chief priest of the Uyeno Temples. From that time the office was always filled by an Imperial Prince, who was looked upon as a hostage for the good behaviour of the Emperor. Iyemitsu did much to make Yedo both splendid and important, one of his regulations being to the effect that every Daimyo should maintain a house in Yedo and pass a portion of the year there. It was under the rule of Iyemitsu and the other Tokugawa Shoguns that the arts of Japan reached their highest perfection; and the Tokyo of to-day still shows many traces of beauty, which neither the harrow of war nor the blizzard of modernisation has been able to efface. Some of Iyemitsu's temples at Uyeno survived a fierce battle which was fought in their sacred groves in July, 1868, between the Emperor's troops and the adherents of the last Shogun, who, more persistent than their master, continued to fight after he had consented to resign. In this battle the chief temple was destroyed by—an Armstrong gun! Its site serves for the Uyeno Museum, a place where I should like to loot undisturbed for days; but the true glory of Uyeno in Japanese eyes is not in its temples or its museum, or even its historical associations, but in the cherry trees which glorify it in the spring, and which I hope to see—next year, "Roses, if I live and do well."

I did not go to the noisy festival, which promised nothing so distinctly picturesque or sympathetic as Uyeno in its quiet weekday garb. The races and fireworks and feasting of last Monday would have seemed to me vulgar and profane; for the Uyeno woods are my temples of peace, where I go and spend long hours listening to the talk of the wise old trees which know so much—so much, that we can never be quiet enough to learn. I think I must have come of the tree folk originally. Oak and palm and pine—they are individual and dear as human kin to me, and I felt at home directly in Japan, the land of trees. It is only since I came here that their hierarchy has been revealed to me. The palm is a holy pontiff; the oak a king, a ruler of men; the pine a seer, sad and faithful; the bay-laurel is a poet whose heart is warm gold; the cypress a penitent soul that will never know its own greatness; the ilex, my Roman ilex, is a pagan

75

still, and believes only in sunshine above and warm cliffs and blue sea below. The rest, elm and ash and willow—well, they are the common folk, sweet and useful, but not royal, not indispensable, like those others.

It makes one rather selfish to be so intimate with the trees, and I grudge the deep glades at Uyeno to the screaming crowd. Also that which they call a racecourse is a grassy road, running wide and low round the lotus lake, called *Shinobazu,* where just now myriads of flowers are holding white and rosy cups open to the sun or stars, while their green velvet leaves, a yard wide, lie on the water playing games with round diamond drops that run up and down on the fine veins trying to find their way back to the cool flood below. And all around the lake fly swarms of gorgeous dragon-flies, their burnished bodies and filmy rainbow wings making them seem living jewels as they dart swiftly through the sunshine. The little children, as bright and gay as they, come in bands to the green path round the lake, and fish for the dragon-flies with long fine threads fastened to tall rods of bamboo. These they fling through the air with a sharp whirl, and the long thread winds itself round the dragon-fly, and he is slipped into a fairy cage, and taken home to be fed and petted; but all his free flying is done for ever.

So—you see why I did not go to the Uyeno festival!

Fujiya Hotel, Miyanoshita, September, 1889

It is only a fortnight since I returned from Atami to Tokyo, and now I am in Miyanoshita among the hills. You will think that I spend my time in flying from one Japanese watering-place to another; but the truth is that Tokyo, just now, is a spot to get away from—on foot, if it could not be done otherwise! The heat gives one no rest, no air, nothing to breathe or live on. Heavy black skies like prison blankets hang over the town, full of hot rain and stored thunder. When they break, we are half drowned; and when the sun comes out after the deluges, the heat is worse than ever—

steady, blazing, steaming heat, more trying than I can describe. The dampness is in everything; shoes and gloves, if left one day shut up, go green with mould, and smell unspeakable things about vaults and tombs. The maids have been spending their time in laying my whole wardrobe out on sheets in the sun (whenever the sun shone) in the upstairs verandahs; but my poor frocks have suffered terribly already. I quite refused to have all my evening gowns and pretty things soldered down in tin at the end of May, as the other women here do; having only just come, with a lot of smart new clothes, it seemed rather hard to put them all away, and wear only pongee and Japan crape for three or four months: but, alas! my pink frock has turned yellow, my blue a sickly green, my beloved black Chantilly has eruptions of grey spots all over it, and so on!

Poor H——— is terribly busy, for all the hard work comes, as a rule, at the hottest time, and Treaty Revision ranges in the Legation upstairs and downstairs and in my lady's chamber. My lady's chamber is empty just now, its mistress having abandoned her post and taken refuge in cowardly flight to the hills, accompanied by one or two friends, the faithful Ogita, and several of the servants, brought, not to wait on me, but because the poor things were badly in need of a little fresh air. Mr. G———, who is H———'s right hand in all the work, is up here too, but will probably be wired for before he has quite done unpacking his things.

The journey to Miyanoshita* is the same as that to Atami as far as Kodzu, where one takes a tram, which runs for five or six miles farther, and stops at Yumoto, a pretty place, with a beautiful Japanese hotel, at the foot of the hills. From there the journey has to be continued in jinrikshas, up a steep and lovely road to Miyanoshita itself. We were fortunate in our weather, for the day was one of shifting showers and sudden sunshine, with faint ethereal mists spreading, rolling, melting away, and gathering again, making exquisite effects of distance when fold after fold of mountain was visible, each clothed in a clinging veil of filmy gauze that seemed to catch and tear on the pine tops. The full and rushing stream of the Hayagawa was beside us for a great part of the way, making

*Murray's *Handbook for Travellers in Japan* (1894) says that the journey from Tokyo to Miyanoshita took about five hours and thirty minutes.

77

pools of light that doubled the sun and the mist, while the grey boulders tossed along its bed broke the water up in airy diamonds. The sense of rest and freshness was wonderful, coming as I did from the choking atmosphere of the town.

I travelled, as usual, in my chair, on coolies' shoulders; and towards the end of the journey we left the road, and took short cuts up through splendid woods, dark and cool and full of the sound of waterfalls. I am never so happy as on such expeditions, when I generally leave the rest of the party far behind, and can have a long *zusammen schweigen** with my friends the trees. The men carried me rapidly and easily, only stopping twice to breathe in the whole long climb. Though I am not very heavy, they were rather spent from the extreme steepness of the path, and I made them stop and have some tea at a tiny brown *chaya,* which leant against the pine trunks like a bundle of brushwood. The little place was poor as a hermit's cell; but it was all sweet with the scent of pine needles, and at the door a tiny runnel of clear water trickled from a bamboo pipe into a hollowed trunk which serves as a water barrel. On its edge was growing a yellow wild flower, which quivered and vibrated with the movement of the water; while a sunbeam crept down through the branches, and danced on the clear sand at the bottom and on the bare back of my head coolie, who suddenly pulled off his blue cotton shirt and plunged it into the water. In a moment he withdrew it, wrung it out, scattering bright drops in the air, and then put it on again with a sigh of satisfaction.

"Why?" I inquired uneasily; for the proceeding looked like a recipe for penumonia—a cold wet garment laid on a steaming human body!

"Cold wet hot wet being-is-not," was the reply, meaning, I suppose, that a garment wrung out in clear water is more comfortable than one saturated with perspiration.

The Fujiya Hotel† is almost entirely arranged for Europeans, the only Japanese rooms being some low buildings in the garden, which are called the Bachelors' Quarters. Mr. G——, his dogs and boys,

---

*Literally, silence together.
†The Fujiya Hotel, established in 1878, was rebuilt after a fire in 1884. Although much altered and expanded it still has much of the old atmosphere.

shook down there; and I and Mrs. N—— had some pretty rooms on the second floor, with wide views down the valley, and not too great a distance of shiny corridors to be pattered over in slippers before we got to the baths; for the baths are Miyanoshita's reason for existing, and are so delightfully pleasant that it seems a pity ever to come out of the warm reviving water. The villages here have grown up round warm springs, and there are no less than six of them in the gorges of our noisy Hayagawa; while one, the hottest of all, is used for baths at Ashinoyu, farther off in the hills, and nearer the source of the river itself in the Hakone Lake. The waters of Ashinoyu are strong in sulphur, and fairly hot, having a temperature of from 90° to 100° Centigrade; as they descend from the heights, they become cooler, and, losing their sulphurous character, take on a little more iron. At Miyanoshita the water is tepid (45–59°), and has no sulphur smell; but it has a delightfully alive feeling as if charged with electricity, and a dip in it takes all the fatigue out of weary limbs after the longest walk.

The baths are comfortably arranged; indeed one is always sure of finding an inviting bathroom in any hotel in Japan. At Miyanoshita the woods of which they are built give out in the warm atmosphere a sweet aromatic smell quite peculiar to the place. Nothing but wood is used for walls or floor or ceiling; and the deep tank where the water flows is of wood too, polished and scented, and smooth as velvet to the touch. The only drawback is that every sound pierces the thin wooden partitions, and people are tempted to make remarks or discuss family affairs with some member of their own party in the next bathroom, forgetting that probably all the others are occupied as well. This applies to the bedrooms too; and I was kept long awake by a cheerful lady on the verandah, who sat there telling impossible stories to a circle of friends till late into the night.

I was up fairly early the next morning, and wandered out in search of some shady corner where I could make friends with a tree and read a little; and I found what I wanted not far from the Bachelors' Quarters, where as I afterwards learned, my appearance in the garden, fully dressed, at ten o'clock in the morning, caused profound consternation among the inhabitants. The men take it very easy in the mornings in summer, and the cool pyjamas, or *yucata,* are not exchanged for clothes proper till various drinks and newspapers have been discussed on long chairs in the verandahs and the gossip of the day fairly threshed out. When the holiday-makers saw me approaching, Mr. G—— says they all fled indoors and began to shave, thinking I was bent on inspecting their domain. He himself, buried in the new dictionary (which just now consists of several thousand little squares of loose paper), could not abandon the treasure to be the sport of the elements and was rewarded for his valour by seeing me subside into a seat with my back to him and his bachelor friends. I had been perfectly unconscious of their presence, and was taken up with wondering how—and if—I could reach the highest point of the surrounding hills, which, in spite of their beauty, troubled me by closing us in all round. That is why I never care for hills so much as for the sea; there is more space to think in, when the horizon is blue and very far away. I found that the hills would be beyond my strength, and went instead up the road which leads along the gorge above the river, to the little village of Kiga, where there are more warm baths and a number of Japanese hotels.

To reach it one has to pass close to a thin sheet of waterfall, which covers the road with spray for many yards, and spreads most welcome coolness on the air. Kiga itself is all built against the cliff, so that many of the houses have the rock itself for their inner wall. It is a pretty, friendly place, with glimpses of pretty tea-house gardens and girls flitting to and fro, and the sound of the Hayagawa everywhere. I sat down for a moment in one of the gardens to admire the flowers and feed the goldfish; and then, since the sun was getting high, I returned to Miyanoshita, and plunged into some of the woodshops in the village—cool dark shops, full of lovely work, on which one could spend many dollars with great satisfaction.

The work itself is mostly wood mosaic,* intermingled in a thousand lovely patterns with fretwork or solid carving. The screens are particularly pretty, having a square of delicate open lattice-work in each panel, mostly in white wood, set in many-coloured inlaid work, and the whole panel mounted in a richly carved ebony frame. These are purely Japanese, and so are the boxes and cabinets; but beside them are writing-tables of cruel ugliness, made to please the European eye. Also one can buy screens and brackets of white wood

*Such wood mosaic is still the souvenir to buy in Miyanoshita.

precisely like those one gets to paint in England. Altogether the foreign element is very strong in the Miyanoshita shops. On the third day of my stay it rained, and I wanted a new book. I had read all that the hotel contained except one—a religious novel, which made much stir a year ago, and which, partly from obstinacy, partly because I prefer to take my religion and my novel separately, I have steadily refused to read. On board ship, in railway journeys, in country hotels, this valuable work has been recommended to my notice—in vain; but I might have been tempted to read it at Miyanoshita that day, had not somebody told me that at one of the carving-shops there was actually a lending library, where one could get books for five sen a day. I at once put on my rain-cloak, and flew down the street, which was quite deserted, and noisy with the rattling rush of the rain. My poor interpreter had to come too, much against his will. When we reached the shop, and explained our errand to the woman who kept it, her face brightened, and she said yes, she had many books, twelve in all, to hire out, and would I like this one? The volume she held out was—the religious novel that I had been running away from across two continents!

For me the real interest of Miyanoshita lies in the family life of the wood-carvers. From the father down to the tiny children everybody helps, and it is evident that woodwork is considered the only honourable or interesting trade in the world. I have haunted the shops just to watch the people, and bought heaps of things I did not want, as an excuse for lingering among them. Many of the workers have no shop of their own, but supply one establishment with various details of objects, which are afterwards put together. There was one little house where I never saw them making anything but red gods of happiness,* little bloated creatures, who resolved themselves into boxes containing smaller editions of themselves in two and three chapters. These were blocked out by one son of about seven-

---

*Mrs. Fraser is here referring to Daruma dolls. Daruma, more properly Bodhidharma, is not the god of happiness but is the name of the founder of the Zen sect of Buddhism. Bodhidharma is said to have lost the use of his legs by meditating for too long in a squatting position. He is almost always portrayed with blank or staring eyes. The story goes that once when meditating he fell asleep, and in self-disgust he tore off his eyelids and threw them on the ground, where they took root and grew into the first tea bushes.

teen, turned on a lathe by another, finished by a third, and painted by the father, whose skilful laying on of his few colours was approvingly watched by the family baby from over the mother's shoulder. But in some of the big shops one sees lovely designs in every stage of completion, every member of the family working at them except the mother, who is always the saleswoman, and whose bright face and cheery talk make you willing to part with a few dollars if only for the sake of the grave ubiquitous baby whose eyes, from his throne on her back, watch you solemnly, and seem to take in every detail of the bargain.

Poor Mr. G—— was wired for after two days, and set off at 4.30 one morning to rejoin the Chief, who is gasping over cipher telegrams and Treaty Revision in Tokyo. It cleared off up here, and we had a day's excursion to Ashinoyu, the sulphurous spring high on the way to Hakone. It was a long climb, through green gorges and up steep mountain-paths; but when we reached a kind of pass behind the solfatara, I felt that I could breathe at last. There were splendid wide views over the country, and far away a deep-blue line which meant my friend the sea. Ashinoyu is a sad place, full of sick people and terribly strong sulphur fumes, and only stern necessity could induce one to remain there. It is, however, a favourite place with the Japanese, who must be less subject to melancholy than Europeans, I think. They walk about a good deal in the hills, and one comes sometimes on parties of young girls, full of fun and laughter, with flowers in their hands and flowers in their hair, springing along light as young fawns on the hillside.

I met a typical group the other day in the woods. It must have been a family party, since it included a handsome elderly man and two boys, besides two or three girls. It was one of these that I saw first, coming down towards me through the green glades, and a pretty picture she made, though one that might have startled an inexperienced traveller. Her robe of soft blue *crêpe* had been thrown off, and was only held on round the waist by a rich silk *obi,* leaving her arms, shoulders, and bosom bare and white to the daylight. Her slender limbs were incased in tightly fitting white silk gaiters buttoned up to the knee, and the skirts of her *kimono* were kilted high through her girdle. Her head was bare, and the sunbeams came down through the leaves on her shining hair and dark eyes, on the sheaf of wild flowers laid in a fold of her naked arm, even on her little feet, bare too, except for light straw sandals tied on with wisps of grass. She stood still for a minute when she saw me, and laughed shyly, and laid down her flowers, and pulled up her *kimono* over her pretty shoulders; then her brothers and sisters burst through the bushes with cries, and laughter, and flying draperies, and bare young limbs, and the whole band ran away from me through the sunny woods.

In such surroundings there seems nothing shocking or unnatural in seeing young human bodies bare to warm air. At Atami one day I was looking out of my window rather early in the morning, and noticed a pile of brightly coloured garments lying on a wood heap. Nobody was about; but I heard laughter and young voices coming from a tumbledown bath-house near by, and then, swift as light, a slender young girl came running out, the water flying in shining showers from her limbs as she sprang at one bound on the pile of wood; there she stood, naked and unashamed, her arms stretched high above her head, laughing out the joy of her heart to the rising sun, and breathing in all the freshness of the new day. I never saw a more beautiful picture of innocence and happiness.

There are lovely walks round Miyanoshita, though all but one or two involve a good deal of climbing. The view from a spur of the hill behind the Bachelors' Quarters of Fujiya's hotel is quite lovely. A sharp ascent leads to a deserted tea-shed, where one can sit and gaze out towards the sea, with the long low island of Eno-shima lying like a dark hull on its bosom; while inland, Fuji's solemn outline dominates the lower hills. The weather is still so warm that I have not felt inclined to push up to Hakone, but was betrayed into visiting the smoking spot called indiscriminately "Ojigoku" (the Greater Hell), or "Owaki-dani" (the Valley of the Greater Boiling). There constant clouds of sulphurous smoke break through the thin crust of earth, and come rolling down the gorge; the earth is everywhere hot to the touch; the rocks are caked grey and yellow with sulphur; and the fumes are overpowering. I never saw a more awful place. There is a narrow path, where one has to follow the guide very carefully; in many places the ground on either side will give to the slightest touch, and there have been some frightful catastrophes, owing to the carelessness or incredulity of people who came to visit the sinister spot. A young English girl whom I knew stepped on this treacherous crust, and at once sank in the seething mud which it concealed. She was rescued by her companions, and did not lose her life, as some have done; but she was terribly burnt, and will carry the marks of her accident on her limbs to her dying day.

There is a distinct fascination about the place. We saw it on a grey day, when the sky seemed dark with coming storm; the air was heavy and breathless, and there was not the slightest current of wind to interfere with the volumes of sullen white smoke, which rose and rolled and curled in a thousand weird shapes in the desolate gorge, where not a blade or leaf can grow. The hill which rises directly behind the boiling valley is clothed in a garment of dense green forest, making a surprising contrast to the scorched foreground of the picture, where everything is white with ashes or crusted with deathly looking sulphur. Japan is certainly richer in hot springs than any other country in the world. They meet you at every turn, and are immensely prized and appreciated by the people.

It was a relief to come down from the horrible choking fumes and ghastly colouring of the boiling valley to friendly Miyanoshita, with its bright shops and sweet wood smells, and its miles of bamboo piping, through which the warm water of the springs is conducted to every inn, almost to every house, in the town. The universal application of bamboo to the needs of man is one of the real successes of Japanese ingenuity. It is always used for conducting water, the sections of its hollow cane fitting tightly and strongly together. Water-cans, basins, boxes, cups are made from segments of the variety which has a solid division at every knot, and which, when mature, lends itself to beautiful polish and carving. Then the building fancies, the garden decoration, the elaborate lattice-work are as charming as they are surprising; and one can hardly believe that the material for all these is supplied by one plant. A bamboo spear is, I am told, one of the most dangerous of weapons, and has been known to transfix two men at once; the leaves serve for more uses than I can mention; and the new shoots make an excellent vegetable. I used to say that I would only live in the countries where grapes were grown; it always made me feel forlorn and away from home to be north of the vine line: but I shall miss the bamboo quite as much, I think, when fate says "Shift!" and sends us back to brick houses and leaden pipes and tin utensils, all as costly as they are hideous.

The heat is lessening. Little breezes come up from Odawara and the sea every evening. There are sure to be heavy storms towards the end of the month, and—I think it is time to go home!

❖   ❖   ❖

Tokyo, September, 1889

I was glad that I left Miyanoshita when I did; for just after my departure a violent typhoon came whirling across the country, and did much damage there. That part of the hotel where I had my rooms suffered heavily, many houses were completely wrecked, and everybody was horribly shaken and frightened. The Nabeshimas (Marquis Nabeshima was at one time Japanese Minister in Rome) were staying in the pretty hotel at Kiga, where I had gone in to admire the flowers and the goldfish a few days before. A great part of it was blown off its rock perch, and poor Madame Nabeshima and the children had to be rescued from considerable danger in the dead of night in torrents of rain. Even here in Tokyo, where we were much farther removed from the centre of the storm, the commotion was terrible. Bricks and slates were flying in every direction, trees were uprooted and tossed about like dry leaves, jinrikshas and carriages were blown right over in the streets, and it rained—ramrods!

This is the first bad typhoon that I have seen on land; and though it is certainly less terrible than when it catches one at sea, it is a sufficiently fearful visitation. It seems to have started somewhere far to the north of Japan,* and to have found its way to us along the warm current which is our gulf stream, giving us palms and camellias in the open air all through a winter which will keep North

*This is probably a slip on the part of Mrs. Fraser. Typhoons normally start in the south.

85

China or Jersey City icebound for months in the same latitude with us. Truly climate is to a country what environment is to individuals. One has to pay in some way for advantages in both directions; and Japan's gulf stream does not seem dear, even at the cost of an occasional typhoon. The storm moved here at the rate of fifty-eight miles an hour, which was nothing like the velocity at the centre, over a hundred miles away. The incessant roar of the wind and the iron rattle of the rain which always go with it make a serious typhoon intensely fatiguing to live through, and I fancy that it must be accompanied by some acute electric disturbance which tells painfully on the nerves. Sensitive people feel unreasonably depressed at the approach of a typhoon some hours before it has declared itself; and those who have lived through many such storms tell me that they always feel that stress of personal conflict and final exhaustion which I experienced during the hurricane. At sea it must have been horrible; some of the skippers say that they never encountered more awful weather, and they and their passengers were amazedly thankful to find that they had really survived it. Of course all the rivers are in flood, and there has been pitiful loss of life in the districts where the storm was at its worst.

Tokyo, October, 1889

The course of Treaty Revision, which was beginning to run a little more smoothly with Count Okuma's help, has suddenly come to a standstill in a rather tragic way. Count Okuma, who has been Minister for Foreign Affairs for several months, is a man of much intellectual power and resolute character. At one time, I believe, he was strongly in opposition to the new ideas; but he has advanced with the times, and is not accused by the anti-foreign politicians of yielding too readily to our demands, and of granting too much in the proposed treaty, especially as regards the retention of foreign judges in Japanese courts. I must say, in passing, that what his countrymen called his absurdly generous terms were indignantly refused by our people on the ground of their complete inadequacy to meet our requirements. Of course poor Count Okuma has not got thus far on the road of progress without making for himself many enemies. With the *soshi* he has long been known as a marked man, and only two months ago one of these gentlemen, called Koyama Katsutaro, tried several times to gain admittance to his presence, but was always prevented from doing so. At last he climbed over the wall into the garden of the official residence, and suddenly appeared, as Count Okuma came out of the house to get into his carriage. Koyama asked if that gentleman were the Minister, and the coachman, suspecting evil, answered that he was not. Koyama was promptly arrested, but proved to be unarmed, and after a short time was set at liberty again.

The Cabinet Ministers are always accompanied by one or two detectives, who follow them about in jinrikshas, generally at too great a distance behind the carriage to be of much use, but near enough to mark it clearly to any one looking out for an official victim. All this escort business was annoying in the extreme to Count Okuma, a bold and self-reliant man; and its uselessness was shown by a sadly practical demonstration a few days ago.

The Count was returning from a Cabinet Council, where there had been a rather stormy debate about Treaty Revision. As the carriage turned into the drive leading up to the house, a quiet-looking, well-dressed young man stepped forward, holding a small parcel rolled up in a violet handkerchief, such as the official employés use for wrapping papers in. Taking aim at the Count, he flung the parcel at him with all his force, and as it exploded cut his own throat and fell dead. The missile did not strike the Count full in the body, as it was meant to do, because the coachman, seeing the man raise his arm, had whipped up the horses, who plunged forward, thus causing the bomb to explode on the side of the carriage; but the splinters struck Count Okuma's right leg, which was crossed over the left, and shattered his knee. The horses were terrified and galloped on, but were stopped at the door of the house, and the poor gentleman was lifted out and taken upstairs. He did not lose consciousness or composure for a moment, and was found holding his knee, or what remained of it, with both hands. Some one who was there told me that the wrecked carriage and torn limb presented a terrible sight, but Count Okuma's perfect calmness and cheeriness greatly impressed every one. That the act was inspired by fanaticism was made clear by the suicide of the assassin.

That, in Japanese eyes, was as it should be. It is the correct and gentlemanlike end to such an affair. The excuse being supposed to be pure patriotism, the deed is not complete unless the doer gives his own life with that of his victim. The man who made this attempt seems for a long time past to have contemplated something of the kind; and that the deed was the result of pure fanaticism was shown by his end. When he cut his throat, he did not know whether he had succeeded or not. His name was Tsuneki Kurushima; he was twenty-seven years old, and the son of a former retainer of Count Kuroda. Poor, partially educated, an eager reader of the newspapers, and especially of those which indulge in violent anti-foreign agitation,* his brain seems to have been filled with vague ideas of patriotism, and he used to tell his friends that he was well qualified to die for his country, having no one dependent on him. He had been thoughtful and silent for a few days before making the attack, and evidently looked upon himself as a martyr to his country.

As generally happens in these cases, the outrage has awakened a good deal of indignation, and sent the weight of public sympathy over to the other side of the scale. But among the *soshi* and the Radicals it seems to have roused the anti-foreign feeling somewhat strongly. We are occasionally met by scowling faces in the streets. The other day, as we were driving through a rather rough suburb, a *soshi* insisted on running beside the carriage for a long time,

*AUTHOR'S NOTE: Some time after these occurrences, I made the acquaintance of the gentleman who was at this time the editor of the *Seiron,* one of the most advanced of the anti-foreign papers. He told me that the proposal to retain foreign judges in the courts of appeal (the arrangement was to be terminable in a few years) roused a storm of feeling in Japan such as even we were unaware of. All patriots looked upon it as an insult to the country's independence and a direct breach of the Constitution. Although a man of high education and much political acumen, he himself felt it his duty to oppose the measure by every means in his power, but was horrified to hear of the attack on Count Okuma, which was the direct outcome of the agitation.

Needless to say Great Britain had no wish to hamper Japan's independence, but only to protect her own subjects during the time when the Japanese were learning to administer their own laws.

certainly not from friendly feeling. He suddenly disappeared, when we could have handed him over to a policeman; but, after all, the roads are free, he had committed no greater breach of the peace than my *bettos* do when they run beside the horses' heads, and it would have been absurd to take notice of the small annoyance. I am sorry to say that once or twice stones have been thrown at the carriage; but here again the offender was some half-grown boy, and it seemed a pity to complicate our very amicable relations with the Government people by constant small complaints; so, as it only happened when I was driving alone, I held my peace, and have not even told H—— about it. I hate to be kept inside the compound, and so go out as usual; while H—— refuses to take the slightest notice of the agitation, and walks all over the town, quite alone, rather to my terror. Mrs. N——, who was horribly alarmed, poor thing, was wailing to me that we should all be murdered, and added that it was a great grief to her that her husband was nearly the same height as the Chief, "for I am sure they will kill him instead of Mr. Fraser!"

This was such a comforting way of putting things, was it not? I was very angry; but of course I laughed, as I always do when people expect me to look solemn. Mr. G——, who knows more of the Japanese than most people, has made me promise not to use the open carriage, or let the Chief show himself in it, as it makes such a mark for a shot or a bomb. A *soshi* would not attack a tall Englishman face to face on foot, says our friend and adviser, but— we will draw the line at the victoria. So H—— takes his usual walks, and I hear occasional pebbles rattle on the roof of the brougham without undue concern.

But I am very sorry for the Okumas. They are some of the nicest of the people here, and have been so kind and friendly to us since we came. He is cheery and full of talk, and the little Countess a dainty smiling creature, exquisitely dressed, and devoted to her home, and her beautiful gardens at Waseda, which are one of the sights of Tokyo. They say she was as calm and courageous as her husband under the dreadful shock, and is nursing him devotedly. He is getting on well, but has had to lose his leg, as it was too hopelessly shattered to be saved. One has a horribly uncomfortable feeling about the whole thing, a kind of futile and unreasonable self-reproach, because the catastrophe was caused, however indirectly, by our Treaty Revision business.

We had just had a proof of the good dispositions of the Japanese Foreign Office in a tiresome little affair of our own, the settlement of which would have been impossible had they not chosen to be amiable about it—entirely out of personal feeling towards H——, as they took care to explain to me unofficially. I do not know why I was told, for as a rule I keep very clear of talking about business, and confine myself to my own domain. The complication began in the flight from justice of a man called Campos, a Spaniard by birth, but a British subject, who had escaped from Hong Kong, where he was "wanted" on a charge of forgery. The Hong Kong authorities traced him to Kobe, and, without asking H——'s permission, wired to our Consul there to arrest him, which the Consul (also without asking for instructions) managed to do outside the foreign settlement, on Japanese ground. Here was the making of an extremely pretty quarrel by "small sword light." The Japanese naturally protested against our arresting malefactors in Japanese territory; our Extradition Treaty with Japan has not yet been framed, and cannot be thought of till Revision is done with, and I think there was a moment of honest bewilderment on both sides as to what to do with Campos. The papers were noisy, and British jingoes (of whom the East is, alas, full) talked of the fine old days and Sir Harry Parkes, and a week or so went by. Then H—— suggested that a simple plan would be for us to set Campos at liberty, and for the Japanese to rearrest him and politely return him to us for extradition, which was accordingly done, everybody was satisfied, and there was no quarrel left to talk about.

No one can imagine how much trouble our own people sometimes make by their tall talk in peace and their tendency to panic in moments of excitement. Somehow the least educated and weakest are always the most disposed to aggression and interference. The higher class of British merchants less often come to the fore than the smaller men, who always seem glad of a chance to give trouble and stop the course of affairs. There are one or two inferior journals published in the Yokohama Settlement in order to air the complaints and offer the advice of this class, which reminds me of Samuel Pepys' description of the French when the Spaniards had beaten them in the fight for precedence at St. James's—"Never saw I a people more overbearing in the beginning of an undertaking, or more abject after the failure thereof." I have stopped reading these rags, which always attack us, or the Home Government, or the Emperor, when news is scarce. I can stand intelligent abuse, or good-natured ignorance; but the two nouns in unqualified conjunction make me tired, as the Americans say.

All these commotions have interfered sadly with a particular design of my own, which, being what the sporting papers call "an event," had to come off in the midst of them, and turned out a great success all the same. This was a big charity concert, given in aid of two things—our Leper Hospital at Gotemba, and a much-needed chapel to be built in the Asakusa district. You know how an undertaking of this kind shunts all one's other affairs off on the sidings of life for the moment, and how one gasps with relief when the thing is well over. This concert gave us no end of work, but has turned out a great success, and we have made more money than we expected. The great hall of the Roku-Meikwan,* the Nobles' Club, was lent for it, and was beautifully decorated with palms and flowers. Everybody who could play or sing offered their help, and the hall was crowded, in spite of the fact that the concert took place on the day after the attempt on the life of Count Okuma, and that, owing to his critical condition, it was ruled that none of the Diplomatic body would attend. I was much disappointed at not being present, and was also sure that my absence would be misunderstood by my collaborators in the work. However, all went well and we shall have the satisfaction of sending a good round sum to both our charities. My own sympathies are strongly interested in the little Leper Hospital at Gotemba, which has already done so much good during its short existence.

The prevalence of leprosy† is one of the few sad sides of Jap-

*A large hall built for official meetings between Japanese and foreign residents, particularly from the diplomatic community. Its name, Rokumeikan, literally the Deer Cry Pavilion, is the title of Pat Barr's 1968 book about Meiji Japan.

†Leprosy has a long history in Japan and was first recognized there over a thousand years ago. Even in 1957 there were thought to be over 12,000 leprosy sufferers in Japan. The missionaries, especially the Catholics, were particularly concerned to help the Japanese lepers, and Father Testevuide established the re-

anese life. Through a kind of false shame the authorities refuse to acknowledge the necessity of either providing special hospitals for lepers or of preventing the spread of the disease. It is generally of a very insidious character, and, except for experts, by no means easy to diagnose in its first stages. The lobes of the ears become thick, also the nostrils; there is loss of sensation in the extremities, and the nails begin to shrivel; the face takes on a dark-red colour, and then the fingers and toes gradually disappear; and in some cases the disease stops at this point, and the sufferer may live many years without growing any worse. This is one well-known form of the sickness in Japan; but there are a multitude of cases of the more virulent sort, producing terrible suffering, and an appearance too horrible to be described. The Japanese do not believe in contagion, the caprices of the malady giving a certain amount of excuse for the error. Sometimes it is contracted at the first contact with the sufferer; but in other cases people may live for years in daily intercourse with lepers, and be none the worse. Among the better class it is looked upon as a terrible disgrace, and never called by its proper name, the sufferer being hidden away in the house and tended in secret. Among the lower classes very little notice is taken of the first approach of the disease; but when the unfortunate patient becomes an object of loathing and horror, when he is most in need of care and help, he is cast out to linger on in misery and die an agonising death—alone.

Such cruelty is really foreign to the national character; nowhere is there more help and kindness shown in the family and the tribe than in Japan, and the treatment of the wretched lepers, horrible as it seems to us, can only be put down to the exceeding loathsomeness of the disease itself and the stigma of disgrace that it carries with it. The Japanese doctors regard it as, to a certain extent, curable, and

habilitation centre at Gotemba in 1889. In 1906, a Japanese who was suffering from an advanced stage of leprosy fell down in front of the British Embassy. The then Ambassador who was just passing by saw the poor leper, rushed to the Ministry of Foreign Affairs, and demanded to know whether in a civilized country like Japan there was no place in which a leper could be looked after. According to a history of leprosy in Japan this accident spurred the Japanese government to take action and care for lepers.

have devoted much science and research to the subject. One in particular, Doctor Goto, has made some successful cures, and the boiling springs of Kusatsu are useful in the earlier stages; but such aids are for those who can pay something for the use of them, and the condition of the pauper leper in Japan remains one of the greatest misery and suffering that any human being can be called upon to endure. One of the Empresses (her name was Kōmyō Kōgo,* and she was a devout Buddhist), many centuries ago, touched with pity for this wretched class of her subjects, founded a hospital for them, where, although she was the most beautiful woman of her time, she was not afraid to go every day to wash their sores and attend to their wants. But no trace of her charity remains now. Lepers are received with other sick people in a very few hospitals of the old simple sort,—I was in one not long ago where I saw leprosy, typhoid, and diphtheria in the same ward,—but the hospital accommodation is still pitifully insufficient. A few very bad cases of leprosy may be put together for the convenience of tending them; but, roughly speaking, no provision is made for such sufferers, and the University Hospital, directed by Doctor Baelz, the Empress's Charity Hospital, and most of the others very rightly refuse to receive lepers at all. Doctor Baelz inclines to the opinion that the disease, as a rule, is not violently contagious here, and assures me that he would rather share the apartment of a leper than that of a consumptive patient; he also tells me that I probably meet many of the former every time I go out of the compound, so perhaps it is fortunate that I have no special dread of contagions in general, such as induces one of my friends here, a very nervous woman, to use only Apollinaris water for toilet purposes!

All this being so, you see how great was the need for the little Hospital which was founded, three years ago, by Father Testevuide, one of the French missionaries here. Like many great undertakings, it had a very small beginning. A poor woman, a hopeless leper, cast out by her family, was dying slowly and quite alone in a deserted shed, when Father Testevuide discovered her, naked, blind, going out from the agony of life to the darkness of death. The priest nursed

*Kōmyō Kōgo (701–60), the consort of Emperor Shōmu.

93

and tended the poor creature, did all he could to lighten her sufferings, and made them more endurable by the hope and promise of a future life beyond the reach of pain. He tried to get her admitted to some hospital, but found it impossible; there was no place for such patients as that.

Then Father Testevuide asked and obtained the Bishop's leave to devote himself to the work of founding a hospital for lepers. A little money was sent to him for charity, and he applied it to this, hiring a small house near Gotemba, a village lying on the lower slopes of Fuji San. All sorts of difficulties had to be overcome. A course of treatment for the patients was recommended by Doctor Goto, who was most kind in letting the Father have what remedies he needed on the easiest terms; but good nourishing food was a part of the cure, and the cost of a patient's treatment could not be brought lower than three yen (about six shillings) a month, and this seemed to be beyond the limits of the income on which the founder could count. However, he started, taking only six patients, and having the pain of being obliged to refuse constant applications for admittance. Then the Gotemba people got frightened, and asked him to depart from their coasts, and take his sick people with him. It seems that Father Testevuide's landlord was heavily in debt, and the village elders threatened to make him pay up unless he turned out the priest and the lepers. But in the end this proved to be a good thing; for a little more money coming into his hands, the Father succeeded in buying a small piece of land, about six acres in all, on which the Hospital was built. The situation is most beautiful, and the air divinely pure. The spot is so far removed from the village of Gotemba, that there is no question of danger to any of the inhabitants, and yet it is sufficiently central for patients to be easily brought there. A little money has come in from different sources, and has been spent with the exquisite care which I have always noticed in the work of holy people. Twelve hundred dollars (less than one hundred and fifty pounds) has bought the land, built and furnished the house, and provided for the requirements of the patients and employés for three years—and paid for one funeral! Some of those treated have so far recovered that all external signs of the disease have been arrested, and they are able to go out and earn their living.

94

The Fathers say that they themselves do not yet believe in a completely permanent cure, and that all they can say to their convalescents is, "Come back again for treatment the moment you find that the symptoms are showing themselves afresh."

Of course the ground on which the Hospital stands is made to yield the larger part of the food for the inmates; and those who are strong enough to do so take their share in the work of cultivation, and have the joy of feeling that they help to maintain themselves. The advanced cases are kept apart from the less acute ones; and, once received, no one is sent away, unless he or she is temporarily cured. For the hopeless it is a home where, until the last minute of life, their sufferings will be alleviated as far as possible, and their hearts cheered by kindness and the hope of a better life. No questions are asked, and the obstinate pagan receives just as much care and tenderness as the born Christian or the convert; but of course the whole atmosphere is warmly Christian. The poor souls for whom faith is pointing to brightness and peace when death shall cure them for good and all—they are eager to bring new-comers in to share the hope which so greatly helps to lighten present suffering. I am sure there will never be a despairing death-bed in the Gotemba Hospital.

The Fathers say that they have found ready help among Japanese Christians for the work of tending the patients. One good man, whose name has at his own request been kept a secret, has shut himself up for life with the lepers, on condition of food being found for his family which he supported by his work. As for Father Testevuide, much has been said about his heroism and goodness, and of course he is constantly compared with Father Damien, the saint of Molokai. The world catches at the name of one good man, and extols it to the skies. We Catholics are rather surprised at the noisy enthusiasm, for we expect these things from our missionary priests. When dear Father Testevuide (whose health is very frail from all his hard work) shall be called home, there will be found many others ready and eager to step into his place.

The autumn has come at last, and the maples are all on fire. Since one autumn, when I wandered through the New Jersey woods as a tiny child, I have never seen such a gorgeous explosion of colour, such a storm of scarlet and gold. Since the spring brought the white of the plum blossom and the rosy glow of the cherry, the colour has been deepening on the cheek of Nature, and has flushed out strong and high in the sunset of the year. All the gardens are mantled in wide panoplies of the wonderful foliage, which grows in a lovely equable way on the branch, each star-shaped leaf coming well to the surface of the mass, so close that no space between it and its neighbour breaks the stretch of colour, but also well spread forth to the light, none crowded out of the honours of the show. I have been to one temple garden after another, and drive almost daily to Oji,* the maple village, which is all alive with Japanese holiday-makers.

That which impresses me most in all these shows is the extraordinary variety of the specimens. I believe our European botanists only admit some twenty species in Japan (America boasts nine in all); but the Japanese subdivide these again and again, and a maple gardener told me that he knew three hundred and eighty separate varieties. Those which please me most are, I think, the kind which grow about ten or twelve feet high, with leaves in five or seven long points, exquisitely cut, and growing like strong fingers on a young hand. They always seem to be pointing to something, and one involuntarily looks round and about to see what it is. They are deep red in colour all the year round, and are constantly grouped with vivid greens, making splendid masses in the shrubberies.

The true autumn maples are quite glorious for these few days during which they last. There is a lovely verse describing them in Chamberlain's book, the classical poetry of the Japanese:

> "The warp is hoar-frost and the woof is dew,
> Too frail, alas! the warp and woof to be;

---

*Ōji is now a suburb of Tokyo and totally built up. Even in 1894, Ōji was being developed with paper and cotton mills.

>For scarce the woods their damask robes endue,
>When, torn and soiled, they flutter o'er the lea."

One storm will rob the trees of their splendours till next year. This beauty is their death ecstasy, and I think the very evanescence of its loveliness must have endeared the maple to the hearts of the people. It has come to be one of the emblems of all that is happy and gay and fragile. One sees its starlike outline on festive robes, on wine-cups, in lacquer and in carving. There is a kind of club restaurant in Tokyo called the "Kwoyo Kwan," or Maple Club, where everything is marked with the maple, from the tea-cups and the carved screens to the *musumë's* dresses. Everywhere the leaves seem to have floated and fallen, and all this honour is only on account of their beauty, for they do not carry the symbolic meaning of the pine, the bamboo, and the plum blossom, which are emblematic of long life, strength, and happiness, and are constantly intertwined in decoration.

A gift is often called "a little pine needle" by the giver, and there is a saying that even a humble pine needle is precious if it is given from the heart. The distinctive name for the maple is *momiji,* but the word *kwoyo* is applied by the Japanese to all leaves which change their colour in the autumn (they are called flowers, not leaves, then); and very few other trees make any show when the maples are flaunting their gorgeous banners in the autumn sunshine, so the name is used chiefly to designate them. The maple is a thing apart from daily life, and yet constantly referred to, as it were. A favourite subject with artists is the fall of the leaf on running water, or down the glassy steeps of waterfalls, where the red wings swarm and float like thousands of drowning butterflies.

With the maples have come the chrysanthemums, the Emperor's flowers, chosen for the crest of the Imperial Household. Everything at Court is marked with the round gold mark, which always looks to me more like the sun than any flower. All the communications from the Palace come on chrysanthemum paper, all invitation cards have it heavily embossed in gold, the Court carriages carry it on their panels, the flunkies on their liveries.

Thursday is the reception day at the Palace, and last week I went to call on the *grande maîtresse* and the Empress's other ladies, who all receive together in a huge crimson drawing-room, reached through labyrinths of the glass corridors which I described to you on the occasion of our audience in May. Relays of servants are posted along the way, and one is handed over from one set to the other, till one reaches a table where a secretary sits with a big book, into which he copies the names off the cards which are handed to him by our escort. Two or three Palace officials stand round the door in the Household uniform; but there are never any Japanese gentlemen in the drawing-room, and the element is so feminine that European men are rather shy of it, and none of our own staff will ever go except under my protection. The little ladies are so bright and sweet, that I prefer these visits to many that I have to make in European houses. They manage very well, too, as to the difficult question of language, so that one need never take an interpreter. The *grande maîtresse,* Viscountess Takakura, is a gentle pale woman, always dressed in some shade of pansy or mauve. She speaks no foreign language, nor does Countess Muromachi, her next in command. This lady is a little older than the others, and is much loved and respected by both the Emperor and Empress, who are said often to take her advice on important matters. She wears soft dove-coloured satins as a rule, while the younger women affect pale blues, water-greens, and rosy greys. Black is not worn at the Palace, except during a Court mourning.

These younger ladies do the interpreting for the others. Two, Miss Kitajima and Miss Kagawa, have travelled a good deal, and speak English fluently. Another, a charming girl, with almost a European type of beauty, has been in France, and talks French well; and yet another can speak some German. So no one need be tongue-tied on these occasions. It has sometimes happened to me to wish that the Japanese ladies understood less than I imagine they do of foreign languages; for some of our colleagues' wives affect an almost brutal rudeness towards them, speaking of them in their presence with sublime contempt, and complaining loudly of an official visit, which perhaps has broken up a more amusing conversation. When, horror-struck, I have expostulated, the reply has been, "Bah, elles n'y comprennent rien!" I was paying a visit at one of the Legations, when a Japanese great lady, Princess S——, was announced, and immediately followed the servant who announced her. It was my hostess's reception day, and she should have had a competent interpreter at hand, as we are all supposed to do on these occasions. Therefore the Princess, although she can speak no foreign tongue, had not brought one with her. As she entered the room our hostess threw her arms in the air with an expression of despair, and exclaimed (I had better not say in what language), "Good Heavens, what am I to do with this creature! What an odious bore! Where is So-and-so (the interpreter)? Somebody run and find him! Could anything be more tiresome?" All this was said at the top of her voice, with gestures which must have made the meaning only too clear to the dignified woman who was thus outrageously received. I did what very little could be done to save the situation; and Princess S——, like the true lady she is, pretended not to understand it for the few minutes during which she remained. I fled when she said what I fancy will be a long good-bye to our hostess, and for the first time in my life I blushed at being a European.

I met this adornment of diplomacy coming away as I was advancing along the Palace corridor on Thursday, and did not get past her without having to hear some noisy criticisms on the manners of the women she had just left, and who, by the way, have loaded her with kindness. Manners! If they were—as in a measure they may be—the passport to heaven, the Japanese women would certainly have reserved places, and many a "smart" European would have to take a back seat. Kindness and modesty, a wakeful, real consideration for the feelings of others—surely these make up for a little unwilling ignorance of the higher subjects which most interest us, and which, to tell the truth, are hardly better known to the "smart" European with her social preoccupations and her rattle of "chaff," than they are to the little hothouse ladies of the Palace.

But this is digression, and I wanted to tell you how amused I was to find that all the sweetmeats of these Household tea parties must represent nothing but the flowers and fruits and leaves in season. On Thursday last the cake plates were filled with every variety of maple leaf, made in sugar and variously flavoured, but so perfectly moulded and coloured that it would be difficult to detect the imitation from the real leaf. Large and small, pale pink, deep crimson, green and orange, with three leaves, or five, or seven, they were piled on the delicate china in such artistic fashion that I could not refrain from an exclamation of pleasure when they were offered to me. With them were autumn grasses and tiny wild chrysanthemums, just the handful of loot that a nature lover would bring back from a walk in the woods.

The maids of honour laughed merrily at my surprise, and told me that the Empress will only eat the most airy of these delicate sweets; so that the Court confectioner has come to be a great artist at producing them. Then nothing would do but that I must take some home with me; and in spite of my protest, a sheet of Palace paper (thickly crinkled, and heavy as watered silk) was fetched, and a large assortment of the bonbons was picked out by half a dozen dainty hands, wrapped up, and confided to a servant to be put in my carriage.

One day in October, after I came back from Miyanoshita, I thought I would go and see one of these ladies, although the regular reception days would not begin till after the Emperor's birthday, November 3rd. I went alone, and asked for Miss Kitajima Itoko, with whom I had made friends before we all broke up for the summer. The servant took my card, and was away a long time, while I sat in the carriage, waiting to know whether the lady was at home. At last he returned, and invited me to enter; and I followed, thinking to be received in the usual red drawing-room. But the man beckoned me past its closed doors, and I followed him on and on, through corridors and across courtyards, and finally up a long flight of rather narrow stairs, which I was surprised to see, as the Palace possesses no visible upper story. Here I was shown into a small sitting-room, papered in pale blue, inhabited by an—army of dolls! No other word will describe the collection, ranged all round the walls in glass cases which stood out quite a yard into the room, and ran up some eight or nine feet in height. A crimson carpet, a few black-wood chairs, a window shut in with paper screens like those in an ordinary Japanese house—that was all that the room contained, except the dolls; and they were so amazing that I hoped I should be left alone with them for a long time. Many of these weird creatures were life size, and so real that I felt as if I must have got into some corner of the Palace which was sleeping a charmed sleep through these times of change and trouble. There were tall Daimyos, with impassive masks, dressed in stiff white robes like cere-cloths. Their fine bluish fingers seemed to be pointing at me in scorn; their black eyes gleamed in the subdued light; and their black hair seemed to bristle under the strange conical caps, blacker even than the hair, and tied under their chins with forbidding black bands. Beside them were lovely women (I cannot help speaking as if they were living creatures), in poses light and dreamy as the swaying of the lotus stems moved by water. Their faces were pale and sweet, and there was a kind of tragic grace in the bent heads, the slender, submissive hands held out in supplication towards their lords. One or two were kneeling, one lying down, all in robes stiff with gold and brilliant in colour. Among these life-sized images were crowds of smaller ones, some gorgeously dressed, some simple old dolls such as any child would love. A few European dolls, horrible mechanical gimcracks in tarnished finery, were given places of honour among the nobles and princesses, who seemed too sad to resent the elbowing of the parvenus from over the water. The room itself was still as death, and I was all alone with the silent inhabitants, enclosed as in a glass tomb; while outside, the ripple and murmur of life hummed through the great Palace: voices of children at play came close to me, on which side I could not tell, and then tinkled away in the distance. A *koto* was being played in one of the near rooms; there were outbursts of girlish laughter, as sweet and full as the songs of mounting larks, which came and went with a patter of sandals and brushing of drapery along the corridors; and across my paper screen (which opened to some balcony flooded with sunshine) shadowy forms came and went, a young head beautifully dressed, a branch of leaves, or the outline of a delicate hand was laid for a moment on the paper. All the place seemed busy and warm as a hive of bees in the sun—all but the silent heart of it where I sat gazing at the portrait-images of long-dead men and women.

Then the slide opened, and Miss Kitajima, in a tightly fitting European gown, came in, and the atmosphere of romance shrivelled up, and left me rather cold in the light of the *fin-de-siècle* day. I asked, of course, about the dolls; but my friend was not communicative, and seemed a little ashamed of them. "They are dolls, foolish things," she said; and at once turned the conversation to some other subject. And I came away disappointed and puzzled, as this is not the time of year for the dolls' festival, which takes place in March, "on the third day of the third month."

The Emperor has been ill, so there is to be no garden party at the Asakusa Palace, and I shall not see the Imperial chrysanthemum show this year. I am sorry; but I believe some of the public exhibitions are nearly as good, and these I have been visiting carefully. As far as the beauty of the flowers themselves is concerned, I give the palm to those which developed naturally and make masses of bloom growing in their own characteristic way, as they are allowed to do in Europe. But for masterly cultivation, for the triumph of human laws over those of nature, for results which look as if they could only have been wrought by magic, the Japanese gardeners certainly take the palm.

The chief place for chrysanthemum gardens is a village or rather a suburb of Tokyo, called Dango-Zaka.* To reach it one drives through miles of quiet ways, bordered with gardens of every kind, whose low bamboo fences with their tyings of black string make a pretty hedging to the brown road, all flecked with sunshine through the overarching boughs, which are getting thin in these autumn days. In the village, and indeed long before you reach it, every gate leads into a garden, where, by paying two sen, you may walk about and look at group after group of historical or mythological figures—all made out of chrysanthemums! Here, at the turn of a path, is a shed built in pretty white wood, open in front, and lined, sides and ceiling and floor, with a pattern resembling old damask, all worked in living flowers, which, having been put in place with their roots behind them, bloom and flourish happily for weeks in these unnatural positions, refreshed by an occasional spraying of

*Murray's *Handbook for Travellers in Japan* (1894) notes: "In the direction of Ōji, are the florists' gardens of Dango-zaka, whither the townsfolk flock in thousands to see the chrysanthemun shows in November. The flowers are trained over trellis-work to represent historical and mythological scenes, ships, dragons, and other curious objects." Unfortunately, these gardens no longer exist.

water. On a raised bridge inside the shed is a group representing a scene in Japanese mediæval history, in which the hero Yoshitsune* has a fierce duel with the strong man, Benkei. The masks and hands of the figures are in carved and painted wood, the expression of the faces is brilliant, fierce, and lifelike, and the hands are beautifully fine and true. The costumes of the warriors are all made in growing chrysanthemums, every detail of the armour being recognisable. The railings of the bridge are also made of flowers. For this kind of living embroidery only the small-flowering chrysanthemum is used, its thick masses of white or red or yellow lending themselves kindly to these strange uses.

But the gardens are not without beautiful specimens of single plants. One of these was trained in the shape of an umbrella, the single stem rising straight for about six feet from the ground, and being of the same thickness from top to bottom. At the top a number of shoots, starting with perfect regularity from the same point, fell downwards, forming a dome of about three feet in diameter. It was edged by a fringe of pale-pink chrysanthemums in full bloom, each hanging from the end of a shoot; three inches farther up was a perfect ring of blossoms slightly less opened, all arrested at the same point of development; three inches farther up, another ring of just opened buds; and close to the stick, a small circle of green balls, buds which showed no sign of colour. Apart from its uncanny artificiality, the thing was beautiful, and probably represented the patient labour of several years.

The crowd of Japanese sight-seers seemed more inclined to stare at us than at heroes or chrysanthemum umbrellas, and followed us as we went on to the other pictures, which Ogita explained to me in his quaint way. Under one shed was a little pond, which was supposed to represent a stormy ocean, out of which a fearful bogy, with horns and tusks and red hair hanging down to his knees, had risen with a pitchfork to frighten some quiet travellers who were crossing the sea in the lightest of skiffs—all made of flowers of course. The passengers represented Yoshitsune and some of his adherents trying to reach the shore, and kept back by a fearful

*The popular legendary hero Minamoto no Yoshitsune (1159–89).

storm roused by the ghost of an enemy whom he had killed in war. He had taken the precaution to bring a holy exorcist with him; and this figure, with a long white beard and venerable countenance, was standing up in the boat, regardless of balance, praying that the demon might be overcome.

In another picture a faithful wife has thrown herself between her sleeping husband and the sword of an enemy, who is stabbing him from behind a paper screen. The masks of the women are far less artistic than those of the men in these groups, denoting subtly the Japanese ideals of male and female beauty. A man should have a fierce, strong expression, and many masks overstep all the limits of art and show the most grotesque contortions of rage and hate; but the female faces are absolutely smooth and expressionless, even when represented in the most exciting circumstances. The only sign of tragedy is the absence of the smile which a Japanese woman is supposed always to wear for her family and friends. She may cease to smile in heavy grief, but no spasm of pain or anxiety must appear on the fair face with its downcast eyes; the countenance must be unlined by the invisible harrow of thought, unstained by tears, unthrilled by emotion. If I painted a sphynx, I should be strongly tempted to make her face that of an ideal Japanese woman. No stone mask could be more impenetrable.

But I must describe to you the finest of the show pieces which I saw at Dango-Zaka, and of which I have obtained a photograph from a friend. This was an enormous ship, the ship of happiness, as Ogita explained; and in it were seated some of the cheeriest-looking divinities I ever saw—the six gods of riches. On the prow was Benten Sama, the beautiful benevolent goddess who has eight arms, so that she can help on sea as well as on land, and give precious gifts to men according to their capacity for receiving them. Her companions are broad-faced smiling personages, Dai-Koku of the big ears and the rice-bags, the white-bearded, peach-shaped god of old age (a very old acquaintance of mine in Peking), and others whose faces are less familiar to me. Everywhere the work is the same, a fine patient flower mosaic built into great lines and bold shapes. One, a god of lightning, I think, was really full of splendid "go" and vitality. The contrast between the violent distortions of the masks and the calm impassive faces of the people who come to gaze at them is rather curious. Of course all the little gardens are crowded with visitors, chiefly of the middle and lower classes. How people who have to earn their living can find time for all this holiday-making is a puzzling question. Perhaps one answer to it is that, with few exceptions, shop life is family life. No one is bound to work so many hours a day. The staff consists of the family, with perhaps an apprentice or two; and if the tailoring, or fan-making, or mat-weaving tasks have not been accomplished in the day, the whole family will sit round the one lamp at night and make up for lost time.

Now that the days are drawing in, it is one of my great pleasures to drive home after night has fallen on the city. Then the little interiors are lighted up, and yet left open to the street, because the autumn days are mild still, and because the Japanese kitchen, consisting as it does of a hole in the middle of the floor, where the fire crackles and smokes gaily, makes it convenient to leave the screens open as long as possible. I am often out rather late (you know the confidential moment at the end of a friend's reception day, when the outsiders have all gone and the intimates really begin to talk!), and as I come home there is a little bustle of preparation for the evening meal going on in almost every home. Here the family of some prosperous tradesman is getting round the *hibachi*. The old grandmother mends the fire, glad of an excuse to be so near the flame. The mother, young and smiling, waits on her husband; while the family idol, the only child probably, laughs and chatters, and insists on being served first, much to the father's amusement. The children rule everything in the little homes—and are not a bit spoilt. When they come to what is considered the age of reason (anywhere between six and ten), they abdicate their sovereignty of their own accord, and seem to grow up in a day; for they at once begin to take their share of the family work, and smile indulgently, just as their elders do, at the baby ways and make-believe tempers of their successors on the throne.

Sometimes there are no children, and one sees a pale woman resolutely turning her head from the sight of the little ones over the way. She must have lost a child, and that little plate of dainties that she is putting aside—tiny morsels of fish and *daikon** and rice—will be placed before the wooden tablet which bears the little one's dead name—the name given at birth is left here with the worn-out garments, the tiny ravelled sandals, and the broken toys; and the soul, new born to another phase of immortality, is given a new name at its passing, that by which it came and went in this world finding its fitting grave in the silence of the mother's heart.

Almost sadder is the glimpse of two old folk, grey and faithful, sitting beside a fire whence all the children have gone; the old woman nursing a cat in a solemn frilled collar, and the old man smoking as he stares at the flame. Or it may be that he is one who, left alone in his old age, looked round among his friends and acquaintances till he found and married a widow as lonely as himself, glad to cheer his and her own declining years by the kindly companionship which the Japanese call, "A party for making tea in old age!" I see many such pictures of humble married faithfulness, as I pass in the darkness of the street—many little homes so poor that thieves would find nothing there to steal, and yet whose in-dwellers seem very rich in peace and kindliness. Truly the best things in the world have no market and no price.

Tokyo, November, 1889

I was much amused a little while ago to hear that the Empress-Dowager was leaving Tokyo, and taking a journey of several hours' duration, so as to enjoy some good—mushroom-hunting! The Empress-Dowager does not show herself in public, and is, I believe, an ardent adherent of the old modes of life and thought in Japan. I cannot find any foreigner who has seen more than the outside of her *norimono*, or closed palanquin; I know her Grand

Daikon is a large, white Japanese radish.

Master of Ceremonies, and one or two Japanese who belong to her especial Court, and they wear an habitual expression of disapproving reserve, of patient deprecation, which has the effect of a dumb protest against changes of any sort, and more especially against the admission of the *stultus vulgus,* the profane foreigner, into the sacred precincts of Japanese life. Perhaps they are chosen for their dignified offices because their peculiar views harmonise with those of the royal lady; perhaps they have imbibed them through intercourse with her, for I have often noticed that the opinions of great personages are extremely contagious. Be that as it may, a high wall of conservative precedent is built round the Empress-Dowager; and when one expresses a desire to see her, one is met by a mournful shake of the head and dead silence, as if to mark the hopeless temerity of the wish. She must be kind and benevolent; for when we had our charity concert for the Leper Hospital and the new chapel, she took thirty tickets, and a message came with the contribution to the effect that her Majesty was much interested to hear of the Leper Hospital, and wished it all success.

Having grown accustomed to the idea of an elderly lady living in absolute retirement, I was rather amused at the thought of her running about the slopes of Kanayama hunting for mushrooms; but I find, on looking into the matter, that this has always been considered as a kind of artistic sport, especially near Kyoto, where the fruit (or is it flower?) grows in great abundance.

Prince Haru has been solemnly installed as heir-apparent, having completed his tenth year on September 6th. The *Rittaishi,* as this ceremony is called, was put off until the birthday of the Emperor, November 3rd, and was then carried out in the Palace according to the old custom. It seems that it is not enough to be born heir to the throne in Japan. The young Prince must be officially recognised by his father, and presented to the nation as such. The reason of this, I imagine, may be found in the fact that until our own times it was not a matter of course that a man's eldest son should succeed to his father's titles and property. A younger child, or an adopted son, or an uncle or brother might be designated as the heir; and Japanese history given countless examples of the exercise of the privilege, which has given rise to many a blood feud hardly healed to-day. In such circumstances a public declaration of the heir to the throne would almost seem to be a necessity; but there is much more than that in this ceremony of the *Rittaishi*— much which is intended to impress the child himself with the fact that manhood is not far off, and that already he must prepare himself to take up its duties and responsibilities. The Empress sent the little Prince two sets of pictures, symbolic of the happiness she wished for him, and the brave heart he must have if he would succeed in attaining to it. Among the drawings illustrative of happiness, one represents the god of happiness accompanied by his attribute, a white stag; others the pine for strength, the stork for long life, the tortoise for riches, and so on. The second set deals with sterner subjects: a hawk symbolises courage; a bear in snow, endurance; a carp swimming up the waterfall is the emblem of perseverance. Although the Empress is not Prince Haru's mother, she is said to have a great affection for him, and one hears of his paying her visits pretty constantly.

The Emperor gave his son the Sword of State which he himself received on a like occasion many years ago. No great pomp accompanied the ceremony, and no Foreign Representatives were invited to be present, at what would be considered a purely religious and family affair, were not the boy a Prince and his affairs therefore the business of the nation. A salute of one hundred and one guns was fired at midday, and a paragraph in a gilt flourish appeared in the *Official Gazette* about his being confirmed in the title of heir-apparent. At the Nobles' School, however, where the Prince has many young friends, fireworks went on all day in the beautifully decorated gardens, and there were rather extensive illuminations in the city. The little Prince is now entitled to wear the uniform of a second lieutenant in the First Life Guards (how odd it sounds over here!) and the Grand Cross of the Chrysanthemum, and his household is put on a more ceremonious and increased footing. A good deal of interest attaches to the sword given him by the Emperor. It is very beautiful, and has been handed down for so many generations in the Imperial family that the date of its forging and the origin of its strange name, Tsubo Kiri (the jar-cutter), are completely lost. The name of the maker is Amakuni, who wrote on the blade that he made it at the command of an Emperor unnamed. The Amakuni family have made all the Imperial swords since the year 701, when the Visigoths were still ruling in Spain, and the seven Saxon kingdoms had not yet been united; so that date does not give much clue to the age of the blade. It is about two feet long, double-edged, with a guard of pure gold, and a handle inlaid with mother-of-pearl, and, as is fitting, it lives in a case of gold brocade. There is to be some sword-forging soon at one of the art exhibitions, and I hope to see the Amakuni at work.

I have looked at a few Japanese swords, and can realise a little what it must be to see them flashing thirstily in the sunshine of a fight. Beautiful and terrible are the only words to apply to them. The perfection of the steel, the blue lights that shoot down its glorious surface, the weight of life and death in the blade, and the exquisite, almost tender beauty of the bird or wave or blossom worked in the gold and bronze of the guard—all make it for me the very manifestation of strength and loveliness, the word by which Matter speaks as man and woman both.

A kind of lull has fallen on the political world since the attack on Count Okuma, which, though apparently the act of an isolated fanatic, was at any rate synchronous with a kind of panic about the foreign ownership of land involved in the proposed Revision of the Treaty. It is significant that several bombs precisely like the one thrown at him have been discovered by the police in Yokohama. That they are made in the country is evident, because two of them were broken up, and were found to contain scraps of Japanese newspapers crushed in among the explosives. The bombs are now supposed to have been charged with dynamite which was recently stolen from some public works. There is a kind of revolutionary club of young Japanese in San Francisco, and people at first suggested that the missile thrown at Count Okuma had been manufactured there and brought across for this purpose, the beauty and finish of the workmanship making it appear unlikely that it could have been made by quasi-amateurs here. But the fragments of newspapers in its newly found companions seem to prove that it was a home-made article after all. Count Okuma is recovering well; but it will be some time before he can take up his work again, and I fancy he will resign as soon as any one can be found courageous enough to step into his place. We are bombarded with telegrams from home, where they want Treaty Revision done with as soon as possible (it has only been on the Chancery table for fourteen years!); but the Japanese seem afraid to touch it, and are making an excuse of Count Okuma's accident to let it lie, until, so to speak, the smoke of Kurushima's bomb has cleared away. The Acting Minister for Foreign Affairs, Viscount Aoki,* will probably take Count Okuma's place if he resigns. Viscount Aoki has lived many years in Berlin, and is married to a German lady, and their house is one of the pleasantest here. He is supposed to be a great advocate of progress, and I have had one or two very interesting talks with him about his country people. He said to me one day, in regard to the anti-foreign agitation: "The whole trouble arises in the ignorance of the people (as to foreigners and their aims); until that is dispelled, the work of progress cannot be thorough. The enlightened classes are almost all on the side of progress; this is a revolution started by the Court and the aristocracy, and opposed by the lower classes. When they have learnt their lesson, we can do our work." Count Ito has resigned the post of President of the Council, Count Kuroda† has ceased to be Prime Minister, and Prince Sanjo‡ has very unwillingly taken his place as leader of the Cabinet. That must be an extremely arduous post, since the present policy of the Government is to include all well-known statesmen in the Cabinet, irrespective of opinions and party. I should think there might be some lively sittings. This Utopian arrangement was advised by Count Kuroda, who now retires, having found it impossible to keep that place with such a political opponent to manage as Count Yamagata,§ who has at last declared himself against the treaty programme as it now stands.

Count Yamagata was requested to hurry back from Europe a little while ago (he had been filling a Diplomatic post) in order to deal

*Shūzō Aoki (1844–1914), Meiji statesman.
†Kiyotaka Kuroda (1840–1900), Meiji statesman.
‡Sanetomi Sanjō (1837–91), court noble and Meiji statesman.
§Aritomo Yamagata (1838–1922), field marshal and elder statesman. In 1888 he was sent to Europe to study local government.

with Treaty Revision, *soshi,* and various minor questions. After his arrival and entrance into the Cabinet, he maintained a strict silence for some time, unwilling to criticise the actions of his colleagues, who were generally in favour of a rapid conclusion of the question. At last, however, he spoke; and being a man of great intellect combined with strength of character, his dictum carried such weight that the Ministers above-mentioned felt that they must either work on his lines or retire from the Cabinet. Count Kuroda retired; Count Okuma has practically done the same, although no public announcement has been made of the fact; and every one expected to see Count Yamagata take the leadership, from which Count Ito and Count Kuroda had retired in succession. But that he has refused to do, foreseeing probably the very difficulties which led to the withdrawal of his predecessors. A Cabinet which may not be composed of one party for fear of giving dangerous offence to the others, but where the old clan spirit is still strongly alive, creating a gulf between the Satsuma and the Choshiu peers, who must be included in fair proportions; public opinion against the treaty programme, and the Government to a great extent pledged to the Foreign Representatives to carry it out,—all this Count Yamagata found, to use a slang term, not good enough, and remains a Privy Councillor. Poor Prince Sanjo, who thought he had entered into peace some years ago (in 1885), has been peremptorily ordered by the Emperor to take the command of the political battalion. He begged in vain to be excused; but there was no one else to be put forward, and he finally accepted under protest, with a rather touching entreaty that "his Majesty would quickly find some person to replace him in a position for which he had neither the strength nor the inclination."

Prince Sanjo's health is delicate, and he gives me the impression of a man who is sadly bored with politics. He falls to my lot at many of the big entertainments, and is always so kind and amiable that I like to have him for a neighbour, although he speaks no foreign tongue. We smile over bouquets and *menus;* he tells me the Japanese names for all the rare fruits and flowers; and when we have to walk in the little official processions, we try to be dignifiedly unconscious of the funny appearance we must present—I looking taller than ever in the absurd trains we are expected to wear here, and he a mass of gorgeous decorations, his head not nearly reaching to my shoulder.

Princess Sanjo is quite charming, though extremely plain. She is conscious of this, poor lady, and the other day asked a friend of mine to tell her in confidence whether there were any women in Europe as ugly as herself. She has a daughter who is extraordinarily handsome, and who speaks English well. The Princess just missed being Empress instead of the Princess Haruko Ichijo, who was finally chosen for that honour. Both ladies belonged to the Regent families of the Fujiwara clan, from whose ranks the wives of the Emperors must always be selected. There are five of these princely families (the group is called in Japanese *Go Sekke,* Five Regent Houses), and their respective names are Ichijo, Nijo, Kujo, Konoye, and Takatsukasa. In the modern classification of the nobles, they were created Dukes; but as I have shown, they are called Princes in the official lists. The title Prince Sanjo now bears was bestowed upon him as a reward of merit for great services rendered at the time of the restoration of power to the Emperor. Pince Sanjo was then Prime Minister, and greatly endeared himself to his sovereign by the splendid assistance he rendered to his cause. His marriage with Princess Haruko (her name is the same as that of the Empress) was a mark of Imperial favour, as it constituted an alliance with the reigning family, although not one which can furnish heirs to the throne. If Princess Sanjo's daughter marries one of the Imperial Princes, as she probably will, I shall have to make *plongeons* before her, and treat her as a royalty. Now she sits in a corner of my drawing-room on reception days, nibbling bonbons and talking nonsense with all the other girls. Her father is building a beautiful European house in Azabu, and meanwhile they are living in their very simple Japanese home, a low house surrounded by mournful yews. The rooms are small, but have beautiful carved lattices in their divisions; the foot sinks noiselessly into the silky floor-mats; and there is an old-time silence and stateliness about the place which suits the inhabitants better than the white marble house on the hill can ever do, I think.

A spring day at a pond in the Asakusa district of Tokyo. Center panel of a triptych print, dated 1889, by Tankei.

A view of the imperial palace in Tokyo. In the lower left-hand corner are the two bridges that are crossed by official visitors. Triptych print, dated 1888, by Ikuhide.

The Emperor's arrival to open the first session of the House of Peers on November 29, 1890. Triptych print, dated 1890, by Kunitoshi.

The imperial family's visit to one of the exhibits of an exposition that took place in 1890 to promote domestic industry and agriculture. Triptych print, dated 1890, by Chikanobu and Nobutsugu.

A main street in the Ginza district as it appeared in 1884. Triptych print, dated 1888, by Tankei.

The hatsu-uma *festival, held annually on the year's first day of the horse by the lunar calendar, at one of Tokyo's many Shinto shrines dedicated to the god Inari. Triptych print, dated 1890, by Chikanobu.*

The Daimaru-ya kimono store, located in what is known today as the Nihombashi district. Triptych print, dated 1886, by Tankei.

A lady-in-waiting using a sewing machine. Sewing machines were first introduced into Japan in 1860. Twenty-one years later, the first Japanese-made sewing machine was exhibited. Left panel of a triptych print, dated 1889, by Shōgetsu.

Tokyo, December, 1889

Did I tell you in my last letter of the delightful surprise we had, in the way of a visit from Edwin Arnold* and his daughter? These last weeks have been very full, as you will see presently; but these guests were of the sort who refresh your few leisure moments, and take care of themselves in your busy ones.

I knew how the poet would enjoy his first visit to Japan, and I wanted to see him enjoy it; so he stayed with us for some little time, and fell so much in love with Tokyo that he has taken a house for six months, where he insists on sleeping on the mats Japanese fashion, much to his daughter's horror. He was brought here, he says, by that enchanting book, Chamberlain's *Colloquial Japanese,* which came under his notice in America. After he had read a few sentences, he decided that it was absolutely necessary to visit this land of glorified politeness, where if phrases are to be believed, a man would honourably sacrifice his own soul, his wife, and children, and all his belongings rather than be convicted of a breach of etiquette. The book which proved such a bait for the great Sanskrit scholar was carefully studied on the journey across the Pacific, in a sheltered corner near the funnel, whence Sir Edwin, I am told, only emerged at stated intervals to take charge of a certain small baby, whose weary mother thus got a few moments for rest and food. He says that sometimes the baby was good, and then he would walk up and down with it on one arm, learning Japanese phrases from the book held open with the other hand. When the baby was fretful, it took his whole attention, and had the Japanese goodnight crooned to it, "Oyasu mi nasai!" (To receive sleep condescend). The pair must have made an amusing picture; and I can believe the story is true, for our servants' children, shy with most people, have made friends readily with the

*Sir Edwin Arnold (1832–1904), poet and journalist. His most famous poem, *The Light of Asia* (1879), is, according to Oxford's 1912 publication *The Dictionary of National Biography,* an epic "in blank verse of Oriental luxuriance" that depicts "the picturesque and pathetic elements of the Buddhist legend." It was noted that Arnold was "fascinated by the artistic and social side of Japanese life. His writings on Japan helped to spread in England optimistic views of Japanese progress and culture." His third wife was a Japanese named Tama Kurokawa. His book *Japonica* was published in 1892.

113

poet of the grey hair and the kind eyes still so full of the blue fire of youth. He made such use of the handbook, that he can speak to the children in their own language, much to their delight.

I called him in the other day to see Countess Kuroda, who had come, by appointment, in a lovely Japanese dress, to have her portrait painted by Mr. Walter S. Landor,* who is staying in the compound at "Number Two," the N——'s house. It sounds rather a complicated method of having one's portrait painted, does it not? But there was no other way to manage it. The little Countess was very anxious to see her pretty face on canvas; Mr. Landor was equally anxious to draw it there; but—well, Count Kuroda is man of an extremely jealous temperament, and his wife clearly let us understand that he would not care to have a foreign gentleman staring at her for hours together in her own house when his own public duties would call him away. How would it be, she shyly suggested, if she said that she was spending the day with the English Koshi Sama's Okusama? Her husband would be sure that she was quite safe if she was with Mrs. Fraser, and—really—perhaps nothing need be said to him about the picture just now, after all! It would be such a nice surprise for him afterwards! As my conscience did not oblige me to tell the Prime Minister that his wife was having her portrait painted, the matter was arranged; Mr. Landor came, and of course picked out for his studio a gaunt north room that we never use unless the house is very full; I filled it with flowers and screens; and then the little lady arrived, dressed in the softest of crapes and the most gorgeous of *obis,* her hair shining like black satin, her eyes dancing with excitement, and a round spot of brilliant rouge (or *béni,* as it is called here) on her lower lip. She was delighted to find that Sir Edwin could speak her own language a little; but did not look at all pleased when he admired her hands, fine and small as a child's. From the Japanese point of view, such personal compliments consitute a breach of etiquette.

"Very dirty, very dirty!" she said, laughing, as she tucked them

*Presumably a son of the author Walter Savage Landon (1775–1864). One A. H. Savage Landor published in 1893 a book about a journey to Hokkaido titled *Alone with the Hairy Ainu or 3800 Miles on a Pack Saddle in Yezo and a Cruise to the Kurile Islands.* Anyone who reads this book will at once understand why he travelled alone.

away under her long sleeves; and I laughed too, not knowing the phrase, which is merely one of polite deprecation when anything of the speaker's is admired. I have since heard it applied to people's houses, clothes, and I think to their dinners, if one had chanced to praise a feast; if one admires a child, it is at once said to be ugly, and anything so intimately a man's own as his wife is invariably called stupid. I remember the Chinese word is much the same; "The stupid person of the inner chamber" being the ordinary name in Peking, if a wife has to be mentioned at all.

At last I got Countess Kuroda installed in a pose which suited her, but which caused the artist a wail in lamentation; for she insisted upon standing, in what she called the only attitude possible for a lady, square to the painter, with both sleeves tightly pulled down to hide her ten fingers. She was a good deal scandalised, on coming round to have a look at the result, to find that Mr. Landor had drawn her hands quite outside her sleeves. She shook her head gravely, and then sighed.

"What is it?" we asked; "is there something wrong with the picture?"

"I ought not to show my hands," she said; "only peasant-women do that! And—oh dear, what a pity I am already so old!"

"Old!" I cried; "why you are just twenty-two!"

"Very old," she insisted, pointing to the picture where Mr. Landor had already got the face in, round and pure and pale. "If I were still young, I could wear paint on my cheeks, and my picture would also have rosy cheeks. But now I am old, over twenty, and I must never paint my cheeks any more!"

This defect was quickly remedied, and she forgave Mr. Landor about the hands when he threw a rosy flush over the little face in the picture. At the second and third sittings the Countess became quite enthusiastic, and seemed to enjoy the change and liberty that the visits brought. When the whole thing was finished, Mr. Landor made a present of the painting to Count Kuroda, who was so pleased that he forgot to be angry; and I have ever since been receiving gorgeous bunches of chrysanthemums or presents of eggs or bon-bons in token of gratitude from his wife.

All this time we have had an invalid in the house, a poor English-woman, who came out as governess in a friend's family, and almost immediately had to undergo a severe operation at the hospital. Her employers have shown endless kindness and forbearance, Mrs. H—— leaving her little children for a month, and shutting herself up in the dreary hospital room with her friend. We brought the sick woman here to recover, and also to give Mrs. H—— some rest; and I cannot say how touched I have been by Sir Edwin Arnold's kindness to this poor soul. I am so busy that I have to be away a great part of the day, leaving her in charge of her nurse and the servants, who have been very good; but the time must often have seemed long to her, and you can imagine what it has been to have such a companion as Sir Edwin for an hour or so every evening. He said nothing to me, but quietly took to dressing for dinner an hour earlier than any one else, and then going into her room, where I found him installed, reading aloud, when I came to see if all was right. I am sure that delightful hour every day has really helped the poor thing to crawl back to life and strength.

I broke down again when she was better, and since I last wrote have had a few days in Atami, the town of the geyser and the long beaches by the sounding sea. I found it much warmer than Tokyo except on one or two days; and then I piled up sweet woods and fir cones in the little grate of my sitting-room, and took quick walks in the crisp air, and mightily enjoyed the scalding baths. My landlord's daughter, O'Detsu, was fired with ambition to learn to knit mittens for her beloved father's honourable cold wrists; so we sat together for hours, she poring over intricate stitches, and I directing her eager stiff fingers. At last, after using all my wools, she turned out a splendid pair, which the old gentleman at once put on. They form an extremely comfortable addition to the wide empty sleeve of Japanese costume.

I had one black wet day in Atami; but it was made up for by one jewelled morning after another—days when sky and sea, woods and waves and islands, were all a vision of immortal shining loveliness; and oh, the music of the long waves on the shore! It always sets life to its own grave sweet cadence, and helps me to think as I never think elsewhere. I went down alone; but H—— came to fetch me, and brought me home over the hills by Miyanoshita, where we stayed a day or two, thinking to take a house there for next summer.

Our journey over the pass to Miyanoshita was a thing I shall never forget. It was a bitterly cold morning when we set out, and a heavy snowfall had turned my world white. The dear old temple and the camphor tree, the empty rice-fields and the village street, were all uniformly dazzling; for the fall had ceased when the sun rose, and he was shining brilliantly in a sapphire sky, as if beyond some crystal dome, which showed us all his glory and forbade his touching us with his warmth. I had not brought my Hong Kong chair this time, and decided to try the Japanese *kago,* the basket litter slung on a pole and carried on two men's shoulders. I had seen my little *amah,* O'Matsu, jump in and out of these things so easily, and look so happy as she was dandled along the road in one, that it seemed worth trying, especially as the only other method of going over the pass would be on foot, and I never was a great walker. "Wo worth the day," as the old ballads say, when I undertook to double my stiff European length into a kind of basket too short to lie down in and too low to sit up in; for the little pent house-roof which ran along the carrying-pole knocked my head even when I had taken my hat off, and was further weighted with various bundles of food and clothing, the property of the coolies who were to bear me be-tween them. The cold seemed all the more intense for that blue sky and laughing sunshine. I was rolled in many rugs; and O'Matsu lighted two fire-boxes before we started, and put one at my feet and one inside my jacket. I think they did much to keep me alive, and perhaps my delight in the beautiful scenery did the rest. In spite of the cold and the intense fatigue caused by the cramped position and the broken trot of my coolies, I would not have missed the sights I saw for anything. It seems to me that the memory of such beauty will follow my spirit long after the bones which ached so wearily shall have been blown away in dust.

On leaving Atami, we followed a raised highroad which runs across the rice-fields to the foot of the mountains, and then scales them for a little way, ending short off in the hills, and obliging the traveller to take to a steep and narrow footpath, which mounts abruptly (far too abruptly!) up the skyey stair. I gasped as I saw my boxes going up this before me on the coolies' backs. The black basket trunks, which had seemed of so moderate size in railway trains and even on jinrikshas, absolutely grew, stood out enormous on these poor men's shoulders, and the sight of a large "Fraser" painted in white on black leather scrambling up the rocks on two staggering brown legs filled me with compunction and dismay! H——, who is an invincible walker, found it all he could do to get himself and his stick up to the top; but, at any rate, he did it at one stretch, while I and my boxes and my coolies had to stop every few minutes, and I felt like a wicked tyrant for letting myself be carried at all.

As we rose higher and higher, the most surprising views spread out all round us. The sea seemed to be climbing the sky, there was such an outspread mantle of it, dimpling in a million diamonds in the morning sun. Peak after peak of the hills rose before us; and at last we saw three seas—one beyond Atami, which we had left behind, and one in a deep bay on either side of us, thousands of feet below but so near that one could see every detail of the houses in the little fishing villages washed up like brown shells on the shores. We were on the highest point of the pass where a deep-runed stone tells the traveller that from this spot his eye can wander over ten provinces of what the old writers called the Kingdom of Japonia. But we hardly cared to look down, for there before us, in midday splendour, rose Fujiyama, white, dazzling, a marble pyramid against a sapphire sky. Mists rolled thick round its feet, as if the mountain-goddess had but just dropped her robe that we and the sun might look on her beauty; then invisible hands seemed to be raising the airy garment higher and higher, till the veil swept over the proud white crest, and the vision was gone.

Once or twice in the course of the day it returned, but never in that perfection. The road was long, and so heavy with snow that the men made but slow progress with my litter, which hung too near the ground for me to get much outlook on the scenery from under its wooden roof. We stopped as little as possible, fearing that the short winter day would close in before we had sighted the friendly lights of Miyanoshita; and this was what happened after all. The last part of the journey, a rather steep descent, was accomplished in the dark, and the coolies tried every step with their sticks before they moved. We knew that we were close to a torrent, because the roar went beside us for a long time; and the cold, which was intense, became even more marked when half-frozen spray was blown in one's face out of the night's black mouth. I was so cold that it seemed impossible I should ever move my limbs enough to get out of that dreadful little litter, and I was greatly relieved at last to see a forest of red and white lanterns, bearing the well-known mark of Fujiya's hotel, come bobbing and dancing through the blackness, and our coolies' shouts were answered by those of the men who had been sent out to look for us.

It was not long before we were housed and warmed, and laughing over the day's discomforts before a blazing wood fire; but I cannot say that I had quite forgotten them, and some trace of stiffness remained for several days. The journey is hardly one to undertake in winter; but I am glad we did it, for it has given me an impression of Fuji which I could never have had in the warmer weather.

Many people go to Miyanoshita for Christmas, especially the foreign colony established in Yokohama. To me there is something so dreary in spending these anniversaries in hired rooms and strange scenery, that nothing would induce me to try it. As time goes on they change their meaning, indeed, and become less gay, but not less sacred. Out here I live my mind life in a curious three time, owing to the enormous distance from home. My Christmas letters had to be written and sent off on November 20th; in a few days they and the quaint collection of gifts that went with them will cause great joy in the little home circle; but I shall have no word of thanks till the end of January, or later. We get in the papers distorted telegrams about events in Europe, but long before the true account of the thing reaches us its very existence has gone out of one's mind; and so, little by little, the vivid interest in home politics dies out, and is replaced by smaller and nearer subjects. But one is not moved or excited about them as one is in Europe. There is so much time here, so much stored leisure to be discounted, that hurry drops out of life to a great extent, and nobody frets when that which should have been accomplished last week is hopefully announced to take place next year. That is the *ambiente,* the moral air of this morning land; and Europeans soon imbibe the easy philosophy.

A curious instance of this trick of willing waiting was brought to sight a little before our arrival. A safe in the Chancery, which had been unused for some years, was opened for some reason or other, and was found to contain a parcel of apparently forgotten medals sent by our Government to be distributed among the Japanese who helped to defend the British Legation against the attack of some *samurai* in—1861! When it was known that these medals would now be distributed, over twenty-seven years after the event, every one seemed inclined to deprecate the precipitation shown by our authorities in such matters. Why not wait till the few survivors of the affray had joined the majority, and then hang the medals on their tombstones all at once, and so avoid unfriendly feeling? The local papers made merry at our expense, and the tiresome people who only live to ask questions to which there can be no possible answer rose like one man, and insisted on knowing the cause of the delay. When at last the truth was told, the delay turned out not to have been of our making at all; it came from the heroes themselves, who in those early days had no desire to be distinguished as the friends and protectors of the abhorred foreigner, although their obedience to orders had made them quite ready to strike a blow in his defence.

The story of the attack is such an old one that you may have forgotten it. It was told me in graphic language by Laurence Oliphant a few years ago; and often in driving past the spot where the Legation then stood that record of bloodshed has come back to my mind. In those days our flag flew from a green knoll in Takanawa, close to the sea, which afforded opportunities of protection by a passing gun-boat. The Shogun's Government kept one hundred and fifty men to guard the compound; but for some undeclared reason they failed to stop fourteen *samurai*, desperate, conscientious fanatics, who made their way into the Minister's quarters on the night of July 4th, 1861, and succeeded in wounding Laurence Oliphant and the other Secretary, and in killing some of the guards, before they were driven back. Once roused, the guards fought well; and it was in recognition of their services that these medals were sent from England, with warm expressions of thanks for their loyalty. But nobody wished to be reminded of the affair, and the Tokugawa Government refused to supply the names of the men who had earned the British decorations, which would at that time have marked out their wearers as traitors in the eyes of the fanatical *samurai* and the country at large. So the medals were quietly put away in a Chancery safe, which, with other valuable objects, escaped destruction in 1863, because the persevering *samurai* who then burnt down the new Legation buildings did so on the very night after they were completed, and before the British Representative and his staff had taken possession.

For this last outrage there was something like an excuse, since the site of the buildings had been, strictly speaking, extorted from the Government at the point of the bayonet. Various beautiful sites were offered when the Takanawa Legation was condemned as being isolated and inconvenient; but our authorities would have none of them, having set their hearts on what was a favourite resort of the townspeople, a beautiful public garden, endeared to the Japanese by the fact that their hero Iyeyasu had held his Court there when he first made Tokyo his seat of Government. It is interesting to remember that Count Ito, to-day the great advocate of progress for Japan, the chief framer of her Constitution, was one of the *samurai* engaged in this incendiary exploit. He laughs over it now, and says that if medals are being given to the protectors of the foreigner he certainly ought to have one, having planned and lighted his bonfire when the new buildings were empty and no lives could be lost.

But I must go back to the story of the safe. It travelled with the rest of the official properties from one place to another, till, eighteen years ago, it was lodged in the present Chancery, a strong little building, well away from the gate, and placed between the Minister's house and the quarters of the two English constables who are all that now remain of the numerous escort necessary in Sir Harry Parkes' days. Then the times changed; and when the Queen sent swords to Count Goto and Nakai Kozo for defending her Representative from the perennial fanatic in 1868, her gifts were received with pride and gratitude. But the medals were forgotten; the keys of the safe were lost; it was supposed only to contain old accounts, which nobody wished to consult; and something very like consternation filled the establishment last spring, when the energetic head of the Chancery said he would not have useless lumber lying about, the old chest must be broken open, and its contents sorted or destroyed, according to their values! Then the medals, silver and gold, with their yellow diplomas, came to light. The active official conscience insisted on their being given to the men for whom they were intended, and a busy search brought one or two of these retiring braves to the light, and caused considerable amusement to the foreign public at large, who, not instructed as to the original causes of the delay, felt delightfully healthy and virtuous in having found such a good case against red-tapeism and official procrastinations, and in proof of the general uselessness of public servants.

1890

Tokyo, January, 1890

New Year's Day was marked by a reception at the Palace far more
formal than corresponding *cercles* held by sovereigns in Europe. I
was glad to have another chance of walking through those beautiful
rooms in the great house across the moat. It was a cold snowy
morning, and there was not much comfort to be found in putting
on a low dress, even with an interminable train attached to it. We
drove off, a goodly procession, preceded by Inspector Peacock, looking very smart in full uniform on "Polly Perkins," an old charger,
who is the *doyenne* of the stables, having come to Japan, it is said,
in Lord Elgin's* time. We have to make a long round to reach the
State entrance to the Palace; and so many carriages were already
drawn up inside the enclosure that I began to fear we might be late.
This reception was for the Diplomatic Corps; but the poor Emperor
and Empress had already held two that morning—one of the Cabinet
Ministers and other members of the Government, and one of the
Peers and their wives; and yet earlier the Emperor had performed a

*Lord Elgin was entrusted with the task of conducting negotiations with China
and Japan. He arrived in Japan in early August 1858, and an Anglo-Japanese treaty
was signed on the twenty-sixth.

123

religious ceremony before the tablets of his ancestors. The afternoon was to be devoted to receiving the military officials, and altogether the programme seemed one which would have taxed the strength of even the "Reise Kaiser" to carry out.

We were received by a number of the Household officials in the entrance hall, and the men waited while we women took off our cloaks in a beautiful little dressing-room full of long glasses and supplied with pins and powder in the most hospitable fashion. I did not want either, but lingered a minute to speak to the dressers who were there in attendance. There were four charmingly pretty girls, two dressed in European frocks of grey silk, and two in their own brilliant costumes, carried out in superb materials. Their smiling faces, and the fine deft fingers which removed my wraps and shook out my finery, made me feel that on the whole Japanese ladies have nothing to envy us in the way of lady's maids. To them I think the whole thing was a delightful treat, and they betrayed a good deal of curiosity as to how the white plumes and the long veil were fastened to my head.

When I came out, we started on that long walk through the corridors which I described in one of my first letters. To-day the endless glass galleries were warmed by steam, and full of bright dresses and uniforms. The great drawing-room where we all gathered presented a beautiful sight; the flower temple in the centre, a mass of orchids and roses, was surrounded by a crowd of men in all the Diplomatic uniforms of Europe, with many military ones scattered among them. The women's gorgeous trains wound in and out like serpents of velvet and gold, and the bright sunshine which had succeeded the snow danced gaily on their jewels as they moved. Outside, the courtyard that I had last seen full of cherry blossom was all a fairyland of snow, and the fountain played above it, throwing rosaries of diamonds about in the sunshine. There were no Japanese ladies to receive us, except the wife of the Minister for Foreign Affairs; and she went to take her stand by the Empress before we were summoned to the throne-room.

This is a large square room in another courtyard, and is at some distance from the drawing-room. As we approached, I saw that the walls of this hall, which I had hardly noticed separately before, are all of glass, except on one side, where the two thrones are placed on a raised daïs, lined with heavy draperies of Kyoto silks. The floor of inlaid woods was so highly polished that I looked at it with some apprehension, having been a little lame with rheumatism of late. We had to wait our turn to enter (the French Minister is just now our *doyen*), and I could watch the ceremony through the glass. The Emperor and Empress stood on the top step of the daïs, a few yards apart, he having the Imperial Princes and his aides-de-camp behind him on his right, and the Empress the Princesses and her ladies on her left. The Emperor, whom I now saw close to for the first time, has a very plain but interesting face. The lower part is heavy and impassive; but the eyes are piercingly brilliant, and the brow that of a thinker. He is of medium height, and has a good figure, which is shown to advantage, as he holds himself extremely well. The appearance of many Japanese gentlemen is spoiled in European dress by their peculiarly short arms; but the Emperor does not suffer from this defect. He looked very dignified in his marshal's uniform, covered as it was with splendid decorations. The Empress was in white brocade, with two of the most perfect diamond rivieras round her neck that I have ever seen. I think they are finer than those of the Empress of Austria. She wore a magnificent tiara, too heavy for her small head; and she looked, poor lady, terribly pale and tired. Her white dress was crossed by the broad orange ribbon of an Imperial order, which was also worn by the Princesses. The effect of this flaming band on a soft rose or pale-green satin gown is rather disastrous.

When it was our turn to make our bow to the sovereigns, I found it a very long way from the entrance to the daïs, and the floor was even more slippery than it looked. However, I got through all the curtseys without accidents. The Emperor and Empress only bowed as we passed before them; the Princesses nodded and smiled in a row; and then we had to back out and down, across more miles of gleaming parquet, and through a door, from which I could stand and watch as the next victim underwent the same ordeal. The whole ceremony did not last five minutes, and I heard more than one of our colleagues grumbling violently at the trouble and fatigue involved. Perhaps I shall do the same next year; but this was the first time for me, and the spectacle pleased me. There was something rather fine about the great sombre room, with its crimson background and glass screens, its sovereigns and their court, all silent as the dead, watching the Representatives of the world file past them as they stood on that daïs-step, which seemed for the moment to be the high-water mark of the country's advance towards friendship and equality with great unseen Europe.

When it was all over, I flew home and tore off my finery to throw myself into the preparations for a huge Christmas tree, the first that had ever grown in our compound, for the children of our servants and writers and employés, who make up the number of our Legation population to close on two hundred, beginning with H——, and ending with the last jinriksha coolie's youngest baby. I could not have the tree on Christmas Day, owing to various engagements; so it was fixed for January 3rd, and was quite the most successful entertainment I ever gave!*

When I undertook it, I confess that I had no idea how many little ones belonged to the compound. I sent our good Ogita round to invite them all solemnly to come to Ichiban (Number One) on the 3rd at five o'clock. Ogita threw himself into the business with de-lighted goodwill, having five little people of his own to include in the invitation; but all the servants were eager to help as soon as they knew we were preparing a treat for the children. That is work which would always appeal to Japanese of any age or class. No trouble is too great, if it brings pleasure to the "treasure-flowers," as the babies are called. I am still too ignorant of their special tastes to trust my own judgment in the matter of presents; so Mr. G—— left the dic-tionary and the Chancery for two or three afternoons, and helped me to collect an appropriate harvest for the little hands to glean. Some of them were not little, and these were more difficult to buy for; but after many cold hours passed in the different bazaars, it seemed to me that there must be something for everybody, although we had really spent very little money.

The wares were so quaint and pretty that it was a pleasure to sort and handle them. There were workboxes in beautiful polished woods, with drawers fitting so perfectly that when you closed one the compressed air at once shot out another. There were mirrors

*Children's Christmas parties have been held regularly in the British Embassy since Mrs. Fraser's day.

enclosed in charming embroidered cases; for where mirrors are mostly made of metal, people learn not to let them get scratched. There were dollies of every size, and dolls' houses and furniture, kitchens, farmyards, rice-pounding machines—all made in the tiniest proportions, such as it seemed no human fingers could really have handled. For the elder boys we bought books, school-boxes with every school requisite contained in a square the size of one's hand, and penknives and scissors, which are greatly prized as being of foreign manufacture. For decorations we had an abundant choice of materials. I got forests of willow branches decorated with artificial fruits; pink and white balls made of rice paste, which are threaded on the twigs; surprise shells of the same paste, two lightly stuck together in the form of a double scallop shell, and full of miniature toys; *kanzashi,* or ornamental hairpins for the girls, made flowers of gold and silver among my dark pine branches; and I wasted precious minutes in opening and shutting these dainty roses—buds until you press a spring, when they open suddenly into a full-blown rose. But the most beautiful things on my tree were the icicles, which hung in scores from its sombre foliage, catching rosy gleams of light from our lamps as we worked late into the night. These were—chopsticks, long glass chopsticks, which I discovered in the bazaar; and I am sure Santa Klaus himself could not have told them from icicles.

Of course every present must be labelled with the child's name, and here my troubles began. Ogita was told to make out a correct list of names and ages with some reference to the calling of the parents; for even here rank and precedence must be observed, or terrible heart-burnings might follow. The list came at last; and if it were not so long, I would send it to you complete, for it was a curiosity. Imagine such complicated titles as these: "Minister's second cook's girl. Umé, age 2"; "Minister's servant's cousin's boy. Age 11"; "Student interpreter's teacher's girl"; "Vice-Consul's jinriksha-man's boy." And so it went on, till there were fifty-eight of them of all ages, from one year up to nineteen. Some of them, indeed, were less than a year old; and I was amused on the evening of the 2nd at having the list brought back to me with this note (Ogita's English is still highly individual!): "Marked X is declined to the invitation." On looking down the column, I found that ominous-looking cross only against one name, that of Yasu, daughter of Ito Kanejiro, Mr. G——'s cook. This recalcitrant little person turned out to be six weeks old—an early age for parties even nowadays. Miss Yasu, having been born in November, was put down in the following January as two years old, after the puzzling Japanese fashion. Then I found that they would write boys as girls, girls as boys, grown-ups as babies, and so on. Even at the last moment a doll had to be turned into a sword, a toy tea-set into a workbox, a history of Europe into a rattle; but people who grow Christmas trees are prepared for such small contingencies, and no one knew anything about it when on Friday afternoon the great tree slowly glowed into a pyramid of light, and a long procession was marshalled in, with great solemnity and many bows, till they stood, a delighted, wide-eyed crowd, round the beautiful shining thing, the first Christmas tree any one of them had ever seen. It was worth all the trouble, to see the gasp of surprise and delight, the evident fear that the whole thing might be unreal and suddenly fade away. One little man of two fell flat on his back with amazement, tried to rise and have another look, and in so doing rolled over on his nose, where he lay quite silent till his relatives rescued him. Behind the children stood the mothers, quite as pleased as they, and with them one very old lady with a little child on her back. She turned out to be the Vice-Consul's jinriksha-man's grandmother; the wife of that functionary was dead, and the old lady had to take her place in carrying about the poor little V. C. J. R. S. M.'s boy-baby.

The children stood, the little ones in front and the taller ones behind, in a semicircle, and the many lights showed their bright faces and gorgeous costumes, for no one would be outdone by another in smartness— I fancy the poorer women had borrowed from richer neighbours—and the result was picturesque in the extreme. The older girls had their heads beautifully dressed, with flowers and pins and rolls of scarlet crape knotted in between the coils; their dresses were pale green or blue, with bright linings and stiff silk *obis;* but the little ones were a blaze of scarlet, green, geranium pink and orange, their long sleeves sweeping the ground, and the huge flower patterns of their garments making them look like live flowers as they moved about on the dark velvet carpet. When they had gazed their fill, they were called up to me one by one, Ogita addressing them all as "San" (Miss or Mr.), even if they could only toddle, and I gave them their serious presents with their names, written in Japanese and English, tied on with red ribbon—an attention which, as I was afterwards told, they appreciated greatly. It seemed to me that they never would end; their size varied from a wee mite who could not carry its own toys to a tall handsome student of sixteen, or a gorgeous young lady in green and mauve crape and a head that must have taken the best part of a day to dress.

In one thing they were all alike: their manners were perfect. There was no pushing or grasping, no glances of envy at what other children received, no false shyness in their sweet happy way of expressing their thanks. I had for my helpers two somewhat antagonistic volunteers—Sir Edwin Arnold, basking in Buddhistic calms, and Bishop Bickersteth, intensely Anglican, severe-looking, ascetic. There had already been some polite theological encounters at our table, and I did not feel sure that the combination would prove a happy one. But each man is a wonder of kind-heartedness in his own way; and my doubts were replaced by sunshiny certainties, when I saw how they both began by beaming at the children, and ended by beaming on one another. I was puzzled by one thing about the children: although we kept giving them sweets and oranges off the tree, every time I looked round the big circle all were empty-handed again, and it really seemed as if they must have swallowed the gifts, gold paper and ribbon and all. But at last I noticed that their square hanging sleeves began to have a strange lumpy appearance, like a conjuror's waistcoat just before he produces twenty-four bowls of live goldfish from his internal economy; and then I understood that the plunder was at once dropped into these great sleeves so as to leave hands free for anything else that Okusama might think good to bestow. One little lady, O'Haru San, aged three, got so over-loaded with goodies and toys, that they kept rolling out of her sleeves, to the great delight of the Brown Ambassador Dachshund, Tip, who pounced on them like lightning, and was also convicted of nibbling at cakes on the lower branches of the tree. The bigger children would not take second editions of presents, and answered, "Honourable thanks, I have!" if offered more than they thought their share; but babies are babies all the world over! When the distribution was finished at last, I got a Japanese gentleman to tell them the story of Christmas, the children's feast; and then they came up one by one to say "Sayonara" ("Since it must be," the Japanese farewell), and "Arigato gozaimasu" (The honourable thanks).

"Come back next year," I said; and then the last presents were given out—beautiful lanterns, red, lighted, and hung on what Ogita calls *bumboos,* to light the guests home with. One tiny maiden refused to go, and flung herself on the floor in a passion of weeping, saying that Okusama's house was too beautiful to leave, and she would stay with me always—yes, she would! Only the sight of the lighted lantern, bobbing on a stick twice as long as herself, persuaded her to return to her own home in the servants' quarters. I stood on the step, the same step where I had set the fireflies free one warm night last summer, and watched the little people scatter over the lawns, and disappear into the dark shrubberies, their round red lights dancing and shifting as they went, just as if my fireflies had come back, on red wings this time, to light my little friends to bed.

Tokyo, January, 1890

I was so taken up with our own doings when I last wrote, that I forgot to tell you anything of the Japanese New Year customs, which would probably have interested you more. It is the time when the people, from highest to lowest, make holiday—the most important moment of the whole year. For many days beforehand preparations were on foot for keeping the feast with due pomp. New clothes were being made in every family—clothes as smart and bright as the winter season and people's purses would allow. Ogita came and represented to me that it was customary to pay all the wages on December 30th instead of two days later, when they would naturally fall due; and this because all debts and bills must be settled before the New Year should dawn. All the servants had new liveries, dark-blue silk robes and black silk *haori,* or coats, with their master's crest embroidered on the back and shoulders. At this time every house is cleaned and put in repair; sweet-smelling new mats are laid down, wherever people can afford them; the sliding screens are covered with fresh paper; and every doorway, great or small, is decorated with garlands of pine and bamboo, gemmed with golden oranges, which twist and swing in the sunshine, while splendid red lobsters brandish their claws among the leaves and fruit. The lobsters are symbolic—of great age; and the gift of one implies a kind wish that you may live until you are bent double like the lobster. They are also a favourite food among the people; it sounds absurd to us to call them decorative, but the Japanese do not think so, and employ them ornamentally with excellent effect. Across the garlanded doorway, the Shinto emblem, a thick straw rope, beautifully plaited and knotted, is hung, to give a blessing to the rest, and to keep out all evil spirits; and on either side is planted a tall bamboo, decorated with its own feathery leaves, and with branches of pine, the never-forgotten emblem of happiness and fortitude. The shops are full of such presents as are fitting for the festival. Some one sent me a ship of happiness, a junk, about two feet long, all worked in sweet clean straw. It was wreathed with twigs of pine, and loaded with tiny models of rice-bags for riches, and lobsters for long life; the mast was a growing branch of pine, and the sails were gold and scarlet paper, bearing auspicious inscriptions. I was rather surprised at seeing the straw ships, having thought that these were only used for the *Bon Matsuri*, the Festival of the Dead, which occurs in summer; but they evidently belong to the New Year as well, for I see many in the Japanese houses.

The streets are crowded with people all through the last night of the year; buying and selling is going on everywhere in the open air, in spite of the sharp cold; and it is only when the dawn has broken that the good folk go home to rest for an hour or two before beginning their round of visits among relations and friends. It is said that in very old times this was the only whole holiday taken by many of the working-classes from year's end to year's end. Be that as it may, they all enter into it with joyful eagerness now. The shops send out ornamental carts, piled high with what are called the first wares of the New Year; and these are drawn through the streets by parties of shop-boys, calling attention to the many useful articles they have to sell. On the 2nd of January, when the excitements of New Year's Day have subsided a little, the first customer in every shop receives a present, and business begins very early indeed, some buyers starting even at two o'clock in the morning to make sure of the gift. All those who can afford it get new clothes at this time; there are few so poor that they cannot spend a few sen on New Year's presents, and the booths show such piles of cheap and pretty things that one begins to think that value and beauty should be calculated here on inverse ratios. Many of the stalls, both in the street and the enclosed bazaars, are devoted to battledores of every variety of design; and probably many thousands are sold on the last night of the year, since on the 1st of January every girl in the town, from the babies up to the brides, will be playing battledore and shuttlecock through most of the daylight hours. The battledore is a bat-shaped wooden instrument, merely painted or gilt on the side meant to meet the shuttlecock; but the back is generally ornamented with reliefs in crape, skilfully combined with painting and gilding. One will bear a scene in history, the faces of the figures being painted, and their garments applied in moulded bits of crape and brocade. Or else a Japanese beauty smiles out of her window, or from the heart of a curling peony blossom; a snow landscape, the white rabbit and the monkey who live in the moon, a fierce warrior, or a bunch of blossoms all jostle each other, and are solemnly judged and contrasted before the buyers decide which to take. Twenty-five or thirty sen (six- or sevenpence) is a good price to give for these perfect little fancies. More lovely, however, are the real flowers, the early plum and dwarf pines, which the florists offer as the first-fruits of the year.

There is a great temple bell near us, which rang in the New Year solemnly at midnight over the heads of the busy, light-hearted crowd. One hundred and eight strokes rolled slowly from the deep bronze mouth, and hung in long vibration on the air; twelve times nine, to ward off all evil from the city for the incoming year. No one seemed to take much notice of the signal, and I fancy many people even stayed out in the streets and restaurants until the dawn, when the more pious ones would go to the eastern heights of the city to see the first sunrise (*hatsu-hi-no-de*)—an event which is sure to bring good luck to the beholder. Then comes a pilgrimage called the "Happy-direction-going," for which a different temple is chosen every year by the bonzes; and after this the visiting and feasting, the real business of the day, begins.

It is very important to start the year with propitious dreams; but as those of its first night might be unpleasantly affected by the conviviality of the evening, the 2nd of January has been chosen as the night whose dreams truly foretell some event of the coming year.

I did not realise the intense difficulty of translating our thoughts into Japanese words till the day after our Christmas tree, when O'Matsu came to me looking very puzzled, and said that she would like to ask a question: why did Imai San (the gentleman who made the little address explaining the meaning of Christmas) say such a dreadful thing about "Jesu Sama"? He had said that Jesu Sama was put into a bucket, such a thing as the ponies have their food in! That seemed very horrible and undignified to her. I tried to explain that in Palestine the animals did not eat out of buckets; but I saw that I made very little impression. Imai San was a man, and a Japanese, and evidently my Bible history carried no weight in comparison to his. A day or two after this I sent all the maids and children down to the Convent in Tsukiji, where my friends the nuns had made a beautiful *crêche* for their children. Here, in lifelike figures, were the Mother and the Babe, Joseph and the Shepherds, and the crib with its straw, all the scene splendidly decorated with pine branches and imitation snow and gold paper stars. O'Matsu came back beaming. "I understand it all now," she told me; "eyes speak better than words. Buckets, indeed!" and she laughed triumphantly. The children, great and small, were enchanted with the nuns' grotto, and came in little parties to thank me for sending them to see it.

Tokyo, February, 1890

Very little of interest has been happening in the political world. Count Okuma has recovered entirely from his wound, and has made a little testimonial to the trained nurses from the Charity

Hospital who tended him during his long imprisonment. He sent them some valuable presents, as he also did to the surgeons who operated on his unhappy limb; and now he pretends to laugh over the disaster of its loss. But he will not take office again at present, preferring to have the rank of Privy Councillor, which admits of his offering an opinion, without holding the portfolio, which would be as yet too heavy a tax on his strength.

His successor, Viscount Aoki, strikes one as a man hardly great enough yet to deal with the question of Treaty Revision, the only question of any importance before the Government just now. But he has knowledge, and patience; also he is modest, and apparently not fired by personal ambition or party feeling, so that greatness may not be far off. I pity him sincerely. The post of Foreign Minister is so little sought after, that, since Count Okuma's accident, it seems difficult to find anybody of the right kind to fill it; and the man who does so carries his life in his hands.

I watched Viscount Aoki drive up to our own door a day or two ago. He was seated in an open victoria with the hood raised, and inside the hood on either hand hung a revolver in a leather pocket, with a heavy chain fastening it to a ring in the carriage frame. The weapons are carefully loaded before the Minister takes his airing, and I fancy that any stranger who tried to stop the carriage or looked into it suddenly would have rather a sensational reception. Three detectives in plain clothes accompany him, as well as a policeman, who sits on the box. The effect is that of a condemned criminal, or a dangerous lunatic out with his keepers. Madame Aoki tells me that the constant watch and guard make life quite intolerable. Wherever she and her husband go, if it be only for a turn in their own garden, the policeman appears, and follows at a not too respectful distance, admiring the flowers and assiduously pretending that he does not hear a word of their conversation. She confided to me that they occasionally amuse themselves by giving their protectors the slip, stealing out like runaway children by a door which opens on a side-street, whence, plainly dressed and on foot, they can take something like a walk. I believe that the consternation is great when it is found that the Minister has really left his own grounds unprotected by the law, and the detectives generally run him to earth and come home with him again.

It all seems rather useless, for Treaty Revision is far less active than it was, and the disputes about the question of Foreign Judges threaten to break up the negotiations altogether. The public here, the mass of middle-class, fairly well-educated people, have outgrown the stage (existing honestly a few years ago) when they would tolerate the temporary employment of foreign judges sitting in Japanese law courts conjointly with the native judges, to ensure justice to any foreigner who might be brought up for trial. The arrangement was only intended to last a certain time, until the Japanese should have shown themselves capable of understanding and impartially administering their new laws, which are not yet entirely codified. Count Okuma and other members of the Government were in favour of the admission of foreign judges in cases where foreigners were concerned; but the vernacular press, the soshi, the people in general, have reached a stage in political development where bumptiousness takes the place of prudence; they consider that the concession would be an insult to their national integrity. But our own Government will not go back on the proposition, feeling that Japan is still too young to the ways of justice to be trusted blindly and entirely with the liberty, the property, perhaps the lives of British subjects. This is the now famous nineteenth article of the proposed treaty. It cannot be granted, and it cannot be renounced; hence a pause in the endless negotiations—a pause during which the Cabinet seems to be constantly unmaking itself, to be built up in a different manner with most of the same names, a process which reminds me of nothing so much as of the children's boxes of coloured bricks, where the same fragments serve as an arch, a doorstep, a fireplace, or a pediment, according to which of its six sides you turn uppermost. No sooner have I learnt which peer holds which portfolio than they all—excuse the smile—seem to toss them into the air, and catch who catch them can in the fall. The Sanjo Cabinet, however, has retired with some majesty. Its farewell was a very earnest appeal, embodied in a memorial to the throne, to increase the responsibility of Ministers and to build up the power and dignity of the Cabinet by first making it responsible in full for all measures promulgated by individual Ministers; secondly, by making each Minister sign the orders for his own department, instead of having to have them countersigned by the Minister President, as is now the

135

case, before they can take effect—an arrangement which, says the memorial, throws too much power into the hands of one man; thirdly, that whatever passes at Cabinet Councils be kept absolutely secret, the obligation of silence not ceasing with the retirement of its members. In fact, the whole memorial is a plea for responsibility, unity, and reticence as the only means by which the Cabinet can maintain its proper position in the State or carry out the functions entrusted to it. The coming elections and the opening of the Imperial Diet are referred to as rendering the proposed measures absolutely necessary to ensure the harmony and efficiency of the Government.

Count Ito kept out of all this very carefully. Watching him as I do from the place of the unlearned, I have come to the conclusion that he has a strong sense of dramatic effect and of the wisdom of inactivity when other people are doing dangerous work or seem on the point of making fools of themselves. His prolonged reluctance to take office probably comes from this acute sense of self-preservation, combined, as I have said, with the other sense of the value of dramatic effect. Is the Cabinet torn with dissensions or in despair because Great Britain will not yield that one little Article XIX., are the *soshi* rampant and the Radical newspapers being suppressed by scores, every one cries out, Where is Count Ito? Where is the man who made the Constitution and brought in the foreigners? Then Count Ito is sure to be in his beautiful villa at Odawara, contemplating the codification of the laws, or the growth of his rhododendrons, or something equally impersonal and removed from the sphere of dispute. He is entreated to return, to advise his sovereign, to strengthen his party, to pacify and reassure the public; and he always comes and does it. And it seems to me at these times that when the others have done all the drudgery, then he reaps the glory of some popular measure; or it goes the other way—an unpopular thing must be done, a bad moment passed, moral accounts faced; then Count Ito feels an irresistible desire for peace and retirement, and his colleagues have to do without him, until the scene is properly set for him to step forward again. He is a very astute yet broad thinker, determined and ruthless, has absolute control of personal emotions and ambitions—all that which constitutes "the moment" with its opportunity or its danger; and any one who knows him would, I fancy, lay heavy odds on the probability of his ultimately attaining any object which he considered important enough to desire.

The regulations have been published for the coming elections, and have caused a good deal of interest. In order to vote, a Japanese subject must be twenty-five years of age, and must have been paying direct taxes to the amount of fifteen yen yearly for at least a year before the day when the electoral lists are made up, April 1st of this year. The actual election day will be July 1st, and stringent measures will be taken to keep it peaceable and orderly. We shall be away in the hills I hope in July; but I shall look forward with great interest to the opening of the Diet in November.

November seems very far away just now. The spring is here, young and weak as yet; but every day adds something to its conquests from winter. Already in January the early plum bloomed in white flakes that might have been mistaken for falling snow but for the crimson knot that held it to the grey branch. These valiant fragile blossoms are greatly endeared to the Japanese, because they come long before one has a right to expect open-air flowers at all. One warm midday hour, perhaps between snow and snow, will give them courage to shed their brown sheath and shake out their ethereal petals to the tepid sunshine. But they go with the snow too; only for a few days do they rejoice us with the certain promise of a yet invisible spring, and then, yielding to wind and snowstorm, they dance on their airy way; the tree is bare of their beauty long before a leaf has dared to show itself, but their message was given faithfully, and the later flowers will keep all the promises that the early plum had made for them. Eldest brother of the hundred flowers, as it is called here, a whole body of poetry and tradition has grown up round the shy evanescent blossom which passes so soon and leaves such a rich harvest of fruit for early summer's garnering. I think I saw the first flowers in Viscount Hijikata's garden on January 13th; but the spot is a sheltered one, and other trees did not follow till much later. Now, in these early February days, the plum-gardens are in full bloom, and crowded with enthusiastic visitors, who, undaunted by the snow, go to admire what they call the "Silver World," a world with snow on the paths and snow on the branches, while snowy petals, with the faintest touch of glow-worm green

137

at the heart, go whirling along on the last gust of wind from the bay. At night, when all is quiet and the second watchman has gone his rounds, an eerie cry is heard; and if I step out on the verandah and look up, I see a string of three or four wild geese passing swiftly between me and the stars, their long necks strained in the speed of their flight, the head cleaving the air as a prow cleaves the water, and the whole body flung after it through space with an intensity of motion shown in the flight of no other bird, I think. Night after night they pass, with the long piercing cry that the north wind must have taught them, and their flight is always northwards; but I think they come back in the dawn when I am asleep, for it is too early for their migration to begin, and they would fly in different order and larger bodies if they were starting on it. We think they have feeding-grounds on the north side of the town, which they are too shy to visit in the daytime. The Japanese, however, connect their migration with the appearance of the early plum, and the poets bewail them for having to fly away from so much loveliness. The plum's own bird is the *uguisu,* the Japanese nightingale, the sweetest of singers; but I have not heard her yet this spring, and last year she did not sing till May, when we arrived.

There are so many kinds of plum trees that one or other of them blooms from now to midsummer. Today's snow blossom will be followed by double white ones and pink ones, deep crimson too, that never bear a fruit; some are long trails of blossom growing obediently in a perfect bell shape round a gnarled morsel of trunk in a pale-green porcelain pot; others make a mist of whiteness waving against the sky from the black branches, stiff and knotted, which the Japanese consider characteristic of the plum, and cultivate with extreme care. The show plum-gardens take rank according to the age and ruggedness of their trees, which furnish a sharp contrast to the delicate snowy petals of the flower. This contrast seems to me to lie at the root of many theories of beauty of the Japanese, and is so desirable in their eyes that they obtain it by means of almost dishonest artificiality. The knotty bark of the plum is emblematic of old age, and the year's first bud is the symbol of extreme youth; therefore the tree must be made to look as old as possible, and the true enthusiasts go to view and rave over the blossoms while they are still hard little buttons with scarcely a touch of white.

This is the condition in which the gardener brings them to decorate my rooms; and when I expostulate and say that I want flowers, not sticks, he shakes his head and draws in his breath, and bends double in a bow, all of which is meant to hide his disappointment at my impatience and want of artistic feeling. The worst of it is that I fancy he is right and I am wrong! He would give me the pleasure of watching the little brown sheaths burst and shed themselves, of seeing the closely crinkled petals unfold to the daylight like a newborn baby's hand, of breathing in the first whiffs of the faint fine scent, so sweet and distinctive that the Japanese say the nightingale can find the tree in the dark by its perfume; all this I should lose if Naratake Ginsemon, the gnome of scissors and string and brown mould, brought me masses of ready spread bloom. So I take patience, and we add warm tea to the water in which they stand, and in a day or two the long hall and the sunny drawing-rooms are a bower of bloom, more beautiful even than the groves of the "Recumbent Dragon" at Kameido, where the old trees almost creep on the ground, and look, in their moonshine mist of blossom, like a withered old witch in a bridal veil.

There is a feast called "The First Rabbit of January," which is celebrated in this same temple at Kameido, chiefly associated in European minds with the splendid show of wistaria blossoms later in the year. Here the memory of a great scholar, Sugawara Michizane is venerated. He lived some sixteen centuries ago but is still believed to take so much interest in literature that ambitious youths write poems in large characters on paper and burn them at his tomb. Anxiously they watch the whirling ashes; and if they are carried high in the air, the scholar may go home satisfied, for his great aspirations will be fulfilled.

People here have carried the power of will and imagination to such completeness that they have succeeded in limiting the winter to a few short weeks which end on December 22nd, when the shortest day is past, and theoretical spring begins. Then the last chrysanthemums are still hanging on in our warm rooms, and seem to look askance at the jonquils propped with pebbles in their flat dishes, brought in by the gardener, who has been nursing them in some dark corner of his house until they were ripe enough, in his eyes at least, for drawing-room decoration. To us they still look cold and raw; but in the first night their grey silk envelope is broken, and morning finds them all staring about the room as if just awakened from sleep. It is thought lucky to have them open for the New Year, an easy matter when New Year's Day was a movable feast, falling near the end of January or even later, as it did formerly in Japan, but involving some effort since the introduction of the European calendar.

Although winter is thus shortened in theory, no one dreams of leaving off winter clothes until April, or even May, for the cold is apt to return at any time, and nobody cares to have brightly coloured garments ruined by a sudden storm. The thick wadded clothes worn make it possible for people to have winter picnics, when they sit in open verandahs, making poems to the moonlight on the snow. The pictures of such entertainments generally give the guests an expression of concentrated melancholy, each looking away from his companion as if he would say, "I refuse to see how miserable you are. It might unnerve me!"

Tokyo, March, 1890

The month of March, in which falls the girls' festival (the third day of the third month), must make up in a great degree to the little Japanese maiden for the secondary place she occupies in the family councils during the rest of the year—secondary, at least, as compared to the one filled by that all-important personage, her brother. His especial festival comes later, when the year is nearer its summer glories, and the sun, low now, will be riding high and hot in the heavens. But March, with its camellias and cherry blossoms and toys, belongs to the girls; and they queen it royally in the midst of their double family, their adoring relations and their submissive doll subjects.

Long before March the 3rd has come, the elaborate preparations for the doll festival have been begun in the families of the nobles and the princes. Away from the house with its inflammable woods, in a safe part of the grounds, stands the *godown,* or store-house, where all the precious things are kept safe from thieves and fire. It is generally an ugly little building of white-washed brick, in two stories, heavily clamped with iron, and having iron doors and shutters often ten or twelve inches thick. Fires are the curse of Tokyo, and have been raging frightfully of late, the wood and paper and mats of which the houses chiefly consist leaping into flame at the first spark that falls upon them. So the rich people keep their treasures in fire-proof store-houses, which I have often seen standing untouched when the rest of the home was reduced to ashes.

European children would be surprised to hear that they were expected only to see their favourite toys for one month in the year, and to consign them to fireproof safes for the other eleven; but the dolls brought to light on March the 3rd are mostly heirlooms, triumphs of the art of a day which worked as if its sun would have no setting, which took no account of labour or time, but only of the passionate straining after perfection for its own sake.

And now March is here, and the girls' festival is being celebrated from Hakodate to Nagasaki. In great houses the store-rooms have been opened, and hundreds of wonderful doll families brought to light to be displayed in all their glory in a special room prepared for them. From generation to generation the dolls are handed down and preserved with that unquestioning reverence which the Japanese bestow on everything they love. Little children are called the treasure-flowers of life, and that which ministers to their happiness is never considered trivial, but regarded as a necessary part of the family occupations. They themselves do not look upon their delicate toys as things to be knocked about in rough play; seeing that the grown people handle them with care, they do the same, and do not repine when valuable dolls are put away in boxes in the *godowns,* and only brought out for this, their special festival.

The origin of the celebration lay in the devotion of the people to an always invisible sovereign. For many centuries the Emperor and Empress were never beheld by any but a few favoured courtiers who shared the seclusion in which they were kept by the all-powerful Regents. So their loyal subjects made images of them, dressed in State garments, and surrounded by all the pomp and luxury due to their exalted rank. In the flowery springtime the images were displayed and worshipped throughout the land with the most eager homage. Even the language retains the impress of this loyalty; for the expression invariably used in regard to beholding the sovereign is not to *see,* but to worship.

I have been paying a visit to the little daughter of one of the great nobles. It was her mother's reception day, and beside the tea-cups on the pretty tea-table stood small bottles of a thick white wine, only used for this festival; I had only been in the room a few minutes, when she said, "Would you like to see the dolls? Pray forgive me for putting you to the trouble of going to another room." Then the heroine of the moment, a tiny girl of five, stepped forward and offered to lead me in. She was dressed in sapphire-coloured crape, shading from pale blue at the foot to dark purple at the shoulder, embroidered in gold in lovely patterns, and girdled with royal scarlet and gold; her hair, gathered in a shining knot on the top of her head, was held in place with jewelled pins; and there was a distinct touch of rouge on either round cheek. With perfect gravity she took my hand, and led me into the farther room, where a wonderful show met my eyes. On rising shelves, covered with crimson damask, several hundreds of dolls were arranged, with all the furniture and belongings that the most ambitious doll-lover could dream of. In most instances an emperor and empress were sitting on their thrones surrounded by their entire court. There were generals, prime ministers, musicians, dancers, all in the costume of a long-past day; the chairs and stools, painted screens, gold lacquer cups and utensils, musical instruments, and weapons of war were all carried out with a reckless expense and patient perfection surpassing the finest antique work of the West. It is very strange to see modern French and English toys among these splendid curios; but this little lady is cosmopolitan in her tastes, and takes special delight in creatures who will walk or sing when they are wound up with a key. After admiring everything, and congratulating her on the arrangement of the show, I asked which were her favourites out of all the vast collection of dolls. With true Japanese breeding she at once pointed to a china baby floating in a bath-tub, which she received from me last Christmas, and then, after a moment's hesitation, to a gorgeous Parisienne sent to her by the wife of the French Minister. This precocious tact so took away my breath that it was hard to find words to express proper admiration of the dolls' country house with gardens, farms, lakes, and pine trees all complete which she showed me in another room. Real flowers had been planted round it in light earth brought up for the purpose; and her mother, when I returned to the drawing-room, told me that "Nobu cho" arranged this part of the show entirely by herself.

The Japanese girl! She is a creature of so many attractive contradictions, with her warm heart, her quick brain, and her terribly narrow experience; with her submissions and self-effacements which have become second nature, and her brave revolts when first nature takes the upper hand again and courage is too strong for custom—perhaps it is too soon yet for me to speak of her to any purpose, and yet I want to tell you how deeply she interests me, how I believe in her, and hope for her in the new developments which the next few years will bring forth. The books I have read on Japan have always had a great deal to say about the *musumë,* the pretty, plebeian tea-house girl, or the *geisha,* the artist, the dancer, the witty, brilliant hetaira of Japan. I suppose these are about as unrepresentative of the normal Japanese woman as a music-hall singer would be of the European sister of charity. That they are very much less objectionable than the corresponding classes at home is doubtless due to the innate refinement of the Japanese woman; but what a gulf is set between them and the girls of whom I would speak—girls surrounded with punctilious care, and brought up with one inflexible standard always kept before their eyes, the whole law of Duty! Inclination may never govern their conduct after they have arrived at years of reason, early reached in Japan; and if they are the brightest children, the most faithful wives, the most devoted mothers, always serene, industrious, smiling, it surely is because Duty is justified of her children.

I think that the simple unfettered life led by the little children here gives the girls a happy foundation to start on, as it were. There is no scolding and punishing, no nursery disgrace, no shutting away of the little ones day after day in dull nurseries with selfish, half-educated women, whose mere daily society means torture to a sensitive well-born child. Here, children are always welcome; they come and go as they like, are spoilt, if love means spoiling, by father and mother, relations and servants; but they grow imperceptibly in the right shape; they mould their thoughts and expressions on those of the sovereigns of the home; and one day, without wrench or effort, the little girl is grown into a thoughtful helpful woman, bent on following the examples of good women gone before her. Very gently but persistently one lesson has been preached to her ever since language meant anything in her ears,—"Give up, love, help others, efface thyself." In real womanliness, which I take to mean a high combination of sense and sweetness, valour and humility, the Japanese lady ranks with any woman in the world, and passes before most of them.

Her lot as a child and as a young girl is an exceptionally happy one; but it cannot be denied that marriage often brings distinct hardship with it. The mother-in-law is apt to be exigent in the extreme, for, by the time she has reached that dignity, a woman's duties are considered over, the young people must provide for her comfort and amusement, and, in the lower classes especially, it does sometimes happen that a woman who has worked hard all her life and suddenly finds herself comparatively unoccupied, becomes fretful, difficult, and makes the young wife's life anything but a happy one. Also, mothers are mothers all the world over; and where is the woman who ever thought her son's wife good enough for him?

An amusing instance of the clashing of nationalities on this ground took place when, some years ago, an English girl married a Japanese professor, and, quite unaccustomed to the ways of the country, came out to live here, in the house of his mother, who received her kindly, but was horrified at what she considered the ignorance and flightiness of her new daughter-in-law. She especially disapproved of Mrs. N——'s having so many dresses out at the same time, wearing first one and then another, according to the fancy of the moment. Expostulation had no effect, and the young bride continued to flaunt her trousseau frocks in the old lady's face. Something had to be done; the Japanese habit is to carefully fold away the last season's dresses, and never look at them again till next year brings the need for them round. In this way the same robes may serve for ten or twenty years; and if fashions never changed, there might be a good deal to say for the custom. Old Madame N—— at any rate made up her mind that it should be enforced. She waited, generously, until her daughter-in-law had gone to a garden party in her best frock, and then she made a raid on her room, emptied drawers of underlinen and wardrobes of dresses, and carried everything away to the family *godown*, the fire-proof store-house which I described just now. I believe the scene was terrible, when Mrs. N—— returned, and found that she was expected to live on her garden-party frock and two pocket-handkerchiefs for three months. The old lady took a strong stand on her rights; but the high-spirited English girl won the day. "You got the things back?" I asked, when she told me the story. "By bedtime!" she replied. "We had a dreadful scene; but it was the last. She saw that I must have my way, and we were good friends afterwards."

I think it would be advisable for Japanese girls to assert themselves a little more when the mother-in-law is inclined to be tyrannical, and it is a pity that the elaborate books which explain the duties of women at every other stage of life do not contain some lessons as to how to treat one's juniors when one has arrived at the envied dignity of having a married son. This is the time to which every woman looks forward eagerly, the time when she will be openly honoured, and repaid for many a silent sacrifice by the devotion of the necessary daughter-in-law, and by the love of many grandchildren, the proudest ornament of old age out here. But the books and teachers are silent on this point, as far as I can discover, and are entirely taken up with telling a girl how great and all-reaching her service to her parents-in-law must be. These rank before her own father and mother, who expect to see very little of her after her marriage; she is completely absorbed into her husband's family, in which alone will she be remembered by prayers and offerings after her death. Her submission to her husband has no limit; but her husband himself owes entire submission to his parents as long as they live. He cannot interfere on behalf of his wife, or at least he very seldom ventures to do so; and if he does, the interference is more likely to do harm than good. There is one bright point towards which the poor little daughter-in-law can look hopefully. The moment she herself becomes a mother, especially if her child is a boy, she is regarded as a person of some importance, and is treated with much more consideration by the old people.

I know a charming little woman whose husband is a Government official. They are Christians, and devoted to one another; but all

145

his affection could not protect her from a kind of persecution inflicted by the selfishness of his mother. Young Mrs. S—— was in delicate health, and needed all the rest and sleep that she could get; but her mother-in-law would not allow her to go to bed until she herself was ready to retire. Like many elderly people, she slept badly, and sat up regularly, reading Japanese novels till one and two o'clock in the morning. Only when the lights were out, and the venerable O'Bassan comfortably rolled up in her *futons,* might the poor young wife seek her rest; and long before daylight she had to be on her knees by the O'Bassan's couch, offering her the early tea. It was she who had to undo the shutters, get hot water, help the old lady to dress, and go through all the services performed for us by our maids, but for the old ladies by daughters-in-law in Japan. Rich or poor, it is the same for all; and if there were an army of servants in the house, it is the weary privilege of the son's wife to attend to these details alone. In this case the result was very nearly fatal. When a son was born, Mrs. S——'s health was so broken down that it seemed unlikely she could survive, and she will all her life be a delicate woman in consequence. Let us hope that she will be merciful to her successors, remembering her own sufferings. Parents of only daughters greatly dread this ordeal for their child, and I am sure it has a great deal to do with the custom of adopting into the family a young man who is willing to take her name and merge his individuality in hers. When this happens, it is done, ostensibly, to carry on the family name and estates; but I believe the dread of a mother-in-law for the petted little daughter has much to do with it, and also the fear in her parents' hearts of having a lonely and uncomforted old age. Although the youth who consents to fill such a position is generally of a class slightly inferior to her own, happy is the girl whose life is run on these lines; her own parents will always be kind and indulgent to her, and her married life is a continuation in a fuller, more perfect sphere, of the sunny years of childhood.

One of the Legation employés married away his daughter this year. When the family came to receive the little present usual on these occasions, I asked the mother if the bridegroom seemed a good and kind young man, who would make O'Sudzu happy. "Oh yes," was the answer, "O'Sudzu will be very happy; her mother-in-law is a good woman, and has taken a great fancy to her." The bridegroom was not even mentioned. As it turned out, he proved to be either very unreasonable or very unkind; for six weeks after the wedding, our poor O'Sudzu was sent home again—divorced! I was dismayed, for we all thought that she was making a good marriage; and although she was plain, we knew that she was a good girl, and well-educated for her class.

"What has happened?" I asked in deep sympathy; for a divorce is a great misfortune to a girl, and marks her as having some distinct defect, bad temper perhaps, or clumsy hands with a habit of dropping the china, or something equally undesirable. But it turned out that poor O'Sudzu was not accused of anything so serious. Her husband came into the room one day, and found her sewing; and as he watched, she threaded her needle, holding it up to one eye as women do.

"Why do you do that?" asked the man.

"Because I see better so, honourable husband," she replied.

"Hold it up to the other eye and thread it," he commanded; and she obeyed. At least, she tried to obey and failed, being slightly more short-sighted on that side.

"Go home," he said, "and return no more. Who wants a one-eyed wife?"

So O'Sudzu came home, and her parents are now seeking for a less particular husband, who will have to be found in a lower class than the one she could marry into before she was divorced.*

There is an old saying in Japan that "Flame is the flower of Yedo"; that flower has bloomed with terrible profusion of late. The end of last month and the beginning of this were marked by some fearfully destructive fires in Tokyo, and whole districts are still lying bare and black, as if people were almost afraid to rebuild on the same spot. I fancy, too, there is some hesitation in the public mind as to the best material for building under present conditions. These fierce fires have always been the curse of Tokyo, the city of wood and bamboo and paper. In old times they were so much a part of life that a whole code of customs grew up round them, regulated by severe etiquette: there was only one costume in which it was proper to assist at a fire,

*AUTHOR'S NOTE: The position of married women has been greatly improved by the new laws which have come into force since these words were written.

147

and this was a particularly showy and elaborate one; there is a whole nomenclature in which every variety of fire is described by a different name—one word expresses a fire kindled by intention, another the accidental outbreak, another the fire caught from the next house, another that kindled by a falling spark, and so on. There was special music, a kind of religious hymn, which was sung by the firemen at their work, and several of their number were told off to stand on the roof with standards on which were painted sacred and terrible symbols, intended to frighten the demons of the flames and arrest their farther progress. Although the fires seem to us both frequent and terrible, the Japanese say that they were still more so twenty years ago, when some part of Tokyo was in flames every night of the week. In the old days there was nothing to quench a fire but hand-buckets, filled from the nearest moat; now there are fire-engine stations all over the city, and a constant watch is kept over each district. One of these stands on the edge of the moat, very near our own gates. It consists of a building for the fire-engine, a small guard-room, and an enormous ladder, set upright in the ground, crowned by a railed platform, very much like the crow's-nest in an old man-of-war. On a transverse beam above the platform hangs a bronze bell, on which the watchman strikes the first signal of any conflagration. The climb to this eyrie looks like a thing of peril; but the wiry fireman runs up like a cat, and then sits on the top rung of the ladder, swinging his legs with splendid indifference over the sixty feet of empty air between him and the ground. When an outbreak is discerned, he strikes his bell, one stroke if it is in the district of his station, two if it is in the next, and so on. Often in the quiet night one is waked up by that first ominous stroke, and then one sits up, listening breathlessly for the next. If there is no second one, the household is astir in a moment; for that might mean fire in our close vicinity.

An old resident in Tokyo tells me that he witnessed one or two of the almost historical fires which occurred here in the early days of foreign intrusion. He and others were students in the Legation when it was established in Takanawa, and, as we have seen, somewhat ineffectually guarded by Japanese troops. The students, mere boys of eighteen and nineteen, were forbidden to leave the compound without an escort, which usually consisted of four or five native soldiers, and at least one English mounted constable; but naturally enough their chief joy was to escape from all this supervision and constraint by saddling their own horses and slipping out unseen to wander at will about the picturesque town. If they met no Daimyo's procession, they were fairly safe; but once or twice they had narrow escapes, and were thankful to gallop back to the friendly shelter of the compound, where nothing worse than a serious reprimand was in store for them. When great fires occurred in the city, the students always managed to see them; and my friend tells me that nothing could be more impressive than the quietness and order with which everything was done to save property, to help neighbours, but, above all, to bring the children into safety. A certain number of men banded together for this purpose, and going through the streets of the district, where perhaps the danger, still unknown, might at any moment become acute, would knock at every door, saying, "A fire has begun; give us the children!" And all the little ones were brought out (the elder ones carrying the babies), and at once took their places in the orderly procession, walking nine or ten abreast, with a man at the end of every fifth or sixth row to keep the order; and so the small people marched away in regiments of three or four hundred at a time, singing little songs to keep their spirits up, and showing no fear in their perfect confidence that they would be protected. There would be no risk of losing a child, since each one wears a label with its name and address hung round its neck, in case of accidents. When the children were gone, it was an easy matter for the parents to collect their household goods into bundles and carry them away if necessary. The most precious objects are the tablets of the ancestors in the household shrine. These must be saved before any other properties, and there is a saying that if the tablets are saved all is saved, but if they are lost nothing will be rescued. I have seen people sitting on their doorsteps with everything portable tied in cloths or piled on a hand-cart, ready to go if the flames or the almost equally destructive hose came too near, but unwilling to leave their houses till the last moment. The furnishings of a Japanese house are so few and simple that they are easily transported; but the delicate wood, the dainty mats, and treasured screens always suffer in these unexpected journeys. If the fire is very sudden and near, there is an indiscriminate rush to save property the moment the children

149

have been removed; and thieves come sometimes in the guise of neighbours, to help themselves to valuable things, which are never seen again. But in general, great kindness is shown to the sufferers, and a whole quarter will open its houses to shelter the people who have been deprived of their homes, and large subscriptions are got up to help repair the damages. The Emperor and Empress have sent a thousand yen, and Prince Haru two hundred, in aid of the sufferers from the late fires here. There is a common saying that these catastrophes occur when the carpenters (who are the universal builders) are out of work; but one must hope that this is a calumny, merely inspired by the fact that they are the only class who benefit by the misfortune. The ground is hardly cold before the carpenters are at work, rebuilding the dwellings which have been destroyed; and it is useless to try to get any carpentering done in other ways at that time; the Kinoshita San is better employed, and I must wait for my wardrobe or table till he is free.

All this consumption of wood must entail a serious drain on the timber resources of the country, and must also mean very heavy expense to somebody. I believe it is possible to insure; but the premium is so high that it puts such precautions quite beyond the reach of the masses, who are, as it seems to me, extraordinarily careless of fire-risk already. The *hibachi,* a box lined with iron, or fire-proof clay, and filled with glowing charcoal rising out of a bed of fine white ashes, serves for tea-making and pipe-lighting chiefly. It is carried from place to place as it is wanted, and has often been the cause of accidents through some end of paper or drapery which floats into it unnoticed and causes an instant flare. The stationary fire in the floor of the room is less dangerous, being deeper and larger. This is called the *kotatsu,* and is used for cooking; an iron pot hangs over it on a chain in the poorer houses, and it forms a center of warmth round which the family spread their beds at night. A fruitful source of fire is the kerosene lamp, a cheap and brittle thing, so universally used that there is hardly a house in Tokyo without it. One of these flimsy glass lamps is often placed on a bamboo stand, quite a yard high, and so slender that the slightest touch will send it over. Round this the whole family gather closely, so as to get light for the work which they often carry on till very late at night. Just as they are all intent on the task in hand, perhaps an earthquake shock is felt, and in five seconds every one is in the street, half paralysed with terror, quite forgetting the lamp on its frail stand. The earthquake has overturned it, and by the time any one gathers courage to return, everything is in a blaze.

I find that here, as in South America, the worst damage done during an earthquake is generally caused by its follower, fire; and in the constant shocks which enliven our existence we always fly to the lamps first, and put them out if the vibrations continue. Were it not for the earthquakes, Tokyo would soon be a city of bricks and mortar, and the picturesque, inflammable, wooden houses would disappear; but the earthquakes will keep the old fashion in dwellings long alive, I fancy The brick house behaves far more violently during the shocks, and does more harm when it is injured. The wooden one can toss and shake a good deal before being really shattered, and there are many instances on record when, the wooden pillars having given way, the peaked roof sank on the ground, enclosing the inmates as in a hen-coop.

It has often been said that the more one sees, or rather feels, of earthquakes, the less one likes them; the Japanese take every other catastrophe with calm philosophy, but the earthquakes really cause panic to every class of the community. It is said that many of the rich people who have built themselves beautiful stone houses, furnished with every possible luxury, steal out of them after dark, to sleep in some old pavilion nearer to the kindly ground.

Tokyo, April, 1890

I have greatly envied the chiefs of missions who were invited by the Emperor to attend the Spring Manœuvres, the first that have been carried out under his own eyes. A great deal of enthusiasm was manifested, when it was announced that the Emperor intended to witness the sham fights himself. It is still and always will be here considered a miracle of graciousness, when he condescends to show himself to his subjects; and there is no mistake about the fervent loyalty of all classes to the person of the sovereign, however opposed they may be to one another. The arrangements were in consequence made on a much more important scale than usual, and a larger number of men were employed, fifty thousand being massed near Nagoya, besides those on board the battle-ships.

The Emperor left for Nagoya on March 28th, and the Empress and Empress-Dowager both accompanied him to the station to see him off. The plan of the manœuvres was based on the supposition that an enemy, crossing the Pacific, had struck at the coast between the two points of Kii and Izu, thus attempting to separate the country's forces and resources. The attacking body in consequence landed at Wakayama at the mouth of the Inland Sea, and tried to penetrate to Osaka and Isé. To turn them aside was the task of the defending force, called the Eastern Army; and a great deal of very smart work was done, which—I could not have understood, but simply longed to see! The weather was awful; but the various battles were fought out with zeal and perseverance, the organisation and commissariat appear to have been excellent, and if the gallant Army of the East was beaten, it had the consolation of knowing that its conquerors were brothers and compatriots. Prince Arisugawa, who framed the official report of the manœuvres, was not sparing of either praise or blame where he thought it was deserved; but the report was sufficiently favourable to give the Emperor grounds for pronouncing himself wholly satisfied with the conduct of the troops and the ships, adding a little word at the end of his speech to the effect that he hoped they would do even better in time to come. Among the battle-ships the *Takachiho* and the *Naniwa* seem to have carried themselves extremely well, and the torpedo-boats did very good service.

Before the Emperor went to the manœuvres, he had inaugurated the great Exhibition at Uyeno, in order that on April 1st it might be thrown open to the public. There was rather an imposing ceremony for the opening, all the Court as well as Japanese and foreign officials assisting; but it was amusing to find that the exhibits were in no way ready to be looked at. They were still lying about the galleries in packing-cases, and it seemed probable that weeks must pass before there could be much pleasure in wandering through the huge courts. Much to every one's surprise, however, the Emperor's visit and the accompanying ceremony (conducted in a temporary pavilion outside the Exhibition building) seem to have given an impetus to the work, and in a few days after that time a really splendid show of Japanese art-work was all in order to be admired, and—for rich people—acquired. It is a great pity that so little announcement or advertising of the Exhibition was done abroad; for many art-lovers would, I am sure, have taken great pains to see this collection of the modern produce of Japan. That it is modern is perhaps its most characteristic feature, and shows conclusively that Japan has not lost her cunning; for the enamels and carvings, the silks and the embroideries, are as fine and perfect as any of the recognised models of the best ancient periods. There are only two things in which the old work seems finer than anything the best modern artists can produce, and these are lacquer and sword-blades. I am in the minority in my opinion of modern lacquer, for such judges as Captain Brinkley consider the modern as quite equal in merit to the old. But there is hardly time to notice this among the exhibits at Uyeno, which are so many, and, alas! so unsatisfactorily arranged that it takes several visits to get a good idea of them. The thing which seems to strike the strongest note in the whole is the new school of painting which has been growing up here, on a battlefield, as it were, so violent was the oppostion it encountered from the conservatives, who cling tenaciously to the old school, while their work seldom shows any of the vigour and freshness which made the work of the old masters in Japan so admirable. The warcry of these Eastern pre-Raphaelites is that nothing can be good which departs in any way from the models created and the canons laid down when Japanese art stood at its highest. Of course this involves both a philosophical contradiction and a confession of weakness. That which is stationary in art or science, or morals, is already on the decline; and the advance party of Japanese artists refuse to admit that the present cannot equal and outdo the past. The use of oil-colours, for instance, is condemned by the purists, because their predecessors have never made use of them; the new school of painters delight in the richness and freedom of tint thus placed at their command, and are producing works which would take a respectable place in modern exhibitions in Europe. I have a series of little oil landscapes by an artist called Yanagi which I should never wish to part with. Fresh and clear and truthful, they put the more simple effects of landscape in Japan absolutely before one, and compare more than favourably with a number of paintings by European artists which hang beside them on our walls.

But strongly as I sympathise with the artistic courage which thus comes forward and asks to be judged by European standards, I confess that where mere private taste is concerned I prefer the original Japanese methods for many reasons; the chief one being that they express ideas and deal with subjects that no other art has touched, and which cannot be even approached through the rich and heavy medium of oil-colours. The transparency and spontaneousness of the old paintings on silk, where perhaps one wash of thin dryish water-colour had to express unfathomed perspectives of cloud or depths of forest, are to me true portraits of the spirit of Nature here; the heavy materials of oil and canvas can only produce her exterior lines, a faithful likeness of a body as it were, with the informing soul left out of the picture. Please do not accuse me of talking nonsense. Nature has both body and spirit like our other friends, and she is not always pressing the spirit on our notice, nor do we always wish to see it; sometimes we are more in the mood for the opulent beauty of matter than for the delicate half-expressed secrets of soul, which imply and command a certain silence and peace and humility before they can be understood. But there are times, thank Heaven! when we can really close the doors of our mind to racket, and emulation, and all the noises of the century; and then—the sweep of a single grass blade on the breeze suffices for our direction; the sight of the blossom shedding its petals softly on the running water that carries them away soothes sorrow into peace; the glory of blown autumn leaves against a golden sunset warms a chilled and tired heart; panting with the dustiness of our daily road we are suddenly cooled and refreshed by the view of a forest glade veiled in wet mists that seem to fall on the brow like holy water from holy hands; and all these things, I venture to say, can only be expressed and brought before us by the old spirit and the old methods of Japan.

There hangs a little scroll picture in my sitting-room which I would not exchange for a Claude* if mere love turned the scale. It

*Lorrain Claude(1600–1682), French landscape painter, draughtsman, and etcher.

has helped me through many long hours of enforced idleness, and has often made pain lighter to bear. It shows a woodland stream overhung by the branches of a wild cherry tree, in bloom and past the blooming; for the flowers are raining down on the stream, blown sideways by the breeze that is shaking the bough. Beyond, a point of rock stands up, and makes a swirl in the stream, and a few of the petals are washing against it like the froth of a ripple. That is all, but it is much. I can almost hear the tinkle of the stream, the delicate hum of the flowers and water against the stone; and when day falls and the evening comes on warm and languid already, the breeze that is shedding the blossoms seems to be whispering through the room.

There is a new art in Japan in which these ethereally delicate effects are well worked out, and that is in the cut velvet pictures which, little known till a very few years ago, have reached great beauty and perfection. The fabric is of extreme fineness, and lends itself well to such details as the plumage of birds or the foliage of trees. I have seen some charming snow scenes worked in this, and groups of wild duck, where the colours were a pure pleasure to behold. My feminine appreciation, however, goes out to the embroideries, which far surpass any that I have ever seen, although we have been collecting them for years. There are, among other things, two *portières* in the Exhibition, about ten feet long and four or five feet wide. The whole of the ground is worked in a warm fawn tint, the stitches consisting of threads of silk laid close together in damasklike patterns, which only show themselves when the surface breaks in the light; these threads are held in place by stitches of a much finer silk at intervals of a millimetre apart, and alternating, so that they make the effect of a slight mottling of the whole background. On one is worked a maze of pine-tree branches, so full and strong in design, so tender and deep in colouring, that they do not affect one like pictured branches, but as the real tree, with all its significance of strength and ruggedness, its friendly needles that do not hurt, its resinous odour and sticky bark. The other curtain, against the same background, pictures a mass of tiger lilies and chrysanthemums, tossing over a bamboo lattice gate in the sunshine, while at the foot of the hedge grow docks and common plants; the stitches vary according to the surface and thickness which they are intended to portray (and splendid effects are produced by merely changing the direction of the thread), and from end to end the great curtain is one stretch of patient perfect work.

It would only weary you, if I went through a list of productions which you can never see. There is a quality in Japanese art which cannot be conveyed by description. When I speak of ivory-carving, people at home think of Hong Kong glove-boxes and brush-backs, or of the Chinese pagodas under glass in the houses of our grand-mothers. Here it is used for the figures of men and women, birds and beasts; and it lends itself to the most subtle shades of expression, to the closest imitation of nature. I saw a group the other day, the figure of a young woman turning to smile at a child who had just run to catch at her robe, and was holding up a bunch of flowers to-wards her. The thing was what we have seen a thousand times, a young mother moving through her house, arrested by an eager little one with an offering to make. One almost heard the cry of the child as he caught at her robe and held up his flowers, half withered in the little hot palm; her face was so lifelike that it seemed to change expression as one looked at it; the mouth was serious, but the eyes were smiling down on the boy in affectionate amusement. When I say that the figure was not more than twelve inches high, you will understand how fine the work must be which can convey such com-pleteness of expression in these miniature proportions. The ivory, when used in this way, is slightly coloured (warmed would be a better word) where face and flesh tints are needed, and the finely wrought fabric of the draperies sometimes flushes into pink or pale primrose; but if there is colouring, it is so delicate that one hardly realises it at first, so imperceptibly does it melt into the warm pale-ness of the ivory.

The enamels are many and beautiful, and there is no shadow of doubt that modern enamel in every way surpasses the old. There are two very distinct styles in the modern enamel, the Kyoto makers preferring to work the true cloisonné, where the design is laid on in gold or copper wire in geometrical (or at any rate purely decora-tive) patterns of bewildering fineness, the colour being applied to the interstices, and often showing the gold surface of the foundation through its shimmering and jewel-like tints. This is the most costly form of modern enamel, and large sums are given for small pieces of it, while the larger ones can only be bought by very rich people. The surface of the finest cloisonné is so perfect that I think I should know it in the dark by the touch alone; and there is no more trace of the original workmanship than if the elaborately patterned surface were the bowl of a spoon.

The Tokyo enameller works on different lines, and produces panels which look like fine paintings on porcelain (landscapes, birds, or animals are the favourite subjects for these), or monochrome vases and dishes, which are a triumph of workmanship, but convey at a little distance no more than the impression of delicate china which carries no particular value. Of course on close inspection the brilliant quality of the colour and its perfect surface proclaim the identity of the piece; but on the whole I care more for the Kyoto than for the Tokyo enamel. Of the latter, however, I have two pieces which I greatly prize. They are rather tall vases, in the deepest sang-de-boeuf enamel, ornamented by heads of grass (those tall crimson grasses which smother the meadows in the Tyrol) growing up from the base, and hovered over by shadowy butterflies. Our old Chinese cloisonné looks heavy and laboured beside all this easy perfection and smoothness; and I think the only piece I still care about is a very ancient bowl, where the *cloisons* were cut deep in the original copper, and then filled up with enamel. It is strange that the chief artists in Kyoto and Tokyo both bear the name of Namikawa, though I believe they are not related.

I have turned out of *Ichiban,* and am inhabiting one of the smaller houses in the compound during the visit of the Duke and Duchess of Connaught,* who arrived here from Shanghai on the 15th, and came at once to Tokyo as a convenient starting-point for their excursions. They brought a good many people with them, and we thought it better to give up our house entirely to them, since, although it looks large, the number of guest-rooms is limited,

*Prince Arthur, Duke of Connaught (1850–1942), third son of Queen Victoria. In 1879 he married Princess Louise, daughter of Prince Frederick Charles Nicholas of Prussia (known as the Red Prince). The Duke of Connaught's career in the British army led him to serve in Egypt and in India. He was promoted to the rank of Lieutenant General in 1889.

and there is absolutely no accommodation for foreign servants. I took this opportunity to do away with the horrible English wall-papers with which the Board of Works had disfigured the rooms, and covered the walls with Japanese papers, slightly embossed with free flower patterns, warm white in tint and with a satinlike surface, which made the rooms look fresh and gay. I brought out a quantity of English cretonnes when I came; but I have never been able to look at them after seeing the Japanese cotton fabrics with their pure colours and true designs, so the cretonnes have disappeared, and are replaced by cool-looking crapes. The Duchess's room was very pretty, all the draperies being soft pink crape showered with cherry blossoms, the carpet dove-colour and the silk quilts and cush-ions pale pink lined with robin's-egg blue. And the cherry blossoms came out to greet the visitors; the gardens were forests of pink rose-like blooms, and I had all the house filled with the branches, so that every place was a bower. The Duchess was delightfully enthusiastic about them, and said that her blossom bedroom was the prettiest she had ever slept in.

Yes, the cherry blossoms are here; and I hope you will not think me wanting in loyalty if I say that they have been almost more of an excitement to me than the royal visitors. I have been very ailing all the spring, and I suppose flowers mean more to me than they do when I am running about and constantly occupied. And this is my first sight of the glory of Japan; for the crown of the year has come at last, and the country greets its beloved Empress's birthday by an outburst of bewildering beauty such as no words can convey to those who have not seen it for themselves. Tokyo is the city of cherry blossoms; every avenue is planted with them in full, close-set rows; every garden boasts its carefully nurtured trees; over the river at Mukojima they dip to the water, and spread away inland like a rosy tidal wave; and the great park at Uyeno seems to have caught the sunset clouds of a hundred skies, and kept them captive along its wide forest ways. In their capricious glory, the double cherry blossoms surpass every other splendour of nature; and it seems but right and just that, during the week or two when they transfigure the world, people should flock, day after day, to look at them, and store up the recollection of their loveliness until next year shall bring it round again. There is a tall grove of cherry trees in my garden, and as I look from my upper window I see the soft branches moving against the sky, and far away, rosy white as they, Fujiyama, the queen of mountains, flushing in the sunset. Then life seems full of promises and peace. The peace will remain; and if the promises are not all fulfilled, it will be because our life is a beginning whose end is the summer of another clime, and therefore, like the spring, it must be here "no perfect thing."

But I must return to my chronicle, which will probably interest you more than cherry-blossom metaphysics. Everybody except myself (I was too ill to travel) went down to Yokohama to meet the Duke and Duchess. The *Ancona* got in half an hour before she was expected; but warning of the arrival was given by the guns of the forts and those of the battle-ships in port. The visitors landed at the Admiralty Hatoba (or quay), where they were met by those of our people who had not gone on board; but they were officially received at the station, where the British residents presented an address of welcome, and a bouquet from the Yokohama ladies was given to the Duchess by Madgie M——. The Duchess was much struck with the wonderful little face. As the royal visitors had been rather overwhelmed with entertainments given them in Shanghai and Hong Kong, the English people here wisely refrained from taking up their time in that way, and they were left free to devote it all to sight-seeing, as of course they wished to do.

The Duchess, indeed, is an ardent sight-seer, and seems to have only one dread; namely, that she should miss some interesting experience which the ordinary traveller would ferret out for himself. Before the party arrived, word was sent that they wished to travel quite unofficially so as to have all possible freedom for sight-seeing; and this desire of theirs tallied with H——'s feeling that it was better for them, in the excited state of the country, not to accept any very pompous Imperial or official hospitality which could attract the unwelcome attentions of the fanatics and the *soshi*. The Emperor would have wished them to be his guests during the whole of their stay, and proposed to put them up in the Enryō Kwan Palace; but in view of their own desire to move about freely, and because of one rather embarrassing misunderstanding in the past, it was thought better that they should not accept the gracious invitation in its entirety. The misunderstanding rose from an event which has never been explained, but which made a most painful impression in Japan. At the time of the Queen's Jubilee in 1887, Prince Komatsu, the Imperial Prince nearest to the throne, went to England to take the Grand Star of the Chrysanthemum to the Prince of Wales, who unfortunately never returned the visit, though Prince Komatsu stayed some time in England. The Princess accompanied him, but very little attention was shown to the Emperor's cousin; and this was the more deplorable because when the Duke of Clarence and the Duke of York had visited Japan some time before, they were received with open arms, honours and kindness were showered upon them, and nothing was left undone which could add to the pleasure of their stay. All this added to the kind significance of the Emperor's invitation, but seemed to point towards declining to put our royal family under still heavier obligations to his Majesty while those already existing had not received ordinary recognition.

At all events the Duke and Duchess have made the most of their liberty, and from the moment they arrived in Tokyo refused to have anything to do with the Court carriages which were sent every morning to carry them about. They did consent to come up from Shimbashi Station in these pretty glass coaches, but an hour after their arrival insisted on going out in jinrikshas, a long procession through the dust, to see the curio shops. Public jinrikshas correspond to omnibuses in London, and official people do not use them. The private jinriksha may be a very dainty and luxurious little affair; but as we ourselves always use carriages, we only keep one such private perambulator for our English servants, and when nine were ordered for the royal party they had to be brought in from the nearest stand in the street, with their dusty bare-legged coolies, who were of course radiant with pride at being employed on such distinguished service.

Two chamberlains and an Imperial equerry have been detailed off to accompany the Duke and Duchess wherever they go. One of these gentlemen pleaded sudden indisposition, and disappeared in the direction of the Palace when the jinrikshas were ordered; the others meekly took their places in the procession with an expression of resigned despair. The Court coachman looked on in profound

160

amazement, and drove slowly after the disappearing chamberlain; and even Inspector Peacock,* the head of the escort, the Chief's right hand in numberless ways, shook his head disapprovingly, and was heard to say it was "most unusual," the strongest term of disapprobation in his vocabulary.

From that moment the visitors have been flying from one sight to another with an energy and persistency which are rather surprising when one considers that they have been for so long in what is supposed to be an enervating climate. Everything that could be "done" from Tokyo has been done thoroughly—Kamakura, Nikko, Hakone, Miyanoshita, Atami; from Miyanoshita the Duchess walked most of the way to Atami over the route which we took in the heavy snow last December. To be sure the road is easier in coming from Miyanoshita than in going to it, since the worst part of the stiff climb up to the Ten Province Stone is an easy drop if one is coming down from it; but a respectable walk of nearly sixteen miles remains, and the Duchess used her chair and coolies very little. I think she rather surprised the small foreign community by the extreme plainness of her dress, generally a light flannel coat and skirt (made by her sewing-maid) and a serviceable sailor hat. She is daintily neat and trim, and when she clicks her little heels together and bows straight from the waist reminds one irresistibly of a smart German officer. Soldierliness is in the blood after all, and the daughter of the Red Prince has an honest right to her share. She is not exactly pretty, but holds herself admirably, and looks so young that her rather shy stiff manner seems to suit the light girlish figure and the erect little head. She is everything that is kind and pleasant, and has the happy gift of getting amusement out of all the vicissitudes of travel, even rough inns and bad weather, and has managed to see more in her short visit than hundreds of people who have stayed months and years in the country.

*AUTHOR'S NOTE: Inspector Peter Peacock is a beloved and familiar figure in the British community in Japan, and has seen long service there. He joined the escort in February, 1867, and has served under Sir Harry Parkes, Sir Francis Plunkett, Mr. Hugh Fraser, The Hon. Le Poer Trench, and Sir Ernest Satow.— 1898.

It is a year since we landed, and I am sure I have not yet seen half the things which our energetic visitors managed to "do" before they left. That which most amused the Duke was, I think, a Japanese play, or that part of it which it is possible to see in one afternoon. Danjuro Ichikawa* was acting one of his great parts, in which he assumes four or five characters of men and women, youth and age, all of which he personates so entirely that it seems impossible to believe that he is anything but what he appears to be at the moment. He is a remarkably tall and gaunt-looking man, about fifty years old, rather like Henry Irving in his general appearance; and yet he personates a dancing-girl, an old woman, a boy, a court lady, with the most bewildering realism. All the women's parts are played by boys or men, in Japan. The Japanese practice of wearing a mask, or a partial mask, on the stage is of course a notable help towards the perfection of the disguise; but it would be easier to make up the face of a *geisha* than to imitate her dancing, with its curious flowing movements like the curves of a pennon on the wind, its sudden agile turns, changing the point of gravity with such rapidity and precision that the dancer's body seems to vibrate like a bow-string whence the shaft has but now sped.

A great actor in Japan is courted and flattered even as in England, openly and secretly. Many a girl in the seclusion of an aristocratic household is never allowed to make acquaintance with a man who is not a near relation; but she is taken to the theatre perhaps once in her life to see some exceptionally moral play, and sits through the whole day in the open box with her father and mother, drinking in all the speeches of the hero on the stage, admiring his courage, his beauty, rejoicing in his triumphs, weeping for his misfortunes. Who can be surprised when the poor child falls in love with the actor, writes to him, bribes her maid to carry presents to him, presents of flowers and fruit and poems, all significant of the most profound devotion and admiration? Love is such a strange thing here. It passes by nine hundred and ninety-nine women, and singles out one poor little creature, who suddenly becomes a heroine, an

---

*Ichikawa Danjūrō, a name used by Kabuki actors for generations.

ideal, a canonised saint of love, throwing the world and life and honour at its feet in a kind of glory of self-annihilation, and as often as not obtaining such martyrdom as death for its sake can give. It is whispered that Danjuro has been much loved; however that may be, he is wonderfully kind and good to his family, maintaining a whole tribe of relations, who keep him poor in spite of his great popularity, and who live on his bounty with kindly indulgence, as is the manner of people here when one member of the family is earning large sums of money.

The Duke was delighted with his acting and dancing, and sent for him to thank him for the pleasure he had given. Danjuro was much gratified, especially by being compared to Henry Irving, of whom he said he had heard much and greatly desired to see. The Duke told him that he ought to come to Europe; but Danjuro replied rather sadly that he should never have time for that, and of course he deprecated his own attainments, as polite people have to do here. Shortly after the interview he sent a present to his Royal Highness, consisting of two plants of rare chrysanthemums in full bloom, a costly offering at this season, and in Tokyo, where valued plants command a price unknown in Europe.

The Duke has bought some beautiful things at the Exhibition, notably two splendid vases to take to the Queen. As nothing may be carried away until the Exhibition closes, there was some little trouble to induce the authorities to allow the fairings to be packed; but all has been made right now. He collected also some beautiful embroideries, *kimonos,* and *fukusas** as presents for various relations; and both he and the Duchess have spent so much on curios in both Tokyo and Kyoto that their visit will long be remembered by the curio-dealers. The record buyer of last year was Mr. Liberty,† who is reported to have spent £25,000 in Japan, and whose influence was felt in a more elevating way; for he had the courage to tell the Japanese that in certain products, especially in their brocades and silks, they were following debased models and losing their sense of beauty by attempting to Europeanise the designs and colours.

*Square pieces of cloth used to wrap gifts. Another type of cloth wrapping that also might have been included with *fukusa* is called a *furoshiki* and is used to wrap up belongings for ease in carrying.

†Liberty's still has a large, high-quality store on Regent Street in London.

They seem to have taken his words to heart, for those shown in the Exhibition are purely satisfactory.

The laying of one foundation stone was asked of the Duchess; and I think she felt that the loyal Britishers had on the whole been pretty forbearing. The stone was the beginning of a kind of Cottage Hospital connected with the Anglican Mission School of St. Hilda's. The ladies who keep the school have one or two dispensaries in the town, which are widely resorted to by the sick poor; and it is thought that much good may be done by this little hospital, which is to start with twelve beds. I do not sympathise greatly with the objects of the school, which only receives girls of a class who can pay very highly, and gives them, in secular teaching, only that which they could have, on a very much higher scale, in the various high schools where the best foreign teachers are employed. The Christian element, although enforced by Bible and catechism lessons, appears most strongly in a kind of rough contempt for all the devout traditions of the Japanese. Ancestor worship, which is such a tremendous factor in Japanese life, instead of being transformed into tender and prayerful remembrance of the dead and a desire to imitate their virtues, is stigmatised as idolatry, and the Protestant dogma regarding departed spirits is put forward in all its brutality as the only recognised truth. No one who has not lived among them can imagine how shocking this is to the feelings of the Japanese; for with them parental and filial devotion rank as the chief virtues, and make the harmony of the family. Minor prejudices and refinements, the duties of hospitality and of friendship, the thousand gentlenesses which give so much beauty to the family life of the Japanese—these, instead of being wisely utilised and encouraged, are pushed aside, ridden over rough-shod, in the attempt to transform the shy, quiet Japanese maiden into the healthy, selfish, rough-and-tumble school-girl of our own clime. The education seems to have little to do with the life which awaits the pupil as soon as she returns to her own home. As for morality, consideration for others, scrupulous cleanliness, duty, economy—all these are as strongly insisted on in Japanese education as in our own, and I think more successfully instilled than in any ordinary English school. I hope I am not being unjust to people for whom I have the greatest personal respect; but I must say that the manners and appearance of girls living in the English and American schools here do not compare favourably with those of girls brought up at home and merely attending school for a few hours in the day after the present Japanese fashion. I was painfully shocked in going over the dormitories at St. Hilda's by the dirty and untidy appearance of the cubicles where the girls slept, contrasting strangely with the expensive finery which they are encouraged to wear; and, system for system, the Anglican one, costly as it is, compares badly with that adopted in our convent schools, where the most rigid economy has to be practised, and considerations of comfort must take a secondary place. A room built full of small cubicles, with barely space to pass along the passage into which they open, gives an impression of stuffiness and darkness very different from the huge upper space at Tsukiji, for instance, where one whole wall is a window opening on a verandah as long as the house, where only white dimity curtains divide the beds, and the air is fresh and sweet on the hottest day. Also, pagan or Christian, I think the girls are glad to see, the first thing in the morning when the sun strikes on it gaily, and the last at night when the little lamp burns low, the figure of the Mother with the Infant in her arms, and the pictured angels, who, as they are told, stand by every white bed all night long, to keep harm away. It would be strange, indeed, if the desolate untidy cell without a single symbol of prayer or sweetness proved a better growing ground for a young girl's heart and soul.

But the Hospital is a different matter, a thing in the management of which Englishwomen usually excel; and I wish it God-speed with all my heart. I am sure the fact that the Duchess of Connaught laid the first stone and said so many pleasant things about it will help it on with its subscriptions. That ceremony took place in a pause between a flight back from Nikko and one off to Kyoto, whence the Duke and Duchess returned here and stayed a day or two, then went to Miyanoshita and Kamakura. At Kamakura they spent one night at the Kaihin-in, and left everybody delighted by their pleasant kind ways. There is very little to do at the Kamakura Hotel in the evening; and the Duchess asked if a band could not be found to play after dinner. There was none in the vicinity; and the nearest place where a band could be procured was at Yokosuka, the naval dockyard a little farther down the coast. A Japanese naval officer who was by chance in the hotel wired to Yokosuka, and the band was immediately sent up. The Duke was very much pleased with the promptness and goodwill shown, and insisted upon inviting all the other guests in the hotel to come and enjoy the music, which helped to pass an otherwise dull evening.

They got back to Tokyo in time to meet the Emperor, who came up from Kyoto on the 6th, and gave a dinner at the Palace on the 7th. Various other entertainments had been given for the royal visitors by the Princes and the Ministers. On the morning of the 8th, Prince Komatsu arrived at the Legation to return the Duke's visit, the Prince taking the place of the Emperor, who cannot pay a visit in a foreign house in his own dominion. When the Duke of Clarence and the Duke of York were here nine years ago, the Emperor called on them in person; but they were staying at one of his own palaces, the Enryō Kwan.

Prince Komatsu came, without warning, at a quarter to nine, and neither the Duke nor the Duchess was quite prepared for such an early pleasure. It was, however, the only time which could have been chosen, since they were to leave for Yokohama before eleven o'clock. Fortunately H—— was dressed, and Prince Komatsu, always the kindest and cheeriest of royalties, took everything in very good part. He brought many messages from the Emperor and Empress, and two gifts of another kind—the Grand Star of the Chrysanthemum for the Duke, and a most lovely little decoration, the Grand Star of the Crown, for the Duchess, who was very much pleased. Then all the good-byes were said, and any number of people accompanied them on board the steamer, which sailed at one o'clock for Vancouver.

In Japan they have left a charming impression, if one can judge by the outbursts of enthusiasm in the local newspapers, and by all the pleasant things said about them by the Court people and officials here. One paper says that "they showed the same kindly and courteous mien to high and low, and that people forgot the honour and only remembered the pleasure of meeting such gracious personages."

There is a sad story which illustrates a very different side of life in Japan, and which for that reason perhaps ought to be told in these letters. I do not want you to think that existence is one long series of cotillon figures out here; it can be very sad and very bitter. I do not think I was ever more sorry for anybody in my life than for a poor Canadian lady whose husband was murdered in a most horrible way a little while ago. Mr. L—— was assistant teacher at the Tokyo Eiwa Gakko, a Canadian Methodist School for boys and girls. The two divisions were quite separate, and Mr. and Mrs. L—— lived in the girls' section, as did one or two lady teachers, young Canadian girls. The school has been established a long time, and is rather a popular one, and Mr. L—— was much beloved by the scholars. They went up to Miyanoshita for the Easter holiday, and returned on April 4th, a day sooner than they had intended, owing, I think, to bad weather at Miyanoshita. The fees of the pupils had just been paid in, and there were some hundreds of dollars in a safe on the ground floor, the keys of the safe being kept by Mrs. L—— in her room. A watchman, such as we all employ, was supposed to make his round every hour through the night, to see that all was right. Only a few girls had returned, as the 5th was the day fixed for reopening after the Easter holidays, and the boys' building was entirely empty. The L——s, tired with travelling, had gone to bed early, and so had the two girl teachers, all occupying rooms that open into the same corridor. Mrs. L—— has a dear little girl, a tiny thing, who slept beside her. The watchman had gone back to his room at eleven o'clock, after making his rounds, when he was terrified by the sudden appearance there of two young men, tall and strong, wearing masks over their faces, and having their gowns drawn up through their girdles as people do here when they are preparing for rough work. They were dressed like labourers, and carried heavy sword-blades fastened to bamboo sticks. They seized and bound the man, and then asked him where the money-box was kept. He told them at once, and also where the keys were, in Mrs. L——'s room, where she and her husband and child were asleep. The watchman's account of the occurrences seems suspicious in many ways; but all the inquiries point to his having only been guilty of the worst of all crimes—abject cowardice.

The next part of the story was told me by Mrs. L—— herself. Awakened out of her first sleep, she sat up suddenly in bed, and saw that her door was open, and that in the light of a lamp which shone

167

in from the hall two poorly dressed men were making their way round the foot of her bed. "Nan deska?" (What is it?) she cried out; and a voice, which she says she knows, answered, "We have business here." She saw what she thought must be sharpened bamboos in their hands, and in sudden fear clasped her baby closely to her. Mr. L—— had been awakened by the quick words, and without an instant's hesitation jumped out of bed and rushed at the robbers, though he had only his naked hands to attack them with. Although they were armed, they retreated to the door; but poor Mr. L——, as any other brave man would have done, followed them, and, as I think must have attempted to wrest their weapons from them. After all, he was the only man in the house, and it contained girls and teachers committed to his care. Being what he was, he could hardly shrink back into his room and let these murderous burglars have the run of the house. So he followed them, and at the door a fierce scuffle took place. Mrs. L——, till then divided between her fears for the child and her fears for her husband, heard the quick rattle of blows, and ran to help Mr. L——, who by this time had followed the men into the narrow corridor outside. He seemed to be unconscious of having received any wounds, and was attacking them desperately; and they were raining blows upon him with those awful blades. Mrs. L—— realised that the men were using sword-blades, and threw herself between him and them; she was frightfully wounded in the struggle, but she could not save her husband, who at last fell, quite dead, at her feet. Then the robbers went as they had come, untracked, undisturbed, except by one of the school-girls, who, poor child, came running from her room at the noise, and meeting them on the stairs took them for house-coolies, and asked them what was the matter. When Mrs. L—— saw her husband at her feet, she gave one terrible scream, which brought out the teachers from their rooms. They saw that he was dead; but she could not believe it, and made them carry him to his bed, since her own hand was useless, two fingers having been severed by the sword-blades, while a gash on the eyebrow had laid her forehead open. She was unconscious of being hurt, and with her left hand quickly dashed water again and again over her husband's face, washed it tenderly, and did all that she and the girls could do to restore him to consciousness. Just think of those three women and that poor dead man, and not a soul to do anything for them! It is surely one of the most pitiful stories I ever heard. Suddenly Mrs. L—— realised it all: her husband was dead, her only child lay beside him, a tiny helpless thing that needed her, and she was bleeding to death as she stood. So very quietly she explained to one girl how to make a tourniquet on her arm, and sent the other to reassure the school-girls in the dormitory; and then, as she told me afterwards, she felt that a terribly decisive moment in her life had come. Unless grace were given her to forgive her enemies fully now, even while her murdered husband lay before her, she knew certainly that she would never be able to do so later; and so, with an intense effort, she forced herself to say, "God bless the Japanese," and she told me that from that moment she never felt rancour or hatred or any desire of revenge.

The watchman is in prison, but no trace has been obtained of the two burglars, although every kind of machinery has been put in motion to find them. That they were burglars seems evident; robbers here constantly supply themselves with swords, which they use freely when attacked. But poor Mr. L—— is the first foreigner who has been killed in Japan for twenty years, and the outrage has excited an intense feeling of anger and apprehension among the foreigners, and one of humiliation and profound regret among the Japanese. Mrs. L—— has had almost a miraculous recovery from her wounds; but she looks terribly shaken, and will not be able to use what remains of her hand for a very long time. A brave woman—the widow of a brave man!

Kamakura, May, 1890

When the excitement of the royal visit was over it was rather pleasant to leave the smaller house, and come back to our own dens, and sit on our verandah in the May moonlight, talking over what has been of late an inexhaustible subject of interest—the building of a Japanese house far away in the hills, where we hope to pass our summers in future. The question of six- or eight-feet wide verandahs, of glass or paper *shoji*, of how few trees need be cut down from the pine grove in which the nest is built—all this has been a constant amusement to me during the spring. At the end of this month I hope we shall be able to take possession of the little home, and then you shall have a full description of it. Meanwhile I have had a pleasant change in spending a fortnight at Kamakura, a little place an hour from Yokahama, very sheltered and quiet, close to the sea. Like Atami, it lies between two spurs of hills, which seem to be carrying it down to the water; and a plain, far wider than the Atami one, stretches inland, covered with rice-fields, and crossed here and there by some ancient avenues of pines—sad old pines, crippled and scarred, and standing at irregular intervals, because their comrades in arms have fallen in the ranks and lie crumbling at their feet. In the daytime a few families of peasants work at the rice-tilling, standing up to their knees in the horrible liquid dressing which nourishes the precious crops; here and there an empty hut, kept only by the family dog, stands close to the road; everything is poverty-stricken and desolate; sand-dunes rise near the sea, and are planted with scattered pines, which seem holding out their arms as if to warn the waves not to come and gaze too near on the desolation which has swept over the site of one of the most splendid cities in the world. The Kamakura Plain, wide as it is, the foot-hills, and the valleys running up into them were all covered once with streets and temples, and full of the clash and the colour of the Daimyos' processions. The air must be thick with ghosts (if ghosts can walk unwearied for six hundred years), and—how one would love to see them! For Kamakura has witnessed some of the most stirring events in Japanese feudal history, and was the very centre of the power of Yoritomo,* that strange man, indomitable, ruthless, astute, a mediæval Napoleon, who took his country into his own hands, and made his history hers while he lived.

Death has conquered at Kamakura. Yoritomo's gorgeous capital was burnt, and only its ashes remain to mingle with the dust and sand of the plain. Tidal waves have helped in the ruin; and now the sea rolls in, empty of ships, to the deserted shores, and the pines along

*Minamoto no Yoritomo (1147–99), the first of the Minamoto shoguns.

the broken avenues seem to be dying willingly, for branch after branch drops with a crash in the wind that is sweeping the dunes to-day as if seeking for something still left to destroy.

But I was wrong in saying that no trace of the old glory remains. There is one which fire and storm and tidal wave have torn at in vain: shorn of its old surroundings, bared of its temple roof, the great Buddha still meets the moving seasons with a front of eternal calm.

It was a mild May night, and the moon rose round over the heaving sea. The wind had fallen, the sighing pine trees were at rest, though one stretched out an arm here and there as in sleep, throwing a twisted shadow across the road where our footsteps fell muffled in the sand of many storms. We passed in silence by the empty fields, the darkened huts, and up the village street, touched to a square of soft dull gold where here and there a light still burned behind the *shoji* for birth or death or unfinished toil, the three strings of our life's lyre. Then the village was left behind, we turned in at an embowered gate, and before us, in a wide temple, roofed only by the sky, lighted only by moon and stars, rose the great Buddha, the monument of peace.

Peace! In the hush of that flood of moonlight the very mantle of peace seemed hanging round him in the silver air. All daylight reds and greens were washed to one luminous grey in that transforming haze; all sounds consoled, fulfilled, harmonised in that vibrating silence.

There are few higher, more perfect works of art in the world than this representation of Amida Buddha, the incarnation of a humanity which, after long struggles to break free from earth, is enthroned in irrevocable peace, but is not deaf to the cries of those who are still stumbling along the thorny road he too has known. The countenance, full of inscrutable majesty, seems only still by the soul's command; behind the deep eyes and the quiet mouth lies a smile gentle and calm, as if rising from the very heart of knowledge. "Having attained," is what the beautiful lips would say, were speech needful. On the brow a silver boss draws the moon-rays to itself; the breast is bare to the kiss of the wind, the feet and hands folded in profound repose. All around, at regular intervals in the pavement, stand the old stone bases of wooden pillars, long ago swept away with the splendid roof that rested on them, with the gates and steps and altars that once surrounded the image and helped to make this temple one of the wonders of Japan.

Yoritomo before his death was inspired by a desire to have in his own city a great Buddha like the one at Nara;* but he died before he could carry out his idea. Some lady in the Court, for love of him, collected money to have such an image made, and in time it was completed, cast in bronze, and set up here to replace a wooden one which had stood for a few years and had been destroyed by fire. No fire or water could injure the fifty feet of towering bronze of the new Buddha; but the sea seemed jealous of its greatness, and broke over it twice, in 1369 and 1494. This last tidal wave carried away everything, except what we see to-day. The temple was never rebuilt, and for four hundred years the sun has shone and the rain has wet the image, which stands like a symbol of the soul, outliving all the trappings of this earthly life.

No farther than the home of Amida Buddha did we go on that night of our moonlight pilgrimage; but there is another temple near, to be seen by daylight—the shrine of the goddess of mercy, Kwannon, everywhere loved and worshipped in Japan. I knew her in China as Kwan-yin, and possessed once a most beautiful figure of her in soft white *pâte,* a lovely mother-woman standing with a babe nestling in her arms, a *mandorla* of blown flame enshrining them both. Here, in her temple† on the hill behind Daibutsu, she holds no child in her arms, but stands, a great golden image in the darkness of a jealously secluded shrine, with hand raised as if to bless, and a smile of love and tenderness on her face. It is as if the other gods had thought her too lavish, too spendthrift of her favours, and had enclosed her here, and set a guardian to keep the gate and to count those who go and come, for fear that all mankind should enter into paradise through her intercession; for Kwannon has a great and faithful love for the human race, and, having already attained to Nirvâna, put eternal joys aside, and returned of her own free will to

---

*Housed in Tōdai-ji temple.
†Hase-dera temple. An excellent guide to present-day Kamakura is Michael Cooper's *Exploring Kamakura* (Tokyo: John Weatherhill, 1979).

this world to save and comfort men and women. Sometimes she is represented as having numberless arms, each of which reaches out some good thing, some desired grace; she never refuses a supplication, except when invoked a second time under one especial title, "Hito Koto Kwannon" (the Kwannon of a Single Grace), for it is not lawful to pray to her twice by that name, although the first use of it compels her compliance. She is the mother to whom all mothers pray in the land, she sends children, and she protects children; and Jizo Sama, the god who tends the children's ghosts, does so at her command. Even the animals she loves, and there are shrines where the peasants bring their horses and bullocks to receive her blessing, and perhaps get the promise of a higher reincarnation when they return to this weary world. Such is the Buddhist picture of Kwannon, the faithful, loving, powerful mother, the type of all womanly grace and holiness. Except by divine revelation, could the heart conceive a more perfect ideal?

Kamakura, May, 1890

As one looks out from the verandah of the Kaihin-in, the one hotel of Kamakura, the sea only shows itself as a blue or grey line made narrow by high sand-dunes, and half hidden by a pine wood which grows in the hollow behind the protecting crest. This wood is just now carpeted with thin green grass, pushing up its way through the pine needles. A few hardy wild flowers swing on the wind, and here and there the tree roots make inviting seats, where one can rest awhile and listen to the cool sibilant talk of the branches in the breeze overhead. A scrambling path leads across the dunes to the wet firm sands, marked with long rosaries of little footprints, undulating as the ripples which break lazily a few yards farther on. Numbers of children come here at low tide to gather the delicate shells, which they sell to the shell-workers of Enoshima, the island which lies behind the promontory to the right.

173

The children are laughing, communicative little people, who walk up and down beside me when they catch me on the sands, and evidently take me for a shell-gatherer too; for they insist on my buying their little basketfuls of shells (generally for a sum too small to be translated into English), and then they run away to their homes among the fishermen's huts, delighted at having earned their money without taking the long walk to Enoshima in the burning heat. I can only understand a few of the things they say, just enough to make out how many brothers and sisters have been left at home, or the age of the baby on the little shell-gatherer's back; but my stupidity seems not to diminish the pleasure that one at least of them takes in my society. She is a bright-eyed little creature of ten or thereabouts, with a very solid baby on her back, to whom she pays less attention than I do to my parasol. She jumps about, slides down sand-hills, hops on one foot, plays little games of "chuck-farthing" with five pebbles in a circle of friends and contemporaries, all without the faintest reference to the solemn baby, who, safely tied to her back with strips of blue linen, falls asleep and wakes up again, cries or laughs, sucks a sugar-cane if he is happy, and bangs his nurse's head with it if he is cross, all without influencing her any more than we can change the weather by grumbling at it.

The children gather in numbers to see the nets hauled in, and it is a sight I seldom miss if I can help it. When the sun is getting low and throwing red reflections along the water and the sands; when the trees on the promontory towards Enoshima are visibly falling asleep in a haze through which they look almost black,—then a light boat rows to shore, leaving a larger one some way out from land, and moving slowly from point to point, where dark objects like human heads are bobbing up and down on the water. They are not heads, but lumps of tarred cork, to which the upper edge of the huge net is fastened. Below, it hangs with weights attached, in many a turn and snare in the water; and now the time has come to draw it in and count the take. All the men but two have come ashore in the smaller boat, and form a line pointing inland, each man holding the rope with both hands; the bare limbs are firmly planted on the sand, and all the brown bodies gleam like bronze in the sunset. Then at a word of command from the first on the line a measured chant breaks out, and a long swinging pull brings the rope some yards farther up the shore. Passing it quickly from hand to hand, the men run down again to the water's edge, never changing their relative positions, and again the toil-song sounds along the beach, as more of the heavy length is retrieved from the sea. The net is sunk so far out that often the men must work three-quarters of an hour before its real mouth is brought to shore; and meanwhile their comrades in the fishing-boat row from point to point where it shows above the water, pushing it gently towards the land. When at last its black drifts are creeping up the rippled shallows close in shore, the rope-draggers leave the piled cable, and, wading into the water, seize the web in armfuls and bring it farther in, to separate mesh from mesh with extreme care, and to catch the leaping fish, who flash their live silver from side to side with a curious rattle and snap against the cords of their wet prison. It is a beautiful sight as the brown men, their loins girded with twisted blue cotton, stand in the water, stretching out the lengths of the net full of dancing silver fish, behind them the sunset sea, and before, the dusky velvet sands. This is the time when the children glean their harvest; and not the children only, but poor widows, who have no man to send a-fishing, and very old people, whose sons are dead, all gather round the fishermen, holding out little bowls and baskets for what they will give; and all that is fit for food and yet not good enough for the market goes to them. When the catch has been a good one, the suppliants go off with their begging-bowls full; when, as sometimes happens, nothing has been taken, then there is no supper for anybody, the fishermen's pensioners separate sadly, and the men themselves, without a word of complaint, pile the net on the boats and row out to sea to drop it all into place again. Once I saw them draw it in long after dark, and lanterns had to be lighted to sort the fish, while the children and old people, waiting eagerly, kept peering forward into the ring of light. It is good to see that there is never a rough word said to the beggars, who, though as poor as the grey grasses on the dunes, do not look despairing or dirty or unhappy. The thanks are simply and duly said, be the gift great or trifling; and there is no grumbling or wailing if it is withheld.

As one stands under the pine trees of the Kaihin-in Hotel at Kamakura, the famous promontory lies on the right hand, hiding the strange island of Enoshima. A mile or so to the left, somewhat inland, runs an old road, where the grass pushes up between the grey uneven paving-stones, and hangs undisturbed from low stone walls on either side. Here and there tall pines, battered and crippled now, show that a stately avenue once led to the temple at whose lowest step the road ends, the Temple of Hachiman, the god of war. The steps are grey, and worn with many feet, and very long and wide and steep. A gallant tree, as old as they, springs from a deep court beside them, and towers far above, its enormous body seeming to almost push them aside, while overhead the branches spread out in thick clouds of leafage, brilliant green, polished, odorous; and this is the thousand-year-old camphor tree of Hachiman, the rival of the one I loved in Atami's temple grove, less great in girth, but marked somewhere in its ringed strength with very noble blood, the blood of Sanetomo, the youngest son of Yoritomo, and the last of the Minamotos.

The tree was younger, but not less green, when Yoritomo used to come to sit in its shade, and look out over his fair strong city of Kamakura. He loved this spot, and often climbed still higher to the slope of Shira-hata Yama, just behind the Temple, whence he could see his war-junks rolling in the bay, and count the white standards of the guards round his place wall in the town.

The end of the Minamoto Shoguns came under the great tree on these steps of the Temple of Hachiman, where I sit to-day, and hear the grasses shiver, and the gulls cry out at sea; and blind insects crawl dustily where the blood made a little sound in dripping from stone to stone. The place is lonely and empty as a rifled grave.

❖   ❖   ❖

Enoshima, May, 1890

The name is so beautiful that I must write it at the top of my paper, although I am sitting in the hotel at Kamakura, and I cannot catch a glimpse of the dream island where I spent my yesterday.

Enoshima!* On a lovely morning of sunshine and showers we left Kamakura, and passed through the low screen of hills which shuts it in to the right. The rain had laid the dust, and the air was keen and saltly sweet; for the night had been a somewhat stormy one. As we rounded down from the hills through deep-cut paths to the shore, we could hear the slow rollers thundering in before we caught a glimpse of the sea itself. Then, as we climbed the crest of a sand-dune it lay wide and near, laughing in the sunshine, moving in lazy billows as if tired with its rough play of the night. A wide stretch of sand, dun in the shade, gold in the sun, and smooth as the cheek of a little child, swept away in a perfect curve that broke once under the climbing waves, and then rose high in a dusky embowered mass, floating in haze and sunshine out at sea, the island of the tortoise, Enoshima. "How can we reach it?" I asked of Ogita; "there is no boat there!" "Boat not in, but honourably walking," Ogita replied; and pointed to a light wooden causeway, which seemed to dance on the water, more like a toy bridge in a lady's garden than a serious link between island and mainland. But Ogita explained: the water was only a foot or two deep beneath the wood-work; and this would not be needed at all, were it not that, when the wind blew violently from the south, the waves washed up far be-yond their usual limit. There was no danger; to-night we could probably return on the sands.

So leaving our jinrikshas, we started on foot towards the mystic island, so full of strange gods and strange presences, so wrapped in the web of story, so little a part of the life of to-day, that one almost expects to see it float out to sea and melt into cloud on the horizon. But not to-day, not until I have passed over the swaying bridge, where the water breaks up lightly, splashing my feet, and even throwing a little spray in my eyes, so that the splendid bronze gate of the sea-goddess's city towers and sways for a moment in my dazzled vision. Then the drops clear away, and I see the *torii* in all its grandeur. Its beautiful shape seems, as it were, to square the circle,

*An amusing and ironic account of a much later visit to Enoshima between the wars is contained in *L'honorable Partie de Campagne,* or *The Honourable Picnic,* by Thomas Raucat (1924). The author's name is invented and is a pun on the Japanese phrase *tomarō ka* meaning "shall we stay [the night]?"

to give all that is strong in angles, all that is lovely in curves; and through its dragon-wrought, wave-swept portal I see the long street of a climbing town, climbing high up to the sunshine on wings of fluttering blue that feather its sides above, on feet of mother-of-pearl, where the shells lie heaped on doorstep and window and wall—shells white and lustrous as bridal moons; shells dazzling and whorled as the snow-queen's crown; shells rosy, thick, thousands upon thousands, like shed petals piled together, as if all the cherry blossoms of the spring had been blown out to Enoshima on one saving breeze, and touched to immortality as they fell on the brown strand of Benten's* magic island.

Enoshima is the home of all the shells† in Japan, and those which the sea does not give it are brought there by the gatherers from far and near. My little friends on the Kamakura beaches have doubtless added their store to the rosy heaps which lie in open baskets on either hand as I climb the steep street. The flutter of blue wings overhead is made by hundreds of shop signs, strange white letters on blue cotton for the most part, hanging close together, and serving as a sign to the passer-by, and a shade to the indwellers of the little houses. To these people the sea is their one treasure-house, the gracious provider for all their simple needs; and they take it and its wonders for granted. To us, outsiders, who go to Enoshima once in a lifetime the visit is a revelation of the riches and beauties of the world of water that laps round our world of earth. How can I put before you any picture of the white and rosy wonders piled on either side of the rough, poor little street? In Europe we never see these things in their glory; occasionally one poor specimen, brought home in a seaman's chest, finds its way to a dull shop, grey and mournful as the northern winter, and arrests us as with a dazzle of tropical sunshine, a flushing of rose, and a call of the southern sea. In my wanderings about Vienna, of all unlikely places, I came once on a naturalist's

*Benten, or Benzaiten, the one female among the seven deities of good luck.
†One shell found in Japan and Formosa has the Latin name *Thatcheria Mirabilis* and has been described as "shell thin, with a striking pagoda-like spire shoulder keeled and angular. Surface smooth, matt with very fine ornament. Outside pale sandy yellow, inside white with enamel-like sheen." The name has no connection with Margaret Thatcher, the present British Prime Minister.

den, where, in a dusty corner, lay one of these incurled cups of the sea, warm ivory on the fluted verge, sunset colour nearer the heart, its curves as free and fine as the soft blown draperies on young limbs which some Greek sculptor saw in the laurel groves of Hellas and reproduced with tears in his slavery in Rome. I knelt down, there in Vienna, and put my ear to the great shell's mouth; and deep in its heart it was singing still, a song of morning seas and velvet sands and fisher-lads, the song that I heard again to-day on the sacred steps of Enoshima. For Enoshima is sacred, from the caves at its foot to the temples on its summit; consecrated at first to Benten, the goddess of love and good fortune, always gracious and helpful to the lads who must make their living at sea. But Benten was a Buddhist goddess, and at the so-called "Purification of Shinto" in the early part of the present reign, she was banished from her temples in Enoshima with other Buddhist divinities, and her island kingdom was given over to the care of Shinto priests. But the people in Eno-shima have not concurred in the Imperial condemnation, and Benten Sama still reigns there, none the less supreme because she is invisible. The first fisher-lad on the shore will offer to guide you to her temple, and in the little silent curious crowd which follows you from place to place deprecatory glances and pitying smiles will be exchanged if you say that you do not mean to climb so far.

And at first, in truth, I did not say I would; for I thought the hours of daylight would hardly see me past the street of shells. The sun was mounting high, and shot down hotly between the flutter-ings of the flags; inside the low shops were a thousand strange things, to be bought for such tiny sums that all my following had both hands full in half an hour; a breeze from the sea, warm and cool at once, and wholly salt and refreshing, lifted the cotton screens and caused them to rustle and snap joyously; and I stayed on, turning from one thing to another in the luminous low shops. The light has a strange quality in Enoshima. All through Japan it is admirably strong and pure; but here it almost has a colour of its own—a colour made of the sheen of mother-of-pearl and the gem-gleams under the sea, and morning haze, and the shadow of the rock on the waves; a million vibrations reaching the eye at once, all dancing, alive, iridescent, melted in one copious wash of sunshine, to me like a bath in the wine of life. Against it all shadows are transparent, cool, just light of another colour, light asleep, no darkness anywhere. The low-roofed treasure-house of shells has no dusky corners; every detail is absolutely clear, every beauty stands out to be praised and catalogued. Here at my feet are the kings and queens of the deep,— huge nautilus shells like hollow pearls filled with moonlight, open shells where Benten (or Venus or Freya, it is but a change of name) must have rested and slept one summer's night, for they are warm and rosy still, and reach out their curved lips laughingly for something to kiss; there are solemn conch shells, that have slept under brown seaweed in autumn starlight, and have caught the rhymed chant of the waves on the shore; open shells of green and grey mother-of-pearl, with shifting crimson gleams on the vigorous edge turned in like an ear strained and alert, where five round holes pierce through in mystic symmetry, as if the sea-king's daughter had been trying her earrings there; and there are little shells in myriads as I have said, thick as the Empress's cherry blossoms in spring; there are showers of spun glass, as sharp and silvery as moonbeams on ice, and these are the glass ropes of the beautiful Hyalonema sponges; there are huge tortoise shields, measuring four and five feet across, but these we would not look at, having been promised a sight of a mythical tortoise whose home is supposed to be somewhere in the Enoshima caves, and who is said to measure twenty-three feet across his old back; there are sprays of shells like lilies-of-the-valley dipped in milk, sea-foam lilies—they are born of a kiss, where the sun met the wave: and besides all these, hundreds of ornaments cut out of mother-of-pearl—big fish and little fish (I bought strings of these all hung together, of the softest pink, and rarely carved), hairpins with moons and rabbits and roses and branches of plum and cherry blossom; and tiny glass cups blown double, with a shell or two and a wisp of seaweed and a gleam of gold-dust loose inside the glass, running down to your lip as you drink, but never passing from the crystal prison unless you break it, when you will lose the value of three-quarters of a farthing, and destroy a thing of fairy beauty which would have told you stories of sea and sunshine to the day of your death!

At last I tore myself away from the shells, and climbed a path that led up by grey stone steps under solemn trees to an inn, which hangs like a gull's nest high on the face of the cliff, staring out to sea. And what a sea! The breadth and the blue of it! From that high place the horizon is so distant that it almost ceases to be; the world is a sapphire globe endomed in sun-shot crystal; earth seems an accident, Enoshima here a seaweed freak that has come up to breathe; I and it may pass away, but sea and sunshine seem eternal in their white empire of noon.

The little inn is fresh and white, and open to the bay as an empty shell. On the side to the sea all the screens have been removed, and the wooden verandah runs past three rooms as open as itself, and then drops suddenly, as it were, down a very steep staircase, shining as lacquer and innocent of a handrail. Also the steps have no connecting planks; and as one goes up or down one sees between them the laughing brown faces of coolies or pilgrims resting in the space below, and much amused to see how high-heeled foreign shoes catch and slip on the polished wood. As I look down through the openings, I see the maid of the inn making my tea with care under Ogita's directions, and Rinzo is toasting bread on his chopsticks over a *hibachi;* so I turn back, and wait for the simple meal, feeling rather ashamed to need food at all in the face of such a view on such a morning! But one is only human after all, and emotions are distinctly exhausting; so I am very glad when the *musumë* comes in, on her knees, and pushes towards me a carved tray in the form of a lotus leaf, with a teapot shaped like a shell, and cups painted with little goldfish swimming round the base of Fuji San.

My companions have gone away, and for a moment I am alone in Japan—that much of Japan which surrounds me here. On the floor are cool wheat-coloured mats, and thin silk cushions in bright silks lie about for seats. The inner screens of the rooms have much white wood about them; and what paper there is, is pale blue, with a sprinkling of silver pine needles on it. The alcove of honour, the *tokonoma,* is framed in by a tree, a beautiful ash trunk, still wearing its fine bark; and a branch reaching out is embedded in the ceiling, and marks the arch of the alcove. Here the paper is very rich, a running melon design in crusted silver, and against it hangs a scroll, with a poem written on it in bold grass characters. Below, on the step, stands a tall bronze vase, holding some sea-grasses and a branch of pine; and on the side of the frame opposite the tree trunk a bamboo stand for fans is hung, and holds two or three of the hotel fans, which are presented to the guests as keepsakes. They are rather violent in colour—on one side scarlet, with the name of the inn printed in white, but the back is softer, with a picture of an enormous turtle with a fringed tail creeping up on a very small rock; the rock represents Enoshima, and the turtle the inn, for it is called "The House of the Golden Turtle."

The *musumë* creeps in to know if I will have some more tea, and I keep her to tell me something about herself. Her name is Ko, she says, and she is seventeen, and very glad that I admire her bright-green sash, which was a present from her brother at New Year. Her brother is a waiter at Atami; and she too goes to Atami in the winter, for then no one visits Enoshima, and the mistress here keeps no maid. Wages? No, she has no wages, but her food and a summer dress; and the visitors are honourably kind. Two English ladies stayed here ten days a little while ago, and they also made pictures— ah! but this Okusama's picture is prettier; and she comes and laughs over the drawing of herself in my sketch-book, and then some one calls for her, and she bows and glides away; and I hear her drop softly down the polished stairs, and slip on her straw *zori* with a little click at the bottom.

And now the time for rest is over, and I must climb the hill and see Benten Sama's Temple, and go down to the caves on the other side, and do many things for which the day seems short. The sun has passed over to the other side of the island ridge, and all the path on this side is in shadow. A light moisture seems hanging in the air, and fern fronds are uncurling, and pine branches seem to be stretching in the cool relief of the afternoon. As we leave the inn and turn up the ascending road, a party of pilgrims passes us, an old, old man with his sons and grandsons, all carrying staves, with the little blue towels which they will take as offerings to the shrine tied to them, done up in gay printed papers. They look at us curiously, and go on, in single file, saying some prayers, I think, for they exchange no remarks on our appearance as they go by. We are taking it slowly, enjoying the delicious freshness off the sea, and in no hurry to face the sun, still hot on the other slope. And so we pass from terrace to terrace of the island stair; for the sides of Enoshima are steep, and rise from the sea in huge steps like the vine terraces of Amalfi. But here there are stone balustrades at the edge, and behind them stone lanterns, and here and there a *torii,* and here and there a shrine, decayed and empty, but not quite forgotten, as the rough bamboo vases filled with still fresh wild flowers testify; and more than once an incense-stick just lighted sends up its close-curling spiral of smoke, blue-grey against the weather-worn stone, and everywhere the background is deep-green foliage growing straight and thick against the cliff.

The three temples of Benten Sama stand one above the other, separated by a wave of dark trees, each sadder and more deserted than the last, till the third drowns the ridge with something of stately desolation. The Shinto reform, whatever it was, seems, like some other so-called reforms, to have been a thing sour and un-lovely, strong only for destruction, and incapable of filling up the shrines emptied by its iconoclastic rage. Where it reigns alone, "purified," as its adherents call it, it strikes one with dull depression. There is nothing in the dusty mirror and the torn *gohei** to inspire hope in the future or courage in the present. The face of Buddha is as the face of a friend, serene, merciful, gracious to poor humanity; but in the mirror of Shinto man finds only his own travel-stained reflection—the picture of that self which must be left behind before he can enter into peace.

Round the entrance of the chief Temple is an enclosing fence, called, I think, the "Jewel Hedge" in Shinto phraseology, but en-closing no jewels here, or at least only the mystic ones which would have no value for mankind at large. The Temple is empty and dusty like the others; but Ogita, with superb contempt for the "purifica-tion of Shinto," persuades me to sit down on a mossy stone, and listen to his stories of Benten Sama and all her goodness and great-ness and beauty. I think she must be Ogita's patron goddess, for he rarely waxes eloquent about any other, and smiles rather pityingly at many a strange idol that I want stories about. But when he speaks of Benten Sama his eyes light up, his delicate aquiline face takes on a flush of colour, and there is quite a ring in his queerly con-structed phrases. He is a *samurai,* a great swordsman still, and a favourite instructor in the noble art; so I am a little surprised at this devotion to the lady of love and luck. As for explanations, ask

Gohei are white paper strips hung at a Shinto shrine.

them not of a Japanese! The springs of action for him and you are separated by an almost impassable gulf. After years of intercourse, he might understand the real drift of your question; more years would have to elapse before you could understand his answer.

But while we were philosophising on the portal of Benten's desecrated home, the sun had passed away from us to the western slope of the island, and we must follow, or night would fall long before we could reach the mainland again, for there is much to see on the western side. Unfortunately, I suppose, I am a very slow sight-seer. That which pleases me must be seen to the uttermost before I want to move on to the next object of interest, even if it be incomparably more important. On the very crest of Benten's island I found some little tea-houses, open to the sea, empty for the breeze to riot through, airy sun-dried nests, where one could sit in the shade of a thin awning, and look out on the blue world of water— water wind-dimpled, sun-kissed, deepest sapphire in the shadow of a rock a thousand feet below me, but fading into tender haze far off on the horizon, where, away to the south, the island volcano of Oshima sent up the thin spiral of smoke which I used to watch for hours from the Atami shore. That light cloud, never changing shape, white by night and grey by day, has a kind of symbolic importance in this coast landscape. It is like the gentle regret of a faithful soul, a shred of mist on the background of life, the sound of a sigh in every pause of its brave music!

Here on the hill a very, very old woman gave me tea, and bowed her poor grey head to the ground when I praised the view. She said her house was poor and mean, and I made Ogita tell her that it was rich in beauty, and her tea most refreshing; whereupon she made me a present of a fairy teacup, of the thinnest china, with the ghost of Fuji San dreamed into it—if you will forgive the barbaric phrase. English is a clumsy, square-toed vehicle of expression, and stumbles along, crushing a thousand beauties of my Japanese thought garden, which a more delicate language (or a more skilful writer!) might have preserved for you. The little old woman was · such a personality, the only soul in sight, for the other houses seemed empty; her grey hair was cut almost short, and gathered in with a comb at the back of her head; her hands were like knotty twigs on old pine trees, and her brown body was so withered and

184

sea-dried that it was more like a weather-beaten shell than anything which still has to consume and decay; her eyes were bright still, even through the tears of old age, and her coarse blue garments were clean and faded, as if they had often been washed in salt water. One son was a soldier, she said, one a fisherman, who had been drowned at sea; her granddaughter had gone down the cliff to wash her clothes, and—august thanks—would the lady return some day—return soon? Sayonara, Sayonara!

We left her standing before the square opening which she called her house, behind her the farther sea, the awning over her head flapping like a dazzling white wing against its blueness, at her feet the first of a long flight of steps cut in yellowish stone, which led down the steep cliff to the famous cave of the Dragon, whose opening is hardly above high-water level. If the Dragon ever lived here, he went long ago—went perhaps with Benten Sama to the underworld; Ogita tells me that the cave only holds its name on account of its shape, like a dragon's tail, twisting and curving and diminishing as it runs into the island's heart, where it is lost in blackness. At the foot of the rude steps (far ruder and steeper than I cared for) one or two natural terraces are formed by rocks jutting out and then shelving down to the water. They are connected with planks, forming rather crazy bridges, much shaken by the thud of the water breaking below. We have to scramble over these to get round to the entrance of the cave; the water has receded now, and left a few pools, where boys are diving for crabs, the little Enoshima crabs which are much prized in Tokyo. Then we find a girl, who must be the granddaughter of our old hostess on the cliff, kneeling on bare knees by a pool, her sleeves all bound back, her skirts kilted up, washing some poor blue wisps of clothing which seem hardly worth the toil. We pass a stone lantern, pass the boys, who want to sell us crabs, and then suddenly our swaying bridge with its broken handrail turns where the sea rushes with a roar into the cleft heart of the rocks, and we follow it dizzily, deafened with the thundering echoes of the cave, and more than once blinded by a drift of spray, breaking high on its wet black sides.

Some little way within the entrance we come to solid ground, marked by a shrine, where a soft gleam of light makes a ring of gold on the gloom—a little wooden shrine, which must, I think, be the one of which Rein says that it has to be removed every spring, and put back several feet from where it can stand in the winter, because, while the south-west monsoon blows, the water piles higher on all the south coast, and then falls again when the monsoon changes. As I approach I find the golden ring growing larger, and can distinguish a number of candles burning behind the shrine; they have been carried into the cave by pilgrims, and are left here as on offering when the exploration is over. A shadowy guardian sells some of them again to us, and we creep into the damp twisting passage, from which other passages branch off blackly. We pass rough gods hewn in the rock, grey and solemn, buried in this eternal darkness near the springs of things, feeling the earthquake rive its way to the light through the heart of the world, hearing the thud of breakers on the outer wall of their island castle; visited day after day in the kindly summer by poor pilgrims, rich in faith and devotion to the only gods their twilight has revealed, left alone in the long months of winter while the salt creeps over their faces like a veil, and the crawling sea things have it all to themselves in the empty passages. What! I must stoop and creep through that black hole to reach the last and most holy shrine? No, Ogita, the daylight is sweet, and holy too; and here there is a drip of dead water, the air is thick and grave-bound. Out to the world again, please; I have no mind to be buried before my time, and I fear to faint in this choking darkness. Ah! there it is, beyond the damp rock walls and the smoking candles, beyond the cave's mouth is my world—a world of sunlit breakers, and scudding clouds, and fresh salt breeze stinging every sense to triumphant life again.

An hour later I look back from the sandy pass over the dune. Enoshima seems to have swum out to sea, and lies a misty mass, its face turned away from me to the dull-red line which shows where the sun dropped but a few moments ago. The night is upon us, quick and cold; we must draw our wraps closely, as we speed along the darkening road. Sayonara, Enoshima!

The summer quarters in Karuizawa were not quite ready, so we came up here for a fortnight, since Tokyo had become unbearably warm and damp. The dampness is here too; for it rains much, and between the rains a soft cool mist hangs on the hillsides and clings to one's garments, and even creeps into the rooms of Muramatsu's hotel, where we are staying. H—— could not leave Tokyo at once, so I came on first with a friend; and a rather adventurous time we two women had of it before we reached this nest in the clouds. There are many things which are still vague, uncatalogued as it were, in Japan, and the measurement of distance is one of them. You ask a weary foot-traveller with a pack on his back how far it is to the next town, and he replies, "A long way—at least five ri" (just about twelve miles). Then you meet a fresh well set-up youth coming out of a tea-house, where he has had a rest and a meal. "Is it really five ri to Ikao?" you ask, in a despairing voice; and he laughs as he replies, "Five ri! No, indeed; perhaps one and a half—not more!" All of which is very puzzling and misleading to us prosaic foreigners, who do not measure distances (as of course they should be measured) by our sensations in regard to them. And so it happened that my friend and I left Tokyo very comfortably towards noon, having four hours of railway journey, and, after that, four hours (as we were told) of easy hill-travelling, which would bring us to Ikao in time for sunset clouds, dinner, and twilight on the verandah and a full moon afterwards. The railway journey was new to me, for I have never travelled on this northern line before. The carriages are much more comfortable than those on the other lines, and by a kind attention of the English superintendent we found a charming little tea-table laid out in the carriage, and amused ourselves with making tea at least three times in the

*Ikao is described in Murray's *Handbook for Travellers in Japan* (1894) as being "a short day's journey from Tokyo to Maebashi by the Takasaki-Maebashi railway in 3 1/2 hours and then some 15 miles partly by tram, partly by carriage or jinrikisha, but jinrikisha the whole way to be preferred. The latter part of the ride is uphill so that two men to each jinrikisha are indispensable. Should the main road via Maebashi be impassible owing to floods, Ikao may also be reached via Iizuka [a distance of 17 3/4 miles]."

course of the short journey. The scenery is rather flat until Maye-bashi is reached; but everything was still in its summer freshness, the little stations along the line are pictures of neatness, and at each one there is always a group of peasants and children and coolies, leaning over the great gates and gazing at the amazing toy, which seems to be no less interesting to them now than when it first ploughed its smoky way past their quiet villages.

At Mayebashi we left the train, and took refuge from the blazing heat in a cool tea-house, where we lingered willingly while Ogita, who had been sent on by an earlier train, organised the usual procession of jinrikshas and chair-coolies; these last took a great deal of finding and bribing, as chairs are quite unknown in this part of the world. My chair had come on in Ogita's train; but before I had been in it ten minutes, I regretted that I had not chosen the humble jinriksha instead, for the men had, of course, not learnt to keep step, and changed shoulder to the poles every few minutes, so that I felt somewhat as Mazeppa* might have done between the four wild horses. I noticed O'Matsu and Ogita having a rather serious talk with the innkeeper, and found afterwards that they had been making inquiries as to the distance to Ikao, neither of them having been in this part of the country before. The answers had been disconcerting, and they concluded that the innkeeper was dishonestly exaggerating the length of the journey so as to keep us at Mayebashi for the night, so they decided that nothing need be said to me on the matter. So we started off, by white dusty roads across the burning plain; the day wore on and on, and the Ikao Mountains looked as far off as ever. We were very tired, and also hungry, for by some mistake Ogita had allowed the luncheon-basket to be sent on in the morning with the heavy luggage, and we could get nothing but Japanese tea and peppermint cakes at the tea-houses on the road.

At last, to our intense relief, a light rain began to fall; but before we had ceased to be thankful for it, it became a deluge. Then the night fell unmistakably, and at last we pulled up at a *chaya,* whose

---

*"Mazeppa" (1819), a poem by Byron that relates the legend of Mazeppa, a Ukrainian noble bound naked to untamed horses, is also the title of a symphonic poem by Franz Liszt (1856).

yellow lanterns and leaping fire stood out pleasantly against the blackness of the great hills looming up behind it. The men were spent, and we and they quite drenched; so we stopped for a short rest. The poor coolies pulled off their straw sandals, caked with mud, and threw them away; then crept round the big fire blazing in the lower part of the inn, the open kitchen where travellers of the lower class are welcome to rest and warm themselves. The *nesan* (or elder sister, as they call the maid) brought them steaming bowls of macaroni,* of which we also would gladly have eaten but for the impossible flavouring of *daikon* which seemed to accompany it. *Daikon* is a giant horse-radish, having a naturally rank and corrupt odour; this the Japanese improve upon by various methods of pickling and long keeping, till, when it is ready for use, it is so pungent and horrible that, as somebody observed of Limburger cheese, it might be employed as a danger signal at sea. I once (perhaps rather unkindly) asked a Japanese gentleman how his people could enjoy such horrors; and he replied, "It is our Stilton cheese, you see!" The truth is, that the staples of food here—rice, macaroni, and a kind of pulse—are all quite tasteless, and must also be eaten in great quantities to sustain existence; so a strong cheap pickle is an absolute necessity to the masses.

Perhaps the *daikon* spurred me on. It seemed too all-pervading to escape from inside the house; and when Ogita, with a very long face, came to tell me that, according to local authorities, it would take us three hours of night-travelling through the pouring rain to reach Ikao, I decided to face that rather than remain where we were, without baggage or European food of any kind, and—with the *daikon*. So, slowly and unwillingly, we set off, hoping against hope that there might be some mistake about the distance. As we climbed into the hills, the darkness was so thick that often only the wet gleam of the coolies' lanterns showed me where my companions were. I had by this time taken to a jinriksha for the more speed; and the last glimpse I had of my chair showed it to me standing out in the village street, while one of the coolies, having got into it, was trying to copy my usual attitude, leaning back with a hand on either arm, and to smoke a pipe at the same

*Noodles.

189

time. He must have been dreadfully uncomfortable, for the rain was coming down on him in sheets; but he evidently felt quite repaid for that by sitting in the seat of honour which had sat so heavily on his shoulders all day.

We had a very weird night ride, through the mist and rain, over solitary moors, where we could only see a few yards of the track at a time. The men came along bravely, never grumbling at the awful state of the path—one cannot call it a road—and even making little jokes at the worst places. The cheery dauntlessness of these poor fellows makes one feel ashamed of growling over any of our much more bearable discomforts. But I was too much interested in the queer experience to feel the fatigue or even the chill of the night rain; there was just enough light to show enormous sweeps of rain-swept mountains, deep valleys full of white cloud armies that rose like awakened ghosts and crept up the hill behind us, pushing us on into the darkness beyond. Suddenly, in a lull of the rain, I saw a great white star moving slowly down towards me out of the sky. Only when it floated close to my eyes did I discover that it was the very patriarch of all the fireflies, though what he was doing abroad on such a night I cannot imagine. Now and then the men would stop to rest, and draw all our jinrikshas together against a bank, where the lanterns hung on the shafts made a faint circle of light in the ghostly air, and showed visibly the hopeless wetness of all near objects. The coolies would get to the lee of our little wooden carriages, and try to light a pipe; and the whiff of their coarse tobacco floated comfortingly for a moment through the mist. Then they would start off again; and in a few minutes the first ones in the long line loomed huge threatening on a rise before us against a pale patch of sky, behind which the full moon should have been shining.

At last we saw lights in the distance, and in a few minutes a whole tribe of little gnomes, carrying big round lanterns and huge oil-paper umbrellas, were bowing and bobbing beside us, and saying, "Muramatsu, Muramatsu,"* over and over again, to show that they

*The Muramatsu Hotel had an advertisement in Murray's *Handbook for Travellers in Japan* (1894) declaring the hotel to be the best in the district. "There are several well-ventilated commodious bed and sitting rooms and also a spacious dining room furnished in European style."

came from the hotel. One last effort of our poor coolies dragged us up through an avenue of dripping firs, so steep that the trees might have been growing up the side of a house; and then we stopped for good under a hospitable porch full of red lanterns and smiling faces. Slowly we unpacked our drenched coverings, and crawled out, stiff and sore, and mighty glad to be under shelter at last. Oh the comfort of the sweet-smelling matted rooms, with their closed shutters, against which the rain beat in vain! In less time than it takes to tell it, our good Ogita and the servants had dry things unpacked, the wet wraps carried away, a pretty dinner-table laid out, with a bright lamp and fresh flowers to cheer us, and food and wine to make us forget the long hungry day. I felt rather like the forlorn little girl in the fairy tale, when the black hillside opened and the kind gnomes took care of her in their warm earth-home.

The view from those particular rooms is rather a celebrated one; so I rose and looked out the next morning as soon as the maid had crept round the balconies to remove the *amados,* the friendly outer shutters, which had kept out the rain of the night. Alas! it was the rain of the morning too; and the wide valley below us and the great mountains of Nikko beyond were only visible in shadowy gradations through the wet grey veil of rain. Not for this were they less beautiful; for the very greyness gives the outlines more grandeur, and the moving film of rain, now lighter, now heavier, now falling straight and sharp, now driven slanting up the valleys by a rush of the breeze, imparts a constant play of expression to the tear-stained face of Nature which it can never wear in the equalising gold of the sunshine. And when the worst is over, and the rain is sucked up into that wonderful mist of Japan, which makes and unmakes a hundred sky-pictures in an hour, each more weird and ethereal than the last, then one cannot quarrel with the rain. As I stand on the covered balcony, and smell the dear wetness of the earth and catch a stray drop on my cheek, my mind goes back to the thirsty lands of earth, —to our Roman campagna, burnt purple-brown in August, and too scorching to touch with the bare hand; to Chile, where every tree is sere by midsummer and the gasping country is buried in its own dust before its ten months' drought is quenched in icy rain; to that "land of sand and ruin and gold," Pechili, where a child may be a year old before the rain has christened it; where I used to go and sit on the baked hillside by our temple home and look across the quivering plain to Peking and—down into the face of an English baby dying of the heat. And I remember there came a day when I said to its mother, "Take courage; if it only rains to-night, he will live! Surely that is a cloud in the south!" And the rain came that night, and the little one lived—to die of another year's heat. Ah, dear rain, it is not I that will be quarrelling with you this day! In the outer life, thank God for the kindly showers that temper the breeze of the sunshine; in the inner, thank Him still more for the grey clouds of anxiety and the wholesome tears of pain, which keep us from being burnt dry and hard in the noonday of our prosperity.

And as I finished these reflections my friend came and stood by my side, and said, "Come, it is lighter now; let us go and have a look at things." Then we went out into the queer terraced town, clinging so closely to the wall of the hill that the main-street is a staircase, and a steep one too. From it the side-streets branch off, herringbone-wise, full of little inns where the bathers stay; for Ikao has hot springs (115° F.), which have been used for the cure of many diseases since very early times, and which still attract great numbers of Japanese to the place. The town is built around and over the springs, which seem to bubble up so freely in this volcanic land, sometimes hot and strong, sometimes weak and tepid, but every-where within the reach of the sick poor, who are able for very small sums to get cures which in Europe are costly in the extreme. Here, some two thousand five hundred feet above sea-level, the hot jets burst out of the green mountainside, and the little town has had to accommodate itself to them. The long street of stairs, full of quaint shops and fluttering signs, ends in a tall shaft of still steeper steps above the town; and these are crowned by a little temple, with stone benches before it, where one can sit and gaze at the enormous hills across the sweep of the upland valley. The temple has stone lanterns, which are votive offerings, and many fluttering banners, which are also offerings, though of a more perishable kind. At the foot of its grey steps is a little terrace, which is all one iris garden in full bloom; the sun suddenly shone down on it as I looked, and a hundred flowers, white and blue and royal purple, shook out flags in the mountain breeze which came fresh and sweet round the spur of the hill from the woods beyond.

The breeze seemed to be showing us the way; so when we had rested a little, we left the temple, and followed a road leading towards a deep ravine on the right. Here a noisy river tears down over boulders the colour of rust, for the water is rich in iron, and coats everything exposed to it with a heavy yellow layer; but the level walk on the side of the ravine is so thickly wooded that the stream is hidden half the time, and only its everlasting song comes up to say it is there. Slowly we went on into the green heart of the hills, the path overhung by deepest woods above, and below, plunging down in sudden precipices to where the torrent literally boils over the yellow stones with clouds of steam and hot spray, and rushes on to turn a huge mill-wheel in the gorge, just as any common cold stream could do! But up on the path all is solitude and quiet, and it seems quite fitting to come unawares on a little shrine with a smiling Buddha sitting on his mat, amid countless offerings of cups and vases, and smaller Buddhas to keep him company. But Buddha took my breath away by smiling benignantly right into my eyes, and rocking forward on his base in friendly salutation. Then I saw that the shrine is only a little china shop, as clean and silent as the heart of a flower, and apparently about as distantly connected with money-making; for without even moving from his place, Buddha let me carry off an exquisite blue cup, for which he received seven cents, and seemed as satisfied as if I had spent seven pounds at his dainty shrine. Beyond him the road became suddenly steeper, and we stood for a moment gazing up its green murmuring arches, broken where a glorious white hydrangea hung out a dancing tent of blossom over the sun-flecked path.

At the end of the path is an inn, with baths and many patients; and one can buy strange specimens of petrified woods, and stone cups, beautifully polished. Here, there is a perfect network of bamboo pipes, supported on tree branches or wistaria roots, or anything else that comes handy; and they run all the way down the valley to supply the different hotels with the mineral water; and in the stream itself lie strips of cotton, which are left there until they have absorbed enough iron to turn them yellow, and are then used as strength-giving belts, much prized by the people.

On our return, I think we must have entered every shop on the way. In one we bought whole pieces of Ikao cotton crape, a rough heavy fabric, with a brilliant reddish-yellow ground, exactly the colour of the iron-coated stones in the stream where the sun touches them; and the maker had the stream in his mind, I know, for up the lengths of yellow crape against the stream swim hundreds of vigorous carp, the symbol of persevering fortitude, amid waves and clouds dashed on in the sharp white and blue of a winter morning. The whole mass takes one's breath away with its rattling bravura of colour, and the eye rests gratefully on a pile of grey-green basket-work, made out of wistaria tendrils, the very tint of the twilight woods imprisoned in the meshes. Then there is pottery of every kind, for every use, but almost uniform in colour—the colour of Ikao, the colour of rust in the sun. There is a delight which I cannot name in finding these subtle harmonies, taken for granted by these people who are still close to the knee of Nature, but only touched by chance among us, who have forgotten our nursery lessons in the dreary board-school of life. I see that in Japanese eyes I am a barbarian even in my buyings; for I take a dozen things which have nought to do with each other, and Ogita and O'Matsu look gravely disapproving when the fairings are all tumbled out together on the mats of my little sitting-room.

There is another walk in Ikao, and this one goes down instead of up the hill, and is quite full of excitements. As we turned down it, I saw a quaint group. A small child was standing stock still in the middle of the road, with her back towards us her hair, shaven away in a neat tonsure on the top of her head, fell from there in a straight black curtain to her shoulders; her fat little body was wrapped in a pale-blue *kimono*; and in one hand she carried a teapot, pale-blue also, and swinging by its wicker handle. Evidently she had been sent to fetch *saké* or hot water; but her little bare feet seemed rooted to the ground, and she was gazing with silent terror into the face of a terrible beast who had set himself down directly in front of her. The beast was a yellow mongrel (Ikao colour, of course), who, by cocking his ears and stretching his fore-legs out as long as possible, had brought his head just to the level of the little maid's, and was looking at her with an expression which said far more clearly than words: "Yes, my dear, I *am* a very terrible dog, and all this road belongs to me, and you have no business here whatever; but *perhaps* I won't eat you quite up this time—oh! who are these awful creatures?" One sight of us was enough; with a long howl, the terrible dog fled down the street, and the little girl clutched her teapot, and shrank to one side as far as the road would allow, and looked up at us pitifully, as if she would say: "You see, the dog didn't eat me; I hope you won't, either!"

So we went on quickly to set her mind at rest, and came on a still funnier sight. A little bath-house, with no door, close to the road, was sending out fumes of steam mixed with talk; inside, in a space not more than a yard square, three dames of the village, with only their heads above water, were having a good gossip. On the edge, among the discarded clothing, lay a baby, trying hard to wriggle into the water too. Of course all the heads turned to have a look at us; two of the ladies hopped out of the water like frogs, and sat on the edge of the bath discussing our appearance, absolutely untroubled by their own, and then hopped in again for another dip. I saw one of them walking home later, with most of her clothes under one arm and the baby on the other. There is so much disinvoltura about Japanese manners!

Farther on we came to a bow-and-arrow booth, where the owner was very anxious that we should have a shot at the painted target; but we were much more interested in a queer grey monkey, tailless as a Japanese cat, who was jumping about as far as his tether would let him, against grey-green rocks the very colour of himself. He too saw that we were foreign monsters of some kind, and showed off all his tricks, and then flashed his fiery red face and human eyes round at us to see if we had been impressed by them, and he was visibly chagrined when we moved on. At the foot of the hill lives a knotty little old man, who looks as if he had been made out of dried twigs. His hair stands up in bristles all over his head, his eyes dance with good humour, and at every word he says, whether he means it or not, down goes his head to his poor old knees in the most engaging bow. This is because he keeps a tea-house with two splendid fish-ponds; and his business is to come out into the road and stop the travellers, and beg them to come into his "dirty house," as he humbly puts it, for a little tea and some good fishing; and that is why he has got into such a habit of bowing that he could not stop if he would. There is a little old woman too; but she sits inside on the mats, and invitingly pushes cushions and trays of tea towards you, if you will only come near enough. I suppose she had legs once, but she must have sat them off by this time, for she never gets up, and there are no particular signs of them anywhere. The ponds are too delightful to be passed by. There are neat benches and planked footways beside them; and by one you can sit, and catch gold and silver fish, like any princess in a fairy tale, for a few cents an hour; by the other you may also sit, and watch how the great fat old gold-fish, almost as big as carp, come and fight for the cakes that are thrown in, how they shove out the younger ones, and kick and splash and struggle till the water is all churned up and the biscuit they are fighting for is thrown high and dry on the bank. Then the fish go off in a rage, and the little old man laughs indulgently, and creeps warily down the bank and throws the pink biscuit out to sea, and the comedy begins all over again. We were not the only guests at the inn of the gold and silver fish; on the bench by the pond sat a middle-aged Japanese, in European dress. He was gravely catching goldfish with a thread and a bit of bamboo; he looked intensely solemn, and frowned visibly when we laughed and chattered on the other side of the pond; and he dropped the "take" with great care into his best top hat, turned upside down for the purpose.

Karuizawa, July, 1890

We left Ikao rather regretfully, and, mindful of past experiences, very early in the morning. The road, all shining in the early sun-shine, did not seem to be the same one up which we had toiled in rain and darkness two weeks ago. The valleys were green and wet below us, and the hills beyond towered against a brilliantly blue sky just flecked with little clouds of dazzling white. The banks of the road were beautiful with blue lilies, and the air was full of song-birds. The Japanese are early risers, and all the little cottage homes were open to the day; in almost all, the business of silk-spinning was going forward, for this is the time when the cocoons are ripe, and the precious threads must be saved ere the moth feels his wings and bites his way through to freedom.

It is a pretty sight, when the little brown cottages are full of piles of the delicate cocoons, light as puff-balls, and generally a snowy white, or soft flaxen colour, but mingled here and there with large cocoons of a pale yellowish green, the production of a silkworm who lives on a certain species of wild oak. As far as I could gather, these cocoons are collected in the woods, and the worm, if reared in captivity, takes to mulberry leaves, and becomes small and tame like any other silkworm. But this may be only a peasant tradition. The silk reeled from these greenish cocoons is of a coarse and heavy kind, and cannot be used with other varieties. The work of reeling off the thread seems to be done in this part of the world by old people, who can no longer do rough work in the fields. I passed one cottage after another where an old man or woman, sometimes an aged couple, sat on the ground among piles of the soft white balls, reeling off the silk on the roughest kind of hand-wheel, to which it passes from a little trough filled with hot water, constantly renewed. The knotty old fingers manipulate the strands very delicately; but the reeled thread is full of knots and inequalities, and could only, I should think, be used for inferior silks. Even in that form it is valuable, and the old people's little crop will probably go far towards maintaining them for the rest of the year.

As we descended into the plain, the cottages were scattered more thickly along the road, and we passed through village streets where every house was full of cocoon piles, making the effect of snowdrifts swept back from the road into the houses. We were making for Iizuka, a station a little farther up the line than Takasaki, from which we could do an hour or so of railway-travelling in the direction of Karuizawa before taking to chairs and jinrikshas again. We had found some firstrate chair-coolies in Ikao, and they carried me down the hilly roads at a swinging trot, and with none of the misery which had attended the upward journey. But the heat was intense as soon as we reached the plain, and no words can describe how grateful and refreshing was the hospitality of the pretty tea-house at Iizuka, where we had an hour's rest before our train could pass. The little upper rooms, cool, matted, open on every side to the air under the wide verandah roof, seemed luxuriously spacious and quiet; from the eaves hung fern-wreaths grown in quaint shapes on wistaria roots, each one having a small glass bell fastened to it, and a bit of paper with a word or two of poetry dangling from the bell. The lightest puff of breeze sets the paper moving, and then the bell speaks in a little musical tinkle like the sound of running water. Our hostess brought up a fairy meal of strawberries and scraped ice and lemonade; and O'Matsu brought a fan, and kept the air cool while we tasted it. By the time the train steamed up, we had forgotten the heat and weariness of the morning, and started out refreshed for the second part of our journey. This stage brought us as far as Yokokawa, a town nestling close in at the foot of the Usui Pass, which leads up into the great dividing range, the central Alps of Japan.

Yokokawa is demoralised by the railway and tram traffic, and has very little that is picturesque about it. The railway stops here,* and the traveller is carried on into the hills by a crazy tram service, composed of tiny carriages drawn by broken-down horses, up a road which is washed away by rain or whelmed in landslips at least once a week. When the cars are not thrown off the line, they jump about so alarmingly that the unfortunate passengers are black and blue by the time they reach Karuizawa; altogether, the journey was considered too sensational for me, and the Ikao coolies had been brought on to carry me up the pass. Some of the party were in jinrikshas, which can follow the tramway line; but for me there was the delightful luxury of a long chair ride through shady paths up wooded steeps, where the tendrils of the creepers brushed my face, and the delicate woodsey smell of fern and pine, wistaria and hydrangea, came in waves out of the solemn greennesses of the forest. Now and then we stopped, that the men might rest at one of those tiny brown dwellings scattered like empty chestnut burrs along the path; always planted near a stream or a trickling waterfall,

*Murray's *Handbook for Travellers in Japan* (1894) says "the construction of the 7 miles of railway leading to Karuizawa over the Usui Pass presented greater difficulties than any that had hitherto been contended with by engineers in Japan, and for this reason a hiatus remained in the middle of the line to the West Coast until 1893, when the Abt system, with its cogwheels working on rack-rails, was successfully introduced."

with perhaps the virgin rock for a background, they consist of one tiny room open to the woods, with a bench for the pilgrim to rest on, a low-burning fire to make his tea over, and a few scrupulously clean blue cups and bowls to serve it in. And how refreshing the Japanese tea is! One of our party had followed me on foot, and was glad enough of the pale gold-coloured liquid steaming in its tiny cups. It quenches thirst far better than any of our luxurious iced drinks, and gives just the amount of nerve stimulant needed during long walks in the heat. The perfume is faint and fine, and has become so connected with our roamings in Japan that, no matter how many years had passed, it would instantly bring back to me the house in the forest or by the roadside, the kind brown faces, the balmy air, the luminous whiteness of the Eastern day.

The woods were left behind at last, and from their cloistered depths we came out on the ridges where not a landscape but a universe seemed to sink away from below our feet, in a wash of warm silver and green gold, filmed with a network of rivers that flowed on from our mountains, in ribbons of level light, towards the hazy glories of the plain. One knew not which way to look; that one supreme moment of a summer day had come, when every tint is purified to a jewel-like perfection, every dell is mantled in living velvet, every rock leaps into amethyst flame, every pool is a piece of heaven, and the sun shines over all, a swimming haze of gold, tender and radiant and warm as the very tears of happiness.

I cannot name the sea of peaks which rose behind and before us. As the summer goes on, they will become individually familiar to me, no doubt; but on this first day their greatness and their multiplicity were too overwhelming for me to even ask their names. Thousands of feet above the dreaming plain, arrested in the cisterns of the hills, a sea of wildly tossing breakers, the white horses of the hurricane, must have been caught and changed to stone at the stormiest moment of their splendid play. Empty as the ocean hollows, barren as the breaker's crest, sharp-edged as the north wind's bite— ah! what can ever put before you all that I saw that day, as I stood on the mountain's ridge between heaven and earth, watching the fires of the sunset kiss the cold crags they could never warm to life?

We dared not linger long, for the night would fall chill in the hills after such a burning day. We let our men rest for a little in the inn of the village which crowns the Usui Toge, a poor grey village, with a temple to keep watch over the pilgrims who pass through it in the summer-time. There are broad stone steps to the temple, and from there the view is glorious; if the contemplation of beauty conduces to holiness, then its priest should be a very holy man. His son, a lad of ten, who stood leaning against the gate, watching us with bold bright eyes, is the black sheep of the village; and we were told sad stories of his pranks by the innkeeper, at which the boy laughed defiantly. He will not go to school, and sometimes tears down the *gohei,* or white prayer papers, which pious souls hang up with straw ropes at the temple gate; he tears his clothes, and loses his father's books; but the worst of all his sins is that he plays practical jokes on that sacred person, his paternal grandmother! Once he killed her cat; another day he nailed a dead crow to the shutters of her house, and then called her out in a hurry, saying that a beautiful procession was going by. Altogether the village seems to have little hope of the young reprobate, and agree in thinking that it is "a sair dispensation for the meenister!"

From the top of the pass we descended quickly and easily for a little way, and then stood for a few minutes to gaze at Asama Yama, the great active volcano which dominates all this side of the hills, and has more than once filled the upland plain of Karuizawa with ashy desolation. It rises very grandly from beyond the green foothills, looking far nearer than it really is. Heavy clouds of smoke pour from the crater, which looks from Karuizawa towards the southwest, and takes the form of a horizontal tunnel into the mountain, as I am told. From that point on the pass there is a wonderful evening effect, as the sun sinks almost behind the peak and rims its heavy clouds of smoke with crimson and gold. We lost it as we plunged into the deep-cut paths below; and when at last we reached our own boundaries, the grey twilight calm was hushing the hills to rest.

And now I am writing in the most lovely study in the world. Over my head the pine branches meet in arches of kindly green; the pillars of my hall are warm brown trunks, roughened in mystic runes by the sun and the wind, and full of sweet gums that catch and cling to my hand if I lay it against the bark; underfoot a hundred layers of pine needles have been weaving a carpet so elastic that the weariest foot must press it lightly; and, lest I should want for music, a stream, deep-running between hedges of wild clematis and white hydrangea and crowding wistaria tangle, sings a cool tune near by, while the hum of happy insects in the air sounds the high note of noon, the hot Eastern noon, when every bird is still.

Very, very early this morning I crept to the verandah of my bedroom, and pushed aside the *amado* and looked out, down the green depths of my woodsey garden, across the foothills below us to the plain beyond, dreaming and blue still in the virginal lights of the dawn. Near by, on either side, the forest spread from our little clearing, up and up to the summits of the hills that guard us on the left. On the right it rolled more gradually to the foot of a green wall, up whose sides some rocky steps lead to what must be a shrine; I can see figures cut in the rock, and a seat below, and a green bough waving far out from some crevice above. All was still and silent, as if just created and waiting for the breath of life to be infused by the Creator. Then, as the silence became too intense to be borne, one liquid rippling note rang out of the sleeping woods in a burst of joy, so breathless, so triumphant that it might have come from the gates of paradise. When it ceased, the clear vibrations still went ringing up through the hills; and in a moment the answer thrilled back from the distant groves below the lonely shrine. I do not know how long I stood listening; it was one of those moments in life which mark an epoch, when time has no value and identity is forgotten. I know that all the other birds listened as silently as I until my Lord and Lady Nightingale had finished their golden matins, and that when other songs broke forth, and the sun touched the hilltops to life, I turned away satisfied with beauty, one more hour of perfect happiness added to that rich inheritance of which no future grief or privation can ever rob me.

We have named our summer home the Palace of Peace; for though it is close to the only track leading up the pass, it is wrapped in green seclusion. The village—there is a village—is not seen till you have passed out at the foot of our garden, between the pine trees that guard the gate, across two streams bridged somewhat shakily, and down a bit of road that turns with the turning hillside. Then, indeed, a few houses are seen; and if you go on, a long poor street winds away before you, reaches another bridge, and passes thence among the wild flowers of the plain, which stretches its level for many miles, bordered on either hand by beautiful green mountains, itself more than three thousand feet above the sea. The plain we see from our windows; but not a single roof-tree breaks the enchanting sense of solitude. Our house is a Japanese one, two-storied, built of wood, with deep galleries running round both floors, the upper one protected by wide eaves, and also by glazed screens instead of the usual paper slides; so that even in very bad weather we need not shut out the light by closing the wooden shutters, as people have to do usually in Japanese houses.

The inner walls are also of glass, where they look on the verandah. The dividing ones between the rooms are papered, and can be removed at will; so that we can have one very huge apartment or several small ones, according to taste and fancy. All the glass walls have in their turn curtains of heavy mosquito netting, which fall from ceiling to floor, with a slit here and there to allow of passing through; and they both keep out the insects, and ensure a certain amount of privacy. There is just room for ourselves and two of the staff, they occupying one verandah and we the other; while servants' quarters and offices go meandering back somewhere into the heart of the hill, whence an ingenious system of bamboo-tubing supplies all the bathrooms (one to every room in the delightfully civilised Eastern fashion), as well as the dinner-table, with the purest, freshest water I have ever tasted. It wells right out of the rock, and the servants bring the bottles down, all misty and impearled with the coldness of it.

Of course all the rooms are matted, and a recess under the lowest stair holds our house-slippers. When we come in from a walk, everybody sits down on the outer step of the verandah, the servants run out with our clean slippers in hand, and not until they are donned do we tread on the delicate mats. These are so fine and soft that I constantly sit on them instead of in my chair; and in warm weather they are delightful to sleep on, cool, resisting, and yet elastic. There are chairs of all sorts of pretty rustic patterns; the whole furniture of my bedroom is made in matting set in soft grey bark, the original untouched tree; the mirror frame is a lovely setting of twigs, the table legs the slender boughs of saplings,—all this being the idea of the Japanese carpenter who made the furniture, and who thought I would like to have something in harmony with the woods around. Everywhere is the smell of sweet new planks and fresh grass blinds and the murmur of streams and pine woods, and—it is heavenly cool! We can use a blanket at night, and I am wearing light flannel dresses in the afternoon.

As we sat on the verandah in delightful repose on the evening of our arrival, a dancing light appeared at the far end of the garden, and came slowly nearer until it resolved itself into a bobbing lantern, which roused our five dogs to one defiant howl. The lantern-bearer paused, then found courage to approach, and a gorgeous person in white uniform, white gloves, and a good deal of gold about him, slowly loomed on our astonished sight, and stopped at the verandah-step with a military bow. This was our special policeman, under whose charge we are to be for the summer. He held out a piece of paper towards us, exclaiming, "My card!" Then he looked at H——. "You—Minister?" he inquired; and when H—— nodded, he proceeded to explain that he had been sent up from Nagano to look after us, and that he should carry out his orders with vigilance and zeal. The English was very queer, and ground out a word at a time; but he would not be helped, and was rather offended when Mr. G—— addressed him in fluent Japanese. His parting salutation was original: "Please! Receive! Sleep!" Then he left us, and he and his lantern bobbed off into the darkness again. He is quartered in the village, and I hear takes advantage of his special mission to swagger fearfully among his colleagues and compatriots.

Karuizawa, July, 1890

The evenings are almost as enchanting as the mornings in this July weather. We sit out till very late, watching the stars shining through the clear air as they never shine for us when we are on the plain. Our green lawnlet (the turf was brought bit by bit from a great distance, and is growing beautifully now) slopes down to a pond where the stars all find their doubles on these still nights.*

I brought a whole library of instructive books up here; but reading is sheer waste of time in these surroundings, and one's eyes are too filled with new and lovely sights to go back contentedly to printed books and other people's thoughts. What book that ever was published brings the sense of strength and peace that the sight of pine branches waving across the morning sky can give? God's books are not all written in printer's ink. On this wind-swept upstairs gallery where I write I am on a level with the second story of the pines, and they are reaching out their green and gold towards me with generous hands. I have just come back from a long walk over the plain; we have had a fearful typhoon; and the first *Lilium auratum* has been brought in: of which shall I tell you first? The typhoon, of course? Ah, well, there is no accounting for tastes.

The typhoon burst upon us last week, happily not quite without warning. When it rains ramrods for twenty-four hours, and the barometer behaves as if it had St. Vitus's dance, we know what to expect in this part of the world, and look to chimneys and shutters, see that the animals are under cover, and, up here, shovel away the dam which turns a part of the mountain stream through the washhouse, and see that the auxiliary streamlet is returned with thanks before the worst floods rush by. But all the precautions in the world cannot make the visitation anything but a very dreadful one; and when it is over, one is more inclined to thank Heaven for that which has not happened than to grumble at damage done. I think I told you that our cottage is built on a three-cornered piece

*The bulk of this entry has been deleted. Mrs. Fraser relates the well-known legend of the cowherd and the weaver-maiden and a separate Chinese story.

of land, bounded on the two lower sides by converging streams, and rising into the hills at the back. The whole is on a rather sharp slope, a fortunate circumstance, for floods and freshets drain off quickly without doing much damage to the house or garden, but wreaking their fury on our communications with the outer world beyond. All through that memorable day the heat was intense, the rain fell with mechanical regularity in straight bars which rattled like iron on all our roofs, made the lawn and paths one moving sheet of water, and churned our toy pond into sputtering froth. All the galleries were safely enclosed with the glass screens; but on two sides the heavy night-shutters had to be put up to keep the rooms from being flooded. Whatever there was of insect life in the garden and woods seemed to be taking refuge in the house. Mosquitoes, moths, huge armed cockchafers heavy as stones—all flung themselves against the glass; and for the thousandth time I was glad that we had not windowed our house with paper in real Japanese fashion—we should have had to sit all day with candles behind closed shutters, as many of our friends did through this very storm.

The poor servants were much alarmed, for they knew as well as we did what was coming. The cook was seen climbing the roof of the kitchen off the shoulders of "Chiisai Cook San" (Little Cook Mr.) to inspect an extra long iron chimney, which he had induced me in a moment of foolhardiness to have put up for his benefit. The servants live so much out of doors, that there are numberless little properties in their own yard to be got under cover, if a very bad storm is coming. Even the dogs lay wise and silent, asking no questions and expecting no walks; not even nosing about under the front doorsteps, where they bury their best bones. Our good policeman (his name is Furihata) came up several times instead of only twice in the course of the day to see if all was right with us; and Mr. G—— visited the waterworks anxiously, fearing either that we should be swamped or else have all our bamboo pipes carried away down the main stream.

The intense oppression and excitement that I have felt in other typhoons was upon us all; we seemed to be fighting the air, hot, choking, evil air, full of enemies to soul and body. Our great volcano neighbour, Asama Yama, had sent out more than one long roar, and the earth had heaved once and twice under our feet, when at last the storm reached us, swept over and round and through us in a concentrated fury of attack. Every moment it seemed as if the house must go, and we and it be hurled down to the drowning plain. The night came down black as wet pitch, and our poor little home, with its flickering lamps and quivering walls, seemed the only point left in the inky darkness. The wooden shutters had all been run into place and tightly bolted when the hurricane broke, for a wooden house of this kind could rise up and sail down the wind like an open umbrella if one lifting gust got under the roof. So all night long we sat, or lay down for a little, with everything prepared for flight should the storm prove the stronger; and again and again it seemed impossible that our wooden pillars resting on shallow stones should be able to withstand the force of the wind, which shrieked and beat and thundered against them all in turn. The whole safety of a Japanese house depends on the wooden pillars which support it (the walls are mere veils of plank stretched between), and an ingenious arrangement is resorted to in order that the pillars may have literally fair play. Each square pillar stands in a socket of stone, the only foundation used at all, and not placed more than two feet below the floor of the house. The pillar is square, and is rounded off at the base; and the socket is also round, and is slightly too large for the post which rests in it, thus allowing the post a chance of moving a very little in earthquake or storm, and righting itself again at once. In slight or medium shocks a house built in this way suffers hardly at all, its elasticity preventing the resistance which would wreck a hard and fast edifice; in the mad destruction of a violent earthquake, I doubt if the house has yet been built which would not suffer, and suffer greatly. Twice in that awful night I felt as if the house must really go, when two great lifting gusts seemed to have got under it; but the long hours passed, and again and again the whole fury of the storm hurled itself against us without doing any sensible damage. As we heard the thunder of the swollen torrents on either hand roll by, with many a crash of timber and cannonade of flying stones, and yet saw that our floors were dry and our roof whole, we took heart to sleep a little, hoping that the tempest would be over by the morning. It had raged for several hours, and all through the night I heard Mr. G—— tapping the barometer violently from time to time to see if it could not be induced to show signs of settling. One of the strangest portents of the storm was the wild excitement of the needle. It danced from side to side, and hardly stayed quiet for a moment till the gale was over; and then it settled to "Fair," and stayed there, in spite of black skies and a deluged world. I suppose it knew what it was about! I am told that this nervousness of the glass is an invariable feature of the true typhoon.

At last the fury of the storm passed away and travelled up through the hills with long wails and half-heard shrieks so awful that they gave the impression of some agonised creature, invisible, close, being tortured to death before our eyes that saw nothing. Fainter and fainter it grew, and only when it passed away did we begin to hear clearly the angry roar of the torrents which had all night acted as an undernote to the tempestuous voices of the gale. As soon as daylight came—such wet grey daylight!—the more daring crept out to see what damage had been done. I was joyfully told that Cook San's dear chimney was none the worse, and I believe he must have made Chiisai Cook San sit on the roof all night to hold it in place. But other things had not been so fortunate. The water-works were badly damaged; several trees which had been planted symmetrically beside a fence had been bowled over like so many ninepins; the road over the pass was gone in many places, the one to the village was under water and torn to shreds; while our own bridge hung over the main torrent on one crazy beam, to be crept across with breathless care. As for the tramway and the telegraph lines, they had ceased to exist, and for five days after that visitation not a message of any kind reached us, and our supplies from Tokyo (on which we mainly depend for food) were entirely cut off. Our poor gardener, who sleeps in the village, struggled up here in the worst of the storm to see if he could do anything for us; and Furihata, our dear little policeman, behaved gallantly. At about three in the morning, when it was blowing great guns, I heard him going on his beat round the house, and, peeping out through a chink in the shutters, saw his faithful yellow lantern bobbing about, protected in some ingenious fashion by his oilskin cloak from the rain and wind. He came up again after daylight to tell us about the dangerous condition of the bridge, and to say that it should be mended immediately; but except that he and two of his colleagues have been seen staring at it with gravity, no steps have been taken as yet. We are in pleasing uncertainty as to where a large supply of wine, some new clothes, and a quantity of groceries have gone to, and I begin to understand the feelings of dear Ben Gunn when he longed for Christian diet on Treasure Island. But now the country is looking so perfect in its fresh beauty after the rain that I ought to be ashamed of repining at such small misfortunes. A harmless breeze is sweeping the soft white clouds into heaps and corners, the sky is sapphire blue between; our pond, composed again, is reflecting it all respectfully; and the air is full of the sound of the leaping streams, which are still having it all their own way for miles around. Through the forest I hear the woodcutter again at work; and farther off, below the stone shrine in the green hillside, a little thread of smoke rises dreamy blue above the pine-tops, showing that the charcoal-burner's family (I discovered them in one of my walks) are again at work.

We have been down through the village and out across the plain since the storm, and had a delightful sense of danger in picking our way over the dancing bridge. The wise dogs refused to trust themselves to it, and all except Bess, the old pointer, had to be carried across. The loose lava of the roads makes them like long ridges of rubble after the floods of last week; but the cool smell of everything and the whiff of vitality in the air make up for a little rough walking.

We had been out beyond the village, and were returning towards it, when a funny sight met our eyes. A bridge at the farther end had been a good deal knocked about by the storm, but still presented a respectable appearance. I saw two men riding towards it from the opposite side; they were smartly dressed in white European clothes and pith helmets such as our inspector wears in summer. As we know every soul in the place, I was curious to see who these strangers were, when the foremost horse stepped gaily on the bridge. Then— he went through it, at least his forefeet did, and he lay amazed, caught in the rotten wood, while the well-dressed stranger rolled over his head, scrambled to his feet, and turned out to be our cook in his new Sunday clothes, followed by Kané, the artistic pantry-boy, dressed exactly like him. Kané turned and fled—why, I know not, since there was no crime in hiring a horse and taking a ride, even if we were on foot at the time. The poor Cook San looked most uncomfortable, but pulled his steed up bravely, and led him aside while we passed. I only asked him if he had hurt himself, and denied myself the pleasure of looking back to see him scramble up again.

One other walk we have had since the storm, up the Usui Toge, to pay a visit to some friends who have taken a house for the summer in the hamlet which crowns the pass. The road was in many places a series of rifts, over which we had to scramble as we could; the loose tufa soil allows the rain to settle and sink through the surface cracks; and when the water has worked a yard or two down, the slightest shock detaches the whole piece, which goes rolling off into the torrent or the valley, leaving one more bare scar on the mountain-side. The clearest tramontana wind blew in our faces, and kept us cool, though it was four o'clock, quite the hottest hour of our August day. The brooks were rushing gloriously down the dells and gorges through which the path winds up, the flowers were full of wet sweetness in the sun, and the landscape was like one great washed jewel in the afternoon light. Our mountains, great volcanic crags, with their feet buried in soft green foothills, were all wreathed in golden haze. On the crest of the pass, we crept out on a dividing spur, a flying buttress of the mountains, whence all the plain stretches away on the left, and that mass of rocks called the Myogi San (the maiden pass) tosses its granite breakers off to the right. Here we sat long, and in silence, watching the rose creep into the gold, the purple into the rose, and some one said, "It will be dark in half an hour"; and we turned to hurry down the steep path while some daylight remained.

Karuizawa, September, 1890

Exactly eight days after our first typhoon, we had a second edition of it, which really worked fearful havoc among the hills, where the soil of the paths has been torn and rubble loosened by the first visitation. Our bridge went altogether this time; but fortunately we found that there is a little one where the stream is much smaller, through the deep hedge at the far end of our garden. The chief bridge is now being rebuilt; and meanwhile we have had to let people pass by the little one, which is intended as a short cut to the path leading off to the charcoal-burner's establishment. On a misty night or after an extra cup of *saké* it is difficult to distinguish the paths. One rather cloudy evening following on a rainy day, we were sitting on the verandah as usual after dinner, when a lantern, evidently in a state of extreme excitement, appeared far down the garden path. I never saw a lantern behave so curiously. First it waved about in the air, then it sank to the ground, then it swung from side to side. As it came nearer, it was carried low, and illuminated two extremely shaky brown legs, which staggered from side to side, tottered, recovered themselves, then began it all over again. We sat in amused silence while this strange creature appeared and disappeared among the shrubs, and at last came close to the verandah steps and revealed its whole identity. The light crept up from the round paper lantern over a sturdy body, very poorly dressed, and crowned by a sleepy face full of irresponsible smiles—a face which waggled joyfully from side to side, and was the colour of old wood; in fact, our neighbour the charcoal-burner, royally drunk.

"This is a very good house," he remarked; "better than the Bansho Kwan (the village inn)."

"What do you want?" Mr. G—— asked. "You have mistaken the road to your house."

"No," replied our visitor, shaking his head as gravely as he could, —"no mistake. House want, house find. Rain soon. Stay here."

He seemed about to sit down on the verandah, when some of the servants appeared; the man spoke in a loud excited way, and they had heard the strange voice.

"You have lost your way," Mr. G—— repeated; "this is not an inn. You shall be accompanied till you find the right path."

Then Rinzo and Uma, looking much amused, took each an arm of the stray lamb. Rinzo relieved him of his lantern, and they walked him down the path, he talking excitedly all the time about the Bansho Kwan, where he said there had been a wedding feast, and just a little—oh! very little—*saké* for everybody. And, indeed, he did not care to go away, although such honourable persons deigned to accompany him; for this was better than the Bansho Kwan—much better than the Bansho Kwan. His voice died off in the distance; and in about ten minutes our men came back, saying that they had put him in the right path, and he could make no mistakes now; besides, it was beginning to rain, and that would sober him, they thought.

The rain did not touch us under our broad verandah, so we sat on for some time, talking of everything under the sun, and unwilling to go and sit near the hot lamps in the drawing-room. The rain fell in soft splashes in our pond, and the trees began to talk, as they always do when there is rain enough to drop from branch to branch. The air was almost too sweet from the masses of *Lilium auratum,* which mark our real midsummer in the hills. The gardener stands them, in huge sheaves, in straight jars a yard high, in the doorways and verandahs; and we were telling wonderful tales of pink lilies, brown lilies, yellow lilies, when—that same crazy lantern appeared coming towards the house, still more erratically than before. As it approached, the sound of heavy steps dragging over the wet pebbles made itself heard between some indistinct remarks about the Bansho Kwan—our friend the charcoal-burner again! He was much tipsier than he had been an hour before, and came with something of a swagger up the wet, slippery path.

"Good house—much rain—very wet. This is a bright house, good for a man to stay in—much better than the Bansho Kwan!"

"Go home at once," said Mr. G——, who thought he was not so tipsy as he seemed. "You must have been drinking a great deal of *saké* not to know that you are making a mistake."

"A mistake no crime," replied the charcoal-burner. "No" (this to Rinzo, who took his arm), "I will not go away; why should a poor man be sent away? Why should a poor man be scolded because he loses his way? Is it a crime to lose one's way? Oh no! I will stay here—here!"

The servants were just about to remove him firmly, in spite of his violent protestations, when Furihata's highly official lantern marched quickly up the path; and at the sight of his cap and white gloves the poor tipsy intruder collapsed, and began to weep over his pitiful fate. He was carried off at last, still wailing about the nice house that was so very much better than the Bansho Kwan; and when the servants returned, they said that the stern Furihata had put

211

the poor sinner comfortably to bed on the mats of the police station, where, as I was afterwards told, he woke up good and happy the next morning, and got home successfully by daylight.

Our garden entrance looks so like a piece of the road, that strangers and pilgrims constantly turn into it, and come wandering up to the house, which some of them take for a foreign hotel. One evening, when we returned very late from some expedition, we were told that two English gentlemen, riding down the pass, had entered the house, and ordered two bedrooms and dinner; they took Dinsmore for the proprietor, and were greatly overcome when they found that they had invaded a fellow-countryman's private castle. Some friends of ours, who have built a charming cottage at Chuzenji, above Nikko, told me that last summer two hot and weary Englishmen burst into their house, and informed the astonished servant that breakfast for twelve people must be ready in half an hour; the rest of the party were on the road. They would have an omelette, beefsteaks, Kirin beer, and I know not how much more. But by the time they had gone into these details, the Japanese "boy" had remembered three words of English. He bowed politely, and then said, "This—European—house!" The unlucky intruders fled without saying another word, and probably found all they wanted at the excellent inn a few hundred yards farther up the path.

Since I have spoken of the pilgrims, let me tell you something about them; for they go by us in great bands at this time of year, and are certainly the most picturesque and cheery devotees that ever walked. On the road that leads up the pass, there is a spot where an old tree has fallen, and makes a pleasant seat. Beyond, the path is steeper, and turns in to follow the trend of a gorge whose sides are all a tangle of wild forest. Sitting here to rest in the breathless afternoon, we hear the phantom of a sound, the tinkle of a bell so far off on the hillside that it sounds unreal, intermittent, and we strain our ears to catch it again. Yes, it is a little nearer now—now nearer still. A little farther up, the road is broken by the storms; and now passing feet are sending the loose rubble leaping down the slope in little showers. Now a chant is wafted to us, with the deep note of the bell; and in a moment a strange-looking train comes out of the green leafage, and winds down the hill. There are nine of them to-day, and they are bound for Zenkoji, the great Temple at Nagano; their dress is that of pilgrims who ascend the holy mountains; and there are no women among them. The foremost is a tall handsome man, who carries a straight wooden standard, with strange characters painted black on its whiteness. He, like all those who follow him, is dressed in pure white, with sacred characters printed on the cotton. The closefitting leggings are white too, and finish with *tabi* and straw sandals, *waraji,* which may be bought for next to nothing at every tea-house, and are seldom worn more than through one day's march. The pilgrim's robe is closely kilted up through his cotton girdle, which, tight as it is, holds his money, his pipe, and any other valuables that he must carry. To the belt is attached that soft tinkling bell which gave us the signal of his coming; and on his head is a huge mushroom hat, made of lightest pith or shavings, and resting over, but not on, the head by means of a bamboo circle, from which spring light supports, so that the air passes in under the white umbrella. The hat is marked with the same ideograph that is stamped on his clothes, probably the name of the pilgrim club of his village or district; and on his shoulders he wears a piece of matting, which hangs round his neck by a string. This is his rain-cloak, his seat, his bed, and is called the *goza.* Then in his hand he carries a staff, with several names burnt into it—the names of the shrines he has visited; and a flask hangs at his side, in which he can bring home some of the water of a sacred lake or pond, such as many of the sanctuaries possess. His sleeves are as tightly tied up as his skirts; and although the costume may sound strange thus described in detail, yet nothing could look lighter or be more appropriate for the purpose of long walking in the heat.

I have described one man's dress, and have thus described the rest; for they are all alike, this being the prescribed uniform for climbing the high and holy peaks. The train looked wonderfully cool and picturesque coming out from the green foliage of the woods. The first man had a handsome face, very bronzed and healthy, with bright eyes, which glanced curiously at us, although he did not break off the chant in which he was leading the rest—a chant which is a constant repetition of one phrase: "Rokkon Shōjō, Oyama Kaisei" (May our six senses be pure, and honourable mountain

213

weather fine). Behind him came a boy; then an old man, who must have made many pilgrimages, and is perhaps near the last of all; then a prosperous-looking tradesman; after him an ascetic, with pale face and immovable expression. The pilgrim club sends people from the counter and the factory, as well as from the farm and the rice-field, to tramp the holy roads together, and bring back blessings for the rest of the villagers or townsfolk, too busy or too old or too weak to perform the pilgrimage for themselves.

The pilgrim clubs are institutions existing all through the country, to enable even the very poor to visit holy places, and to get an immense amount of change and amusement and interest on the way. Hundreds of people (and often thousands) belong to a club, which can be started anywhere by anybody who chooses to obtain permission to do so from the authorities of his particular sect (and sects are numberless), and who has the energy or the necessary personality to get his friends to join him. A tiny entrance fee of a few cents is required, and the subscription varies from eight to fifteen cents a year. When all the expenses are paid, the remaining money is raffled for, and the winners (perhaps 2 or 3 per cent. of the whole number) spend their gains on the pilgrimage; but no one is debarred from going at his own expense if he pleases. The president of the club is always the leader, and his expenses are paid as a matter of course. He knows the road, he knows the shrines and the priests and the innkeepers; but he is not required to see to actual payments, a treasurer being elected, who has to give an account of all these. The inns take pilgrims at reduced prices, and the cost of even a very long expedition is so tiny that we Europeans in our stupid vulgar extravagance would hardly know that we had spent it at all. It is a matter of cents, and yet the Japanese manages to get weeks of travelling on it, to visit one holy or historical spot (it is the same thing very often in his country) after another, and to make acquaintance with endless numbers of his countrymen, all bound, during the few summer weeks of pilgrimage-time, on the same errand.

As the pilgrimages are really made on foot, of course the summer months are usually chosen, as the fine weather and long days add greatly to the pleasure of tramping through the country; indeed, the shrines on the peaks can only be visited between the middle of July

214

and the beginning of September. Then the rest-houses are opened, the roads have been mended, the tea-houses are all ready to receive the guests, and the mountain is called "open." There are many holy peaks; but of all, Fuji is the greatest, and the ascent the most painful. Women belong to the pilgrim clubs, and have also clubs of their own; but they are not allowed (were not would be a better word) to mount to the summit. They were considered too common, made of too base a stuff, to tread the sacred ground of the mountain's crest, and were stopped at some distance from it; and in consequence they flock to the lowland shrines, where they are welcomed and made to feel at home. They travel constantly to the great Temple of Zen-koji, which lies to our west in the town of Nagano; and to judge by their beaming faces and happy chatter, they must enjoy the expedition mightily, though most of them are old and grey, having handed over household cares to the useful daughter-in-law, and feeling now free to attend to their souls and their amusement. I once asked one of our servants about his mother—how she passed her time, what her occupations were. "No work; she not work now—too much old! Little temple go, little theatre go—very happy!"

The "O'Bassans" of the pilgrim parties are often accompanied by a grandchild, a bright little maid of twelve or thirteen, who waits on her grandmother, and stares amazed at barbarians like ourselves. It is surprising to find how far these old women and little girls can walk, carrying all their baggage in humble bundles—such tiny bundles! Some of them seem to be as little troubled with luggage as a migrating swallow.

So in the pleasant summer-time, through the length and breadth of the land, the roads are all alive with gay parties of people visiting the shrines of their own sect, and then those of any other sects which seem attractive or profitable. For in the curiously mixed condition of religious ideas, sect becomes confused with sect, not in principle, but in personality; for a person may belong to more than one at a time without prejudice to either. Some pious persons spend their whole time in making pilgrimages; but I must say that this kind of piety does not seem to interfere with their catching cheerfully at every straw of amusement that comes along. There is also, I fancy, much respect and consideration shown to pilgrims after they return to their own villages, and for all their lives they will rank higher in their townsmen's estimation than the people who have never performed them. A pilgrimage confers a kind of diploma of holiness, and is also a claim on the gratitude of the stayers at home, since it is hoped that the blessings prayed for by two or three at the distant shrine will descend individually and richly on the generous subscribers who enabled them to visit the sanctuary.

Very different are the laughing bands of the Japanese pilgrim clubs to the companies one meets just across the water, in China, where people never laugh. There is an eminently holy temple near Ningpo, where day after day, year after year, tottering painfully on the horrible swollen hoofs which are the inevitable evolution in age of the "golden lilies," the broken feet of childhood, bands of forlorn old women come with prayers and tears to entreat the merciful gods that in their next transmigration their crushed womanhood may be laid aside, and that they may return—as men.

We stood aside one day to let some pilgrims pass us on the road. One of the men could hardly get past me at all, overcome with amazement at his first sight of a blue-eyed creature in strange garments, the foreign barbarian woman. The road was rough, and he stumbled heavily almost at my feet. His companion laughed heartily. "That is what comes of staring at the elder sister!" he cried; but the astonished one picked himself up, passed on and out of sight with his head turned and his eyes still fixed on myself, as if expecting to see me turn into a fox on the spot, or send my head after him like the snake-woman of the Japanese ghost story.

We had a visit from a dear old woman pilgrim one day, as we were sitting at afternoon tea out of doors. She was very old, and partially blind; but in spite of this was evidently the leader of two younger women who accompanied her. They were all peasants, burnt in face and limb from long standing in the rice-fields under the scorching sun. The old lady had her skirts kilted very high, and a blue towel tied coquettishly round her head. As she came up the path, she seemed to share the feelings of the lost charcoal-burner; for she kept exclaiming, "How beautiful, how grand! Whose is this honourable beautiful house?" The servant explained; and then she said that it was the first time she had seen a foreign house, or garden:

216

might she humbly ask that she and her companions should be allowed to stay a little and look at it? Of course she might! So she went over the funny little domain, and looked with the greatest interest at the cooking arrangements, and inquired if that honourable animal (the Brown Ambassador) with the honourable long tail were really an honourable dog? What great and wonderful people these honourable foreigners are, to be sure!

Tokyo, October, 1890

Our return to Tokyo was followed by the usual autumn typhoon, more destructive than ever this year. The catastrophe which has saddened us most was the loss of the *Ertogroul,* a Turkish battle-ship, which went down with the admiral and five hundred and fifty men. The poor admiral was always afraid that something would happen to his horrible old tub with her worn-out engines, and only a short time ago was heard to say that she could not possibly live through a bad typhoon. He had warned the authorities at home of the state of the vessel, and solemnly rejected any responsibility for what might occur. He was a charming man, and had made himself so much liked here that the tragedy has cast quite a gloom over our small circle. He had fifty cadets on board, and they were all lost. About sixty of the men were rescued, and have been treated with the greatest kindness by the Japanese. A Russian man-of-war offered to take the poor fellows home, and the offer was accepted by the Cabinet, and went up to the Emperor to be approved. To every one's surprise, the Emperor was most indignant; the men, he said, were his guests, and as such they should be taken home in one of his own battle-ships with all the honours. This is accordingly to be done. Our own fleet gathers in force just at this time, before going south into winter quarters, and we have been very busy. It is rather an imposing sight, when the European squadrons are all gathered in Yokohama Harbour.

I am always glad to return to Tokyo, and to greet Fuji San from my windows once more. With all the splendid scenery of the hills, I miss the great white mountain when we are in Karuizawa, and feel more at home in Japan when its perfect outline is the first thing I see in the morning, the last at night. There are a thousand beautiful stories told about the mountain; they hang round its name as the mists hang round its feet, and the love and reverence of a hundred centuries have wrapped it in a mystic robe of holiness, so that to look at it is to have the mind raised to higher things, whether one will or no.

Tokyo, November, 1890

The month of maples, chrysanthemums, Imperial garden parties, the beginning of our queer little gay season, has been marked by an important event, not unaccompanied by disaster. The event was the opening of the Diet in great state by the Emperor, and the disaster— the storming of the Russian Legation the same day. The inauguration of the Houses of Parliament has been the point towards which great preparations and precautions have been tending for many months past. The elections took place quietly and successfully in July, when we were in Karuizawa; the Japanese are a profoundly lawful people (if I may use the word in its old sense), and there were few or no disturbances. Of course here and there some irregularities crept into the proceedings, and one or two elections were invalidated on account of bribery; but as those things are not unknown in England, the very cradle of representative government, we must not be surprised at their occurring here on the first trial of the new methods, and doubtless many a strange scene will be witnessed before the huge unbroken team of deputies settle down into their working stride.

The present Houses of Parliament form a group of roomy wooden buildings, intended only to serve until the permanent and costly erections planned for the purpose can be completed. With admirable good sense the Government decided that, until the needs of the Diet had been shown during a working session, the permanent Houses for its accommodation should not be put in hand, and also that no national vanity should induce them to spend more than was absolutely necessary on these temporary buildings. A very small sum, 80,000 yen, was voted for the work; but as it went on, various portions had to be added to the original plan drawn out by Stegmüller, the German architect to whom the task had been entrusted, and the final cost has proved to be about 240,000 yen (£24,000), a small sum when one considers the necessities of the case. Although carried out in wood, the structure is dignified and harmonious. It covers a very large area; is surrounded, of course, by a garden, planted with full-grown trees; and contains Chambers of Session for the House of Representatives and the House of Peers, each containing three hundred and twenty-six seats, and accommodation in the balconies for four hundred visitors. Besides the great halls, there are over a hundred rooms fitted up as committee-rooms, libraries, and so forth; fire-proof warehouses for archives; and two official residences for the Chief Secretaries of the Upper and Lower House. Huge stacks of chimneys show that the winter session need not be a cold one; and the electric light is used here as in the Palace. The decorations are in such beautiful colourings (pale rosy terra-cotta, dull green, and rather dusky gold), that the absence of elaborate ornament is not even noticed; and certainly the comfort of the members has been carefully consulted. The seats and desks look most inviting. In the Chamber of the Upper House, above and behind the President's table, a large alcove, almost like a chancel, has been built into the wall; and here stands the throne, where the Emperor will sit on the rare occasions when he attends a session. The President's seat and table would then be removed, and the sovereign would preside alone over his lieges. The decoration of the throne place is most beautiful, the baldachino and drapings of heavy Kyoto silks, and the front shut in by a richly carved railing. When the Emperor is absent, a curtain is drawn across the alcove, and the view of the throne shut out. The Empress, the Imperial Princes, and the Diplomatic Corps have boxes, made as comfortable and pretty as possible;

and on the second floor a large reception-room for the Emperor is built over the entrance hall, and opens on a balcony, where he can step out and show himself to the people if necessary.

There had been some delay about the opening ceremony, arising from the fact that the whole organisation of the Diet had to be elaborated before it could take place. When the day came, the excitement was intense; although, apart from the invitations sent to the heads of missions, and other officials, only the most tardy announcement had appeared as to the hour when the Emperor would leave the Palace. From early morning the streets were crowded with people, and the great open spaces round the Houses of Parliament were packed with dense crowds, such as always gather eagerly when there is a chance of beholding the sovereign. The police had their hands full, as they were responsible for keeping the public back to a line drawn twenty yards from the main route on all the streets intersecting the road from the Palace,—this not to isolate the Imperial procession, but to keep space open for the hundreds of vehicles which must pass conveying visitors to the Houses of Parliament before the Emperor's arrival. The result was perfect; for there was not a single block of any kind, or the slightest difficulty in finding the carriages and jinrikshas when the ceremony was over. A very stringent regulation forbids that any one should look down on the sovereign from an elevated position. There were hardly any upper windows on the route, which passed by the great avenues along the Palace moats; but one or two youngsters who had audaciously climbed trees so as to get a better view were pulled down sternly by the police, and the attempt was not repeated. A very large body of troops lined the entire route four deep before the Emperor finally left the Palace; but this was done merely to add to the pomp of the procession, for his Majesty would have nothing to fear from any class of his subjects except too warm a demonstration of loyalty, and even that would always be tempered by the religious awe with which even the most violent Radicals here regard his sacred person.

The invitation named ten o'clock as the hour for arriving at the Houses of Parliament, and by half-past ten the rush of carriages and jinrikshas was over, and a broad empty way was left for the procession from the Palace. It was headed, of course, by Guards and outriders; and then came three carriages full of Imperial Princes (cousins and uncles of the Emperor) old enough to take their seats in the House of Peers; then the beautiful State coach, with its glass sides and golden phoenix crown, its six splendidly caparisoned horses and gorgeous attendants, passed slowly by, carrying the Emperor in his marshal's uniform and many decorations, attended by Marquis Tokudaiji, the Lord High Chamberlain, who sat on the opposite seat. A body of Life Guards followed the Emperor's coach; and then came a number of State carriages containing the Cabinet Ministers and Court officials. When the Emperor arrived at the entrance to the Houses of Parliament, he was received by all the great functionaries, headed by Count Ito (who has been elected President of the Upper House), and then proceeded to wait in the great reception-room while all those who had accompanied him were sorted into their places. A separate reception-room was set aside for the Diplomatic Corps, whose younger members were indignant at finding all the windows impenetrably veiled to prevent their looking down from this upper floor on the Emperor's arrival. They had, however, the privilege of accompanying him to the Chamber of Peers, and told me that it presented an imposing sight when he entered and took his seat on the throne, surrounded by that great concourse of subjects and courtiers. The Commons were all gathered in the hall, some of the lower seats having been removed to give them standing room; the Empress, with the Princesses and her ladies (the only women present), took their places in the box prepared for them; and the Strangers' Gallery, as well as every available corner, was crowded with smart uniforms and brilliant decorations. The members of the Lower House were almost all in plain evening dress, and it was maliciously remarked that they looked fluttered and delighted; while the Peers, conspicuous in their gorgeous military and official uniforms, preserved the impassive dignity and calm which mark the Japanese aristocrat.

When the marshals entered preceding the Emperor, the House rose and stood in breathless silence, and then bowed like one man almost to the ground as he took his seat. The first sound heard was the Emperor's voice, when, standing before the throne, he made his first speech to his first Parliament. It was one of those incidents which strike the hour, clear for all men to hear, in the course of a country's history; and no one then present will forget the solemn moment.

Here is the speech:

"We announce to the members of the House of Peers and to those of the House of Representatives: That all institutions relating to internal administration, established during the period of twenty years since Our accession to the Throne, have been brought to a state approaching completeness and regular arrangement. By the efficacy of the virtues of Our Ancestors, and in concert with yourselves, We hope to continue and extend those measures, to reap good fruit from the working of the Constitution, and thereby to manifest, both at home and abroad, the glory of Our country and the loyal and enterprising character of Our people.

"We have always cherished a resolve to maintain friendly relations with other countries, to develope commerce, and to extend the prestige of Our land. Happily Our relations with all the Treaty Powers are on a footing of constantly growing amity and intimacy.

"In order to preserve tranquillity at home and security from abroad, it is essential that the completion of Our naval and military defences should be made an object of gradual attainment.

"We shall direct our Ministers of State to submit to the Diet the Budget for the twenty-fourth year of Meiji, and certain projects of laws. We expect that you will deliberate and advise upon them with impartiality and discretion, and We trust that you will establish such precedents as may serve for future guidance."

So much for the event. Now I must tell you of the riot which broke out and threatened to wreck the Russian Legation while this majestic ceremony was going forward in the House of Peers.

As the Emperor was going thither, the procession had to pass the corner of the Russian Legation grounds, where two wide streets form an angle, and where a small pavilion perched on the garden wall gives a view down both streets. True to their orders, the police were keeping back the crowd which would have poured down from the side to the main street; and it may be that the people were indignant at seeing a number of foreign ladies and children standing on this point where they could see the Emperor from an elevated position quite forbidden to his own subjects. His Majesty at any rate entirely understood the situation, and glanced up, smiled, and nodded to Madame S—— and her daughter. I was not well enough to join them that morning, as I had intended doing; but they described to me what followed.

As soon as the Emperor had passed, the populace, composed largely of young students, tried to force the blockade of the main street. They were vigorously met by the police, who, seeing that they might soon be outnumbered, struck a few sharp blows with their sword-scabbards to reduce the mob to order. The ladies in the summer-house above were watching the contest with rather alarmed interest, when a cracker was exploded in the crowd with a snap and a puff of smoke, rather startling in the circumstances. Somebody in the pavilion gave a little scream, and there was a laugh among the rest, when they suddenly became aware that stones were being thrown at them from the crowd, first singly, then in showers, and increasing in size; a brick very nearly struck Mademoiselle S——, and, much to her mother's wrath (for Madame S—— is a gallant lady, who objects to retreating before a mob), the little group had to disappear from their position in the pavilion. By that time the stones were also flying over the front gates which open into the side-street, then crowded with a surging mob, and some terrified servants came rushing to say that the people were beginning to climb the gates. As all the gentlemen of the staff were absent with the Minister, there was no one to appeal to. Madame S—— sent the servants back to barricade the iron gates, which are fortunately strong and high, and then smuggled one man out of a little side-door in another part of the garden to call some of the policemen to enter by it and defend the place within. Her visitors and their children had taken refuge in a remote part of the house. Meanwhile, outside the gates, a pretty fierce fight was going on; the police were working bravely to get to the gate itself; and the men-servants had posted themselves in the pavilion, and were returning their assailants' fire by a shower of bricks, which had been piled for some new building in the garden, and which naturally did not tend to improve the temper of the mob. Madame S—— told me that her relief was intense, when she saw a little company of policemen file through the forgotten door and march to the gates and the pavilion. As soon as the crowd saw that the police were in force inside the enclosure, they lost something

223

of their courage; but they were still surging against the gates in great numbers and much excitement, when the carriages containing the Minister and the Secretaries returning from the Diet drew up on the outskirts of the crowd, finding it impossible to penetrate through it. Knowing nothing of what had occurred, Monsieur S—— imagined that a fire must have broken out, and was much alarmed for the safety of his family. When at last a way was opened for him to drive up to his own gates, great was his amazement to see that they were held by a body of police, one of whose number sat astride the top bar with a revolver in hand, prepared to shoot any one who tried to follow him. The crowd quickly melted away after the Minister's return, but not before several arrests were made. The incident has naturally created a very unpleasant impression; but we are told that it really has no political significance. I have noticed that the actions of an excited crowd seldom have, especially if the apologist be a member of the Government.

Nevertheless there is a good deal of rampant *soshiism* abroad, and it manifests itself in quite unexpected ways. Hearing of the trouble at our friends' house, I ordered the carriage late in the afternoon to go and tell them how sorry I was for their fright. Just as I was ready to start, H—— came in and told me that he had sent the carriage back to the stables, as the streets were not safe for me to drive through. I was greatly surprised, as I have never been prevented from going out, even in last year's anti-foreign agitation. I learnt afterwards from Mr. G——, who was walking with him, that quite close to our own gates they had suddenly been surrounded by a band of *soshi,* armed with their favourite sword-sticks. An attempt had been made to distract the Chief's attention by hustling him behind, and at the moment when he was intended to turn his head a sword was drawn to strike him in front. But he refused to look behind him, and kept his eyes fixed on the face of the man in front, who lowered his sword at once. H—— laughed a little, and went on and finished his walk; but his companion told me that had he turned his head he would have been run through at once, for the *soshi* was closer to him than Mr. G—— when the thing happened. The Chief was in greater danger than any one had been in the riot of the morning. There was deep dismay in the Japanese Foreign Office when the matter was reported, and profuse apologies were of course made.

H—— improved the occasion to insist upon the abolition of those horrid sword-sticks. Every turbulent *soshi* in Tokyo carries one, and they constitute a real danger in any excitement. We cannot imagine why the Government should be so shy of controlling the *soshi*, who are now wild misguided youths, and will be later very unmanageable and dangerous citizens.

And now let us turn to gayer subjects. A pretty little compliment came out for Prince Komatsu* the other day, the Grand Cross of the Order of the Bath, with which, I think, his Imperial Highness was very much pleased. We went with much solemnity to his Palace, and H—— gave the Queen's message and invested him with the collar, which is really a beautiful bit of gold and enamel work. All sorts of pretty speeches were made, and the Prince (who has the most good-natured face I ever saw, with a Disraeli curl on the forehead) kept us to lunch, and the Princess went through all the pretty speeches in her own royal-feminine language, quite a different dialect from the royal-masculine speech, which in its turn is quite apart from the speech of ordinary men, who must be careful when speaking to the Princes to use certain words consecrated only for the ears of royalty! Is this not a puzzling sum? Of course all the conversation is carried on with the help of interpreters; for though the Prince speaks some English, it is not enough to carry him through an official occasion, and the Princess will not admit that she knows any English words, though I suspect that she often understands what I am saying long before the interpreter has repeated it. She has the most lovely Paris frocks, and, though not pretty, is always extremely well put together. My wicked Dachs, the Brown Ambassador, fancies himself greatly in white satin, and generally picks out the smartest gown in the room to lie down on, with the air of paying its owner a great compliment. After the Prince had been invested with the Bath, he and the Princess came to dine with us. The Princess had a beautiful dress of white satin brocaded all over with gold feathers; and as we women were sitting in the drawing-room after dinner, Tip observed the gown from afar, and decided that it would suit his complexion.

*Prince Akihito Komatsu (1846–1903) studied in England from 1870 to 1872. In 1870 his family, which was descended from the Fujiwara clan, received the name Higashi-Fushimi.

Giving one bound through the air, he landed on it with all his four fat paws outspread, and looked round to be complimented on the feat. The Princess screamed, taken off her guard by the sudden onslaught, the lady-in-waiting turned pale, and poor Tip was carried off in sad disorder. He is a source of the greatest amusement to the Japanese ladies who come to see me; they think his tricks quite miraculous; and he sits up before each one in turn to be fed with sugar and told that he is *rippai* (splendid). He is a born courtier; for he goes round on my reception days, speaking kindly to any strangers who come, holding out a solemn paw to be shaken by Europeans, but making a long Japanese bow with his head on the floor before the little ladies of the country, who go off into fits of laughter at the sight, and I am sure believe that I have taught him his absurd tricks.

I have at last seen the Palace chrysanthemums, which are extremely beautiful, and almost more interesting than beautiful, on account of the complete triumph of art over nature which they proclaim. The gardens devoted to them are those of the Aoyama Palace, on the eastern heights of the town. This was the Emperor's residence for several years, while the new Palace was being built, but it is now the home of the Empress-Dowager. The Emperor's birthday party is always given in the gardens of Aoyama, the chrysanthemum being his flower, even as the double cherry is that of the Empress, whose own birthday party is always given at the Hama Rikyu, the cherry-blossom Palace by the sea. As no party was given last year for the Emperor's birthday, this was my first view of these famous chrysanthemums, and I was quite dazzled by the extraordinary variety and size of the blooms.

The Aoyama gardens are very large, and are laid out, according to Japanese rules, in lakes and islands, bridges and arbours, pavilions, rocks, little dells full of maple trees, and little hills crowned with strangely shaped stones of enormous value in the eyes of the Japanese. But at this season one hardly notices the other features of the grounds, because everywhere are armies of chrysanthemums, sheltered in large pavilions of pure white wood, open on one side of their length to the gaze of the admiring crowds who have been invited to behold them. These garden parties are wonderfully well arranged, and always seem to follow the same precedent. An hour is named on the card of invitation well ahead of the time when the

Majesties intend to appear. The carriages put us down at the gate, and we have quite a long pleasant walk over the green lawns and through exquisitely kept grounds before we reach the place of gathering. All through the gardens the air is full of music, the bands being stationed in picturesque spots sufficiently far from each other not to distress the sensitive ear; the paths are full of all one's friends and acquaintances; the crowds of smart frocks and bright uniforms make the gayest of pictures under the trees. When the goal is reached, one finds a huge tent, all draped in the broad stripes of severe black and white, which are the mark of the Imperial Household; a tremendous feast (no better word quite expresses the fact) is laid out here for the world in general; and at one end is a smaller pavilion in which the sovereigns receive us, and where we have tea at little tables with the Court people. But the sovereigns are kind, and do not arrive until we have had time to walk about and look at all the show of flowers.

And what a show! There is one plant, standing alone under a carved roof, which has grown, as it was told, in the shape of a great junk, with a poop at either end, and double decks and all the rest of it. The central stem has become a tree, covered with solid bark; and it has thrown out this year nearly four hundred blossoms, all exactly alike, of the same size, and of a pale-pink colour, the whole thing occupying a space about fifteen feet long, and standing quite ten feet from the ground. When one can tear oneself away from this beauty, there are, as I have said, armies of flowers planted in terraces five or six rows deep, each entire row being so perfectly uniform that there is no single difference of petal or leaf all along the line; for the Japanese gardener would reject as failures the most beautiful blooms if the leaves grew unevenly up the stem. He succeeds in producing a hundred specimens, each flowering to the same point, with the leaves sprouting in perfect regularity at the same distances on the stalk. My simile of an army is really a correct one, for in looking down the lines there is no more dissimilarity to be discovered than in lines of well-drilled troops. And not only this, but between the lowest line and the topmost one our garden magician has managed to show us the growth from bud to bloom; the lowest line, standing hardly a foot from the ground, is all in bud, the next slightly more advanced, the next still more so, and so on till the highest of all shows us the full-blown beauty of the flower. In the very long thin-petalled specimens now in fashion here, the disc is spread out like a white or crimson sun, over a delicate frame of copper wire, many inches across. In some specimens the petals are so long that they hang over the edge of the wire in a flowery fringe; in others they are spiked, and bristled with what look like fine hairs growing out of the surface; others are curled, thick, pompous; some like full moons in perfect roundness, some all rays like a midday sun. In every shade of rose and crimson, brown, scarlet, yellow, pale lilac, sunset purple, they almost fatigue the eye with colour; and I turned gladly to look at some lovely pale globes whose foamy petals curled inwards over a green as alive and transparent as the wave on the shore or the glow-worm's lamp in the grass.

Going from one to another with a Japanese friend, who was giving me the national appreciations on the subject of chrysanthemums, I was almost sorry when the Majesties' arrival was heralded by the Grand Master of Ceremonies, who waved us into two lines, through which the Emperor and Empress walked together, followed by the Princes and Princesses and the rest of the Court. The ladies' dresses were of lovely Kyoto brocades, as near the tints of the chrysanthemums as possible. The sovereigns merely bowed as they went by, and then a long procession formed after them in couples, according to the usual order of precedence. I found myself in charge of the Minister for Foreign Affairs, and we played a decorous kind of "follow my leader" through the grounds, until the Majesties came to a halt in the pavilion marked out for them; their interpreters stood beside them, and we went in, in detachments according to precedence again, to have our little conversation and make our little bows, and slide off to leave room for the next batch. When all the greetings and bowings were over, the business of ices and champagne began, and was treated with proper solemnity. Then a tiny shower came down, and the Court rose as one man, the sovereigns took leave of us with some little precipitation, and they and their people made for the main building of the Palace, where they would at any rate be safe till the rain had passed. The last I saw of them was a string of little ladies carefully holding up their delicate satin gowns and racing along under black umbrellas.

We broke up at once—not at all according to precedence! We

had no umbrellas, of course; but everything is foreseen in Japan. As we issued rather ruefully from the royal tent to traverse the long piece of wet garden which separated us from our carriages, a number of servants suddenly appeared from among the bushes, carrying sheaves of umbrellas, at least five hundred of them, all alike, ornamented with green silk tassels. One was put, ready opened, into each guest's hand, and, as we stepped into the carriages at the farther gate, another little army of servants was in waiting to relieve us of the precious umbrellas, which were all carried back in bundles to the Palace—to wait for next time.

Nikko, November, 1890

Do you wonder that I have waited so long to write the name of the most beautiful, the most solemn place in Japan? In truth, I have feared to write it sooner, have feared to visit it until now. It seemed to me that a certain initiation should be gone through, a certain standard of judgment on Japanese thought attained, before I went to stand face to face with the supreme expression of beauty and solemnity. So I visited other temples, stood in the shade of other groves, listened to other waterfalls and other nightingales, taught my strained Western senses to forget the golden-tinted ruins, the jewelled hills, the gorgeous colour feasts of our blazing South Italian home; and then, when the spirit's eyes were rested from the sunshine, when they had learned at last the value of cool shadow and grey distance and whispering pine branch under an autumn sky— then I was not afraid to come to Nikko, I could hope to understand.

I could not come all the way through the grand cryptomeria avenue, because the travelling now is mostly done by rail;* but even from the carriage windows we could look up at the splendid

*Murray's *Handbook for Travellers in Japan* (1894) says, "Nikkō is reached in 5 hours from Tokyo by the Northern Railway, carriages being changed at Utsunomiya."

trees through which the line cuts again and again, wantonly, as it seemed to me. The last two or three miles are done in jinriksha, and make up for the rest of the noisy smoky journey. One creeps slowly and with a certain reverence to the heart of Nikko, the village of Hachi-ishi, which is the centre of the district; for though we foreigners distinguish this one town by the name of Nikko, that properly belongs to the whole of this range of hills, which lie some eighty miles to the north of Tokyo.

To the north-east of Hachi-ishi rises the volcano of Nantai San, extinct since prehistoric times; and in its side is a huge cavern, from which in ancient times (so the story goes) there issued frightful storms which devastated the country every spring and autumn. Popular legends say that, on account of these twin storms, the country was called Ni-Ko San, or Two-Storm Mountain; and that the great saint and scholar Kobo Daishi* in the year 820 exorcised the storm demons, and called the place Nikkō San, the Mountains of the Sun's Brightness, which name it bears to this day.

This atmosphere of a great past hangs over [Nikko] everywhere, and even noisy tourists who respect few things are impressed and silenced by its calm majesty. Foreign residents from Tokyo and Yokohama come here in the summer and take houses, and have their futile picnics and tea parties, and make no more effect on the place than do the sand-flies on the face of the great bronze Buddha. One of my reasons for going in the autumn was that they would all have flown back by this time to thick carpets and coal fires; for though the maples are still in all their red beauty, it is cold in Nikko, and the river brings down icy breaths at night from the tempest-haunted caves of Nantai San.

Now the river is the first thing one sees, the central spot of all one's mind-excursions here. It divides the place in two, coming down very full and angry between the deep-green hills, and spanned, just where the sides of the glen are steepest, by a perfect bridge, thrown in one scarlet arch across the white water, from the black green of this side of the golden green of that, where the sun lingers

*Kōbō Daishi (or Kūkai, 774–835), famous priest of the Shingon sect of Buddhism. Kōbō Daishi founded the temples at Mount Kōya and is credited with having developed the *hiragana* syllabary.

230

longest ere he rolls down to the plains and the sea. Why are not all bridges scarlet, latticed, lying between green steeps? The inevitable wise man will say that they should be things of use, and not of beauty alone; but, then, he has never been to Japan. This bridge is not for use; only grass-grown paths unopened to traffic lead anywhere near it. Should the Emperor come to visit the shrines, his sacred feet might tread its scarlet arch—his, but no others. He would have to walk alone, as of old the Shoguns walked; for the bridge is too holy for unanointed feet. At one time pilgrims were allowed to cross, because of their consecrated mission; but this is no longer allowed, and the lovely bridge has not felt the tread of a mortal footstep for many a day.* Do the ghosts of holy men come to do the repairing the these autumn nights, I wonder? No human hand has mended it for two hundred and thirty years, and they say the wood is as fresh and strong across its eighty-four-feet span to-day as it was when it was put in place.

Lower down the river than the bridge of beauty comes the bridge of use; and when we have crossed it, to-day seems left behind, to-day with its hotels and railways and endless fuss and friction chafes us no more; we seem to have entered into the avenues that lead to change-less peace. The pines, the solemn, pontifical pines, are standing shoulder to shoulder in serried ranks, their enormous roots reaching up like brown buttresses against the central spire, their heads far away near the sky, whence their murmur comes down to us fitfully, like prayers that pass the lips long after they have been prayed in the heart. Between the trees long stairways of grey stone climb from terrace to terrace, ledge to ledge, of the dusky hillside, ending perhaps where stone lanterns are set as if to catch the early sun-rays, and whisper the good news of his coming to the deep shadowy courts from which the stairways rise. It must be highest noon ere the shadows lift from those embowered courts, tracked with grey stones laid in leisurely sequence along the rich dark soil, showing the path to a favourite shrine, or to the well where pure water

---

*AUTHOR'S NOTE: When General Grant visited Japan, the Emperor had the bridge thrown open, and invited him to pass over it. The General was much touched by this mark of honour, but refused to accept it, saying that he considered himself unworthy to do so.

bubbles always for the pilgrim to wash in ere he enter the holy places. Beside the stepping-stones grey lanterns stand, stone too, each with a recess where a light may be placed, in memory of the giver or the giver's dear ones. In one a light is floating in its cup of oil; in another an incense-strick, just lighted, sends up its blue spiral of smoke, as it stands in the mouth of its rough bamboo holder.

The air is mild in these sheltered courts, and the ground dry and scattered with pine needles; so I sit down at the foot of a flight of steps, and my good Ogita, who has a bad cough, and cannot walk far in these days, tells me the story of Iyeyasu and Iyemitsu* and of their coming to be buried here.

As usual, I have been carried away by the human associations of this great home of great shadows, and have told you nothing as yet of the visible treasures which it contains. Behold, are they not all written down in the indispensable pages of Murray? And yet I wish I could show you some of them; for it seems as if specimens of every art had been stored here to honour Iyeyasu's memory. From highest to lowest, his country-people have contributed their gifts. Ogita tells me (but I find no corroboration of this in any of the handbooks) that the famous avenue of cryptomerias was planted by a great Daimyo, the Prince of Chikuzen, before Iyeyasu's body was brought to Nikko, that the road might be worthy of the traveller. The first gate is a splendid granite *torii*, sent by this same Prince from his own quarries two years after Iyeyasu's death; then comes an exquisite pagoda, over a hundred feet high, and richly decorated, presented a little later by one of the great vassals of the family. The Gate of the Two Kings† is a marvel of carving and painting and symbolism, which it would take days to describe; whichever way one turns, the most amazing elaboration of ornament meets one's eyes, and yet all is harmonious and subdued, dominated by the great stone stairways and the dark pine trees, and lit in the luminous even whiteness of Japan's noonday. The light here, as elsewhere in the Islands of the Dragon-Fly, is soft, yet entire; the magic mountains

---

*Tokugawa Ieyasu (1542–1616), founder of the Tokugawa shogunate, and Tokugawa Iemitsu (1604–51), the third Tokugawa shogun.
†Ni-ō-mon.

seem to cast no shade; in the depth of the woods, as in the golden Temple storehouses, everything is calmly clear to the eye.

There is one tree which stands alone, surrounded by a stone railing —the square stone railing of temple architecture which gives such character to all these scenes. The tree has a right to special protection; for it is, says local tradition, the one which Iyeyasu (who must have loved pines as I do) carried about with him for years in his palanquin, when it was a tiny sapling in its pot. Near it stands a stable, where a white horse is kept, in case Iyeyasu should return and want a charger in a hurry. He must have sent for it this morning, for the stable is empty. Then we are taken to see various relics of Iyeyasu, his helmet and shield, bronze objects so overlaid with green patina that their very shape is obscured; then a wonderful library of Buddhist books, in a revolving bookcase, scarlet and gold. But that which pleases me most are the finely carved panels of the splendid halls intended to accommodate the Shogun and his train when they came here to worship. Every bird and beast seems to have been pressed into the service of decoration, every device which unlimited treasure and redundant imagination could produce has been lavished on these temple rooms, each more beautiful than the last. The very architects seem to have feared the envy of heaven for their perfect work; and one pillar has its carvings done upside down, that the voluntary defect might appease the jealous gods. It is named the "Pillar of the Aversion of Evil."

The tomb of Iyeyasu is beyond all these splendours, a small pagoda cast in a single piece of bronze, of a golden colour, standing alone on the hillside. And this reminds me of the splendid tomb of Yung Chung, in the northern hills beyond Peking, with its vast hall, its hundred scarlet pillars, its lonely state; and beyond it, on the hillside, a nameless green mound, as large as the Temple itself, in whose depths the great Emperor's bones were laid secretly and unmarked, so that no enemy might disinter them, no envious god shatter their resting-place in his jealousy of its beauty.

Only one thing will I tell you of the tomb of Iyemitsu, great Iyeyasu's grandson. In a small iron storeroom, entered by a low and heavy door, I saw the finest piece of illumination which the world contains, eight feet long, four feet wide, the whole surface covered with a series of paintings so delicate, so patient, so perfect, that I have never seen anything in European collections to approach it. The artist seems to have actually dipped his brush in sunshine and star-dust when he painted it. It represents the Buddhist heaven, with glorified spirits crowding round a central figure, which makes the impression of giving out light. In that small dark treasure-house, the old priest spread it out for me to see, and murmured explanations of the picture; to me it was like a piece of sunshine imprisoned since the morning of the world, when the sun must have been more gladly golden than now. How strange to think that grey pine-shrouded Nikko should keep this jewel buried in its bosom!

At last we left the temples, and wandered back to the bridge, near which a flight of stone steps leads up to other holy spots, temples and shrines crowding one another on the hillsides. One stone marks the grave of Iyeyasu's favourite horse, the one he rode at the great battle of Sekigahara,* which was the turning-point of his life. The old horse was turned loose in these sacred hills after its master's death, and lived many years in freedom among the pines. At the end of the walk from the bridge, by the bank of the river, stands a long, long row of strange little Buddhas, all exactly alike, their gentle faces quite obliterated by moss and spray, only their outline telling what they are. The torrent keeps them always wet, and sings here such a loud rushing song that one's senses get dazed, and no one ever counts the moss-shrouded images right. The Japanese call them the five hundred Buddhas; but there is nothing like such a number as that. I think they object to being counted. Tradition says that no two people have ever counted them alike; and, indeed, when the river is running high, it is not easy to get to them all. They look intensely weird and lonely, and a profound melancholy seems to hang around the long grey line. Some time ago, in a violent storm, one of them leapt from his place, and went bounding down the stream as far as Imaichi, the village at the foot of the hill; then he turned and stopped, with his blind face towards his old home, and there he stands to this day; but none of his companions have found courage to follow him.

*The battle at Sekigahara in 1600 confirmed the domination of Tokugawa Ieyasu and the establishment of the Tokugawa shogunate.

234

Wisely had we chosen the moment of our visit to the Nikko hills; for, beyond the sombre mantle of the pines, the mountain-sides were clothed in a curtain of scarlet and gold, a curtain woven of the star-shaped leaves of innumerable maple trees, hanging to the cliffs as children hang to the skirts of their mother. The path up to Chuzenji* was all aglow with them; and where it wound directly under their branches, fired from above with the noonday sun, the effect of colour was so strong that it caused sudden dizziness, and I had to close my eyes for a moment before I could support it. All the waterfalls on the way (and Nikko is the home of waterfalls) were studded with a spray of jewel-tinted leaves, mingling with the iridescent showers; every pool was the harbour where thousand-sailed fleets of golden leaves rose and fell on the delicately ruffled surface of the flood; the path was all paved with crimson stars, laid on a soft mosaic of bronze and orange; and everywhere was that delicious fleeting smell of autumn woods where the summer has breathed its parting sigh. I was happily surprised by finding the maples up here so late in coming to their glory; for ours in the Tokyo gardens, exposed to sharp winds, are already curled and brown. But the woods were always gracious to me, their worshipper; and the leaves have hung on in the sheltered dells to give me the greeting that Caesar heard of old, "Morituri te salutamus."

At last the wooded steeps are left behind, and we reach a level road that leads, with a bend and a sudden turn, right out on the edge of a lake; an upland lake, of crystal water and sun-searched deeps, with all the sky to dream over it, all the daylight to smooth its frets of blue and gold to one wide white calm. The hills fall back a little from its sides; the woods stand shyly off from its silver strand; all the world just now seems to culminate in this perfect jewel, held up in the palm of the hills for heaven to gaze upon. I too will gaze, for I shall not see the like of this untouched peace again. The rest may wander and climb, and even try the steep ascent of great Nantai

---

*Murray's *Handbook for Travellers in Japan* (1894) says, "The road is practicable for jinrikishas with two men. . . . But owing to the steepness of the hill which has to be passed on the way, ladies and persons unable to walk, are recommended to take chairs or horses. Chūzenji, which is 4,375 feet above sea level, is only occupied by pilgrims for a few days in July or August, the period for the ascent of Mount Nantai (8,150 feet)."

San; but not I. I will sit and drink the light here, and learn the silences of peace, and hear the wordless music of the ripple at my feet, as soft and even as the breath of infancy. Space to breathe with one's face to the sky, solitude, and the ceasing of this world's voices, speechless beauty all around, and the blue dome of the heart's home above,—why go farther? Here is the City of Rest.

1891

Tokyo, January, 1891

The New Year has come round again; but it has brought such a frightful visitation of influenza that our little society has hardly had strength to exchange the usual greetings and good wishes. I am told that the scourge was let loose in Tokyo at an innocent Christmas party in our house, where we had ventured to gather together all our European and Japanese friends round a huge Christmas tree, to the great delight of the little Japanese children, to whom the sight was as surprising as it was to the compound children last year. We had placed our tree in the inner part of the hall, where the great staircase makes its three turns round a square space, usually filled with plants and easy-chairs. That day everything was turned out, and the tree spread it branches right up to the level of the second floor, where, by the way, a kind of fire brigade was stationed in case of accidents. All this was impenetrably curtained off from the entrance hall, until all our guests had arrived and the whole of our Tokyo world gathered together; then, at a given signal, one of the old Christmas carols burst from a choir hidden in a recess, the curtains were drawn aside, and the pyramid of light shone out in all its completeness. The sight was fairylike, and the cry of pleasure that rang from one end of the hall to the other quite repaid me and the

237

many kind friends who had been my helpers for any trouble and fatigue that the thing had cost.

Then came the distribution of our little gifts (a serious business, for there were at least two hundred children, besides all their grown-up relations); and this was followed by a sight which to me was as pretty as the tree itself. The house is not very large for a gathering of this kind, and all the available rooms on the ground floor had been turned into supper-rooms for the grown-up guests; so we were obliged to lay the children's feast in the long gallery in the second floor, running the whole length of the hall below. This had been decorated with green wreaths and quantities of lanterns, and here little people of every nationality sat side by side and made friends over the bonbons and crackers. Count Saigo's three splendid boys, in the gold-laced uniform of their military school, insisted on helping to wait on the others; and it was pretty to see the dark aristocratic heads bending over the fair-haired English babies, who smiled up confidingly at the kind big boys. Everybody sat down where they could find a place; a small Princess Sanjo, dressed in dazzling garments of crape and gold, her hair held up with gold and amber chrysanthemums, made friends with a dear little person of three who is one of my great cronies, a Yorkshire Margaret, with the reddest hair and the bluest eyes I have ever seen. Her little fat fingers already sticky with sweets, were eager to explore the wonders of the little Japanese lady's embroidered pocket-book, with its gold and coral chains hanging out in a fringe over her splendid sash. The tiny Saigo girl, another small friend of mine, had been to foreign parties before, and ran about as if the place belonged to her; while her mother followed her everywhere with an amused smile, and making many excuses for her daughter's forwardness.

The grown-up people crowded in such numbers round our beautiful battalion of children, that there was hardly room for the attendants to wait on them at all; but the European little ones looked after themselves pretty effectually, and Japanese children of the upper classes will not eat in public; they take a bonbon out of politeness, but it does not enter into their code of manners to be eager about food or to partake of it before strangers. They would, until quite lately, have expected to have their portion of the feast packed up in pretty boxes and put into their carriages, or sent to their houses after they had gone home. A reminiscence of this custom has brought me a charming collection of Imperial wine-cups; for whenever H—— lunches or dines with the Emperor, one of these is put into the carriage wrapped up in Palace paper. They vary a little in design, but are always of transparently thin white porcelain decorated with gold chrysanthemums. At the dinners given by the Imperial Princes, the parting gift is generally a silver or enamel box, sometimes of beautiful workmanship, filled with bonbons; and wherever one dines, we women at any rate carry away baskets or bouquets of most lovely flowers.

But to return to the Japanese children. I told you, I think, last year, how charmingly the servants' little ones behaved (the tree was repeated for them this year too); and I was glad to compare their manners with those of the small nobles whom we had gathered together this time. Well, except that the nobles showed rather more gravity of demeanour, and were far more beautiful to look at, there was really nothing to choose between the classes. The same suave calm manner, the same quiet thanks for gifts bestowed, the same self-effacement and consideration of others, were shown at both my parties; and I feel that there must be a great deal to say for a system of education which, without robbing childhood of a moment's bright happiness, can clothe little children of every condition with this garment of perfect courtesy. I have rarely seen its match, except once or twice among little Austrian and Italian royalties; but there inheritance and environment, as well as the high standard of behaviour insisted on in all noble Catholic families, royal or otherwise, had had full scope, had moulded the little personality from the very outset of life.

Here, explain it who can, it is in the blood, and can be counted on with absolute certainty. It is, to me, most comforting to see that all that is desirable in the little people's deportment can be attained without snubbings or punishments or weary scoldings. The love showered upon children simply wraps them in warmth and peace, and seems to encourage every sweet good trait of character without ever fostering a bad one. Japanese children are never frightened into telling lies or hiding their faults. Open as the day, they bring every joy or sorrow to father or mother to be shared or healed, and their small likes or dislikes are quite as much taken into account as those of their elders. True, from the time they can begin to understand anything, axioms of honour, kindness, filial duty, and above all patriotism, are repeated and explained to them with a good faith and solemnity which would send our English schoolboys off into fits of scoffing laughter. The nursery catechism takes somewhat this form in Japan.

"What do you love best in the world?"

"The Emperor, of course."

"Better than father and mother?"

"He is the Lord of Heaven, the father of my father and mother."

"What will you give the Emperor?"

"All my best toys, and my life when he wants it."

And so on—and it is all true, and has been and will be proved again and again. But there are no scoffers in Japan. There are bitter haters, and perhaps as many criminals as can be reasonably expected after only thirty years of intercourse with civilised nations, the delays in extending the railways, and the tiresome perfection of the police system; but the most hardened criminals have not yet learnt to scoff at virtue and patriotism, to heap contempt on honour and courage and humility. This grave belief in abstract things (which in England to-day could only be mentioned with an apologetic smile for one's own weakness) is still the foundation of education in Japan, and gives the parent or the teacher a strength and authority in dealing with the young spirit which our poor schoolmasters can never exercise. I have known many of these unhappy men, and have not yet found one who was believed in by his pupils. Indulgent tolerance from big boys, who can afford to say, "Old So-and-so is an awful humbug, but not half bad when you're big enough not to be afraid of him"; hatred and fear from the little fellows, to whom all morality is made horrible because their chief torturer is probably their preacher as well,—this is what our dominie gets at home, this is what I have seen and shuddered at for so many years in dear Protestant England, that it is an unspeakable relief to be among people where the teacher is still venerated, where the position of master in a school is considered honourable enough for the eldest son of a great noble to accept it gladly, where education leads youth unblushingly back to the feet of those great schoolmistresses the cardinal virtues, and still has for its object to make gentlemen, scholars, and patriots out of Japanese subjects. In this reverence for truly great men and things lies the real strength of the people—a strength which may or may not be assisted by modern armaments and modern legislation. I am certain that it will never be called upon in vain, and will never be finally vanquished by evil.

No one can deny that there are turbulent students in some of the Japanese colleges; and occasionally where a teacher has given real dissatisfaction (generally from wishing to introduce some unpopular innovation) the whole class or the whole college will strike, and refuse to attend any of the lectures until the obnoxious professor has been changed. But there is no want of respect for his office involved in the rebellion, in which as a rule the strikers are warmly supported by their relatives. It is the man, the individual teacher, who, as they consider, fills the office unworthily; and since there has never been any necessity for promulgating laws forcing attendance at school in this country, the scholars are not breaking the law by staying away. They troop back to their class-room the moment that the grievance is removed, and, as far as I can judge by reading accounts of such *pronunciamientos,* do not abuse their power. On the whole, they do not much care about foreign teachers; and though some have become greatly beloved, others have been violently unpopular, on account of their rough methods, more approaching the familiar brutalities of the English clergyman-schoolmaster when dealing with very small and weak boys. Terrible trouble has been caused here in girls' schools, chiefly in those recruited from the upper middle classes, when a foreign mistress has so far lost her temper as to strike a pupil. Then the whole body of girls would leave at once, and only consent to attend again when a proper apology for the insult had been offered and accepted.

A terrible scene took place in one of the college playgrounds some time ago, when two foreign teachers, instead of entering by the proper gate, jumped over a fence to join the boys (youths of seventeen and eighteen) in a game of football. The lads flew at them, and maltreated them very severely, one gentleman having the impression that he had barely escaped with his life. The onset was cruel and unprovoked, as far as the victims of it knew; but some slight excuse may be found in the fact that it took place during a time of intense anti-foreign excitement, that *soshi* principles and false views of patriotism were everywhere in the air, and that every boy in Tokyo was boiling with rage at an absurd story which had got about that a well-known missionary teacher in Tsukiji had refused to take off his hat when the Emperor drove by. The unfortunate teacher in question had to claim British protection, and was so pestered by threatening letters and excitable young patriots that he wisely decided to leave the country for a few months and take a short holiday. All this sounds very absurd and unreasonable; but is it not the *défaut d'une qualité*, the one weak point in a tower of strength, the hard shadow cast by a blazing sun of patriotism where none would have been visible in the dull grey light of indifference?

I have wandered from the congenial subject of Japanese children to the more puzzling one of their elders; and yet it was about the children that I meant to write to you to-day. I have several small friends amongst them, and I think, when they are not made to play tunes on the piano or repeat French fables for me, that they are really glad to see me. They do not readily join in the noisy games of our young English friends, who invade the compound on Saturday afternoons, and make the place ring with those delightful squeals of joy such as only English lungs can produce. But in their quieter way they enjoy things quite as much. One of the prettiest sights of last year was a fancy-dress ball, where the little Japanese nobles came in costumes of war or the chase, the most elaborate and splendid that I have ever seen. Every detail was carried out in antique stuffs; the weapons and ornaments were the original ones used by children of the family hundreds of years ago, and kept as precious relics through all wars and revolutions. The solemnity with which these were worn was pretty to see. Evidently the little boys attached something of religious veneration to the things which they were permitted to handle on that one day. The girls were quite as splendid; but their every-day dress is so brilliant and rich that one noticed the change less in them than in their brothers. One or two had on robes given them by the Empress, who is fond of children, and often sends for the little ones to come and see her. When they were all assembled, the master of the house (an artistic, appreciative English man, who is legal adviser to the Japanese Foreign Office) marshalled the small people in a long procession, where fierce-looking young gods of war led fair-haired Red Riding Hoods by the hand, where a little carter in his smock-frock and long whip was accompanied by a small damsel out of a fairy tale, wearing trailing robes of purple and gold, looking as gay and delicate as a Brazilian humming-bird. One of the loveliest there, little Madgie M——, an English child, so beautiful that we all took a sort of national pride in her, has passed away to the country where she will be young and fair to all eternity. One misses the little angel face at this year's gatherings.

A little while ago we went out to spend the day at Meguro,* Countess Saigo's† beautiful place in the country. I say Countess Saigo's, because her husband laughingly disclaims having anything to do with such a feminine domain. "Look at all these flowers, and the silkworms, and the children!" he says; "does it look like a rough sailor's house?" And it certainly does not, though the way everything revolves round the First Lord of the Admiralty tells how he is loved and honoured there. After an elaborate lunch, we women rose from table, and my hostess beckoned to me to follow her. I knew whither she was leading me—to look at the portrait of her eldest son, a brave and brilliant boy, who died while at school in Europe, and whom she never forgets, even when surrounded by all her other children. There is always a little sadness in her smile, a grave note in her gentle voice as of pain accepted and forgiven. I followed her in silence; and her three-year-old daughter caught her dress and toddled along at her side. A little off the hall we entered a small quiet room, where, near a window, so that all the daylight illuminated it, was the portrait, a life-size head, of the dead boy. There were fresh flowers on either side, incense-sticks burning fragrantly, and in front, on a small table like those used in the temples for presenting offerings, a collection of tiny plates containing atoms of food from all the complicated French dishes of the lunch from which we had just risen.

It is some years since the boy died; but from every meal partaken of in the great house his share has been set aside—he is not forgotten. The little sister, who never knew him, stands up on tiptoe in her flowery robes, and gravely examines the small dishes to see if all

*Meguro is now a busy Tokyo suburb.
†Countess Saigō was presumably the wife of Tsugumichi Saigō (1843–1902), the younger brother of Takamori Saigō (1827–77), who led the so-called Satsuma Rebellion (or Seinan War) in 1877 but later came to be regarded as a popular hero.

is in place. She would no more think of touching the dainties than of striking her mother's beautiful face. "My brother," she lisps proudly, as she pulls at my dress and points to the picture. But the mother has turned her face away, and, with one deep salutation to her son's picture, leads us out. We join the rest, and spend a long gay afternoon in wandering about the grounds, picking flowers, and examining the great house full of silkworms, who provide all the clothing for our hostess and her daughter.

"I send it to Saikyo* to be dyed and woven," says the Countess. "See what a pretty pattern I have chosen for my daughter's new *obi!*" And she holds out a piece of French ribbon, with Louis XV bouquets and love-knots in pink on a pale-green ground!

"But it is a European design!" I cried. "Don't you think your own are much prettier?"

Then the Count spoke, laughing as usual. "Yes, please tell my wife that she should not venture on European costume. She looks as large as—a *saké*-tub in those tight-fitting things." Which was a deliberate untruth, for he and we and the Countess herself know that she is one of the few Japanese ladies who have what our dressmakers call a figure—the only one who looks as well in our costume as in her own.

"Don't listen to him, Mrs. Fraser!" she retorted, laughing gaily. "He only lives to tease; and if it hurt, I should long have ceased to live."

Then the Count has a portrait to show me, and I am taken indoors again to see a most villainous full-length painting of the little daughter in her *kimono* which was given by the Empress; and I try to conceal my feelings about the crude production, which is barely recognisable as a likeness. Both father and mother seem to worship the small girl, who is the most benign of family tyrants now, and whose character is forming visibly in the maturing sunshine of her home. I was much impressed last autumn by seeing her, tiny as she was, insist on taking part in some egg-and-spoon races which were going on at a children's garden party composed chiefly of Europeans. The little Saigo girl was the youngest there; but when asked if she would run with the others over the grassy

*Saikyō refers to the western capital, that is, Kyoto.

little racecourse, she nodded gravely, took the egg and spoon in both hands, and started off, her long robe with its delicate colours sweeping the turf, her little feet skurrying along under it in their miniature sandals, and her whole soul concentrated on getting the egg to the goal in the spoon, although she had not the slightest idea why the feat had to be performed. It was evidently a highly honourable thing for a *samurai's* daughter to do, so—come on! She was so small that the roses and lilies of the garden over-topped her little head, and in a minute or two all the other children had left her far behind; but she would not give in, and pressed bravely round the whole course, her lips quivering, large tears rolling down her cheeks, which had lost all their colour except the two spots of rouge, her little chest heaving pitifully, while her mother, who walked by her side. tried to persuade her that the game was for bigger and stronger children. No; she had begun, and the *samurai* spirit would brook no defeat. A hundred eyes were on her when she neared the goal, and something uncommonly like a cheer went up from the society crowd when she reached it. She did not break down even then, but gravely returned the dreadful egg and spoon to her hostess, bowed her due thanks when a prize dolly was presented to her, and then walked back to her seat beside her mother, as if egg-and-spoon races were her usual exercise!

Yet she is not very strong. When the cold days came, she pined, and lost her appetite (she and her brothers are brought up on European food); and her mother took her down to Numadzu,* where the sun shines warm among the pine woods even in winter, because the Kuro Shiwo, the warm stream in the sea, bathes all that coast. I went to see them when they returned, and found them installed in the official residence, a big European building in the town. "How is O'Ione San?" I asked. "Much better," her mother replied. "Doctor Hashimoto has ordered her to learn dancing as a gymnastic exercise, and it has done her so much good!" Just then a servant held open the door, and O'Ione San entered,

*Murray's *Handbook for Travellers in Japan* (1894) says of Numazu, now an industrial town in Shizuoka Prefecture, "There is much marshy ground in this neighbourhood. Most persons, rather than stay in Numazu itself, prefer to go on 25 minutes by jinrikisha to the village of Ushibuse, on a beautiful landlocked bay which offers excellent sea-bathing."

and came to greet me. "Will you dance for me, O'Ione San?" I asked; and the sweet round face lighted up with pleasure. "Then," said her mother, "O'Ione San must go and put on her dancing clothes." "I like dancing clothes," she replied. And at a nod from her mother the maid carried her off to be dressed.

This was evidently rather an elaborate business; but at last the doors were thrown open with some pomp, three women musicians in dark silk gowns entered, bowed profoundly, and ranged themselves on the floor against the wall; they were followed by a maid, who spread a square of fine matting over the carpet; and then came the little lady herself, dressed in a strange black-and-white costume, much more severe than anything she usually wears, and opening robe over robe in front to give her small feet play. Her hair had all been done again, and was full of ornaments; and her expression was as grave as her gown. She came and stood on the mat, then knelt down and touched her head to the ground, and then the music began, strange strident notes, with a strong humming accompaniment, and quick beats through it like pursuing feet and sobs as of labouring breath, that weird Japanese music which is to me the saddest in the world.

But this time I hardly noticed the music in my wonder at the precision and freedom, the grace and the strength, of the child's dancing. Every movement had been learnt to perfection; her little body swayed over to this side or that, recovered itself at the right angle, seemed to be rising from the ground on those long winglike sleeves, or striking it in anger with a little white heel that stamped with the sharpness of a hammer on the ground. She turned and twisted, whirled her skirts like a wheel, or slid round her square with them clinging closely to her childish limbs; and when the dance was over knelt again and knocked her head on the floor, and stood up to begin another, giving her orders to the musicians in one authoritative word. They were women with refined faces and delicate hands, women of the *samurai* servant type; and they smiled proudly at their little mistress as she showed off her new accomplishment, mastered in a wonderfully short time, for she had then only been learning for about three months. The finest dance she kept for the last; it consisted of some wonderful evolutions with a fan, which flew hither and thither, opened and shut, and wheeled about with such rapidity and verve that it seemed like a live thing, and the sharp click of its slats opening and closing kept time to the hurrying music. When she stopped at last, it was without a sign of fatigue; and I found, on rising to go, that she had been dancing just an hour!

All our pleasant engagements have been broken up by the influenza, which seems to have taken the gathering of our small world round my Christmas tree as a convenient occasion for spreading itself over Tokyo. The next day whole households were in bed, and within a week the town was one large hospital. In the Palace there was hardly any one left to attend on the Empress, who was very ill. One lady-in-waiting only was spared, and she was nursing all the others and the Empress as well. In many houses there was not even a servant who could light the kitchen fire; and one of my friends, too ill herself to go downstairs to do it, kept her family alive on Liebig's extract cooked over a spirit-lamp beside her bed. As for us, we fared better than some of our neighbours, because our loyal little servants endured everything rather than let the kitchen fires quite go out; but—we had thirteen people in the house down with it at once, including ourselves. My own first notice of its arrival was an attack of such sick mental despair, that I thought I must be going out of my mind; then I felt myself falling on top of my little *amah*, O'Matsu, and just called out to her not to get killed—and the rest was black darkness, from which it took me a long time to recover. Every engagement was cancelled; people were too ill to ask if even their best friends were still alive; and as soon as we could crawl down to the carriage, we went off to Miyanoshita to try and recover strength. Miyanoshita was soon full of other victims, who came on the same errand; but as we were all suffering from the inevitable after-depression which the scourge leaves behind it, we avoided each other sedulously, and when we had to meet were all as grumpy and reserved as if we had just left England for the first time and were afraid of making "undesirable acquaintances."

Miyanoshita worked wonders, and the weather was glorious, though bitterly cold. Enormous icicles hung over all the bridges; the fairy waterfall on the road to Kiga was just a film of frozen spray. But the sun shone in the daytime; we made roaring fires of pine logs and cones in the sweet-smelling wooden rooms; Kelly and Walsh,* the beneficent booksellers in Yokohama, sent us piles of new books and papers; and in a fortnight we found that we could answer a plain question civilly, look at food without nausea, and trust our feet to take short walks. Then uprose the great question of neglected work, unread despatches, unregulated affairs. "Let the things lie," I pleaded; "who wants to hear from such a hotbed of sickness as our unlucky compound?" But my arguments were ruled away as beside the mark, and, feeling still rather shaky, we returned to our stricken home.

"I wonder if there is a session going on," I said, as, driving up from Shimbashi to the Legation, I noticed a crowd gathered at the end of the wide road which leads to the new Houses of Parliament. Then the coachman turned, and drove down the road itself. There were no Houses of Parliament there. Forty brick chimneys rose straight from the ground, which was layered with ashes. Smoke was still rising from them in a dull spent way here and there. The Chamber of Representatives, the Chamber of Peers, the committee-rooms and reception-rooms and fire-proof archive-rooms, had all been burnt to the ground. The electric wires had ignited, and the fire had taken exactly five hours to consume the whole building, in the early morning of the day on which we travelled down from Miyanoshita.

A formal reception at the Palace has had to be given up. All the electric wires there were at once disconnected after this catastrophe. No other means of lighting the huge place was ever contemplated, and the ladies of honour say that really it is better to go to bed by daylight than to sit up with one candle—after one has had the influenza!

*Kelly and Walsh according to an advertisement in Murray's *Handbook for Travellers in Japan* (1894) were located at No 61, Corner Main Street, Yokohama, and described themselves as printers, publishers, booksellers, stationers, news agents and tobacconists.

Who was the Irishman who declared that the population had been "decimated by one third"? The description might apply to Tokyo since the visitation of influenza. It spared nobody, falling first upon the foreign community, and then on the Japanese; from the Emperor and Empress down to the last coolie, every one seems to have had it. Society has put up the shutters, and Tokyo is so dull that I find myself regretting the mountain walks round Miyanoshita, where, as I told you, we went up to recruit. The last of my walks I took late in the day before we left, and the memory came home with me here. The sun had set, but had left a crystal clearness in the sky, which was just beginning to turn lilac behind the enclosing hills. A new-born moon, like a silver feather, hung over the flush of amethyst, and the pine trees were beginning to make black fringes on the mountain-edges against the sky. The air was intensely cold, but full of the sound of unconquered brooks, some boiling hot and sending up wreaths of smoke as they rushed down in a neck-and-neck race with a cold rival fringed with icicles, as if to see who could reach the gorge first in the sight of the watching woods. I went up into the valleys behind the house, right towards the sunset. I relapse into savagery in the country, and commit many *bassesses* to get my walks alone. There is only one thing in life which for dear comfort equals a solitary ramble among the hills on a grey winter afternoon—and that is the Ninth Symphony!

The universal epidemic has broken up some little readings in which I had been much interested from two points of view—a selfish and an unselfish one. As most actions are none the worse for being shown off in the best light, I will tell you of the unselfish one first. In some of our long conversations with Japanese ladies, I noticed how eagerly they listened to any story of valour, heroism, or filial piety. Very often, not knowing quite how to amuse our visitors, we have shown them pictures and engravings, all of which had to be explained and illustrated clearly to their minds. They think it impolite to pay a short visit, so as a rule there has been plenty of time to develope our themes. I have found the strongest interest excited by anything connected with our Queen; and a splendid old copy of

Pyne's *Royal Residences,* out of my American grandfather's library, was almost the most popular of the picture-books. Then, seeing how shut off from intellectual amusements is the life of the Japanese lady, a friend and I put our heads together to see it we could not provide some little entertainment for these dear women, who have shown us such endless kindnesses since we came. My friend should have by far the greater credit for any success that we achieved. She is spending all her time, money, and strength on helping the Japanese ladies in those directions where from tradition and circumstance they are narrow and stunted. She is frankly a missionary, in her own quiet independent way, and can talk to them of Christianity as it would be quite unfitting for me to do. But she is so *grande dame,* so Japanese in her intense consideration for others, that she has won their complete confidence; they send their boys and girls to her to be taught English and English modes of thought, even where they are not inclined to become Christians themselves. I constantly meet the Saigo children there, and little Princess Kujo, Princess Sanjo and her daughter, and many another; and no one ever speaks of the mistress of the house except as "Dear Mrs. K——." She looks upon me as a bigoted Catholic, and I tell her that she will be saved by her invincible ignorance, *i.e.* good faith; and then we leave controversy on one side, and work our little schemes out together with perfect harmony and success.

Now for the other motive, the selfish one. I want to be brought nearer to the lives of these Japanese women, both from the interest and sympathy I feel for them, and because, although on some points my knowledge is wider and more accurate than theirs, yet there are many others where I am glad to learn from them.

I think it was in October that I had what the papers called an official tea party, at which we collected all the women of importance in our little world, and asked them if they would care to come to me once a fortnight to hear "pretty stories" read and talked over. I could give them as an example my English reading society, where twenty or thirty women meet and read and discuss English literature with very keen interest. The idea was new, and pleased them greatly; though I think one or two feared that, as my coadjutor worked so frankly for Christian interests, this might be a scheme to forward them. However, they all accepted, and have been most faithful about coming. Of course there were many things to be thought of and prepared. The first story had to be one which would appeal to their sense of all that was fit and proper. After much deliberation, we fixed on a tale of filial piety, the immemorial "Exiles of Siberia," with its wonderful story of a daughter's devotion to her parents. Then the translation had to be put into flowery language full of pretty conceits, or else the sensitive ears of these dainty Court laides would not listen to it for a moment; and the business of finding a proper translator brought me into contact with my first friend of the professor class in Japan—a woman so cultivated and modest and charming, that I shall always feel the richer for having known her. Her husband is a professor in one of the colleges; and she has had a very modern education, and writes for Japanese reviews and magazines (how funny it sounds!), of which more are published here than foreigners imagine. She had long desired to be of use in cheering the rather monotonous lives of her countrywomen, and, while deploring, as in (Japanese) duty bound, her own unworthiness, yet set about the task of translation with great enthusiasm. The long story had to be abridged, and much left out which would have been incomprehensible to our audience; but at last it was ready, and our little ladies gathered in force to listen to it.

It was with a new sensation, called, I believe, shyness, that I found myself explaining to them what we were going to do. Our translator-reader had arrived, dressed in softly tinted blue crape with her little monogram on back and shoulders. Every detail of her costume was fine and harmonious, her hair piled in a shining crown on her small head, and her splendid *obi*—the most expensive article in a Japanese lady's dress—kept in place by a thick silk band buckled with pure gold. At first she stayed near the door, explaining to me in her pretty deliberate English that she was too small and humble a person to go up to the top of the room among all those great ladies. As it was impossible for them to hear her from the door, she was at last prevailed upon to take a more prominent seat. The others quite understood the hesitation, but received her very graciously, and expressed their thanks beforehand for the trouble she had taken. Then I was asked to read the English before each paragraph of the

Japanese, as some of my guests, especially the Empress's ladies who understand it, wished to compare the two. And at last we began. Well, it really was a success. The translation delighted them by its elevated style; and the story was after their own hearts: an unhappy parent, a devoted child, an all-powerful Emperor who grants her prayer,—why, the whole thing might have happened in Japan! Who would have thought that foreigners had such a high morality? (This of course was not said to me.) Evidently there were devoted children all the world over,—and so on!

Every two weeks we have a meeting, alternately with my English one, which is one of my great interests now. We finished Elizabeth, and then gave them a tale of wifely heroism, Lady Nithsdale's* rescue of her husband from the Tower, which appealed to these daughters of the *samurai*, and drew tears of admiration from their eyes. They laid aside their studied calm for once, and became absolutely enthusiastic over the heroine's courage and wit. When I went out in the world, the husbands of some of them came and thanked me for the "splendid story," which had been repeated all through the family circles word for word. At the end of every reading the Empress's ladies make the same polite little request to be allowed to take home the manuscript, "so as to read it again." And that is what happens to it, being read aloud to the "august ears," only too glad of some new thing, I fancy, in the dulness and pomp of a childless life. The Empress is fond of writing verses—a very touching one appeared the other day: "The world is great, and full of men and women, who can tell each other of the grief or joy in their hearts. My heart is also full; but that which it containeth I

*A. L. Rowse, in *The Tower of London in the History of the Nation* (1978), describes the escape of Lord Nithsdale who had taken part in the Jacobite rebellion in Britain in 1715. The Earl of Nithsdale, along with other Scottish lords, was arrested and lodged in the Tower of London. The night before the execution of two of his companions, the Earl of Derwentwater and Lord Kenmure, Nithsdale escaped. His wife had made a difficult journey from the North and had succeeded in gaining entrance to St. James' Palace, where she appealed for mercy to King George I. Unsuccessful, the Countess gained access to the Tower with some women companions, and, in the ensuing confusion, she was able to throw a cloak and hood over her husband and get him past the guards disguised as a servant of the Venetian Ambassador. Nithsdale then crossed the English Channel to safety.

tell to God alone." She composes music too, and is, it is said, the author of the national anthem, a very solemn and stirring chant.* I sometimes have fancied that the extreme faithfulness and earnest attention of her ladies to our little readings was not given entirely on their own account. The next story on our list was a life of gracious Queen Margaret,† the saint of Scotland, whose shipwreck on its shores was a very sunrise of love and faith and gentle rule for the rough country and its rougher Court. Where, in these stories, the action turns on faith, we give the religious element its full value; and the audience never takes offence. "Hearts are alike in Europe and Japan," one of them said to me; "English ladies are very brave and true to their duties—that is what we admire." "You could teach us more than we can teach you on that point," I sighed, thinking what Japanese women would make of our just laws, our honourable equal marriage rights (equal in all except evil, where our prosaic old legislators must still argue on the ground that woman is a naturally pure and elevated creature, and shall never enjoy the indulgence necessarily extended to her fallen companion!)—of what my little friends here would be, surrounded by the chivalrous institutions of the West; and I was also thinking of what we Western women could make of our world, had we the heroic humility, the faithfulness to duty, the divine unselfishness of our Eastern sisters.

You will say that the exaggeration of a virtue is revenged in Nature's exacting balances by the formation—somewhere—of a fault. I must grant that, and unnatural heroic unselfishness does often encourage a distorted selfishness in base natures quick to seize their own advantage from another's generosity; and Japanese husbands, especially those of the upper classes, have fallen into this sin, and do fall into it every day. A man who for his father and mother will support every privation, make every sacrifice, is cold and indifferent, perhaps, to the blameless woman at his side. She is too much a part of himself for him not to be ashamed to lavish outward testimonies

*The words of the Japanese national anthem "Kimigayo" are from a 31-syllable poem of unknown authorship from the *Kokinshū* collection of poetry (compiled 905–22).

†Queen of Scotland (d. 1093), daughter of Edward the Atheling. Canonized in 1250.

of regard upon her. She is the other self of the inner life, which, for all their apparent disregard of privacy, is so truly the inner life that a Japanese never even speaks of his wife unless absolutely obliged to do so. As far as European life has touched them, the Japanese are willing to conform to our usages as regards the treatment of women in public. The wife of an official accompanies him to pay me a visit. Since the husband is in office, the wife may only appear in European costume, and she passes before him, according to European traditions. Perhaps the next time they call he has resigned his portfolio; then Madame is in her own pretty dress, and Monsieur enters first in his own pretty way!

The truth is that marriage is not, and never can be here, the supreme relation of life, as it is in Europe. Love, in our sense of the word, has nothing to do with the matter; and the experience of this great passion, which holds such a paramount place in Western lives, is here an exceptional thing, a destiny, generally condemned to be a sorrowful one, and eliciting pity, and something of the praise we accord to martyrdom, when, as constantly happens, the poor lovers, seeing their union impossible in this world, commit a double suicide, and travel to the Meido* together, sure of reunion in the shadowy realms, where, for us, marriage ties are said to be dissolved. As marriages are always arranged by parents or friends, the young people's consent only being asked at the moment when they have had their first interview, a very small amount of personal feeling enters into the contract—at any rate in its early stages. An English bride would blush angrily were it hinted that she was not, as the phrase runs, in love with her new husband; that rarest of passions, pure love, is supposed to preside even at the most fashionable weddings. Not so in Japan. The young girl here would reply that such passion is for the women whom she need never meet; the very name of it is unknown to her, unless she has seen it illustrated in a play at the theatre; who would think of mentioning such a low feeling, where the solemn duty of wife to husband, and husband's father and mother, is concerned? Her marriage is the passing from childhood's happy careless life to the responsibilities of reason. Body and soul, mind

*Meido is the land of the dead.

and spirit, must all tend to one thing—the giving entire satisfaction to the new master and his family.

This seems very dreary and cold to us; and the best European woman, educated in the full consciousness of her own value, would feel that she lost her integrity by entering such bondage. That it is done by hundreds of girls every year without any thought of love or duty either, but simply for the sake of having a luxurious home and plenty of fun, does not touch the case at all. Our typical high-minded English maiden despises these weaker sisters, is ashamed for them as for some blot on womanhood itself. The best of her gods is still naughty Cupid; and if he is to be shut out of her life, she would rather give up the struggle at once.

And yet all English history can show no record of higher, stronger love than the Japanese wife has again and again laid at her lord's feet. It would seem as if that rare passion of which I spoke just now may, in fact, be born in what we call bondage; may grow great in its nameless glory in these quiet lives; and when the time comes, may claim life, and everything which is dearer than life, with the certainty that all will be given entire. You exclaim, as you hear of some amazing piece of heroism, "How the woman must have loved the man!" And your friend, your little Japanese friend, looks up into your face with her childlike smile and some surprise in her dark eyes: "Oh no, it was her duty; he was her husband."

It seems to me that the common amusement called "falling in love" has absolutely nothing to do with the affectionate and careful fulfilment of the duties of married life, and that the crown of an all-absorbing worship of one human being for another may be, and often is, granted without that passing preliminary ailment having been contracted at all.

Nor does what is mistakenly called "the plurality of wives" seem to interfere materially with the true wife's happiness, or her regard for her husband. Steeped as we are in the laws and prejudices of the West, it is not easy for us to judge of these questions; but since my sympathies naturally go with the woman, the wife-woman, who alone can carry the noble name, alone takes the responsibility of all the children's education, no matter who their mothers may be, we shall at any rate apprehend one aspect of the truth if we can grasp her point of view—a point of view which in ordinary circumstances would not have the defect of over-leniency at any rate.

In the first place, there is but one wife properly speaking,* and it has rarely, if ever, been heard of that any attempt was made to intrude any other woman into her place. Her dignities as responsible head of the household, as wife and mother, as ruler of the home-world and dispenser of its hospitalities—these could never be taken from her; nor would they ever be given to a concubine, if the lady of the house were to die. Into her hands is given her husband's income, great or small; she apportions it as the best interests of the family require; and the great ladies show a profound power of organisation, making property yield its highest value, controlling all expenditure with a good sense and economy seldom shown by European women, unless they have had very special training in the management of great affairs.

Where the property is very large, the lady employs a steward to collect the rents and see to the more outside matters; but she never drops the reins, and it is to her, and not to the master, that all claims or complaints are made. The steward is always called *her* steward, and may never come into contact with the master at all. This all entails very hard and constant work, and quite precludes the possibility of spending a very idle life, as rich men's wives are popularly supposed to do. Her other task, twin to this, is the entire management of the children's education while they are still young, and her responsibility for their health and morals.

Motherhood is what may truly be called the supreme relation of life for the Japanese woman. It crowns her with honour and glory; and although her children, if they be boys, are considered superior beings to the mother who bore them, yet she shines with every glory or distinction they achieve; every success of theirs is a jewel in her crown. As in the Bible, so here, the names of great men's mothers are handed down with those of their sons; and the nation says, for instance, of the Empress Jingo Kogo† in her brilliant con-

---

*Both Emperor Meiji and Emperor Taishō were sons of second wives.

†Jingū Kōgō ruled during the late fourth century. She is a legendary figure who is said to have led an attack on the Kingdom of Silla in Korea.

quest of Corea, "No wonder that she did valiantly! Was she not carrying her great son Ojin* in her bosom at that time, to inspire her with wisdom and courage? Like son, like mother!"

It seems like a compensation to Japanese women for their judicial inferiority to men that the ruling passion of a woman's heart, love for children, is recognised as a national virtue; that the reverence for childhood has developed a system of kindness and care and protection of childhood such as would be the dream, the unrealisable dream, of many a broken-hearted mother in England, powerless to protect her children from the drunken cruelty of the brute who is their father, or, in a superior class, from the more refined torture inflicted by schoolmasters and other bullies. There is no baby torture here, no beating, no starvation, none of the indescribable horrors exposed and punished in some degree by our only too necessary Society for the Prevention of Cruelty to Children. From one end of Japan to the other, a child is treated as a sacred thing, be it one's own or a stranger's. Each little one carries its name and address on a ticket round its neck; but should it, indeed, stray from home, food and shelter and kindness would meet it everywhere. Do not shudder—a man will kill his child outright, scientifically, painlessly, if he sees that there is nothing but want and misery before it; but while he lives the child will not suffer.

A terrible case came under my own notice last year, when something very like famine desolated the land. The rice-crop failed, and the want was terrible. Relief camps were opened, soup and bread distributed from various centres in the city, one of the most efficient managed by Archdeacon S——, the (Protestant) Legation Chaplain (he and his wife people of such merciful goodness that everybody in trouble flies to their house, and is sure to find refuge and comfort there. Their hearts are of pure gold, and their house must be built of india-rubber—I wish one could say the same of their income!). But it was impossible to reach everybody, and starvation ploughed the poorer quarters of the city. At the worst moment a coolie came to the gate of our Convent in Tsukiji,

*AUTHOR'S NOTE: Ojin was after his death deified as Hachiman, the god of war.

257

leading two little girls. All three were frightfully emaciated. The poor father entreated the nuns to take the children, and bring them up among their orphans. He said he could no longer earn a livelihood for them; their mother was dead; he had nothing left in the world. Alas! he was not the first who had come on the same errand. During the few weeks before, one child after another had been brought to the good nuns, or left helpless at their gates, the parents certain that it would be cared for by them. Every corner was filled with sick and hungry people; the nuns had given up their one sitting-room, and were living in terror of the supplies giving out, for many a time the Superior has gone to bed not knowing where the money for the next day's marketing was to come from—and this with over three hundred mouths to feed! "It is God's family," she has often said to me; "so it is God's affair, and the money will surely come, or the food. He does not intend that we shall make debts! But on this day the Sister was frightened. It did not seem right to crowd the children's dormitories any further, and people were sleeping on the floor in the passages already. She gave the poor man food, and a tiny sum, all she could possibly spare, in money. "Leave me your address," she said; "and the moment I have room I will send for the poor little girls. Have courage; I will not keep them long waiting." So the man went, taking his children with him; and the nun, seeing the despair in his eyes, was troubled all night about it, and sent down the first thing in the morning to tell him that she would risk it, he might bring the little girls back. Both children were dead. My dear blameless Sister Superior weeps whenever she remembers them, and that is very often. In that famine-time she saved many a child from being sold to a much worse fate than death. The parents were mad with trouble; the Yoshiwara* man offered money, would never be unkind to the girls; prostitution was a misfortune certainly, but no disgrace, no crime; why not let them go?† Then the poor little girls, in their terror of the unknown, would cry out,

*Yoshiwara was the red-light district of Edo.

†AUTHOR'S NOTE: Such traffic is forbidden by law, but is unfortunately still carried on in secret. It is quite distinct from the apprenticing of girls to masters who train them as *geisha* (or dancing-girls). These are highly educated according to Japanese ideas, and are not necessarily disreputable. Their training is extremely

"My cousin or my friend is with the Tsukiji Virjen Sama; take me to them, Ottottsan!" And that was one reason why the Convent was so terribly full just at that time.

I must say a few words more about the woman's life here before leaving these grave subjects for gayer ones. Perhaps it is really a hardship that a young and charming woman should have to call herself the mother of several big girls and boys who could not by any chance be her own children. I am always inclined to smile when such a woman gravely speaks of "my daughter," nodding to a girl nearly as old as herself, and perhaps without a trace of her own delicate features and innate high breeding; but my impression is that my friend herself sees nothing derogatory in it, although she may be very well educated and a Christian as well. The *mekake,* or concubine, is in her own way a perfectly respectable woman, probably taken from the class of small shopkeepers, who do not consider her accepting such a position as any disgrace. The woman herself very likely acts as a servant in the house; always kindly treated and provided for to the end of her life, she yet has no part in her children, and must only tend and love them as an upper nurse might do. This is the real hardship of her lot; but in the simplicity of the Japanese points of view there are many things which soften it for her. Although never for a moment usurping the mistress's place, she is treated with a good deal of consideration by the whole family, on the principle of her being a favourite with the great lord and master, round whom they all revolve in different circles indeed, but all with equal dependence on the domestic sun. If he be a very rich man, he will probably give the *mekake* a home to herself in another part of the grounds; but there will be no enmity between her and the great lady, the true wife, who mothers all the children. A young married woman came to see a friend of mine, arriving rather late for an appointment. "You look tired," my friend remarked to the visitor. "I am very tired," she replied; "we have had a dear new baby born in the house. I was up all

severe, and every gift of mind and body is developed to the highest point. Many have married men in prominent positions, and those whom I have known, although not warmly welcomed by Japanese ladies, have shown great sense and dignity in the conduct of social and domestic affairs.

night with the mother. We thought she would die, poor thing; but I am glad to say she is all right now!" This lady was a Christian too; but—the King can do no wrong in Japan.

One very good result comes from the frank way in which these matters are treated. There are no illegitimate children, as we understand the term, because every child takes its father's name, and he is forced to provide for its maintenance. Even in former times the son of the true wife was looked upon as a man's natural heir; but failing him, the inheritance passed to his brother, whoever the latter's mother might have been. Failing a half-brother, it passed to a daughter of the true wife, and failing such, to any other daughter whom the man might have had. Such was the rule; but where each man was absolute master in his own house, distinctions of favouritism were often arbitrarily exercised. A man could, in fact, choose which son should inherit his honours and estates, or he could put all his own children aside, and install a stranger as head of the family. Nothing mattered except that my lord's whims should be carried out. But now things are different. A man is responsible for all his children, whoever their mother may have been; but his title can only be inherited by the eldest living son of his true wife, and, failing such, must go to the nearest collateral legitimate heir. The next heir to the throne after Prince Haru must be the son of his Empress, or, failing him, the son of the true wife of the Prince nearest to the throne. This new regulation is a death-blow to the old system of adoption; and while rendering far higher honour to the true wife than she had heretofore enjoyed, inflicts disabilities on the children of concubines, which will gradually bring discredit on the whole system. At least, so it strikes me. It seems to be the thin end of the wedge of external respectability according to Western ideas, applied to the spot where its touch will be most keenly felt—the honour of the family. I doubt if the new regulation will add to the happiness of the Japanese home, which for decorum and harmony so far compares more than favourably with the ordinary European one; and I see in it a danger to the permanency and strength of the tie between father and child.

Where the man is no more a Christian than the ordinary society man in London; where he has taken no vows, however flippantly, binding him to one woman; where every day humanity does not take the sacred name of love in vain,—there I think that decency, order, and the family ties are less outraged by the existence of the quiet faithful concubine and her children than by the revolting arrangements resorted to in Europe, where men, who as the saying goes "are not straight to their wives," are brought without shame or regret into the society of women from whom the poor Japanese *mekake* would shrink with horror.

The counterpart of that class exists here. Compared to the poor creatures who compose it in Europe, the Japanese women are models of refinement and disinterestedness. But society shows stern disapproval of the men who frequent their company; a wife may protest against such lapses without any infringement of the respect she owes her lord, and it would be considered her duty to do so.

As a last word, I should say that there are many Japanese families of the upper class where it has been for generations the custom to make the wife supreme in every way, and to admit no *mekake* into the family. Concubinage is an expensive luxury confined to the upper classes, and is greatly on the wane even among them; among the poor it is unknown; and divorce, though still fatally easy, is not often resorted to.

Tokyo, March, 1891

A profound gloom has been cast over the capital by the death of Prince Sanjo; he was such a familiar figure at all the Court functions, he and I had sat through so many dinners, walked in so many processions side by side, that I had come to look upon him as an old friend; he was always kind and cheery, and the wife and daughter had been among those whom I saw most constantly. They are in terrible grief; and I shall not see them for many months, as a long period of seclusion will separate them from the world. They were all with us on Christmas Day, and the poor Prince took influenza almost immediately afterwards. His lungs were never very strong, and he could not weather the attack of inflammation which set in. If companionship is any comfort in grief, his family ought to be comforted; for the whole country mourned for the Emperor's friend and councillor, the quiet, duty-loving statesman, who has done so much for progress, justice, and peace.

If there were a Libro d'Oro in Japan, the name of Prince Sanetome Sanjo would be among the very first in its pages. A Kugé (or descendant of an Imperial Prince), his pedigree goes back to Kamatari (A.D. 626), the founder of fourteen out of the sixteen Kugé families existing to-day.* Prince Sanjo was always devoted to the Imperial cause, and in very early youth flung himself, his influence, and his fortune into the struggle to put down the usurpations of the Shogun and restore the sovereign to the reality of power. I have described this struggle in an earlier letter. Prince Sanjo was but a boy when it began; at its close, after fourteen years of constant warfare, he was only thirty years old, and had proved his devotion and ability so completely that he was at once raised to high rank in the Government, and was ever after looked upon by the Emperor as the most trustworthy of his councillors. In 1871 (he was then thirty-four) he was given the post of Chancellor of the Empire, the highest in the Administration. He held it for fourteen years, by far the most difficult years in Japan's stormy history—years during which all the changes that we admire to-day were introduced and consolidated without the slightest shock to the national strength or integrity. The country came through the ordeal, accompanied as it was by civil war, rebellion, intrigues without and within, with perfect safety; with the Emperor firmly seated on his throne, never to be touched again by the ambitions and intrigues of the Shoguns; with enemies transformed into loyal servants, friends rewarded for faithful service, the empire ready to work like one man at the task of setting its army and navy, its legislation, its organisation on the footing which befits a great power. It is, I fancy, rare to hear of a Prime Minister holding uninterrupted office for fourteen years; and it is in our experience unparalleled that any nation should so have transformed itself in that period of time. Prince Sanjo had no personal ambition,

*AUTHOR'S NOTE: If pedigrees may be trusted, there is no body of peers in Europe who can out-class the present peerage of Japan. It numbers four hundred and seventy-three members of the old nobility, and, of these, four hundred are the direct descendants of Emperors, and possess written records going back for thirteen or fourteen centuries.

and several times begged for permission to retire from public affairs, which were then advancing safely and smoothly. This permission was at last unwillingly granted, in 1885; he was made Keeper of the Privy Seal, and did not again enter public life till the end of 1889, when he reluctantly took the leadership of the Cabinet at the Emperor's command after the attempted assassination of Count Okuma. Every one recognised in him a man of intense conscientiousness, wisdom, and intrepid courage, whose every good quality acquired a double value through his complete integrity and disinterestedness.

There are distinctions in Japan which are only granted to dying greatness. When we heard that the Emperor was about to visit his faithful servant, we knew that but one visitor would succeed him in the quiet house; the sovereign was the herald of death, and he conferred the honours which Sanetome Sanjo must take with him to the Meido, the shadow realm, for he could not enjoy them here. As soon as his desperate condition became known, the Emperor hastened to his house; and while the Prince was still conscious, told him that he had come to thank him for his life-long devotion, and to bestow on him the highest rank that it is possible for a subject to hold. The people who accompanied the Emperor tell us that all his assumed calm fell away from him when he looked on his friend's face, and that it was with the greatest difficulty that he controlled his emotion as he spoke words which must have been very sweet even to dying ears. This is what the sovereign said:

"In the early years of my reign, while I was still but a youth, you were my greatest help. You, not shrinking from the gravest responsibility, lent me assistance so constant, so ready, and so true, that you were to me as a teacher and a father. Never did you fail in the discharge of your great duties. All my subjects should look up to you as a model. In recognition of your great services and faithfulness, I confer upon you the First Class of the First Rank."

This last, Sho-ichi-i, is a distinction which has not been granted to any subject for over eleven hundred years, when it was borne by one of Prince Sanjo's ancestors, who died in 738. They say that the poor Prince made violent attempts to rise and salute the Emperor properly. A few hours after the visit he passed away, and the world is much the poorer by the loss of a good man.

The Imperial family practise the "pure Shinto" form of religion, and Prince Sanjo's State funeral was arranged altogether by Shinto rules. These forbid pomp, but enjoin the use of white robes, white woods, quantities of flowers, everything simple and cheering and pure. I have heard the reproach of heartlessness again and again made to the Japanese, on account of the calm and cheerful countenances with which they accompany their dead to the grave. But their long and tender remembrance of the dead surely exonerates them from the accusation. Their belief is that those who die beloved, and for whom remembrance is constantly made, do not suffer in the shadowy peace of Meido, that home of departed spirits, which is not a prison, and from which they constantly come to visit the living, to protect and comfort the bereaved. Is it possible that this humble impersonal faith can sustain the survivors in the dreadful emptiness of the stricken home? I think it helps them so greatly, because it is a part of eternal truth—just that portion of it which they are fitted to apprehend now. The great Teacher does not insist upon making all His children learn the same lesson the same day.

Our friend's funeral was very beautiful and very simple, its greatest pomp being that which we should all love to share in—the true sorrow of grateful hearts. The white-robed priests and mourners, the white lotus flowers with their silver leaves, the exquisite whitewood coffin with its snowy panoply—all seemed to fit the passing of his pure spirit to its rest. But the whole country mourned his loss, and there never has been seen such a concourse of people in Tokyo as that which lined the route of the procession. The procession itself was two miles long, and passed over some six miles of distance, from the solemn house among the fir trees where he died, to the Gokokuji Temple, where the funeral rites were to take place. It is a beautiful place, with great gardens full of flowers, in which wander young bonzes from a college kept here for them. The Temple is the mortuary chapel, as it were, of the Imperial Cemetery, a part of the grounds having been set aside for that purpose, now that Emperors live and die in Tokyo. The place is never opened to the public, except when some silent Prince or Princess comes knocking at the gate.

All along the line of march really sorrowing crowds watched the train go by, amid a hush of intense respect. The troops who accompanied it remained outside the gates, and the rest passed in, up long flights of steps which led to the sanctuary where the service was to take place. All those invited to the funeral had already assembled here. The heralds of the train were a number of white-robed men, carrying quantities of green branches of the *sakaki* (*Cleyera Japonica*), sacred to the dead. Then came the offerings, which would later be placed before the coffin; these were enclosed in a case, white and plain like all the rest. A great troop of Shinto priests followed, all white-robed except the high-priest, who wore purple. Then, to the sounds of the weirdly sad Shinto music, came a great white banner, on which were inscribed all the Prince's titles and honours; and after that quantities of people carrying the *sakaki* sprigs, the placing of which forms a part of the funeral ceremony, and others carrying silver halberds and enormous trophies of flowers such as people here send to a funeral instead of our wreaths and crosses. Eight separate decorations, the most honourable in the Emperor's gift, had been bestowed on the Prince at different times; and these were carried on cushions by eight bearers, all dressed in white; and then came a goodly company in the same costume, the chief servants of the family. It was their privilege immediately to precede the bier, which was of a lovely shape, like a small temple, all carved out of spotless white wood, the spruce which the Japanese call *hi-no-ki*. It did not look like a coffin, but like a closed litter, with beautifully chased golden mountings, and fresh green bamboo blinds closing its little windows. The roof rose at the four corners in delicate ornaments, and tassels of pure white silk hung against the blinds. Raised on a system of poles crossed and recrossed, the bier was carried by fifty men, all dressed in white. We were told that it covered a double coffin, made also of white wood. A thrill of real sorrow seemed to run through the great crowd as it passed, and then all hearts went out to the boy and girl who followed as chief mourners, for their mother was too prostrated by grief to appear. The girl was my little friend, Princess Chiye, her beautiful face absolutely rigid, and white as the robe which showed under her black cloak and brown *hakama*, the kind of divided skirt worn on all occasions of ceremony. Her little feet were roughly sandalled, and she walked the whole way from her father's house to her father's resting-place, bareheaded, without betraying a sign of fatigue. Her brother, dressed in black and white, and wearing the same common sandals, walked at her side; and behind them came four little girls, the younger sisters,

who wore no black, but white crape robes without a single ornament, and having their long hair tied back with white ribbon and
hanging far below their waists. They were followed by a crowd of
relations, and in this order the procession passed at last in at the Temple gate, and up the many steps, till they stopped under a tent or
porch which had been erected before the door of the Temple. Here
were two pavilions, in which the family took their seats, together
with the Imperial Princes, the Ministers, the Foreign Representatives,
and the other guests.

The tent was all draped in the sombre black and white stripes
that I have so often seen used for Court functions. In the centre,
just before the steps, the bier was placed on a stand prepared for it;
the banners and flower trophies were disposed on either side of the
space leading up to it; and the Prince's Orders were laid on little
white-wood stands around. Then came Shinto chants; and the two
chief priests with their acolytes prayed before the bier, and bent in
homage to the dead. Then the chief priest took the offerings of food,
and placed them on other stands prepared for them; and he read
aloud, in a high-chanting voice, two orations of farewell to the dead.
In these all the good and great acts of the Prince's life were re-
counted; and at the end came the phrase, "May thy soul have eternal
rest and peace in heaven," so like our "Requiem eternam dona eis,
Domine, et lux perpetua luceat eis," that a very deep chord of sympathy was touched in those who could understand the words.

But the ceremonial was terribly long for the poor children, who
went through it, as *samurai* and nobles should, without a single
change of expression on their young pale faces. How the eldest
Princess bore it I know not; for she worshipped her father, and the
tie between them was that of the most complete confidence and
intimacy. When the orations were over, the priests distributed sprigs
of the *sakaki* to every one, beginning with the young Prince, the
Imperial Princes, and the envoys of the Emperor and Empress.
When these had reverently laid the branches before the bier, the
poor little Princess and her four sisters slowly advanced, holding the
sacred boughs in their hands, bowed to the very ground in the last
act of homage to their beloved father, and laid the green boughs on
those already lying before his coffin. This was a terrible moment, and

seemed likely to be too much for the eldest daughter's fortitude; but she conquered it, laid her offering on the rest with a hand that trembled pitifully, and led her sisters back to their place, unconquered by grief.

Something like two thousand people followed to render this green tribute to the Prince's memory; and when that had been done, most of the guests returned home, only a very few having been invited to attend the actual burial in the cemetery. The road to the grave was all a double wall of flowers, standing high on either side of a long carpeting of fine matting. Every lovely bloom that could rob death of its terrors had been collected there; under the bright Eastern sunshine a beautiful canopy of white wood hung high over the open stone vault. In the gardens around, all life was rising to its spring, and stately trees, the guardians of the place, seemed to have been waiting long for this honoured and welcome guest. When the white coffin had at last been placed in its quiet home, amidst a silence woven of love and reverence; when the green boughs and the flowers and the insignia of earthly glory had been laid at the door, through which the honoured dead must pass alone, —then those who had been bidden to his farewell crept away, leaving the poor children to say their last good-byes. And in that morning smile of nature, in that perfect peace which seems to have robbed death of its fear and bereavement of its sting, I trust that the good-byes were not despairing ones.

These things happened in the end of February, and this is the beginning of March. Alas! the spring has robbed me of another friend, and one whose like I shall not find again. Ogita, our *samurai*, guide, interpreter, my right hand in a thousand matters of life, has passed away, unable to recover from the effects of that awful influenza. He had been ailing for long, coughing, and looking very thin. We think he hurt himself by giving lessons in the exhausting Japanese fencing, which Dr. Baelz, one of the strongest men I know, and trained, as all Germans are, to such exercises, told me was so terribly fatiguing that the learning of it nearly broke him down. Poor Ogita was a great swordsman, his family was large, the Government pay none too generous; so nothing was said when it was found that he was giving lessons in his spare time. After Christmas we sent him down to Atami to keep him out of the way of the epidemic; but he took it there, and came home at last, with death written on his face. Do you wonder that I tell you so much about a mere servant, a Chancery writer? He has been so helpful and faithful, has carried out all my whims with such gentle patience, has piloted me through so many journeys, taught me so many quaint stories, that a part of my Japanese life has died with him.

He had a little house in the grounds, where I went constantly in the last days. The old mother, the wife, the five girls and boys, always received me with an air of gay satisfaction, and never let me see them break down at all till quite the end. In the bare little house on the worn mats lay my poor friend, too weak to speak, but with a light of welcome always shining for me in his eyes. He was a tall man, of soldierly bearing, and there was something very pitiful in seeing him lying, so long and weak, on the floor of the tiny room, which seemed so much too small for him. Behind him, to keep off any draught, was a six-leaved screen out of my sitting-room, with gay summer landscapes and dancing waterfalls painted on the panels. What comforts could help him he had; and though the rooms were small, at any rate the house was his home, and he was surrounded by all the love of mother and wife and children. The children were greatly on his mind; but when their future was provided for to his satisfaction, he was quite content to die, and said to me once or twice, "Okusama is very kind; I would get well if I could; but I can never travel with her any more, and I am too tired to live." To the very last his two hands always went up to his brow when I entered, even after he could not speak; and I used only to stay a minute or two at a time, for fear of exhausting him. We had had many a conversation about the future life; but, alas! he had lived too long among careless Christians to have any special regard for Christianity. He had seen in his twenty years of Government service bad men and good, among the Christians as among the sects of his countrymen—less good, perhaps, among the former than among the latter. There was no ground for a conversion here, and he went out among the shadows a valiant, humble, upright soul, a *samurai* and a gentleman to the last; and I do not believe that any true gentleman was ever shut out of heaven yet. They left me alone with him for a while the day after he was dead; he lay very straight and stiff, with a smile of peace on his thin face. His hands were crossed on his breast, and his long blue robes were drawn in straight folds, all held in place with little packets of tea, which filled the room with a dry fragrance; the coffin was lined with these, and his head rested on a pillow of the same. Beside him on a stand lay his most precious possession, his sword; and before the weeping wife left me kneeling there, she touched my shoulder, and pointed to the sword, bowing her head in reverence, and whispering, "Samurai, Okusama!" Incense-sticks were burning in bronze vases at either end of the sword, and freshly gathered flowers stood on the floor near the coffin head. Behind was still my screen, not turned upside down, as it should have been in the presence of the dead (perhaps because it was mine); and in the little room, bared of all except that which was left to honour my poor friend, the summer landscapes and dancing waterfalls spoke of hope and new life and a world where a tired spirit might rest earth's weariness away.

So they took our *samurai* home; and after the first bursts of grief, far less restrained among the poorer women than among the nobles, I think the old mother and the wife and the little girls have found comfort in visiting the quiet grave in Shiba, where Ogita lies. All little gifts are stored up to carry there; O'Ione San, the baby girl of three, whom her father worshipped devoutly, saves up all the pretty cakes that find their way from my tea-table to her little brown hands. "Ottottsan's!" she says when they are given to her; and a piece of paper has to be found to wrap them in, and they are put in the alcove in the place of honour till she and her mother pay their next visit to Shiba; and then they are laid with many a tender word on his grave, to comfort him if he is lonely or hungry in the Meido. Good-bye, kind friend and faithful servant. "May thy soul have eternal rest and peace in heaven!"

And now, as I have spoken of Shiba, I must tell you something of those Shiba Temples* which are the pride of Tokyo—temples built mostly as tombs or temporary mortuary chapels for the

---

*The only building of this complex to survive earthquake and war was the main gateway, which was built in 1605.

269

Shoguns of the Tokugawa Dynasty. Its founder, Iyeyasu, lies at Nikko (as does his grandson, Iyemitsu); but during his lifetime he suddenly realised that he had no especial temple of his own; "and that," said he, "is a thing unheard of for a great general! I must immediately select a temple, where I can pray during my life, and where others will pray for me when I am dead!" The result of these pangs of conscience was the choice of the great Temple of Zōjōji, in what is now called the Shiba Park, as the one where his *ihai* (mortuary tablet bearing his posthumous name and titles) should be set up. The Temple was administered by priests of the Jōdō sect of Buddhists; it was extremely rich and splendid, but was burnt, in revenge it is said, when in 1873 the Buddhists were banished, and the Temple given over to "pure Shinto." A smaller and poorer one was built, which seems out of place behind the magnificent triple gate (Sammon) which remains from the days of its predecessor. But the mortuary temples (not intended for public worship) were fortunately not burnt, and contain wonders of lacquer and painting and carving. The great red gates, with their scarlet columns and big lanterns and wheeling flights of pigeons (tame as those of San Marco), are quite beautiful to look at; and I often drive past them just to see the pigeons gathering round the feet of some girl who stands in the great opening feeding them with grain bought at the little booths which line the terrace, while behind her the sun touches hundreds of huge stone lanterns in the grey inner court. And when the spring has come, when the tall camellia trees are flinging the petals and the perfume of their single rose-coloured blossoms all abroad (petals so delicate that it seems wrong to walk on them, perfume so fragrant that one longs to store and carry it away), then the courts of the Shiba Temples are happy places to wander through; its flights of grey stone steps make seats where one can rest and dream a sunny hour away with much profit. For the sun is the master of the house; and unless you find him at home, you may as well leave your card and come another day. The dusky splendours of the sacred buildings will be invisible to you unless he illuminates them; the paintings and carvings withdraw into space, and none of the fairy-work will show itself rightly, except at the touch of the great magician.

The friend who took me there the first time had spent days and weeks in making drawings of some of the wonders of decoration on panel and roof; and he would not let me go near the temples, until one glorious morning when it seemed as if a hundred suns were shining at once. Then the wide courts, with their armies of lanterns, their limpid fountains for the washing of the worshippers' hands, their stately stairs and fern-set walls, all seemed so attractive, that I had no great desire to enter the dark buildings. But my want of enterprise was taken no notice of, and I was glad, for the contents of the casket were equal to the outer covering. Through a splendidly carved dragon-gate, we passed to an inner court, where are two hundred and twelve bronze lanterns, very stately to behold. Beautiful, also, is the cistern for holy water, perpetually brimming with a crystal flood which never overflows. Then we pass to an inner court still, whose galleries are adorned with elaborate paintings; over our heads a beautiful winged woman hovers, painted in the purest and most brilliant colours; and everywhere are endless interweavings of those wave and wind patterns which symbolise the original principles in nature, the Fûng Shui (wind and water spirits) of China. It would take many days to note all the changes, the beautiful elaborations worked from these through hundreds of developments, in each of which the artist gives a new shape and meaning to the rush of the hurricane, the curl and spray of the wave. But we pass on from the gallery intended for the Daimyos, who accompanied each Shogun when he came here, to his own temple, to pray. They might not go with him to the inner sanctuary, the Honden; there he entered, and offered up his devotions alone, while they sat, the greater divided from the less, in perfect silence without. All this painting and gilding and carving must have proved a great interest and solace, if the Shogun was long at his prayers. We passed on to the inner sanctuary, having slipped off our shoes so as not to scratch the polished and lacquered steps with our hard heels.

I believe there is in the human being a profound hunger and thirst for beauty for its own sake; there are chords in our hearts which thrill at the sight of piled gold and rippling jewels, at the miracles of perfect priceless decoration, as they thrill at great music or a splendid sunset. Now and then in life this hunger is satisfied by a feast, and more than a feast, of beauty; the soul is intoxicated with the new wine of gold and colour and magnificence, and understands in that triumphant flush some secret of the permanent and divine essence of beauty which it never can apprehend, or affects to forget, in the sober daylight of its working existence. When I found myself face to face with the marvel called the Octagonal Shrine, I felt that I was in presence of the supreme effort of art in one particular direction—that this vision of the eight-sided shrine of pure gold lacquer, from whose depths trees and hills, birds and beasts, have been as it were resolved for us to see, whose sides and pinnacles shine with gems and fairy-work of rainbow enamel, this indeed could rank with my visit to the green-draped shrine in the Dresden Gallery where the Sistine Madonna reigns in the silence, with golden hours passed under Michelangelo's cypresses in the gardens of our home, with our sailings in the summer moonlight past the islands of the syrens to the violets of Pæstum: here was one more piece of perfect beauty, mine for ever in the inalienable kingdom of remembrance. I have but to close my eyes, and there rises before me this golden flower of beauty blooming on its petalled base in hazy glory; the sun falls on it down the softened air, and seems to kiss it into warmth and life. The columns all around reach up, as if they had grown of themselves in bars of pure gold, to fence the treasure in from floor to ceiling; and the roof itself, with all its sombre splendour, seems a shadowy reflection of the jewelled casket below. It contains——. But who cares what it contains? The perfume of the rainbow and the elixir of life most like! No, only a little image of the Shogun Hidetada* and his mortuary tablet; and the Shogun himself lies deep in the ground below our feet, rolled in vermilion and charcoal to preserve his bones. Gladly must his spirit hover over the place where his memory is enshrined in all that beauty!

There are other chapels and other shrines in Shiba's magic courts—shrines of surpassing richness and loveliness; and if we ever go there together, you shall visit them first: we will linger in the great hall of the books, where the sacred scrolls lie swathed in silk, each in its lacquered box on its lacquered stand; we will see paintings and carv-

*Tokugawa Hidetada (1578–1631), the second Tokugawa shogun.

ings, angels and demons, peonies and lotus flowers in a hundred lovely tints; and then, when you are inured to hardihood through this orgy of colour and decoration, we will visit the tomb of the Second Shogun. We will see it undazzled, sober still, if possible, but shall want no more sights afterwards. *Sufficit!*

Tokyo, May, 1981

The Empress's own cherry blossoms were in all their glory in April, when she invited us to come to her Palace garden by the sea to look at them. Something interfered with the festival last year, so this was my first visit to the Hama Rikyu,* or Enryō Kwan. Everywhere the cherry blossoms have been perfect this year; our own garden is a dream of loveliness. There has been just enough rain to bring on the flowers without drowning them, and at one moment the whole place was like the rose-coloured wedding that we once had in the family. Do you remember the transformation of that December day? Winter seemed a thousand years away, when we went down to see the Empress's cherry blossoms. The Hama Rikyu consists more of gardens than palace; for the house, though pretty, is small, and is chiefly used for the accommodation of illustrious visitors. It was there that our two young Princes were received when they visited Tokyo. The Empress stays there for a few weeks in the late spring, to enjoy the freshness of the sea breezes, which blow in at the wide windows. The sea rolls up to the foot of the walls on one side; and the garden is built out into the water, like Miramar, near Trieste. The flowery alleys wind about amongst lakes and canals, where real waves come beating boldly against the toy bridges. There are islands with quaint pavilions perched on their green summits, and arbours,

---

*Hama Rikyū, or Hama Detached Palace, is now a public garden surrounded by warehouses. No palace remains, but the area where ducks used to thrive has been preserved. It was still used in the 1890s for imperial duck netting parties. The lake with its many different bridges is still very attractive.

and boats, and all the furniture of a fairy tale; and everywhere, above the floating strains of the gay bands, above the murmur of talk and singing of the wind in the trees, comes the august chant of the sea— the chant that began when all this rich country was a reed-grown marsh, when the wild foxes were the only courtiers, and Emperors and Empresses of Japan were called Prince Fire-Shine and Princess Fire-Subside, and the Flood-Tide Jewel and the Ebb-Tide Jewel, in the play-grounds of mythology. The sea is with us still, and has never turned courtier. As we walked through the gardens in the usual official procession behind the sovereigns, we looked, with all the uniforms and finery, like some huge dazzling snake, gliding in and out of all the narrow paths, hanging on red bridges, losing its lengths in green dells; and the breeze rioting in from the bay rained down cherry blossoms on our heads.

Suddenly we came out on a wide terrace close to the sea; the salt water was lapping against the stones at our feet; the sea-gulls flew inland with wild cries, the afternoon sun turning their wings to dull gold; the gardens stretched back towards the town, their mountains of rosy bloom seeming to break like spray against the black-green pines on the steeps of Count Ito's garden. And just then, in the tearing breeze, a native boat, with its great white sail set square to the wind, seemed to be rushing down on us for a moment—came so near that for one breathless space we heard the water cutting cold against the prow; the brine from the new-made wavelets came salt on the air, and a rim of spray hung between us and the sun; then the boat turned and tacked, and fled up the bay, carrying some stray pink petals lodged in the hollow of the sail. It was just a piece of bare delicious nature, let down before our eyes as a contrast to all the artificialities of the Court. Perhaps even that is less artificial here than it would be over the water. Our dainty Empress, who has the soul of a poet, had ordered from her own looms a robe of pale apple-green brocade, with bunches of rosy cherry blossom scattered over it. The effect was quite lovely. A soft green velvet mantle, and a bonnet of white lace and jewels, made one forget that the gown had to be made in European fashion; and the Empress herself seemed very happy that day, as if she were frankly enjoying the flowers and the sunshine, and even the bonbons, cherry blossoms and brown twigs and fairy grasses, all done in sugar by that famous Court confectioner! She kept me with her longer than usual, asking many kind questions about some theatricals which we had had for a charitable object, an infirmary which was much wanted, and for which she had kindly sent me a generous cheque.

It was the first time that I came away with regret from one of these stiff parties; the whole thing was so wonderfully pretty and fresh. But I suppose we shall soon see the gardens of the Enryō Kwan again, since the Cesarévitch, who is expected for a visit to Japan, will be lodged there.

Very great preparations are being made for this royal visit. The apartments in the Palace by the sea have all been furnished and decorated anew; there are to be triumphal arches and illuminations and Court balls; and the Emperor intends to lavish honours—and fun—on his guest. The S——s at the Russian Legation have transformed their somewhat dingy house into a bower of flowery beauty; I have just been going over it, and rather envied the Grand Duke the two thousand pots of lilies in bloom which are to line the great staircase. They must have spent an enormous amount of money, for they have had to build an immense ball-room out into the garden; and as there was no time for painting and papering, the whole place has been lined with Japanese crapes in brilliant colours, palms, and ferns, and creeping plants. I could not help condoling a little with Madame S—— on the endless bother of the whole thing. "How can you say such a word!" she cried, with flashing eyes, "*Bother!* It is a joy to do anything for our sovereign's son. I wish we could have done fifty times more!"

And now, since it is May, and since the Cesarévitch cannot be here for a few days yet, let me tell you of the strange symbolic rejoicing called the Boys' Festival, which is peopling the town with flying-fish, rising and falling from their gilt poles on every breeze—fish of every size and colour, but all of one shape, the shape of the *koi,* the undaunted, unconquerable carp.

When the fifth day of the fifth month has come, the streets of Tokyo and of every city in the empire are alive with these quaint banners fluttering in the wind. A stranger might congratulate himself on having arrived at a moment of public rejoicing; and I shall never forget the amazement with which I regarded the flying-fish and their golden rice-balls, when I first arrived here, in May, two years ago. Now they are a part of the spring; and it seems as if its best days were past, when they no longer hover over the low brown roofs.

For all its festal aspect, no crowds or knots of holiday-makers are to be seen in the streets of the city; no drums are beating the time of a religious festival: everything is quiet. The shops are open; customers are coming and going; brown little children with bare legs play with bean-bags in the roads; the young girl walks slowly along in her clattering *gheta* (clogs) and silken *kimono,* followed by her attendant maid, who carries her books from school; the business man in native costume and "bowler" hat wheels by in his jinriksha to his day's work. Busy life seems going on everywhere, undisturbed, beneath the rustling wave of bright colour which floats over the town. Bright, indeed! The banners which fly from almost every house are all in the shape of gigantic fishes, painted blue or red or grey, with silver scales, made of paper or cotton cloth, and hollow so that they swell and rise, shrink and fall, as the wind takes or leaves them. Very realistic, indeed, are their gaping mouths, huge eyes, and fins, and the sheen of their scales glinting in the sunlight. They are of various sizes, though always large, and all made after one pattern—that of the *koi,* or carp.

The *koi* is the emblem of a male child and of luck; and this is the Boys' Festival, O *Sekku* or *Tango,* as the Japanese call it.

Fish in Japan takes the place of beef in England, and next to rice is the staple product of the country. On the birth of a son, the support of the house, the relations and friends send or bring with their congratulations live *koi* swimming about in tubs of water; and at this feast parents are entitled to display a paper fish for each son, the younger the child the larger the fish, and *vice versa.* This toy fish is attached to a long bamboo pole, which is hoisted in front of the house, often with other ornamental flags and signs, such as a wind-wheel or a gilded wicker basket, which may stand for the puffy ball of rice paste with which the real fish are fed. Several fish may often be seen flapping round one pole; and proud is that house, for it means that the master is blest with many sons.

But the carp does not stand (or swim) only for luck and good cheer. That wonderful feat, only accomplished after persevering efforts, of swimming up the rapids (*taki nobori*), is, as I think I said before, the symbol of the brave youth who overcomes the difficulties and obstacles of life. I do not think European carp ever attempt the enterprise, and it was only when I came to Japan that I learnt that it is possible. Here it has passed into a proverb, and is a favourite subject with the native artists, the valiant carp being now synonymous with the abstract virtues of perseverance and fortitude. The legend says that when he has scaled the waterfall a white cloud from heaven sweeps down and catches up the triumphant fish, who then becomes a dragon. The brave *koi,* undaunted by the most fearful difficulties, is pointed out to the boy to impress upon him that the prizes of life are not for the sluggard or the coward, and its presence in lifelike similitude at his birthday feast is meant to act as an incentive to manly action and unflagging courage.

His birthday feast it is, at whatever time of the year he may have been born. Except for the purpose of casting a horoscope, the real day of his birth will be seldom remembered; and just as every girl's festival is March 3rd, so every boy's festival proper is May 5th, although the whole month is more or less his, and the fish float triumphantly from their enormous flagstaffs until the heats of June. It is on May 5th that the little feast is kept inside the house—every house, rich or poor, that Heaven has honoured with a son. And in all we should see the same symbols, the same flowers; for sons belong to the poor as well as to the rich, and are counted as the props of the home.

First of all, in the matted dwelling, one notices that in the floral arrangements, which are a distinct part of every ceremonial, a marked preference is shown for the long graceful leaves and spirited flowers of the iris. On the raised daïs, the place of honour, in the chief room, one will see a fine lacquer table supporting a vase, or more often a flat dish, of these lovely flowers, every leaf and blossom shooting up at exactly the right angle of strength and grace—the result of an hour's work or more, but looking so exquisitely natural that it seems incredible they should not have grown so by themselves, up from the limpid water where a tiny wedge of bamboo is really holding them all irrevocably in place. In another room is a wicker basket, or bamboo hanging vase, pierced in two or three places; and from this the swordlike leaves emerge with a will of their own, and the delicate flower-de-luce hangs its petals over them like white and purple flags well-wishing them through the fight.

At this time of year the table at a Japanese dinner party is a study of what can be done with these most characteristic flowers. I was at one a little while ago where all the decoration consisted of green bamboo, of the most perfect and polished surface, cut into sections of different lengths, and set upright in perfect gradation in three groups, spaced down the long table. In these natural organ pipes were arranged thin screens of iris flowers, ranging from deep purple to pale mauve, with their pointed leaves shooting up like swords among them. Every grace of stem, every vigorous breaking of flower from sheath, of leaf from leaf, was displayed with unerring knowledge and decision; and the result—forgive repetition—was the most perfect picture of strength and grace that it is possible to see.

But to return to our little Japanese boy and his festival. To-day Yasu, or Saburo, or Takenori would in old times have expected to find the entrance of his house all decked with iris leaves in the morning; and he and his friends would have plaited little toy swords, and have done some sharp mock fighting, just to mark the day. For fighting was what the young *samurai* had to learn; and a friend tells me that, in order to harden young boys and make them absolutely indifferent to suffering, he and his young townsmen were obliged to rise from their warm beds between three and four on a winter's morning, and go in a single robe, bare of head, and bare of foot, to the fencing-ground, where many a hard blow was dealt, and the young blood, warmed by the fight, threw off the rigour of the icy cold, and knew that it had won one victory more over sloth and weakness. He was quite accustomed to this terrific *régime* when he was eight years old!

So while our Japanese boys are playing, like others, at war, they know more of its hardships than one would think who only saw them with green swords in the mild May morning. The bath has preceded the play, and in the bath the irises too have their service. It is still credited with strength-giving powers, probably on account of its remarkable vitality and the varied character of its growth through the changing seasons. Great bunches of the leaves are thrown into the ocean of hot water called a bath in Japan. Thus used, the plant was supposed to inspire the spirit of patriotism and valour. Tradition held that the dew was an indispensable agent in developing this property in the herb, which was therefore employed the day before the festival in decorating the house-roof, being exposed there all night, to be taken down in the morning for the bath, in which the eldest son was the first to bathe.

But in the best room of the house, the honoured "guest apartment" as it is called, there are many things besides flowers set out—warlike figures, and toy weapons, such as would appeal to any boy's heart, in East or West. But here the figures are not toys—they are portraits; and each one tells its tale of glory in the ears of the Japanese child. These models of men, clad in armour, standing in attitudes of action or menace; the horses, richly and minutely caparisoned, pawing the ground as if impatient for battle,—they are the images of the warriors and heroes of this strange land, accompanied by their chargers, whose names have also been handed down for veneration. That warrior to the left of the bronze bowl is Iyeyasu, the maker of Yedo, the general whose tomb we have seen among the solemn pines of Nikko, the man whom the Japanese consider the greatest ruler the country has ever obeyed. Beside him is that famous charger, who outlived him for thirty years, wandering free among the sacred groves. His tomb also we have seen. Yonder is the figure of the mythical Raiko, the Japanese giant-killer, who delivered Kyoto from a fearful cannibal demon; and shoulder to shoulder with him is the effigy of another hero, Momotaro, the peach-born boy, who accomplished prodigies of strength, and freed his country from a stronghold of devils.

Standing up among the bows and arrows, the swords and spears, may be seen the model of a very strange-looking battle standard, or *umajirushi*. The head of this banner is composed of a number of small gourds, golden in colour, clustered round a larger one, and all placed on a rod. Underneath the gourds, a little way down, strips of bright scarlet cloth are suspended round the stick. No one looking at the pretty toy could imagine its romantic origin or the wonderful part it has played in the history of Japan. The gourds and scarlet cloth represent the *umajirushi* of Toyotomi Hideyoshi,* the greatest adventurer, and perhaps the greatest general, in Japanese history.

*Toyotomi Hideyoshi (1536–98), soldier and ruler of Japan, took control of the country after Oda Nobunaga and was succeeded by Tokugawa Ieyasu.

By telling these stories to their children, the Japanese believe that they sow the seeds of reverence and admiration for the best and noblest examples of their ancestors, the seeds of self-reliance, and belief in the invincible power of their country; and though to us, perhaps, the courage seems exaggerated and the ideals unattainable, yet I think it bears no mean fruit in the Japan of to-day. Loyalty and courage are the undoubted inheritance of the nation.

And so for the little boys of Japan the brightly coloured banner and the gay toy warriors have a real and moral significance. The children's hearts are stimulated, unconsciously at the time no doubt, and their ambition roused to become worthy compatriots of the brave men gone before them. I think the hour will come again, as it has in time past, when these things will be of use to them, whether in the war with evil for good in their own hearts, or on the battlefield face to face with the foe.

Tokyo, June, 1891

The most terrible blow fell on this unfortunate country on May 11th; and now, weeks afterwards, it is still impossible to think or speak of anything else. The Cesarévitch, whose coming was so eagerly anticipated, for whose entertainment every resource of the empire was to be called upon, whom the Emperor intended to honour as no foreign Prince has even been honoured before—the Cesarévitch was attacked, deeply wounded, all but killed, by one of the policemen set to guard his way.

No words of mine can describe the consternation and dismay which took possession of this place, when on the afternoon of the 11th those horrible telegrams came pouring in, to the Russian Legation, to the Ministries, to the Palace. It was a lovely afternoon, and I was returning from a drive, when I met, not far from home, my friend Mrs. K——. She stopped her carriage, and got into mine, telling the coachman to drive to the Russian Legation, and on the way she told me what she had just learnt from one of the officials.

The Cesarévitch had been attacked; no one knew yet whether the wound was mortal. We were met at the entrance to the Russian Legation by scared-looking servants, who led us up the big staircase where all the beautiful floral decorations had just been completed in expectation of the Prince's visit to-morrow. The fear of death seemed to be on every one, and the very gloom of it to hang over the great flower-filled house. What made it more terrible for Madame S—— and her daughter was that they were alone there, the Minister himself being in attendance on the Cesarévitch. As yet no one knew whether a riot had taken place, whether Monsieur S—— were also hurt or not; but to tell the truth, I do not believe the two poor loyal women could have then suffered more anguish of soul if he had even been killed. I learnt for the first time what loyalty meant; with what a passion of devotion the blood of some races leaps to the call, mad to be spilt for the sovereign and his family. My poor friends were utterly prostrated by the blow, which had fallen some two hours before, while I was far out in the country. They had wept till they could weep no more, and Vera S——, a most charming and brilliant girl, was raging up and down the room, wild to slay the doer of the deed, who, I think, would indeed have had a short shrift if her little fingers had once met on his throat. "Our Prince, our Prince!" she sobbed; and there were no other words but those. "Our Prince, our Prince! God have mercy on our Prince!" I am certain that at that moment both mother and daughter would have gone to death joyfully and unhesitatingly, if by so doing they could have assured the Cesarévitch's life. The Russian Bishop was there, doing what he could to comfort them; and telegram after telegram was brought and read to us by the Secretary, who himself looked as if he had heard his death-warrant. "Two deep wounds on the head; recovery impossible," the first message had run; then, "Prince better; most courageous," "Returning to Kyoto at once," "Great loss of blood—I am safe" (this had been added at last by Monsieur S—— to reassure his family a little); I do not think he himself cared two pins whether he was safe or not, and he very nearly killed himself by running for three-quarters of an hour to the Otsu Station holding one side of the Prince's jinriksha, while General Bariatinsky, his Governor, ran on the other to defend him from any further possible attack.

How it all happened is a strange tale. The Cesarévitch came over from China on April 27th, attended by a squadron of Russian warships, to begin a tour through Japan which was to occupy a month, and during which he was to be shown everything which could possibly interest or amuse him. The visit had been under discussion for many months, and was intended to cement the bonds of friendship already existing between the two countries. We had heard of the many negotiations on the subject, and the coming of the Cesarévitch was to be the event of the year in Tokyo. When all the arrangements were completed, Monsieur S—— still felt uneasy about the safety of the heir-apparent. The Czar was allowing him to come on the Minister's representation that no danger whatever could possibly assail him on Japanese soil; but the Minister himself (I remember his telling me of it) was not absolutely satisfied with the arrangements made, and finally told the Emperor of Japan that he did not consider the guarantees sufficient. Then the Emperor made an answer at which some of his own people were almost indignant. "I take," said his Majesty, "the personal responsibility of the Cesarévitch's visit. His person shall be sacred as my own; I answer for his safety with my own honour."

After that there could be no more hesitation, and the Cesarévitch came, accompanied by his cousin Prince George of Greece, and by a numerous train, including a number of Russian officers. Prince Arisugawa was deputed to meet him, and the people were honestly and truly glad to see him. The Emperor's guest was received with the most hearty enthusiasm, when he landed in Nagasaki from the *Pamiat Azova,* the war-ship devoted to his especial service. The road from the quay to the Governor's house where the Cesarévitch lunched was lined with crowds for the mile and a half of its length— crowds who received their Emperor's guest with every mark of welcome. From Nagasaki he went to Kagoshima, where he and Prince George and the whole party were the guests of Prince Shimadzu for several days. There some splendid shows were organised, all the sports of the old feudal court were revived in a kind of tournament, and the Russian Minister told me afterwards that the display of antique armour and weapons had been quite wonderful. Presents of great value were offered to the Prince and his companions, and he is said to have much enjoyed all the novelty of the entertainments provided. From Kagoshima he came up to Kobe, where he landed and took train for Kyoto. He was attended by several great Japanese officials, among others dear Mr. Sannomiya, whom we always call the guardian angel of the foreigners here. While the Cesarévitch was visiting Kyoto, Mr. Sannomiya came up to Tokyo to see that everything was in readiness for his reception here by the Emperor; and it was during his absence that the blow fell. I shall never forget his face, when he came down to the Russian Legation that evening, just before the special train started carrying most of the Princes and all the Ministers down to the scene of the disaster.

Of course, we sat there speculating wildly on the motive of the horrid crime, and longing to hear more of the details, for it was as yet impossible to gather from the excited telegrams anything but the merest outline of the facts. But more accurate news came on later in the evening, and by midnight we knew pretty well all that there was to be known, and could also estimate the gravity of the misfortune. The poor young Prince suffered a great shock, with after-pain, fever, and weakness. But Japan seemed to have been suddenly arrested in her march to the vanguard of nations, to have been thrown back fifty years in her history of civilisation, to have fallen into a great abyss of bitter and humiliating trouble.

And yet it was such a simple story! Had it happened in Europe, it would have been looked upon as a great misfortune, but no more. No deductions would have been drawn from it; no enemies could have brandished its record in the stricken face of the nation to show that no civilised peoples should have friendship with her, that treaties were an absurdity, equality a dream. All that happened to poor Japan, smarting under the wound, to her the most bitter of all—a wound to her honour. The Emperor's welcome guest had been betrayed.

He had gone from Kyoto to see Lake Biwa, the Lake of the Lute, whose waters are called the melted snows of Fuji. The party had lunched with the Prefect of the District at a little place named Otsu, the usual centre for some lovely excursions in the neighbourhood of the lake. As the roads do not allow of using carriages in that part of the world, the Prince and his following were in jinrikshas, each drawn by two coolies. The Cesarévitch was in the fifth of these little vehicles, those in front being occupied by the Governor of the Province, the Chief of Police, and two inspectors. Behind the Cesarévitch came another Japanese official, then Prince George, then one or two other members of the party, and finally Monsieur S——, the Russian Minister. The streets were lined with police on both sides, the men being set at short intervals from each other, all picked men who could be relied on to do their duty. But no one dreamed that their services would be really needed. It is the boast of new Japan that the foreigner can travel from end to end of the Empire without ever receiving the slightest molestation; and this foreigner was the beloved Emperor's guest!

Among the policemen stood one called Tsuda Sanzo, an old sergeant-major in the army, where he had earned a decoration for services rendered in the Satsuma rebellion. A self-centred and somewhat bigoted man, he was yet one of the quiet, steady, tried servants who would be chosen for such a post as this. As the Cesarévitch passed him, he drew his great Japanese blade, and aimed a deadly blow at the Prince's head. The jinriksha was going at a fair pace, and the sword slid, caught the hat, and inflicted a second blow. Then it fell as Tsuda himself fell; for one of the coolies, dropping the shafts, hurled himself unarmed on the policeman, and the second coolie snatched the sword and dealt the assassin two serious blows with it while he was still wrestling with the first man. The Prince himself, blinded with the flow of blood, leapt from the jinriksha as the shafts dropped, and ran forward towards the ones occupied by the Governor and the other Japanese officials. In an instant the Governor was supporting him, and led him aside into an open shop, while the whole train was thrown into the wildest confusion. Guards threw themselves on Tsuda and secured him, and Prince George, in intense anger and excitement, came and struck him violently with his stick. Monsieur S—— jumped from his jinriksha, and flew past the rest to where the Prince was standing in the little shop. He was bathed in blood, but refused to sit down; and when Monsieur S—— in his wild anxiety threw himself at his feet with a cry, the Prince raised him quietly, and said, "Do not be anxious. *Ce n'est que du sang.* I am not really hurt!"

He was very much hurt, poor young fellow; but not dangerously so, as in the terror of the moment somebody wired that he was.

They bound up the long cuts on his head, thanking Heaven that the hard hat and the thick hair had helped to turn the blow; and then they got him back to Otsu, Monsieur S—— running by the jinriksha, and holding it on one side, while General Bariatinsky did the same on the other. A special train brought him back to Kyoto, where, in spite of his calm cheerful manner, he was only too glad to lie down at last and have his wounds properly dressed.

And Tsuda? Of course after the event there were plenty of people who were sure that the man was insane, that he should never have been chosen for the service which brought him into such close contact with the heir of the Czar. It transpired that there had been insanity in his family, that one or two of his intimates had heard him speak with fear of the aggressions of Russia, just as a certain small class here write and speak. Their minority makes them insignificant; and nobody has done more than laugh when these wiseacres pretended to see the visit of a spy in the coming of the Cesarévitch; when, in obscure newspapers, they reminded the people of the Russian principles of aggression, as shown by Russia's taking Saghalien, which was, after all, deliberately exchanged for the Kurile Islands. Japan is rich in fanatics. One of the men who held these doctrines committed suicide before the landing of the Prince, in order, as he said, to be spared the sight of his country's humiliation. A legend exists to the effect that the late General Saigo, the chief leader of the Satsuma rebellion, was not really killed, but had succeeded in escaping to Russia, where he is supposed to have remained all these years, awaiting a favourable moment in order to return to Japan and once more raise the standard of revolt. A story got abroad that the Cesarévitch was bringing him back in his suite, and the absurd rumour caused a good deal of excitement in some districts. Such ideas had probably preyed on Tsuda's mind, apt to be unhinged because of that strain of madness in his family, which was quite unknown to the authorities; and when he was named as one of the guardians of the road for the Russian Prince, the insane resolve to make away with him probably formed itself in his brain. The instant onslaught of the two jinriksha coolies prevented him from taking his own life, which would undoubtedly have been his next act.

But he has brought profound sorrow on the whole empire. So

much was expected and hoped from this visit, in the way of friendship with the great European Powers. It was to have been in a way Japan's first step in the Social Polity of the world; and one cannot but feel the most profound sympathy with her in her distress.

Two hours after the first news of the attempt reached Tokyo, a Cabinet Council had been held, and a special train was starting for Kyoto, carrying Prince Kitashirakawa with the Emperor's own surgeon, Dr. Hashimoto, and various officials to the spot. An hour or two afterwards another train went down with some of the Ministers, more of the Court people, and all the distinguished medical men of the capital; and early the next morning, amid an outburst of public grief and indignation, the Emperor himself, with all his staff, started for Kyoto. But before he left, an Imperial Rescript appeared, which told the nation of what had occurred, and of the intense pain caused in the Emperor's breast by the horrible deed. Here is the Rescript:

"It is with the most profound grief and regret that, while We, with Our Government and Our subjects, have been preparing to welcome his Imperial Highness, Our beloved and respected Crown Prince of Russia, with all the honours and hospitalities due to Our national guest, We receive the most unexpected and surprising announcement that his Imperial Highness met with a deplorable accident at Otsu whilst on his journey. It is Our will that justice shall take its speedy course on the miscreant offender, to the end that Our mind may be relieved, and that Our friendly and intimate relations with Our good neighbour may be secured against disturbance."

The Ministers paid a visit to the Russian Legation before they left for Kyoto—a visit in which it was intended at any rate to convey the expression of the profound regret of the Government to the wife of the Russian Representative. It was a most distressing ordeal for everybody, the official finding absolutely no words sufficient to convey their dismay and sorrow; while Madame S——, who is always a delightfully impetuous and impulsive person, and who was just then in a frenzy of loyal indignation, seems to have found no difficulty at all in expressing her feelings.

Meanwhile there was one person who could do nothing to help the poor young Prince or to punish his assailant; the valiant gentle Empress forgot all the repressions of her up-bringing, all the superb calm which as a part of her rank she had shown in every circumstance of her life, and for the whole of that wretched night walked up and down, up and down, weeping her heart out in a flood-tide of grief. Those who told me of it said that all night long and for days after the Empress had but one cry; not a cry of despair for her country, humiliated in the eyes of the whole world, condemned perhaps to find bitter enemies where she had looked for friends—all that seems not to have touched her at all at first; her only thought was for the boy—and his mother. "The poor mother, the poor mother!" she wailed. "She cannot see her boy! She will not believe he is safe! Poor mother! how can I comfort you?"

That was all. And she who is supposed never to change expression or show the smallest weakness before others walked up and down her lovely rooms like a caged creature, with the tears raining down her face. Her ladies were terrified and overcome; they thought she could not live through such a storm of grief. Message after message was sent to the Czarina, assuring her of the profound heart-broken sympathy with which the Empress regarded her trouble, and promising that the Cesarévitch should be nursed and tended as if his mother were with him. As soon as she recovered from the shock sufficiently to travel, she went to see the wounded boy, who was deeply touched by her sorrow and her kindness.

He behaved all through like a Prince and a gentleman. Not the slightest sign of rancour ever appeared in his voice or manner; and when, at his parents' command (it is said, at his mother's entreaty), he gave up the rest of his Japanese tour, and was carried back on board his own ship to be nursed, he softened the act by every kind word that could possibly have been used, thanking the Emperor warmly for all his kindness, and saying how great a deprivation it was to him not to visit the Emperor in Tokyo; because "for reasons of health, as he was still somewhat weak, it was considered wiser that he should return to Russia at once."

Mr. Sannomiya told me that the meeting between the Emperor and his guest was affecting in the extreme. As for poor Princess Komatsu, who went to visit him, she utterly broke down when she saw the poor boy, deathly pale from loss of blood, his head enveloped in bandages, and yet smiling at her kindly as she entered the room. The lady-in-waiting thought the Princess would faint;

but she pulled herself together, and only cried quietly. Indeed, though perhaps it sounds heartless to say so, I should think the Cesarévitch (who has had a good deal of fever) would have got over his accident more quickly with fewer visits and less excitement. However, sympathy is a great thing; and this atrocious attempt has called forth such overwhelming expressions of national sorrow and sympathy, that the Prince can never forget it as long as he lives. And as for the Emperor, I doubt if even he knew what his people felt for him until it was announced that the Emperor mourned—was in sorrow for his subject's sin—and the whole of the population in all its millions left its work and its pleasures, deserted the farm, closed the shop, turned from all its recreations and amusements—to sorrow with him.

I have never seen anything like it,—and you see I am learning lessons in loyalty! The theatres were closed, the shops and markets abandoned; everywhere people spoke in groups and with profound sadness in their tones. The little daughter of Viscount Aoki, the Minister for Foreign Affairs (she is ten years old), heard the announcement of the outrage with a stony face, and went away in silence to her room. There, for hours, she lay on the floor in an agony of grief and shame, moaning, "*I* am a Japanese! *I* must live with this shame! I cannot—I cannot! I cannot bear it!" At the Nobles' Club there was one opinion only—how could those at the head of affairs, those who were responsible for the Prince's safety in his journey, support life any longer? Why had they not already wiped out their dishonour with death? There was only one thing for a gentleman to do in such circumstances—commit *hara-kiri* or some other decorous kind of suicide!

Among the people the sorrow took two forms: one, the intense desire to make reparation to the illustrious guest and his family for the insult and outrage which he had suffered; the other going deeper still, the yearning—no other word quite expresses it—to lift some of the load of sorrow from the Emperor's heart, to do something by which the "august" would cease to mourn. "Tenshi Sama Go Shimpai" was the word in every mouth—"Great Augustness, worshipped Sorrow"; and rich and poor, old and young, strong men and little children, all did what they could, gave more than they could, to undo the wrong.

People who were on board the Cesarévitch's ship told me that it seemed like to sink with gifts; the decks, the saloons, the passages, were encumbered, and still they came and came and came! The universality and spontaneousness of the manifestation gave it an overwhelming value, which the Prince here and his parents at home were quick to appreciate. Rich people gave out of their riches, and objects of unexampled beauty and rarity were brought out from the treasure-houses and sent with messages of love and respect to the boy who lay healing of his wound in Kobe Harbour. The poor sent the most touching gifts—the rice and *shoyu,* the fish and barley-flour, which would have fed the little family for a year; poor old peasants walked for days so as to bring a tiny offering of eggs. The merchants sent silks and porcelain, lacquer and bronze, crapes and ivory, according to their merchandise; telegrams poured in, expressing intense sympathy, and more intense indignation at the outrage. In the first twenty-four hours after the occurrence, so many thousands of these were sent that it was almost impossible to deliver them; twenty thousand persons called during the first two days at the hotel in Kyoto where the Prince lay before he was removed to his vessel; every corporation and community, town and village and guild sent either a deputation to carry its condolences or a letter to express them; and many who could ill afford the outlay telegraphed messages of sympathy to the Czar and Czarina in St. Petersburg, and always added a protest of horror at the wicked deed.

The perpetrator of it is not yet judged, and some care has been necessary to keep him from being torn to pieces by his indignant countrymen, who "are ready to eat him," as the saying is here. The newspapers vie with one another in condemning the criminal, who, after all, seems to have been a common madman, all the more dangerous from having earned the confidence of his superiors.

Rather an amusing story is told here.

The Emperor, it seems, sent word to the judges that the wretched Tsuda must be executed at once; the judges replied, "Your Imperial Majesty may remember that you have graciously granted a Constitution, in which it is promised that criminals shall only be judged and condemned according to the laws which have now been promulgated; in those laws such a case as this was not foreseen, and therefore we can only award to this man the punishment incurred by one who assaults and wounds any other person of any class whatever. We regret that we cannot carry out your Imperial Majesty's wishes. Tsuda Sanzo will undergo a term of imprisonment."

"Tsuda Sanzo will be executed," the indignant Emperor replied. "Let it be seen to at once."

"Then," said the courageous judges, "your Imperial Majesty will dispense with our poor services, and find some one to carry out your august commands who has not taken the oath to administer the laws according to the Constitution."

But the Emperor was too upright not to see that they were in the right, and it is said that he was pleased with their justice and courage. Tsuda is undergoing a term of imprisonment—I think ten years is the time mentioned; but I am sure that if he ever comes out alive, he will have to change his name.

The two coolies who undoubtedly saved the life of the Cesarévitch have been magnificently rewarded by the Russian Government. They are young, good-looking fellows, who, from being members of the poorest class of Japanese subjects, have suddenly become rich men, with decorations and reputations of which the Japanese think even more than of money. Their own Government awarded them each a medal, and a little pension of thirty-six dollars a year for the rest of their lives—a sum quite enough to keep them from want, living as they would with the ingenious frugality of their race. But the Russian Government has done things very magnificently. Each man has been awarded a thousand dollars a year for life; the Cesarévitch himself has presented each of them with a sum of two thousand five hundred dollars, and a Russian decoration has been added to the Japanese one. The two heroes, it is said, were completely stunned with this munificence. The sailors of the Prince's vessel made a tremendous feast for them on the day when they came on board to receive their reward; and I hear that they have gone back to their homes in a distant province to buy rich farms and live at ease, doubtless to marry the girls of their hearts, and to tell the tale of their courage and good luck to the third and fourth generation.

But the last note is a sad one. It is impossible not to be sorry for the Governor of the Province and the Chief of Police, who were held responsible for the outrage, and who really and truly had done all that it was possible to do to ensure the Prince's safety. They have both been dismissed, one degraded as well. In spite of all messages of forgiveness (and the Russians have been very generous), a most painful feeling remains, and painful memories must be carried for many years. The sovereigns and their people mourn together for the wicked madness of one man

A little *samurai* girl, a mere child of sixteen, I think, was in service near Yokohama. She travelled to Kyoto, dressed herself in her holiday robes, composed her poor little body for death by tying her sash tightly round her knees after the custom of *samurai* women, and cut her throat in the doorway of the great Government offices. They found on her two letters: one a farewell to her family; the other containing a message, which she begged those who found her to convey to the Emperor, saying that she gave her life gladly, hoping that though so lowly it might wipe out the insult, and she entreated him to be comforted by her death. Her name, they say, was Yuko, which means full of valour.

Tokyo, July, 1891

My third summer in Japan is well on its way. I shall not see a fourth—in succession, at any rate; for we go home on leave next year. Europe draws one back with a thousand cords; but even there I shall regret the little Palace of Peace among the Karuizawa pines. Before transporting the family to those heights, I have been taking a long holiday by the sea at Horiuchi,* a place about an hour's drive from Kamakura; Doctor Baelz has a Japanese cottage there, and kindly lent it to me for the time. Our station was Dzushi, and there I alighted one warm afternoon with one friend, one interpreter, and Rinzo, Matsu,

---

*Horiuchi, between Zushi and Hayama. Murray's *Handbook for Travellers in Japan* (1894) describes Horiuchi as "lately risen into favour as a sea-side resort, which commands a lovely view of Mount Fuji."

and our "Big Cook San," the gentleman who tumbled through the bridge last summer. The poor fellow has been suffering from bad lungs ever since the influenza epidemic, and I thought a change would do him good. I only mention him because when they all turned out of the train I was so amused by the mass of baggage he had brought. Evidently the rumour had gone abroad that Horiuchi was a place quite in the wilds, and that all our comfort there would depend on what we brought with us. Big Cook San descended to the platform, jingling like a gypsy tinker with all the saucepans that he had hung round himself at the last moment. An omelet-pan and a bain-marie, miraculously tied together, hung over his shoulder; a potato-steamer from his waist; in one hand he carried a large blue teapot, and in the other a sheaf of gorgeous irises, carefully tied up in matting, for fear that there should be no flowers at Horiuchi! A whole vanload of goods had preceded us, so these were after-thoughts, trifles gathered up at the last moment. We let the servants and baggage start before us from the station, and followed in a leis-urely fashion, stopping our jinrikshas every now and then to admire the lovely glimpses down green gorges, through which the road winds and turns again and again before it comes out on the beach near Horiuchi. This is a tiny village, built in the round of a bay with-in Odawara Bay. The hamlet is as poor as possible; but the air is so pure that people have been tempted to build a few villas there for *villeggiatura*. The Italian Minister has a gorgeous one on the ground that rises from the beach; but it does not compare with the doctor's cottage for beauty of situation. This is planted so that when one enters the front door one looks right through the house, and the most beautiful picture of Fuji across the bay is seen framed in by the pillars of the verandah; and when one comes, as in duty bound, to stand beside the pillars and salute the queen of mountains, the sea is almost rolling to one's feet, just stopped by a low stone wall and a green dune, planted with pines that sing night and day as the salt breeze rustles in from the sea.

There are but six rooms in the house, all floored with sweet-smelling mats the colour of wheat; the bathroom is of clean polished woods, and the great tank in the floor is always bubbling with oceans of hot water, where one washes all fatigue away in these warm days. As the house was meant merely for a bachelor's bungalow, it contains one jug and basin, which are kept on a shelf in the bath-room, where we went in and used them by turns. At our first lunch we discovered that, although the table was gorgeous with Cook San's irises, nobody had thought of knives and forks; two sets were found in a luncheon basket; and then a runner was despatched over the hills to borrow some from the hotel at Kamakura. But I did not mind at all. The irises were far better than knives and forks; and with the sight of the sea rolling in so close in crisp wavelets, the music that sea and pines made together, and above all, that vision of Fuji San and the Hakone Mountains across the blue spread of the bay, one felt ashamed of needing food at all. All the first day the beloved Fuji seemed to be gazing at us, making us feel small, but very happy. This morning a little good-natured gale has been tossing the trees about, and the sacred mountain has wrapped herself in clouds. I suppose I have said it again and again; but I feel impelled to say it once more,—in Japan one cannot think of Fuji as a thing, a mere object in the landscape; she becomes something personal, dominating, a factor in life. No day seems quite sad or aimless in which one has had a glimpse of her.

Last night her black shadow looked intensely solemn, with the stars above, and hundreds of torches in the fishing-boats floating on the sea beneath. I asked today why the sea was so full of stars last night,—I had never noticed it at other times, but only in these July days. And then I was told the story of the Festival of the Dead, which I had heard spoken of in Tokyo in a scornful, superficial way, but which I hear is kept religiously in the provinces still.*

I have been boating in the little Horiuchi Bay, and have gazed down for hours into the depths below through a glass-bottomed box let down over the side of the boat. It is a perfectly simple contrivance: the glass rests on or just under the water, and the wooden sides shut out all reflection; a series of small holes allow any water that splashes over the glass to run off,—one looks through it,—and suddenly one seems to be at the bottom of the sea. Great fish and little fish go darting in and out among the wet, sun-touched forests of the ocean bed; the rocks are shining palaces, guarded by fierce

*AUTHOR'S NOTE: See Lafcadio Hearn's beautiful and complete description of the Festival of the Dead in *Glimpses of Unfamiliar Japan*.

red starfish who crawl slowly backwards and forwards on their beat. The shells open and close, and swim about full of the strange soul-bodies which are their only life; there is colour, movement, expression, continents of clean silver sand, bordered by little reaches of golden woodland waving lazily on the water as our tree boughs wave in the wind; the fish have physiognomies, and meet, and fight, and bend, and dart away, all with their own little life to see to, their own extremely important affairs to conduct. And the sun laughs down through the moving liquid sheen, and makes many a pool of radiance in the quiet spots, and flings on the sand whole networks of living light that recall the flashing mail of the goldfish, or the pattern that wind and sunshine will ripple into the corn, or the gleam that the warmth of aeons has flushed into alabaster, where milk and honey made marble still let the light shine through. Ah! these are all the vintages of the wine and the warmth of life; whatever the shape they take, the source of their beauty is one,—and would I could know its name!

And all through a pane of glass and a bit of wood? Ah! well, a less thing than that may open a world to our eyes. The glass makes the surface calm, the wood shuts out the misleading reflections of other things. It would be good to apply it to life sometimes, I think.

All my peace took wings at the sight of a telegram calling me back to Tokyo long before I was ready to go. Very cross, indeed, I was to leave the cottage in the bay; and my temper was not improved when I found that the summons meant an unqualified series of official *corvées*. Some people who had a right to ask it wanted to be presented to the Emperor and Empress, who, alas! are in anything but a gay mood just now; but they were kind and good-natured, and so were the Princes; and my philosophy, which had suffered greatly at being recalled to Tokyo and audiences, was made quite serviceable again by finding one of the dearest of old friends waiting for me in town, whose coming I would not have missed for worlds. We talked of nothing but Rome and Villa Doria anemones and old friends for days, and took a deep draught of the wine of pleasant memories laid by in the Roman summers of our youth.

There was one bit of that week in Tokyo which will be added to the store of my memory picture gallery. A lunch was given for our distinguished visitors in that Palace by the sea where three months ago the Empress's cherry-blossom *fête* took place. It is called a Palace; but it consists mostly of a series of pavilions, lovely little Japanese buildings open to the view, and having hardly any decorations except the exquisite quality and colour of the woods used, and the perfect taste which makes them seem as much a part of the scenery as the fairy islands on which they stand or the blue water lapping round their steps. For in this dream garden (forgive me, if I told you of this before!) the real salt sea is everywhere, running its tides in and out of tiny lakes and winding canals, spanned by red bridges, delicate as if built with the slats of carved fans. The great sea fish come swimming in, and a number of fishermen had been brought with their boats that we might see the fishing with the circular net, which is an old Japanese amusement.

The boat is low and slender, and one man sits in the stern with a long single oar rather like the one used by the gondoliers in Venice. He pushes hither and thither till the spot seems promising for a throw. The fisherman his companion stands on the prow, which rises a good deal at the point. I do not know whether these were picked men, but I never saw straighter or goodlier lads than these fisherboys. Their firm brown limbs looked as hard as bronze; their bright eyes and set resolute faces showed the resource and courage that come of long training in a difficult art. The pose of the one who was waiting to throw the net was the most perfect expression of strength in rest, but ready for the hunter's spring. As they floated across the lake, whose water was ruffled by a coming storm, I longed for an artist to be at hand, and make the picture one that would keep for ever. Do you know that lurid light which comes before a storm, when all the sky goes black as ink, but from some sharp rift an angry shaft pours down and seems to be absorbed by the greens of the trees and grass, until they positively glow as if with some indwelling radiance of their own? So it was that day in the Hama Rikyu sea garden. The black of the sky, the gold greens of the foliage, the red of the bridges, and the storm light on the water made a harmony almost too vivid to be borne; and on that background floated the slim boat, twisting and turning like a watersnake, while the boy standing high on her prow gathered the black coils of his net under one bare arm, poised his body in a bold curve far over the point, and with a sudden movement flung the net with a rushing noise out on the water, where it lay, a perfect round, for a few minutes, before it began to sink in search of its prey. Then slowly and very gently it was drawn back by a length of rope to the hand that had thrown it; the thrower sprang down from his point of vantage, and sat in the boat, drawing in fold after fold of the fine black mesh, and taking from its snares great fighting fish whose scales gleamed unbearably bright as they turned and leapt in their furious struggle for life under the dun glare of the coming storm.

Then I looked up, and outside our green embankments a great square sail, blown out with the strong south wind, went hurrying up the bay before the storm, as sublimely indifferent to Empress's gardens as its white companions the sea-gulls, who flew backwards and forwards from the free sea outside to the captive lagoons within, shrieking news to each other about the storm.

Karuizawa, August, 1891

Our Palace of Peace seems even cooler and greener than last year, and has already some of the atmosphere of home about it. It is a very wet home to-day; this is supposed to be the last day of the rainy season, and our world of woods and hills is drinking in the gracious flood, and promising, to the ears that can hear, a rich harvest of wild flowers and woodsey shadiness and emerald turf to make up for these grey wet hours, which, by the way, we are all enjoying after our own fashion. The Chief is writing, as usual; it is now past five o'clock, and ever since nine or thereabouts this morning the sounds of dictionary work have reached me from the other side of the wooden house, where Mr. G—— and his writer Okamoto San discuss and disagree over the possible and impossible meaning of all the Chinese words in the language. The third volume of the precious dictionary must have grown as much as the grass and the trees during this long day of rain. The very dogs are subdued and quiet, lying recklessly where people are sure to walk over them, gazing out with the calmness of despair, knowing that no human being in his senses would take down hat and stick to give them a run across country to-day. One beautiful Gordon setter, eldest son of Floppy Flo (a British subject, who came to us off a kind of pirate sealer, where several murders had been committed, and whose captain, when sent to prison, made the most careful arrangements for his dog's welfare), began to weep pitifully the first time he woke up, in the cold dawn of the hills, far from his mother and his sister Sōdeska, who were left in town. The rain was blowing into his kennel; and I crept down in the grey of the morning to comfort him, and found the faithful D—— there before me. It seems he had been very cross with the noisy puppy till the nature of the trouble was made clear; and all day long he was reproaching himself and making excuses for poor baby Gordon, whom he treats exactly as if he was a two-legged baby instead of a four-footed one.

Another faithful person is once more with us, to my great joy, and that is Furihata, the good policeman. We have not been without news of this hero since we parted; for at the New Year H—— sent him a little present, which was acknowledged in English as follows:

"To Hon. Fraser

"Dear Sir,—Accept my best Thanks for Your very kind present as it New Year's compliment. That is valuable in itself; but I shall doubly esteem it as a gift from You.

"Yours very truly,
"F. Furihata.

"416, Nagano Streets, Nagano Ken."

On reading this, I felt sure that Furihata had made great progress in English; and as we must have an escort in these solitudes, asked before leaving town to have him awarded to us again. I was rather disappointed to be told that, much to the regret of the Foreign Office, my request could not be granted, as the man had left the service. On inquiring what had become of him, we learnt that he had got tired of wielding the strong arm of the law, and had taken a place as railway porter at Shin Karuizawa Station, about half an hour from here. Then I thought no more about the matter until the day I came here. Our journey was, as usual, extremely sensational.

Train, jinriksha, sedan-chair, and "shanks's mare"—as our old nurse used to call going on foot—were all tried by different members of the party, not to mention the jumping matchbox called a tram-car, which nothing would induce me to enter, although I consented to let it carry my precious luggage. There was so much of this that it filled the whole car, the only one to be had, leaving just room for one "boy," an inexperienced creature, who jumped in with the courage born of ignorance. He was left in town last year, and knew not the horrors of that winding, precipitous mountain road, about three feet deep in black mud. The servants who had tried it last year turned from it like one man, preferring a four-hours' walk up the steepest paths of the mountains to a repetition of their previous sufferings.

It was early in the afternoon when we finally started from Yoko-kawa to make the ascent. Only three jinrikshas could be found in the whole town; my own chair had been brought from Tokyo; and after great efforts a *kago,* or basket-litter, was got from another village with two coolies for my little *amah.* It was about as big as a good-sized workbox; but she packed herself into it with great ingenuity, and smiled, as she always does at everything, from presents to scoldings. Most of the dogs had gone on already with Mr. G——; so we had only Tip, the Brown Ambassador, and the elephantine Gordon, who had cried aloud all the way from Tokyo. Even the experienced Tip had been very unhappy in the train; and now they both trotted delightedly through the mud and wet grass for two or three miles, and then politely but firmly asked to be taken up. We had not yet parted company with the jinrikshas; so Gordon was solemnly installed with the Chief, and Tip got on the little foot-board of my chair, standing well over the edge, as dogs always will do, and sniffing excitedly at the wet mountain breeze, which doubtless brought him news of pheasants and rabbits. Once he lurched, flopped hopelessly over the edge, and hung in his leash for a second, till I pulled him up again, a sadder and a wiser dog.

As we mounted higher and higher among the lonely hills, a fine wet mist came down, wrapping us round like a veil, and making the figures at the head of the procession look huge and indistinct to those at the end. The mountain shrubs and all the nameless flowers gave out their bitter-sweet perfume; and many a wet branch shook its rain of cold drops on my neck, as I passed rustling through the leaves, borne high on the shoulders of the men. At last the point came where things on wheels must part from things on feet; the Chief took the *rikisha* road, and I and the *kago* and the walkers began to climb the other. The walkers included, of course, Rinzo, O'Matsu's husband, who considers himself entitled to go with me on all the expeditions; "Small Cook San," an absurd fat boy, very proud of his European clothes (his commander, "Big Cook San," who is about half his size, had gone on before); and, bringing up the rear, Kané, the artistic pantry-boy, who spends his time in worshipping my English house-keeper, Mrs. D——, for whose benefit he makes the most wonderful Japanese landscapes in washtubs or old boxes, with bridges and waterfalls, and little men and women, miniature lanterns and goldfish, and pine trees three inches high—perfect curiosities of imagination and dainty handiwork. His bit of a room is always a study of art-arrangement, his hanging pictures and ornaments all in exactly the right places. He is quite the tallest man in the servants' quarters, and had caused me nearly to choke with laughter that morning when he appeared at the station got up in a military suit of dazzling white, frogs and buttons complete, and crowned by an enormous pith helmet. The whole costume was so carefully copied from that of our Government official, Inspector Peacock, that I thought for a moment it was he as I saw him pass in the distance.

Kané looked quite as neat and dazzling, after his long tramp up the wet mountain paths; every time that I turned my head to see how my poor retainers were getting on, a succession of beaming smiles met my gaze, one behind the other, fading away into the enwrapping mist, like that of the immortal Cheshire cat. The top of the pass was nearly reached, and I, looking before me, had forgotten my companions, and had been enjoying the divine misty solitudes for two hours or more, when, a few yards higher up the steep path, a sudden frantic commotion of wagging tails became visible, followed by an outline in the grey haze that soon resolved itself into Mr. G——, surrounded by all the dogs. In two seconds more the columns were, as war correspondents say, involved in inextricable confusion. Three dachses, two setters, and the old pointer Bess were jumping over me and each other in the wildest transports of joy. When the dogs subsided a little, I had a chance to notice another spectre in the mist, an official spectre, standing at attention in a policeman's uniform. "Furihata?" "Not yet," said Mr. G——. "This is the inspector of the district; but you will find Furihata at the house. On hearing of your wish to see him again, a paternal Government ordered him to give up portering and return to the service of his country. Of course he obeyed, and you will have him all summer!"

And so it was. When I came within sight of the cottage, Furihata, gorgeous in white and gold, came towards me accompanied by his sergeant, and exclaimed, with a melodramatic gesture and a voice of triumph "My Furihata!" I said, of course, that I was very glad to see him, and to know that he was to be attached to us during the summer. He escorted us solemnly over the threshold of Peace Cottage, and then, on the steps, gathered himself up for a grand effort, and exclaimed with a gasp, "*My*—protection—British Legation—Karuizawa!" He was so pleased with this phrase that he came back twice that evening to say it again, and has, I hear, repeated it to several of our friends who have taken houses here for the summer; only for them the wily creature substitutes "foreigners" for British Legation.

I wrote you so many letters from Karuizawa last year, that I fear there are few new things left to tell you of now, except two expeditions which had not taken place then: one to the Iriyama Toge,* and one to Komoro, a Buddhist monastery in the hills. I will begin with Iriyama Toge, the Cathedral Rocks, as foreigners have named the place. You remember that our home here is on the northern edge of a plain made by a wide sweep between two parallel lines of mountains, all at such a height that, as a prosaic British friend of ours puts it, "one has left all that bamboo tropical rubbish behind." No bamboo grows here, no camellia trees or palms, only pine and oak and chestnut clothe the hillsides; but the *Lilium auratum* blooms in profusion, and our cottage is like a hothouse just now with the

---

*Iriyama Tōge, or Iriyama Pass, is described in Murray's *Handbook for Travellers in Japan* (1894) as "1 hour, by the base of the hills skirting the moor. . . . The summit commands probably the finest view obtainable of the valley leading towards Myōgi-san [Mount Myōgi], and, looking backwards, of the wide stretch of moorland at the base of Asama-yama [Mount Asama]."

masses of splendid flowers, lilies, white and scarlet and golden, blue-bells, hydrangea, and a most superb white blossom like gardenia growing on trees twenty feet high. These and many others the gardener brings in every day from the woods, and our few tame garden flowers look poor and weak beside them. As I was saying, we have our home among the foothills of Asama Yama, the never-sleeping volcano, which is the background of our view. From us the land drops for a little way, and then one finds oneself on the level flowery floor of the valley, about four miles wide, and extending some six or seven miles towards the south before it begins to drop in sheer terraces down to Nagano, Naoetsu, and the sea-coast. The Iriyama Toge is the fence of hills which rise softly on the southern boundary of our upland valley; softly on our side indeed, but between them and the distant plain below comes one of those amazing successions of crags and peaks, gorges and ravines, grey rock and green woodland and mossy slope, which look—as if some Titan had been sampling creation in the smallest possible space. If ever there were Titans, this country must have been one of their homes. Asama Yama is active enough now; but we have seen, thank Heaven! no such play as she used to indulge in—play which covered her southern slopes with boulders, some of them a hundred feet in diameter; which in 1783, during the most frightful eruption the world has ever seen, continued for six weeks to shake the empire of Japan to its very foundations, while, as the writers of the time tell us, "the mountain was on fire from the crown to the base," and never ceased to pour out lava, mud, rocks, and ashes (these fell two inches thick eighty miles away), while the roar and smoke seemed to go up to heaven itself. Over fifty villages were then destroyed; valleys were filled up to the brim with stones; our upland plain, which had been a rich rice-bearing district, was covered with something like four feet of solid scoria, while the streams which watered it were turned aside; the loss of life could not be counted; the lava stream ran thirty miles in sixteen hours down the northern slope, and lies there a black scar to this day. No wonder that the country is deserted, that the two or three hamlets are poor and miserable! Who would build good houses near such a devouring monster? who that could help it would come within reach of its devastating breath? I never realised until

301

we came here that it was our beautiful Asama Yama that had done all this mischief, or I doubt whether I should have had the courage to settle so close to its sides. They tell me that the height at which we have built, and the intervening foothills, would make us quite safe in case of a new eruption; but I am inclined to pray for peace in our time, all the same. As we go across the plain towards Iriyama Toge, the layers of scoria are clearly shown in the cuttings made here and there in a fruitless attempt to find an arable surface. For all time the lovely plain can be nothing but the mountain's outer court, as it were, Asama's garden, rich in wild flowers and in nothing else.

Through these we went, knee deep in "aster and in golden-rod," across the plain, to where our horizon-line rises in grassy slopes that look as if they had been shaped and smoothed by a gentle hand; but here and there a stern rock stands out, like an ascetic in the world, protesting against the ease and softness with which he sees himself surrounded. One of these rocks, high up near the crest of the hills, stands out huge and four square in natural granite, with a place for the preacher in the centre; and this the foreigners have called Pulpit Rock. But we pass round its base and over another crest; and then we are on the ridge of the Wami Toge, and can look down over the weird and beautiful valley of rocks, through which a deep-cut path winds off towards Takasaki and the distant plain. The surprise of this sight is perhaps its especial characteristic: at one moment you are strolling leisurely, after something of a climb, up a slope which seems to end in a grassy ridge a few yards farther on; you have left great rocks and hills behind, the turf is soft under your feet, and you say to yourself, "We will just rest a little on the knoll, and then we will be getting home; for there is no more to see now. This is like the Asama foothills."

And in a minute you stand on the green ridge, and a new and magic world—a world of bower and castle, keep and buttress, soaring minister and deep-cut fosse—lies spread beneath your astonished eyes. King Arthur's Court might come riding out in golden array from that grey portcullis; King Arthur's Queen might lean over that skyey parapet, waiting for one upward glance from her hero-traitor knight. What deeps are in that ravine, where some laidly worm might coil its dragon scales! What heights in those distant spires, melting in golden haze, where a wandering King might dream the hours away with Morgan Le Fay and her airy sisterhood! The turf creeps in green velvet folds to the castle's foot; the drawbridge lies for ever across the empty moat; the sunset floods with squandered gold the unpeopled bastions of the fort; only the wood-pigeons whirl round the eaves of the Queen's high bower; no step or cry is heard, save that of a poor man in blue coat and straw sandals who urges a heavily laden pack-horse up the dark road which winds, so deep-cut that we can hardly see it, round the castle's base. We are in the heart of the central mountains of Japan; the great castle is a nameless rock; King Arthur's fortress a bit of nature's forgotten play; and I, a dreamer, who sit here for hours, weaving the worlds together in my dreams, East with West, Past with Present, Legend with Truth, till my comrades gather round me, telling strange stories of hair-breadth climbs among the rocks, calling high and long for two who seem to have lost themselves in the labyrinths of this granite city. At last we see them far down, looking weirdly small, waving their hands to us from a point which they have scaled. They are two who often get lost in company; so we turn, smiling, and leave them to linger as they like, while we make our way home across the plain, clinging to the skirts of the daylight as they sweep all too swiftly from us. Sweet is the slow walk home across the evening fields; the grass is all in twilight at the root, but the last light lingers softly on the billowy surface, where pale-purple asters and white stars of Bethlehem float as on a cloud. Hundreds of sunset lilies are turning their pale-gold faces to the west, as a signal that day is done. In the hot hours they sleep, and as we passed at noon every cup was closed in the sunshine; but now that the twilight cools the air, they open wide, and stand in starry multitudes along the plain; behind them the misty mountains and the hushed empurpled sky; at their feet a tangle of low grasses steeped in dew; and "God's peace over all, my dear, God's peace over all."

Far away, where the plain turns sharply to the south, stands a little town called Komoro*—a town of eager industries and uninteresting surroundings, far less picturesque than our shabby village where every house is decaying, every screen is torn, where the chil-

*The former castle town of Komoro is on the railway line between Karuizawa and Nagano.

dren and the cats scatter into wretched-looking homes as we and the dogs pass by. Poor old Karuizawa was a grand place once, a stage on the long Nakasendo road, where every Daimyo must pass on his way from Kyoto to Yedo. Now only mountain pilgrims and crazy foreigners like ourselves ever go near it; the railway has turned two miles aside, and the place has become so poor that it has not even a public bath!* Since our coming this year our butcher, our rice-dealer, and our own laundry man have all set up their signs in the village, proclaiming that they are specially appointed to attend the British Legation. The place is a favourite one with the populous Canadian missionaries; and I hope their patronage, combined with our own and that of our friends, will bring a little prosperity back to the town. But Komoro is quite a different thing; it lies right on the line of railway, has good inns, and thrives on making saddles, tools, and carts for the whole province.

When we went to Komoro the other day, it was not to stay there, but to make an expedition to a strange Buddhist convent† far back in the hills that overhang a river, whose name, I am ashamed to say, I have forgotten to ask. The road, after leaving Komoro, goes for some way between rice-fields, over the very hottest country I have yet traversed in Japan. The fields are separated by little dykes just wide enough to walk on; and these are intersected again and again by temporary canals of the most minute kind, patted into being with the back of a spade so as to conduct the water from one level down to the next, and so on. For all rice-fields must be laid out in terraces, so that as soon as the water has thoroughly overflowed one field it may drop a foot or so to do its work in the next, and so on through field after field till every plant is fed. Between the fields the dykes are green now, and here and there a lonely blood-red lily waves like a signal in the air. The colour is an intense scarlet, and partakes in some way of the nature of flame, since it can be seen at distances where all other tints, including white, would pass unnoticed. I

*Karuizawa is now a thriving resort with numerous hotels, golf courses, and summer villas.

†This would seem to be the Nunobiki Kannon temple, still a beautiful spot to visit from Karuizawa.

had brought my chair, and was, as usual, far in advance of the rest of the party, who had chosen to walk—a great mistake on such a burning day. Soon my men turned from the dusty road between the evil-smelling rice-fields (alas! agriculture, to be successful here, must—excuse the word—stink), and took to a path which, after crossing a fairly full river, penetrated into a rocky range of hills on its northern side. How welcome was the shade and coolness of the groves! I think the men walked faster than they do on cooler days; and while my companions were still struggling up the sides of the slope, we were racing along the crest of the ridge, all our troubles over. It was just midday when the path dropped again, in the direction of the river's noise (the stream itself was invisible), and the dull-red gate of some sacred building showed at the end of a short alley thick-set with oak trees. A still farther descent, and we were inside a grey stone court, with very old buildings round three sides of it, while in front a terrace spread between two walls of rock which rose straight on either side. The place was set in a very cleft of the rock, like a sea-swallow's nest. No sun came here, although above and behind us high noon lay on the land. Before us the rocky walls ran a long way out, and between them, far away, bathed in noontide glory, the country beyond the river seemed to swim in the blazing heat.

I have at home a picture of the gentle lady Murasaki Shikibu, who eight hundred years ago retired to just such a spot as this to meditate on the romance which by command of the Empress she was to write. It was in August, by the light of the full moon, that she sat all night on the balcony of a temple between the rocks, far uplifted from earth, and gazing down on Lake Biwa as we here gaze on the distant river. If her temple was like this one, I do not wonder at the power of inspiration which, overflowing her mind, caused her to write the chief incidents of her story on the back of a roll of Buddhist Scriptures till all the space was covered. Next day, when the sacred frenzy was over, she discovered what she had done, and in time copied out the whole book anew to make reparation.

Here, in the rocky monastery of Komoro, all was still, and the light was not light, but clarified shadow, an even dusk, in which all objects were perfectly to be apprehended, but none smote the weary eye-balls more strongly than another. I cannot give you the sense of remoteness, of isolation, of tempered peace which the atmosphere inspired. Coming from the sun-stricken world outside, it was like turning from some wild passion of love that scorches and kills, to the impersonal tenderness of a motherheart, to pre-natal dawns ere individual suffering had stamped the soul with the individual immortality which it must carry, for better, for worse, through eternity. Peace was in the brown earth where the dust fell softly from one's feet as if knowing how tried they were; peace in the hermit trees which had chosen to grow in small hard clefts far above the noises of river and plain; peace on the grey-faced rock and all along the patient steps and ledges by which a path had been wrested inch by inch from the butting crag, so sharp in its dizzy drop to the river's bed that the eye hardly dared to follow where a brown-winged falcon, whirring out from its eyrie, fell like a falling stone on its unseen quarry below; and peace, in armfuls, heartfuls, where at last, after passing by bell and shrine, by gateways cut in the edge of the cliff against an empty sky, by narrow steps round the brinks of chasms that sank out of sight in the darkness, the path came out on the bare crag's top against a rock that shadowed it still, and watched, like a sentinel, over—a dying man.

Lying on the scant grass, his face to the sky, his limbs doubled under him, was a poor Japanese, a man of about eight-and-twenty, dressed in thin cotton, and gazing out with eyes where suffering was not yet subdued in unconsciousness. He groaned pitifully, but shook his head in refusal of the help that all were longing to give. The bonze, who was acting as guide, explained. The man was doing a voluntary penance, fulfilling a vow. Eight days and nights he had passed here, without touching food or drink. He had still two days more to suffer, but would probably die first. It was his own wish; there was nothing to be done; it was better to leave him—in peace.

And surely you are at peace now, poor brave martyr to the only god you knew? God is not One who will reproach you for giving more than He asked.

Father Testevuide is dead. Father Vigroux takes his place.

Such is our news from Tokyo; and ever since it came, somewhat late, to our solitudes, I have been thinking very sorrowfully of the little Hospital in the hills, where profound grief will be felt for the loss of the dear missionary who has been father and mother to the poor sick people there. Thank God, I cannot help saying—thank God that he went before the disease had fastened on him! His death was for his people, nevertheless. For months at a time, when funds were low, he used to starve himself, in order to spend on his sick the money which should have gone for his own food. Besides the lepers, he had many poor, and was sometimes the only priest in a very wide district; so that the hardest work constantly fell to his share—as, indeed, it does fall to all our priests here, where the demand far exceeds the supply.

Do you know what our priests have to live on in Japan? Fifteen yen (thirty shillings) a month. Out of this they must pay house rent if there is no dwelling-house attached to the chapel, food, clothing, the expenses of getting from one part of their parish to another, and (do not laugh) their charities! I cannot make out that any one of them has any private income; if they had, it has all been given *pour les œuvres,* and thirty shillings a month is what they receive—and live, or die, upon!

"Why—why?" I cried in indignation, when I first learnt all this. Because there is no more to give; the Church is in the straits of holy poverty. The class who, especially in France, used to contribute so generously to mission work has been obliged to devote those moneys to voluntary schools since the name of God has been eradicated from all the public ones; and missionary work would be paralysed if the priests could not live—like paupers: dear, kind, clean, holy paupers, but just that. I have heard it said that the sum spent by different sects of Protestants in Japan equals that which the Holy Father has at his disposal for mission work throughout the world. I do not know how true this may be; but, watching the two systems at work, close beside me, I have come to the conclusion that in these matters money is of secondary value, of next to no value, as compared with prayer, self-sacrifice, and the Heaven-taught discipline of a holy life. It is impossible for the most hardened scoffer to make the acquaintance of one of our priests or sisters of charity here without feeling that he is in the presence of a power for good. As I heard one man say, "Well, people don't do this kind of thing to amuse themselves! 'Pon my soul, the poor chaps deserve to succeed!"

And here let me render a tribute to the scoffer, as I have known him in the East, the British or foreign bachelor, popularly supposed to be so immersed in his own comforts and pleasures, in his club and his whist and his billiards and—other things, that it would be in vain to turn to him for assistance where the poor are concerned. Well, after a long experience of charitable work, I must say that the jolly foreign bachelor is the only creature (barring the Empress of Japan and some ladies of her Court) to whom I have never once turned in vain. Generally a hopeless pagan himself, and often living on very small pay, the moment one speaks of orphans or lepers or earthquake victims, his hand goes into his pocket, and out comes all (and sometimes a good deal more than all) he can possibly afford. Never was there a more kind-hearted and generous creature; and many a time, where I had asked for a real necessity with regret and hesitation, the regret and hesitation have been transferred to the acceptance of a sum which must have made a large difference in the giver's banking account. Once the dear Tsukiji nuns had their house so full of sick and poor that it was absolutely necessary to start an infirmary at once, and a relatively large sum was wanted to do it. We had a charity ball or something of the kind coming off for another object, and I could not compromise its success by appealing to my usual public for this new need. Five gentlemen, quite unsuspected by the world of philanthropic tendencies, made up the sum for us between them, and the infirmary has been full from that day to this; numberless cures, baptisms, and conversions have taken place there, which must surely in great part be put down to the credit of my five friends. And the kindness of the bachelor to the little children and the sick! The toys and cakes smuggled down to the nuns for the little ones, the sums of money sent "just to give the poor little beggars a bit of a treat," the touching way in which my beloved Soeur Sainte-Domitille will say, when everything else has failed, "Eh bien, il faudra écrire à Monsieur un tel," with the certainty of not being refused! It is all very instructive, and makes one think even better of human nature than one did before.

Père Testevuide's place has, of course, been filled at once, by a Father whom I have known well in Tokyo, Père Vigroux, who is the Apostolic Pro-vicar, and whose hands have always been as full as they could hold of work. It will be impossible for him to drop his other tasks at once; but God only knows how he is going to accomplish them and look after the lepers as well. The Archbishop wrote to him asking him to undertake the Gotemba business, and he accepted promptly. But Gotemba is just now a problem of a very anxious kind. There is next to no money to keep it going; there are thirty in-patients there, and others are asking for admission all the time; poor creatures to whom the treatment would be of inestimable benefit, whether as arresting the still curable symptoms of the disease or as palliating and softening the horrible sufferings of its more advanced stages. But how can they be received if there is no money to pay for their medicines or their food? The original Hospital, built with such pathetic economy by Père Testevuide, was already far too small for those whom he received; and before his death he managed to throw two wings out from the main building, and with these it could now accommodate eighty patients. But the founder just managed to feed thirty by going about and begging food for them himself. He knew the district, and was greatly beloved; and yet he could never quite carry out the desires of his heart. No wonder that good Père Vigroux felt, even while undertaking it, that it was an enormous task.

From reasons which I think I told you before, scarcely any provision is made for lepers here; and every now and then some tragedy occurs which just tears at one's heart-strings for pity.

I must tell you a story; please forgive the horror of the beginning, for the sake of the end. A month ago, up here in the hills, where of course our papers come a day late, I was horrified to read in the *Mail* an account of a poor leper who had been found (and left) dying by the roadside in a suburb of Yokohama. The indignant Britisher who wrote said that in the course of a walk his attention was attracted by the cries of some one in great pain. Coming near the spot, he found, to his horror, that a crowd of Japanese boys were pelting with stones a poor creature who was rolling on the ground, naked, in agony, in the very last stages of leprosy. The Englishman, I am sure, dispersed the boys, and probably gave the poor wretch some money, but in his letter mentioned nothing but the pitiable condition of the man, which he described as such that it required the greatest courage to come near him. Of course one would have given worlds to help; but Yokohama is far indeed from Karuizawa, it was already evening, and all that night I was made miserable by the thought of the leper's suffering, which I could do nothing to alleviate. In the morning the thought came to me to write to the nuns of the Convent in Yokohama, and get them to look into the case; there would be no need to ask them to help, when once they knew of it.

Tokyo, October, 1891

You have, I fear, a right to be puzzled at my apparently indiscriminate use of the title of *samurai*. You say that I describe a prince, an interpreter, and a waiting-maid all by the same term, and that such carelessness is misleading. But it is not carelessness, and the appellation is appropriate to them all; so it is not misleading. It simply applies to the whole of the class who had a right to carry arms, and their descendants; and it is the fault of Japanese ideals if it has come to express everything that is heroic and dignified and honourable.

All courage, all calmness, all indifference to self—these were and are what *samurai* men and women have a right to expect of each other; and should the nation ever again be plunged in war, I fancy the *samurai* spirit will have much to do with carrying it through and over its difficulties. This spirit was curiously shown the other day. A very great friend of ours, Mr. Sannomiya, of whom I have so often spoken to you, met with a serious accident. He and several others were posted along the sides of artificial canals, up which the Japanese beaters drive the wild duck for the guns. These canals are deep and narrow, having high green banks on either side, with a bamboo fencing at the top, pierced here and there for the guns to pass through. The place will look utterly deserted, and yet be bristling with guns rendered quite invisible by these screens. Well, by some mistake poor Mr. Sannomiya received the whole of a charge of duckshot at precisely the distance when the charge had expanded enough to cover his whole person. He was very much hurt. The unwilling assailant was ready to commit suicide from despair; but this would not have helped poor Mr. Sannomiya, who was taken to the Red Cross Hospital in a very critical condition. His wife told me afterwards that the surgeons were anxious to administer chloroform before extracting the shots. They warned the patient that the operation would be painful in the extreme; but Mr. Sannomiya scoffed at the idea. "Who ever heard of a *samurai* taking chloroform?" he asked, and lay still while thirty-six pellets were cut out from his head alone. Very high fever and six weeks of painful convalescence in the Hospital followed—weeks during which he never uttered one complaint; and when I saw him at last, he looked like the ghost of his old cheerful self. With my usual brilliant tact, I managed to invite him and Marquis K——, his assailant, to dinner on the same day not very long afterwards. I only remembered the unfortunate combination too late to alter it, and I think that the *samurai* spirit was shown quite as much by the urbane kindness and gentleness of both the men that evening as it had been by poor Mr. Sannomiya's silent stoicism in the Hospital.

Madame Sannomiya is one of the ladies who have done most for the Red Cross Society here, of which the Empress is the President and the ruling spirit. We all belong to it, and have beautiful little medals, which we wear at the functions connected with the Hospital. Anybody who likes may become a member, and the meetings are crowded by a very representative gathering of the population. The first one to which I went was quite a revelation to me of the way in which the Empress has managed to draw the people to her. An immense enclosed hall in Uyeno is set aside for these meetings. For the avoidance of crushing, it is divided into sections, which run down both sides of its whole length, leaving a path up the middle. A high platform at one end is reserved for the Empress and the Imperial Princes and Princesses and we have our places on benches at the side. The great space was so thickly packed with people, that it seemed as if there would not be standing room for another pair of feet, and every class except the very poorest seemed to have furnished members. But I do not think it was entirely interest in the Hospital which had induced them to pay their little or big subscriptions; I think the crowd came (and only subscribers are admitted) in order to see the Empress stand on the daïs, and to hear her read the report of the year. The Empress, amidst a silence of intense excitement and respect, stepped forward with a paper in her hand, and in a clear voice read the report it contained. This was what was so truly amazing—the most modern thing I have yet seen in Japan!

After she had finished, those who were to be newly enrolled went up the steps of the daïs, and received their medals and diplomas from Prince Komatsu, who said a few words about the Empress's gratitude to all who helped this charitable scheme so dear to her. There was a great deal of bowing and band-playing and then the Empress retired, and we went off to look at some sword-forging, or rather sword-damascenings, which had been got up for one of the Princes in another building. I am afraid I do not know anything about blades; but I was immensely interested in the old sword-smith and his work. He and his two assistants were dressed in white ceremonious-looking costumes; a kind of white square tent had been erected over his ovens and bellows; and he kept up a running fire of orders to his assistants in a low voice during the whole process. The blades were handed to him one by one, when he drew on them a lovely design, apparently without forethought, in a black substance; the blade was heated white hot; and then, with tools which to me were nameless, it was welded and hardened, and fused in the fire and welded again, polished, cooled, and then handed up to the Prince's aide-de-camp, who showed it to his master. The result was most beautiful, and purely Japanese; but the Prince seemed indifferent, and barely glanced at the blade. The old man looked profoundly discouraged, and started on another at once, as if hoping to please him better the next time. I was very sorry for his disappointment. It was nothing to the descendant of a hundred generations of sword-smiths that we, ignorant foreigners, should admire his work; but that his own Imperial Prince, in his gorgeous military uniform, with a foreign sword at his side, should not care for the weapon of honour, "the soul of the *samurai*," that evidently cut very deep indeed.

I was speaking of service a little while ago, and of how the servant shares in the honour accorded to his master. All our servants belong to one clan; and I was warned on first coming to live here that it would be a mistake to introduce strangers, as they would be very badly received. I cannot quite make out who governs the politics of the clan; but I see that my *amah* and her husband are extremely powerful in it. Once or twice, when necessity has induced me to take some highly recommended servant from a friend, the experiment has always ended in the new servant's coming to me with extreme regret to announce that a grandmother in a distant province had been taken dangerously ill, and required the presence of all her relatives at once. Sympathy was received with silent respect, a small present of money, although perhaps much needed, somewhat unwillingly, because at that time I did not know that to give money not properly wrapped up in paper is all but an insult. Then the new servant would disappear, to return no more. Only one have I lost in a different way, and then I confess that my wrath was extreme; but it was a question of the internal government of the clan, and my poor little housemaid had to go—to Honolulu.

Her name was Toki, and she was a widow, with one little boy, about ten years old. She was very small and delicate-looking, with a fine oval face, high-bred features, and a beseeching gentle expression, as if life might be softened into treating her more kindly in the future than in the past. The women's work in the house is so very light that there was no hardship in the service. I found that even O'Matsu did not insist upon the attentions she usually claimed from Toki's predecessor, having set up a servant of her own, a nice little girl of twelve or thirteen, whom she bullied gloriously. Toki had been several months with us, and I had got quite accustomed to seeing the slight graceful figure shadowing my path, when one day Mrs. D—— came up to say that there was terrible trouble in the servants' quarters; Toki was weeping bitterly, and said she must go away. Rinzo and O'Matsu had decided that she was to go away.

I bounded on my chair, and then Rinzo and O'Matsu were called and interrogated. They send Toki away? Never! They loved her as a daughter, and it was breaking their hearts that the dear girl insisted in the most headstrong manner on going to Honolulu, to marry a member of the clan who had lost his wife since he emigrated. But he was a good man, rich, chief cook to a foreign gentleman; doubtless Toki would be happy. Still, they would miss her very much, and were *so sorry* that she was going!

There is an omnivorous emigration agent for Hawaii here, who is, they say, highly paid for all the Japanese he can send across. I had never come into collision with him before; but if I could have laid my hand on him that day, he would have heard what the tracts call "a few plain words." I was certain that the most dreadful pressure was being brought to bear on my gentle little Toki, who was devoted to her son, and, in a minor way, to us. The next interview I had was with her. I told her that no power on earth should take her away if she wanted to stay; and that I was sure it was her duty to remain with her son. She cried bitterly, poor soul; but said that her kind relations had apprenticed her boy to a jeweller on the *Ginza* (the street of shops), who would certainly make his fortune; that it was her own unprompted wish to go to Honolulu to marry the rich man's cook whom she had never seen; that Okusama was too kind, too much kind (oh dear! oh dear! and more floods of tears), but she would sail on the 17th.

And so she did. O'Matsu took her down to Yokohama, and was in black disgrace for a month afterwards, during which she too wept copiously over the missing of the headstrong Toki and Okusama's unkind suspicions. At last she had to be forgiven on account of her charming manners and her general usefulness. Then, with surprising regularity, I was told that Toki had written to say that she was very happy, to say that her husband gave her five meals a day all of the best rice, to say (by the next mail this) that she had a kind Japanese doctor and three large gold rings, to say, by the next mail again (O'Matsu forgot to state who wrote this letter), that—she was dead.

Sayonara, little Toki.

On October 28th, early in the morning, we were roused by the most terrifying shock of earthquake that I have yet experienced. The disturbance took the dangerous form of violent verticle movement, accompanied by fearful rumblings and the crashing of stones. We were all asleep; but even in sleep that apprehension never leaves one, and before I was awake I had reached the door, and was trying to get out into the gallery. Sometimes the door gets jammed during an earthquake, and in any case it is not easy to open it when the floor is tossing like a ship at sea, and the roar and crash are so awful that you cannot hear the voice of a person standing at your elbow! As a rule the shock has a duration of from thirty to sixty seconds, and that feels like hours in the horror of dismay that it inspires; this first one of October 28th went on for seven minutes, and was followed by lesser ones for many hours. For all its terrors, it did only minor damage here; but in the south it has practically wiped out a large and thriving district, one which had always been considered exceptionally free from such visitations, and as yet the loss of life and property cannot even be estimated.

It had another most unusual quality of earthquake shocks: it had been predicted. On what grounds precisely it is impossible to say, but with confident certainty, at any rate. The last really severe earthquake (I am not speaking, of course, of volcanic eruptions, which are generally accompanied by shocks of more or less violence) took place in 1854; and it was prophesied that there would be another in thirty-seven years—a prophecy which has just been fulfilled. As, for twelve hundred years, there is no record of precisely that interval between one earthquake and another, it sounds like an arbitrary prediction. Thirty-seven is one of the Japanese mystic numbers; when that period after a death has elapsed, the survivors perform certain rites for the benefit of the dead—ornament their shrines and make offerings to them. And doubtless many of those who perished in that earthquake are being so remembered now. But this catastrophe has, I think, surpassed in horror all those remembered by living people. The centre of the disturbance was at Gifu and Nagoya. At this last place seven hundred shocks of earthquake were registered between October 28th and November 3rd. Professor Milne's beautiful seismographs were quite incompetent to register the strength of the shocks, which far surpassed anything that had been contemplated when the machines were invented. The description of the visitation at its centre is awful past belief. Two towns and many villages are completely destroyed; railway lines are twisted like wire; huge bridges tossed into the air and snapped like matchwood, the stone pillars on which they stood being sliced smoothly through their whole diameter. Mountains have slipped from their foundations; a new lake has been formed; three hundred and fifty miles of river dykes injured—one half of this totally destroyed; a grove of bamboos was taken up and flung sixty feet from where it stood; the earth has opened in frightful fissures, and in some cases closed again over the houses and bodies it had swallowed. The lowest estimation puts the houses totally destroyed at 42,345, those partially ruined at 18,106. As for loss of life, that will never be known, I fear; every turn of the spade brings dead and dying to light, and many of the wounded were so frightfully hurt that it was impossible to save them. As all the telegraph communication and railway traffic was interrupted, it was not easy to bring assistance immediately to the sufferers, and the first doctors and nurses who got to them were on their feet for days and nights, and did more than seemed humanly possible to help the poor creatures. At Ogaki Hospital, two surgeons dressed the wounds of six hundred patients in forty-eight hours.

The misery and destruction were as usual enormously increased by the fires which at once broke out. What the earthquake left the fire devoured; and now, with the winter coming on, at least one hundred thousand people are without houses, without food, having lost their means of gaining a livelihood, and everything else in the world. Of course every kind of assistance is being given by the Emperor and the Empress, by the Government, by public subscriptions, and private individuals; nurses and doctors have flocked to the afflicted districts, and relief camps have been started, where allowances of food are dealt out; but with all that, the suffering is awful, the want all but impossible to satisfy. Here we do nothing but collect money and clothes, bandages and blankets; and the railway companies carry it all free of charge down to the scene of the trouble. I am glad to say the English trained nurse from St.

Hilda's was sent down at once, with two Japanese nurses and a doctor, at the mission's expense, and they have been doing good work among the sufferers, who are, every one says, perfectly patient and resigned. There has been no murmuring even at their misfortunes, and their patience and gentleness make it easy to organise and carry out the plans for their help. The excellent organisation of the Red Cross Society has shown itself now; and the indefatigable efforts of doctors and nurses have certainly allayed much suffering and saved many lives.

I hardly know Dr. Hashimoto, the director of the Red Cross Hospital. He is utterly devoted to his work, and never goes out; neither does his colleague, Dr. Takagi, of the Charity Hospital; but I have been brought more often into contact with him. He took me over the wards the first time I went there, and explained to me the evolution of that extraordinary disease *kakke*,* which seems to be a purely Japanese ailment. The muscles of the legs become useless, without any symptoms of paralysis, and gradually waste away, leaving the limbs cold and shrivelled. The disease attacks men, and hard-working men more than any other class of the community, and is frequent in districts where the people live on rice alone as their staple food. My *amah* tells me that in her province, where a kind of rough oatmeal is mixed with the food, the disease is almost unknown. The soldiers suffer from it a good deal; but it is hoped that the meat diet lately introduced in alternation with the native rice and fish food will do much to overcome the weakness. In the navy the men are generously fed on meat, rather to their own distaste, but very much to their physical well-being. I think I told you that Count Saigo, the Minister of Marine, is a firm believer in European food methods, and carries them out in his own family.

At Karuizawa, or rather about a mile away from the village, in a pretty gorge, is a little spring of warm mineral† water which is supposed to be very beneficial to *kakke* patients; and numbers of soldiers from some military hospital used to be sent up to bathe there. They were lodged in the inn and seemed to be under no es-

---

Kakke is the Japanese name for beriberi, a disease caused by a deficiency of vitamin B_1, or thiamine, in the diet.

†Perhaps Mrs. Fraser meant Kose Onsen, or Kose hot springs.

pecial control; but a milder, gentler set of fellows it would be impossible to find. They made friends with every child in the village; and as soon as they grew a little stronger would generally carry a baby friend about with them. They used to go off in bands of nine or ten at a time to the little tumble-down bath-house in the gorge; they were all dressed in a dark-blue *yucata,* with the number of their regiment worked on it in red, straw *waraji* on their feet, and nothing by any chance on their heads except the shock of bristling black hair which is induced by the constant practice of shaving the head in childhood. How often in our queer journeys I have seen the careful mother shaving her baby's head while he was asleep! The little one never stirred; and when the process was over, the mother would reach out for the small green mosquito net, supported on split bamboos, and put it down over the baby in a safe square, and then creep away to her household work. This shaving is very irritating to the poor infant's skin, and induces forms of eczema the most distressing and obstinate. The nuns have no end of trouble in this way with the children brought to them.

In going over the Charity Hospital, the University Hospital, or that of the Red Cross (chiefly devoted to accidents and surgical cases), one sees none of the anomalies that I have noticed in some of those conducted on more elementary lines. No infectious or contagious diseases are received in the wards devoted to ordinary patients; the nurses are admirably trained, and, if wanting in initiative to meet a sudden responsibility, are at any rate religiously obedient to the doctors, and invariably kind to the patients. I have had many sieges of illness since I came (the climate is anything but favourable to the highly nervous organisation of the European woman); but I have been partly repaid for these by the delight and amusement of making the acquaintance of one who is now a real friend—my first Japanese trained nurse. I shall never forget the day when she first loomed on my astonished vision.

She was barely four feet high, her complexion was dark in the extreme, her feet were encased in white linen socks with divided toes, and shod with dainty straw sandals with green velvet straps. Her figure, the shape of a very soft feather pillow which has been hung up by one end for days, was draped in a tight-fitting white apron with a large bib, and she was kept inside her buttonless and stringless clothes by a cruelly tight and wide leather belt put on over apron and all. Into this belt, holding her breath for a long time first, she could, with a great effort, push her fat silver watch, her clinical thermometer, two or three yards of a Japanese letter (which she would read, a foot at a time, when she thought I was asleep), her carefully folded paper pocket-handkerchief, and the relentless little register in which she noted down, from right to left, strange cabalistic signs, with which she and the doctor conjured every morning till they knew all the sins my pulse and temperature had been committing for the last twenty-four hours. Her name was O'Tora San (Honourable Tiger Miss), but her ways were those of the softest and most harmless pussy that ever purred on a domestic hearthrug, and oh, what a nurse she was! So gentle, so smiling, so very delightfully sorry for one! It was quite worth being ill to revel in such seas of sympathy. I have often caught the tears running down her little brown nose when the poor Okusama was extra bad; and through long nights of pain has she stood by my bed, or sat on her heels on a corner of it, fanning me ceaselessly with the all but imperceptible flutter of the fan's edge—a movement only possible for those wonderfully sensitive Japanese fingers, but most refreshing to the fanned one.

When it was time for her to have her meals, my chief maid, O'Matsu, a dainty-looking princess of nature herself, would creep into the room, having shed her sandals at the door, and after inquiring about my health, would make a deep and graceful obeisance to the Honourable Tiger Miss, and inform her in a respectful whisper that her honourable dinner was ready. The polite little Tiger would jump up, return the bow, ask my leave to depart, and slip out to feed on fish, pickles (such dreadfully strong-smelling pickles!), and rice, washed down, as they say in the Waverley Novels, by thimblefuls of green tea or fish soup. After about fifteen minutes of solid feeding she would return, come to my bedside, and express her gratitude for the meal supplied to her. Then she would drop down on her cushion in the corner, and with the calm unconventionality peculiar to her race, let out a couple of holes in the leather belt. Another polite summons would be brought to her with more bows at about eight o'clock every evening, when the Japanese bath in the back yard had been heated to boiling-point. O'Tora San was always invited to take "first wash," before even No. 1 boy, *amah,* or chief cook. This was a great compliment, for the hierarchy downstairs took its bath according to rank with as much exactness and punctilio as if its members had been ambassadors being received at Court.

O'Tora San had the real nurse's gift for feeling the time, and waking at the right hour; and for eight days and nights I think she never failed to come to my bedside every two hours to replenish the ice-bags in which I lay. Once she had to go away for two days for some family reason, and was replaced by a dreadful person, who had never nursed in a European house before, who did not know a warming-pan from a smelling-bottle, and who further irritated me by reading endless Japanese newspapers printed backwards on pink paper. How glad I was when on the afternoon of the second day my little Tiger returned, smiling sweetly as usual, with an enormous sheaf of Japanese pinks in her hand, and looking so nice in her own soft grey silk *kimono* and sash, instead of the hideous hospital apron and leather belt.

Many of the Japanese trained nurses have come under the influence of Canadian Methodist missionaries, and their phraseology is sometimes startling in the extreme. A colleague of my little Tiger was nursing a friend of mine, the wife of an American clergyman. O'Take San (Honourable Bamboo Miss) was rather pretty, and on being questioned admitted that she had been married—once. My friend became all sympathy, expecting to hear of early widowhood and a broken heart. She asked timidly what had become of the husband. She was electrified by the answer. "Wal" (O'Take San had an aggressive twang, acquired with much care), "I guessed he didn't love his Saviour 'nough, so I sent him right away. See?"

I will add here two little letters which I received from O'Tora San and a friend of hers, written to bid me farewell in the summer of the next year. The first is from O'Tora herself, and wonderfully well-spelt and written:

"TOKYO CHARITY HOSPITAL."

"MY HONOURABLE MADAM,—I have a great honour to get an opportunity to write you. I am very sorry that I could not meet you before you leave Japan. Indeed, I was always thinking to visit you; but as my body is not free as a nurse, I could not succeed my purpose. Once I had been at Yokohama as a nurse, my engagement was finished, and I returned Tokyo. Alas! you were not in Tokyo. Will there be no time to meet you again? If my thought goes so far as this point, I always burst into tears. Madam, permit my negligency. If I may have an honour to receive your letter, I shall be very much obliged of you, and will keep it as long as my life as the memory of yours."

O'Tora's friend, to whom I had been able to show some trifling kindness, wrote more than once to thank me. Indeed, one often feels very small at accepting the lasting and effusive gratitude with which little services or gifts are received. Her letter runs thus, and shows that she had come under missionary influence:

"MY HONOURABLE MADAM,—I have great honour to write you. . . . Miss Matsui (O'Tora San) told me that you were ill, so I was quite astonished, and tried to visit you; but, alas! you were then for Europe. I therefore have nothing for you but only to welcome you again in Japan. I am sure that you will be again in our country. I am, madam, working at hospital, and for me nurse is suitable. For the glory of Almighty Father I am eagerly studying nursing. . . . Indeed, our hospital is just like some Christian school; Rev. Wada, pastor of Shiba Church, gives us important sermons every Saturday evening, and we are to attend Church every Sunday morning, and in the evening there are Bible lessons constructed for us. . . . My heart is filled with joy and thanks. . . . By God's mercy I am quite healthy and strong in spirit and body. Some day when I get leisure, if you return, I shall have an honour to visit and thank your kindness orally.

"I remain, dear Madam, always
"Your faithful servant,
"SAWA TANAKA."

1892

The end of the year was marked by the marriage of young Princess Sanjo (her name is Chiye) to Prince Kotohito Kanin,* one of the Imperial Princes, who has spent some years in France studying naval matters. The wedding itself was conducted in private; but a great dinner was given in the evening at the Aoyama Palace, to which we all went. There were most of the Imperial Princes and Princesses, crowds of officials and colleagues, and the whole thing was rather brilliant. It was so funny to be solemnly presented anew to the little bride, and to make her the profound curtseys which the royalties here expect. I am afraid we both laughed; and when the ceremony was over, she made room for me on the sofa, and we had a good talk. She looked quite charming in her first white brocade, her first diamonds; and the little new airs of dignity sat very prettily on her, I thought. She never went to these solemn evening parties before, the Japanese not expecting girls to appear at them; and I should think it must have been rather an ordeal to have to receive such a number of people at once. All through the long dinner, the first

*Prince Kotohito Kan'in (b. 1865), a descendant of Emperor Higashiyama (r. 1687–1709).

she had ever attended, she was as gay and composed as if she had been doing nothing else all her life, and some of us remembered her wonderful fortitude and courage after the death of her father last year. Her mother has never quite recovered her strength since the blow; and Princess Chiye tells me that she has had a great deal to do for her four little sisters, who look to her for guidance as well as companionship, and who will miss her sorely now that she has been carried off to a palace of her own.

The young Prince, the bridegroom, might be taken as a typical representative of the old Japanese aristocracy. His slight figure, delicate and beautiful features, his tiny hands and feet, all make him one's ideal of the mediaeval boy Emperor, kept from all contact with the rough realities of life, served, worshipped, and—irrevocably enslaved. But Prince Kanin is a free man, and his erect bearing, clear voice, and flashing eye show that there is nothing of weakness below the slight and boyish exterior. He is immensely interested in his own profession, and ambitious to see the Japanese navy put on the most efficient and splendid footing. His French is fluent and clear; and through the long wedding dinner, where I had the honour of being his neighbour, he talked well of many things, and thanked me for what he chose to call the kindness I had shown to the Princess in these past years. The dinner was long, but admirably well done, and the flowers, all carefully chosen as the lucky and joyous ones, most exquisite. In all the decorations the beloved pine branches, with little cranes and tortoises perched on them, were freely used; the wedding cake was an artistic presentment of Fuji San, pure white, with little pine trees and the lucky animals climbing round its base. After a great reception which followed the dinner was over, and the royalties had retired, I told the Prince's *grand maître* that in England a wedding cake was always cut up and distributed among the guests. This was evidently a new idea; but it was at once adopted with enthusiasm. The *grand maître* made the first incision, and then handed the knife to me, as if uncertain whether I wanted half or a quarter of the enormous thing to take home with me. However, he was not long in doubt; and the moment I had cut a tiny wedge, all the other women present came and begged for a piece. Sheets of the pretty Court paper were produced, and when I went away I carried off a little pine tree, a white crane, and a green tortoise, as well as the flowers and bonbon-box which I had found at my place. The tortoise is a most enchanting creation, with a great flat back, a beseeching waggly head, and a long tail of pure green silk, which distinguishes him from all other tortoises as the only one symbolic of riches. The pine is for happiness, the crane for long life. I hope dear little Princess Chiye will have both!

And now, in these winter days, what can I tell you that you have not heard already? For this is my third winter in Yedo, and I begin to fear that I have related enough to weary you of all its ways and customs.

Tokyo, April, 1892

Spring is, after all, Japan's loveliest season, when the country smiles and weeps, pales and flushes, like a maid decked for her bridal. I have seen it three times now, and yet it comes as a long-expected joy, eagerly watched and waited for. Everything seems lovelier than usual this year; and though my heart has made a thousand journeys over the westward water, and Europe is drawing me with irresistible compulsion, yet it saddens me to think that I shall not see the cherries bloom next year, nor the wistaria arbour flush from grey to purple, sink back from purple to green. I shall not write many letters after this, and I am wondering which, of all sights and scenes yet undescribed, you would rather hear of on this soft spring day.

Did I ever tell you of my delightful visit to the Uyeno Museum and the School of Art, under the guidance of the director, Mr. Okakura?* It always seems to me that, if I see things at all, I have the good fortune to see them in the most charming way. The Uyeno

---

*Kakuzō Okakura (1862–1913), author of *The Book of Tea*, *The Ideals of the East*, and many other works. He remained with the museum and school from 1889 to 1898. In the earliest years of the twentieth century he was instrumental in forming the collection of Chinese and Japanese art at the Museum of Fine Art in Boston.

Museum is a store-hourse of art treasures and historical memories, and to have the delightful and learned director for my companion there was a great joy. It was one morning in the beginning of April that I drove up through the flowery avenues to the great building where he was waiting for me. From the brilliant sunshine and the waves of cherry blossom that seemed breaking like foam through the dark branches of the pines, we passed to the twilight dignities of the great halls, where all the legacies of the past—weapons of war and robes of gold, lutes and fans, swords and drinking-cups, embroideries and lacquer and enamel, all the discarded pomps of a splendour-loving people—are gathered and set, line by line, case by case, as if for burial. There is something strangely like death in the still untroubled air of such places—air so separate, in its irrevocable calm, from all the joyous pulsing of the live world in the sunshine without, so sealed and set apart from the vibrating existence of to-day, that I almost doubt if the ghosts (Japan is full of ghosts) of those who made these things, and who doubtless hang round them still, would acknowledge a descendant, a compatriot, in the modern Japanese, the man of science, who took me past them, and told me in quiet, somewhat scornful tones of their histories and values.

My guide, who is perhaps the greatest existing authority on these subjects, was dressed in his own dignified costume, and seemed outwardly in harmony with the Japan of the past. He has large brilliant eyes, and a low clear voice; his English is fluent and complete. He rather laughed at my delight over the first object that met my view, a magnificent bullock-cart, which used to be the Imperial travelling carriage. It is as large as a small room, with heavy wheels, that must have turned with august slowness over the august roads; time could have been of no value to the august travellers then. Heavy beams of the most splendid black-and-gold lacquer support a four-square tent of lacquer and carving, with jealous curtains, heavily tasselled with silk, closing the openings of the front and sides. Very long poles run out, also in lacquer; and these were attached to stout white bullocks, who advanced, step by step, their hoofs weighted with the pride of drawing the Son of Heaven, who, sitting in his gilded shrine, and passing through his fair domains, must have found it very easy to believe that he had the makings of a deity in him, at all events.

Not always was it an Emperor. Sometimes the car was surmounted by a golden phoenix, and then the brown men and women in the rice-fields of "reed-growing Japan" knew that their Empress was passing by. I have a print, a Japanese print of the last century, full of figures in trails of purple and rose, and pale carmine and primrose gold. The colouring is that of the iris gardens of Hori Kiri,* when the sun is setting softly behind the translucent, silky-bannered ranks, shining here purple, there white, there gold or copper, as the flowers grow. And in the crowd of lovely figures there are movements and swayings so like the iris shapes that in my mind I call it the iris picture. Now the central thing in my picture is the Imperial bullock-cart, exactly as I found it in the Museum. The beautiful shape, graceful for all its square strength and roominess, is hung with curtains of delicate blinds, each held in place by a great tie of silk; its poles have that splendid curve of strength as if of themselves they had leapt forward in the royal service. In my picture the phoenix does not crown the roof; and there are no bullocks, but a crowd of lovely maidens, gathering close round their Empress, who has descended to the ground. So many are they, so eager to serve her, that I think they must have been trying to draw the cart themselves; but if so, it had been too much for their slender strength, so now the Empress stands in the midst of them, still between the shafts, her wonderful drapery blown a little about by a rebel wind, her beautiful face with a sad little smile bent down on her breast, where her two hands are trying to hold her splendid robes together. You can see her figure swaying to the wind. And the girls, in draperies scarcely less splendid, have taken each some part of her princely baggage: one a crown on a cushion, one a *jui,* or fairy sceptre, one her bow, one her arrows; others carry musical instruments, some hold the shafts; and past them all the rebel wind is sweeping, playing with streamer and gown, and causing the heads

---

*Horikiri is described in Murray's *Handbook for Travellers in Japan* (1894) as a "favourite flower resort, lying some little way beyond Mukōjima [Tokyo], . . . famed for its irises which bloom in June."

to bend for fear that the wonderful wings and coils of hair should be set straying by its force; and to it they all oppose the yielding strength of the iris. Their faces are far paler than their robes, and in my picture even these are fading now, so I know that they are long dead; doubtless the wind had its way in the iris garden.

And my guide wondered that I cared to stand so long looking at the old bullock-cart!

Well, at last we went on, and he led me through hall after hall of strange things: prehistoric were many of them, arrow-heads and knives, and spear-heads in stone—the things on which humanity seems to have, so to speak, cut its teeth simultaneously all over the world; strings of those strange "jewels" the *maga-tama,* stones curved like an ear, and the *kuda-tama,* like straight tubes, worn as ornaments once, and then coming to be regarded as talismans and holy things. Only in one part of the Emperor's dominions does their use still survive—in the Loo-Choo* Islands, where many a grim old custom is carried on to this day. Of all living races that I know of, the Loo-Chooans are the only people who have the courage to face the worst horrors of corruption in their care of the dead. These are laid away in caves, and for five dreadful years it is considered the duty of the living once a year to take them from the kindly shroud of the darkness, bring them to the light and wash the poor remains, then wrap them again in their coverings, and lay them by. After five years the body is supposed to be sufficiently reduced to be put in boxes and placed in the household shrines. The Japanese Government have repeatedly forbidden the practice, but find that it is still carried out by stealth, to the great danger of the population after any epidemic. I had a curious glimpse of some Loo-Choo people last year, which I will record here, as I think I did not tell you of it at the time.

I had taken a huge party of children and young people to—switchback in Uyeno Park! Yes, a splendid switchback was set up under Iyeyasu's pines, and was much patronised by the Japanese. Well, just as my English boys and girls tumbled out on the platform after their third ride, a grave party of Loo-Chooans came and paid their fee. They were (as we found out) well-to-do merchants, who had made up their minds to see the wonders of the capital. The

*Ryūkyū Islands.

party consisted of two middle-aged men, one youth, and a most reverend senior, an old man with a beautiful white beard, erect head, and piercing dark eyes. All the men had larger eyes and smoother darker skins than the true Japanese, and much of the gentle look of the Malayans. In their dress a dark-purple colour predominated, and there were some slight variations from the ordinary Japanese costume, but not enough to attract attention. All my gay young people stood aside to let the strangers have their turn, and these took their places with a solemnity evidently mingled with awe. The old man sat down on a front seat, and spread his robes in geometrical lines over his knees, joined his hands as if in prayer, and looked straight before him. The younger men got in, and off they went at a breakneck pace. The youths clutched the seat, and screamed; the middle-aged men clutched the seat, and were silent. The old man came back precisely as he had gone; his beard was nearly blown off his face, and his garments were all over the place, but he had never turned his head or ceased to look solemnly before him, and his hands were folded as if in prayer. My young people made an entreaty through our interpreter that he would go again. The sight was entrancing to their young imaginations. No, thank you. It was all doubtless most clever and beautiful; but the gods had been kind. Let us not presume on their favours. Good-bye.

I left you in the Uyeno Museum, you say? Did I? Well, the switchback is only just outside!

> "C'est bien de moi! Quand je chevauche
> L'hyppogriffe au pays du bleu,
> Mon âme sans corps se débauche,
> Et s'en va comme il plaît à Dieu!"

You must take my stories as they come, or not at all!

Yes, I saw many things that day. Are not the lists of them in the helpful pages of Murray, written by two of my great friends? The director asked me if we cultivate the nose in Europe. I turned my profile to him with just pride; but that was not what he meant. The art of smell has been brought to its perfection here; and I was shown little bronze burners in which one, two, three—a dozen different kinds of aromatic stuff can be burnt at once, the puzzled guests being required to name every ingredient used. At one time these perfume parties were very popular, and Mr. Okakura told me that he knew people who could detect each and every perfume of any combination, there being over fifty kinds of incense in all.

Then I stood for long by the relics of the Japanese embassy to Rome, when the great Daimyo of Sendai, Date Masamune,* sent one of his nobles with a huge train of followers to acknowledge the supremacy of the Pope, and to ask for his prayers and assistance. There is an oil-painting of the ambassador, in early seventeenth-century costume, praying with folded hands before a crucifix; in a case are various objects of devotion—rosaries, crucifixes, and so on; and close by are the horrible blocks of metal, generally stamped with a crucifix, which in the persecutions were laid down before the feet of those suspected to be Christians—they must walk over these or die. How many thousands refused, how many pure souls left their martyred bodies to their enemies, how many delicate women and little children kept their faith and lost their lives, we can hardly tell. Christianity was stamped out as a national religion; but I think the martyrs prayed for their beloved country, cruel as it had been to them. And a little germ was kept alive. Nearly thirty years ago, some missionaries landing near Nagasaki found whole villages hidden away in the hills by the sea, where the old prayers were still said just as they had been learnt two centuries before, where baptism was administered and marriages and burials prayed over faithfully, although never a priest had set foot there since their first pastors had been killed. The poor people's joy was overwhelming; but even at such a recent date persecution found them out again. They were exiled, and dispersed for a time. But only for a time. Universal toleration was proclaimed in 1873, and on the twenty-fifth anniversary of their discovery, after my arrival in Japan, the Catholic Bishops and their priests went in state to celebrate a great

*Datè Masamune (1567–1636), a military leader who sided with Tokugawa Ieyasu and received the fief of Karita in Mutsu Province (present-day Miyagi Prefecture). In 1613 he sent his retainer Hasekura Tsunenaga to head a mission to Spain and Rome, but though received by the King of Spain and the Pope they failed to achieve their objectives, which were to open up trade relations with the Spanish dominions in the New World and to establish a bishopric in Mutsu.

religious festival among these faithful people. A friend of mine who accompanied them told me that nothing could be more entire or beautiful than the faith then shown. The people came flocking on foot over the hills, whole fleets of boats covered the sea, and the good souls wept for joy, crowding round the Bishop to touch his hands, his robes, his feet.

Let us forget the persecutors: has not every nation numbered such at some moment of her history? I like to remember that all those faithful martyrs were Japanese; that in their sweetness and constancy "le Bon Dieu a fait des siennes," as an old nun said to me one day; and that everywhere in the island empire we may feel that we are surrounded by true hearts and brave spirits, loyal to the best that has been revealed to them.

We finished the morning in Mr. Okakura's especial domain, the Art School, situated in the same grounds, and not very far from the Museum. Here students were carving, painting, drawing; and many a bright face was turned upon us as we passed from room to room. That which interested me most was the making of lacquer—a long and complicated process, which I had never beheld before. In little rooms the men sat one or at most two working together, in just the silent, patient way which seems fitting for the production of that marvellous material. From the first handling of a thin bit of wood to the point where decoration pure and simple may begin, thirty-seven separate processes must be gone through. A very fine and thoroughly seasoned wood is used for the foundation; the first applications of lacquer are rubbed away again and again; a fine textile substance is spread on the surface, layer on layer, as one by one absorbs the rare varnish; then these are polished again, each drying being effected slowly in moist darkness; then, in fine red lacquer, comes a layer of gold-dust, laid on thick and moist, and entirely covered again by that gorgeous scarlet, its only use being to make the red richer and deeper; and at last, after weeks and months of preparation, the decorative work comes, a marvel of richness, bird and beast and flower in raised gold, where every modelling is clear and effective, yet the whole smooth to the touch as the inner walls of a sea-worn shell. It is almost indestructible: you can fill your bowl with boiling spirits, you can drown it for years in the salt sea (I have seen beautiful old specimens of lacquer recovered from wrecks), and it will always return to you, whole and smooth and golden as on the day it first saw the light.

When it became necessary for me to tear myself away from the lacquer studios, the chief artist, Fukumatsu, who, Mr. Okakura told me, is considered the greatest living worker in lacquer, had a long conversation with the director, and I was told that he wished me to have a little specimen of his work, which he would make for me from the very beginning, allowing no one else to touch it even in the preparatory stages. It should be something with my *mon,* or crest, upon it, and he came down to the carriage to have a look at the "stag's head proper erased" on the panel. That, however, did not strike him as artistic, and I was asked whether some other presentment of a stag would do as well. Any other animal would do as well, I thought, in Mr. Fukumatsu's inspired fingers; and after thanking him for his kind thought, I said farewell to the director and his lacquer magicians. Life was very full just then; and though I did not forget my visit to the school, Mr. Fukumatsu's benevolent intentions went clean out of my head.

Six weeks later a packet was brought me, wrapped in covering after covering of soft yellow silk. When these were shed away, a tiny black box lay in my hand, decorated with a golden stag—a thing so fine and perfect that it might be worn as a gem. The inner surface (the whole thing is barely an inch and a half across) is a tangle of golden weeds on a powdered goldstone ground, and the two halves fit together so that you can hardly see where they close. A letter from Mr. Okakura accompanied the charming gift, asking me to keep it in remembrance of my visit, and saying that Fukumatsu had begun it on that day and had just finished it now. It will be one of my pet treasures, the materialisation of a most pleasant memory.

1894

Tokyo, April, 1894

Two years have passed since I wrote my last letter from home to
home—years in which all the old threads have been taken up and
strengthened and renewed; and now I am once more in this half-way
house of the world, whence a step to east or west brings me nearer
to Europe. I do not think I have really been so far from Japan that
I did not sometimes see the cherry blossoms drifting on the wind,
did not sometimes hear the scream of the wild goose through the
winter sky and the long roll of the surf thundering up on the Atami
beaches. Whatever life brings or takes away—and I came with a
heavy heart to this other home of my love, as if life or death, I knew
not which, were chanting some final dirge in my ears with every
break of the sea against the ship's side—whatever comes, Japan will
always be my second home. One cannot explain these things. I have
lived in many countries, north and south and east and west, and,
except in the Rome of our childhood, in none have I found the spirit
of beauty, the spirit of peace, the skirts of Nature's robe ever at hand
to cling to, as I have here, "east of the sun, west of the moon," in
the land of the gods, reed-growing Japan.

Fuji smiled on me as of old beyond my bower of cherry blossom
to-day; the garden has gone mad with some jubilee of growth,

333

throwing out thousands of gorgeous roses even so early as this, before the azaleas have done flaming over their fairy hillocks; every palm tree in house and garden is going to flower this year; the bamboos are all a-feather with new shoots; the great wistaria arbour is a dream; and I have a crimson carpet spread under the translucent green and purple, and sit there whole days just watching things grow, and seeming to hear the sap bubbling up to intoxicate the world with beauty.

There have been some splendid Court functions to celebrate the silver wedding of the Emperor and the Empress. The anniversary fell on March 9th, just after our arrival, and for many days we lived in a kind of pageant of pomp and colour. I shall never forget the nō dancing at the Palace; but I had better tell you the story from the beginning, if I can.

On the morning of the 9th there was a great reception at the Palace, which, from entrance to audience-chamber, was full of the most beautiful flowers. We mustered in force; and when it was our turn to go in and congratulate the sovereigns, H—— and I led quite an imposing staff up to the steps where they stood. Of late I have been the only woman in the party, and it was delightful to have dear Mrs. L—— with me this time, looking quite charming in her mauve-and-silver Court gown. I had found a brocade all over strawberries, and in spite of H——'s sarcastic quotation, "Ce n'est plus la mode de s'asseoir sur son blason,"* wore it bravely. We were received in a small drawing-room, as we usually are for a private audience.

The Empress was wearing such a mass of diamonds that you could hardly see what her dress was made of. Everything was white, and in the brilliant sunshine that glowed on white jewels, white satin, white flowers, I remembered my first real sight of Fuji, with the blaze of the winter midday lying white on its dazzling snows. The Empress's fine little face was as white as all the rest; but her dark eyes shone very happily under her diamond crown, and there was quite a ring in her voice as she answered all our pretty speeches; indeed, she talked more gaily than I have ever heard her do before.

*"It is no longer the fashion to sit on your arms."

The Queen's message arrived just an hour before we started for the Palace, and we were profoundly thankful that it came in time for H—— to deliver it at the audience. The Emperor looked like a piece of the sun himself in his brilliant uniform and splendid decorations; and he, too, had for once laid aside the cold calmness of his usual manner, and laughed and talked as if he were in the best of spirits. After the stock phrases had been exchanged, he told me that he heard I had brought a wonderful dog from England (a new Dachs, who took command of Tip and all the rest the day he arrived); and I felt cold for a minute, fearing that politeness would require me to place Toney Bones at his Majesty's disposal. But—I did not!

There was a review in the afternoon; but I did not go to that, preferring to reserve my strength for the evening, which promised to be long and interesting. The Emperor and Empress, by the way, began their day with a religious service in their private chapel two hours before they received us. The Emperor's taste in religion, as in other things, is for extreme simplicity; and the chapel, which I regret not to have seen, is of course pure Shinto, containing the *ihai*, or mortuary tablets, of his Majesty's ancestors. All the Imperial family and the chief dignitaries of the empire assisted this morning at the service, prayers being offered in turn, and incense burnt before the *ihai*. All the day had gone in giving audiences and reviewing troops, and I thought their Majesties had a right to be very tired, when the time came for the evening's entertainment to begin.

It consisted first of a dinner, given to eight hundred people in different banqueting-halls of the Palace, the Imperial Princes acting as hosts for the Emperor, who presided at the table in the great dining-room, where two hundred guests were accommodated. I had been through the room again and again, and had often wondered how it would look filled with people and lights and flowers. So I saw it now, lighted from end to end with soft shining candles (no electric light has been used in the Palace since the burning of the Houses of Parliament), lined with flowers, the long table which ran round three sides of the room just one line of light and silver and hot-house blooms. The seats for the Emperor and Empress were tall gilt armchairs, and behind them the wall ran back in an alcove, a reminiscence of the *tokonoma,* the alcove of honour in the chief room of a Japanese house. This was a bower of flowers, and in the midst of them were set two quaint little figures of a very old man and a very old woman, the Darby and Joan of Japanese legend, who, though humble (they are always represented in poor clothes, and carrying implements of work—the old man a spade, the old woman a broom), lived in the greatest contentment and happiness to extreme old age, never having quarrelled in their lives. I have often seen the quaint figures, with their smiling, wrinkled faces and snow-white hair, at lowly festivals and in poor people's homes. There was something rather touching about finding them here, put up as the types and patrons of married happiness, in the midst of all the pomp and magnificence of the Imperial feast.

Just opposite the sovereigns' places, the silver ornaments took the shape of sculptured cranes, each over four feet high, with silver pine trees beside them, and great silver tortoises at their feet. These were presents to the Emperor from some of the Princes of the Imperial family. The work was lovely, and they made a beautiful effect, rising out of the sea of flowers and silver and gleaming glass. Beside the plate of every guest stood a miniature crane, with a tortoise at his feet, exquisitely worked in silver and enamel, forming the cover to a casket of bonbons. These were the Emperor's gifts to his guests, and certainly mine is a curio that I should be sorry to part with. The dinner was admirably served—no small triumph when you remember that European methods, with all that they entail of utensils, glass, porcelain, silver, and linen, do not enter into the daily life of the Palace at all. The service was perfect—a footman to every two guests; and all this crowd of men did not get in each other's way, attended quietly to one's wants, and made, in their dark liveries of crimson and black and gold, an effective background to the long rows of guests, where the women were almost all in white, relieved with gold or silver and covered with jewels, the men with hardly an exception in all the glory of smart uniforms. Only the chiefs of missions and their wives had been asked to the dinner, and there were but four of the latter, so my place was very near the Emperor and Empress; and I had quite enough to keep me good and amused while the feast lasted. There were people present that night who rarely show themselves in public: old pretenders to the throne; old leaders of rebellions; fierce fighters, the story of whose feats would make one's blood run cold but for the hot white fire of heroism that lights them up. How strange it was to sit opposite to these men here in the Palace; to watch the calm dark faces veiled by that mantle of cold suavity more impenetrable than an iron mask; to listen to the quiet small talk of an official feast; to watch the decorations rise and fall on breasts that were heaving to madness with the lust of war or the pride of race or the desire of revenge only a few years ago! Tokugawa, Mori, Iwakura, Kido, Saigo, the brother of the Satsuma leader, Kawamura, who so tenderly washed the beloved rebels' head while the brother wept over it—name after name down the long table spoke of that recent history of the country which to-day's Japan has left a thousand years behind. All the heads bowed one way, all the glasses were lifted with a gesture of devout, passionate loyalty, when the Emperor's health was drunk; and the Emperor, sitting there, not talking much, but smiling kindly on all within his vision, must, I think, have felt warm at heart with the conviction that at last he has prevailed; he has carried out the dream which worked in his restless brain in the many splendours of Kyoto, in the long fight against bonds which had grown with the growth of centuries, which burnt into his spirit all through his boyhood, till he risked all to snap them, and—prevailed. He rules alone to-day, in spite, perhaps because of, all that he has granted in reforms, in public freedom, in representative government, and individual liberty. I do not believe there is a man of any party in Japan who would not be glad and proud to lay down his life for his Emperor. If a war should come, Japan's armies will gather of themselves from every home in the empire.

But I must not talk of war now, for the silver wedding was a festival of peace. When dinner was over, the Emperor and Empress held a kind of *cercle* in one of the drawing-rooms, where all the vases and wreaths of flowers had swarms of silver butterflies hanging over them. There was a little pleasant talk, and then we all went to the throne-room, where the *nō,* the ceremonious dance, was to be performed.

Here we found a crowd of people, all the other guests indeed, waiting for the sovereigns' arrival. The room itself had been a good deal altered, and I hardly recognised the five hundred square yards of polished parquet over which I have had to skate with slow dignity on various occasions. The throne, which is usually here, had been removed, and a high daïs had been erected, where two *fauteuils* were placed for the Emperor and Empress, with seats below on either side for the Cabinet Ministers and for the Foreign Representatives, running a little way down the two sides of the room; but close to the throne behind were seats for the Imperial Princes and Princesses and for the Empress's ladies. They looked charming, all massed together in their shining dresses and jewels under the lights. The Empress was wearing a still more gorgeous gown than she had on in the morning—a cloth of silver with a design of phoenix plumes in the brocade, I think. She looked very white and fragile against the dark silk hangings behind her chair, a little wraith of royalty, wrapped in trails of misty silver, the long gleams breaking from the diamond stars in her crown as from the edge of a sword whirled in the sun.

The place was already crowded, and the moment we had found our seats some curtains which hung over the glass screen at the farther end were drawn back, musicians came in, made a low obeisance to the sovereigns, and crept to their places at the back of a low square platform, which, covered with green cloth, occupied the centre of the room. It was only slightly raised above the floor, and was well below the daïs on which the Emperor and Empress sat.

And then the *nō** began. Here is a translation of my programme card:

"THE 9TH DAY OF THE 3RD MONTH OF THE 27TH YEAR OF MEIJI.

BANZAIRAKU.

Music composed, 1,300 years ago, by the Emperor Yomei. It represents the joyous flight of a Bird of Paradise in the Golden Age.

*Mrs. Fraser witnessed a performance of Bugaku—the ceremonial music and dance practised at the imperial court—not Nō.

338

ENGUIRAKU.

Music composed, 987 years ago, by Fujiwara Tadafusa, General of the Life Guards. The accompanying dance was composed by Prince Atsumi.

TAIHEIRAKU.

Music rearranged, from the Chinese original, 1,037 years ago. It represents the idea of the establishment of peace by the regulation of every disorder or discrepancy.

BAIRO.

Music from India transmitted to Japan, 1,160 years ago, in the reign of the Emperor Shiomu. It is also called Baïro-Hajinraku, and represents the idea of the submission of enemies."

Such is the programme, indeed; but how can I describe to you the extraordinary scenes and sounds to which these few bald sentences and unintelligible names introduced us? The first effect of the low, grinding music, with its threatening drum effects and stormy cries, was painful; a feeling of tension, anxiety, unnaturalness, took possession of me, and I wanted to get up and move about, to do anything that was absolutely impossible: but when the Bird of Paradise came floating over the floor, with golden wings and flowing draperies and outspread arms, as if seeking for its mate, the sense within me had found its air, and breathed with a gasp of joy. For the Bird of Paradise seemed to be a beautiful girl, very slender, and so light that she rose and fell, as it were, on the wings of the music, which followed and wafted her on, backwards and forwards, floating and sinking, just as the spring wind carries the birds that have flown too low in my garden. There was nothing sudden or unexpected about the dance at first. The Bird of Paradise sunned itself in the light; then another, its mate, came gliding towards it, and there were two of them, darting, swaying, whirling hither and thither across the dark stretch which in some way gave the impression of being empty air; faster and faster the quick, darting movements came; more rapidly the draperies' soft floating reds and golds were blown in ever-recurring twists and folds round the slight figures; then the music died, and the dancers knelt with their heads low on the ground in homage to the Emperor, who smiled, and said a word of precious praise, sure to be treasured for a lifetime.

There was a pause, and I awoke from the kind of trance that had fallen on me, and looked round slowly, trying to remember where I was. A Japanese friend leaned forward from behind me, and began to tell me some more of the fairy tale. These were not girls, but boys; all the nō at Court are performed by men alone. Yes, doubtless they were not bad; indeed, there should be none better, since for eight hundred years the same family had always provided the Emperor's dancers, and were trained to these exercises from father to son, father to son. But see, the new dance is beginning, a martial measure. Those men are dressed in armour; the music is harsh and loud; they wheel and turn, they retreat and advance; the light strikes on cold pale faces and gleaming eyes, on helmets towering with some dragon crest, on gloved hands grasping a spear, on mystic fell of fox or badger wrapped for a charm round the up-curved sword-sheath. And my obedient spirit follows on, to dreamland, fairyland—to a new and yet old country of my thoughts, where these strange rhythms, these triumphant measures, have meant more to me than I can remember to-day. I cannot understand the little buzz of talk which breaks out after each performance, as if those around me were glad to warp back, like a spent bowstring, to the common lines of life. I can sympathise with the Emperor, whose face lights up, whose eyes dilate, as he watches the mysterious nō; he has ceased to talk, and sits in silence, waiting for the next lifting of that curtain of the dreamland of history.

Ah! this is the Indian music—a strong, many-throated strain, with tender intervals and pauses and swelling notes of sober joy. Who knows what voices gave it birth four thousand generations back in the country over the sea? Strange, indeed, are the dresses of the dancers now, six tall men, straight as palms, lithe as the spear cut from the young bamboo, with close-shod feet, and close-wrapped sleeves that show every turn of the fine wrist as it darts or draws back the spear that compels the submission of enemies. Are the men six, or one, I wonder? Faultlessly matched in height and figure, they go through their rapid evolutions with such precision that every streamer and end of drapery makes the same curl on the air at the same moment. Their dress seems like a close-clinging tunic and under-robe of some soft silk tissue, in which threads of red and gold are closely intermingled, so that the folds which seemed red in the shadow break in dusky gold where the light falls on them. But the whole costume is composed of ribbonlike bands of material, which hang close when the wearer is in repose, but shake and part and float on the wind of his motion; and as the movement swings on in a triumphant step, these bands fly aside, all at the same instant, at the same angle, and reveal gleams of splendid armour beneath—breastplates where the light twinkles on gold and lacquer, arms where a sleeve of mail clings to the supple muscles—show the sword-hilt on the hip, and a long straight blade hanging by the swift straight limbs. Six great spears dart upright, cross their points, are laid out in a square on the cloth while the dancers thread quick steps across and across them; and at last, as the music screams for victory, the men fall back, each in his place, stretched almost on the ground, his head by the spear's head, his feet at the spear's foot; they hang for an instant, as if in the act of falling still, and at a sudden note spring to their feet with their draperies whirling behind them, they drop the spearpoints in low obeisance towards the Emperor, their heads touch the ground in uniform homage, and they are gone; the screens have closed behind them. See, the royalties are moving; they pass down the lines, smiling a kind good-night to all. The ninth day of the third month of the twenty-seventh year of Meiji, the Period of Enlightened Peace, is over, and the curtain of To-day has fallen, grey and tangible, over the dreamy splendours of the Past.

Index

Fuji (*also* Fuji San *or* Fujiyama), mountain near Hakone, 118–19, 218, 292–93, 333, 334; pilgrimages to, 215

Fujiya Hotel, 76–85, 119; Frasers' stay at (1889), 76–85; description of, 78–79

Furihata, special policeman at Karuizawa, 203, 205, 207, 211–12, 297–300

Gakushuin, see Nobles' School

gardens, viii, 12, 137–40, 273–75; Frasers', 273, 333–34; of the Hama Rikyu, 273–75, 295–96; Imperial, 17; iris, 277–78, 327

geisha (dancing-girls), 143, 162, 258

George, Prince, of Greece, cousin of the Cesarévitch, 282–84

geyser, at Atami, 58–60

gifts, parting, 238–39

girls, Japanese, 143–47

Girls' Festival, 140–43

Go Sekke, Five Regent Houses, 112

Gotemba, Leper Hospital at, 91–95, 307–9

Goto (Gotō), Count (Shōjirō), statesman, 31, 36, 121; attack on, 36; description of, 31; wife of, 31

Goto, Doctor, 93–94

Grand Duke of Russia, see Cesarévitch

grande maîtresse, Viscountess Takakura, 97–99

Grant, General Ulysses S., xviii, 231

Guards, 87, 220; Life, 221

Gubbins, J. H., C.M.G., secretary to the British Legation with responsibility for dealing with the Japanese authorities, 13, 35, 67, 89, 224; dictionary being prepared by, 80, 126, 296; at Karuizawa, 203, 205–7, 210–11, 296–300; at Miyanoshita, 77–80, 82

Hachi-ishi, village in Nikko district, 230

Hachiman, the god of war, 257; temple of, 176

Hakone Lake, 79, 82, 83

Hakone Mountains, 293

Hama Rikyu (or Enryō Kwan, Detached Palace), Empress's summer home, 22, 159, 166, 226; description of, 273–75; visits to, 273–75, 295–96

hara-kiri (ritual suicide), 288, 291

Harris, Townsend, 30–31

Haru, Prince, heir-apparent, 40–41, 107–8

Haruko, Princess (later Sanjo), 112

Haruko, Princess Ichijo (later Empress), 112

Hasedera, temple, of Kwannon, 172–73

Hashimoto, Dr., Emperor's surgeon and director of the Red Cross Hospital, 245, 286, 317

Hideyoshi, see Toyotomi Hideyoshi

Hijikata, Viscount, garden of, 137

hills, 5, 9, 199–200; descriptions of, 9, 199–200; as summer refuge from the heat, 5

home life, Japanese, 105–6

Hori Kiri, flower resort near Mukōjima, 327

Horiuchi, seaside resort between Zushi and Hayama, holiday at, 291–94

Horiuchi Bay, boating in, 293–94

hospitals, 317–18; see also Cottage Hospital, of St. Hilda's; Leper Hospital; Red Cross Hospital; Tokyo Charity Hospital; University Hospital

hot springs, 93, 192, 317–18; see also baths, hot

house, the Fraser's (*Ichiban,* Number One), 126, 127; summer (or vacation), see summer house

Household, Imperial, see Imperial Household

House of Peers (Upper House), xi–xii, 219–22

House of Representatives (Lower House), xi–xii, 219–22

The "weathermark" identifies this book as a production of John Weatherhill, Inc., publishers of fine books on Asia and the Pacific. Book design and typography: Miriam F. Yamaguchi. Layout of illustrations: Nobu Miyazaki. Composition of the text: Korea Textbook Co., Inc., Seoul. Printing of the text: Kenkyusha Printing Co., Tokyo. Engraving and printing of the plates, in four-color offset: Nissha Printing Co., Kyoto. Binding: Makoto Binderies, Tokyo. The typeface used is Monotype Bembo.